INTERNATIONAL MONETARY FUND

WORLD ECONOMIC OUTLOOK

Growth Slowdown, Precarious Recovery

2019
APR

Cover and Design: IMF CSF Creative Solutions Division
Composition: AGS, An RR Donnelley Company

Cataloging-in-Publication Data

Joint Bank-Fund Library

Names: International Monetary Fund.
Title: World economic outlook (International Monetary Fund)
Other titles: WEO | Occasional paper (International Monetary Fund) | World economic and financial surveys.
Description: Washington, DC : International Monetary Fund, 1980- | Semiannual | Some issues also have thematic titles. | Began with issue for May 1980. | 1981-1984: Occasional paper / International Monetary Fund, 0251-6365 | 1986-: World economic and financial surveys, 0256-6877.
Identifiers: ISSN 0256-6877 (print) | ISSN 1564-5215 (online)
Subjects: LCSH: Economic development—Periodicals. | International economic relations—Periodicals. | Debts, External—Periodicals. | Balance of payments—Periodicals. | International finance—Periodicals. | Economic forecasting—Periodicals.
Classification: LCC HC10.W79

HC10.80

ISBN 978-1-48439-748-0 (English Paper)
978-1-49830-610-2 (English ePub)
978-1-49830-611-9 (English Mobi)
978-1-49830-611-9 (English PDF)

The *World Economic Outlook* (WEO) is a survey by the IMF staff published twice a year, in the spring and fall. The WEO is prepared by the IMF staff and has benefited from comments and suggestions by Executive Directors following their discussion of the report on March 21, 2019. The views expressed in this publication are those of the IMF staff and do not necessarily represent the views of the IMF's Executive Directors or their national authorities.

Recommended citation: International Monetary Fund. 2018. *World Economic Outlook: Growth Slowdown, Precarious Recovery.* Washington, DC, April.

Publication orders may be placed online, by fax, or through the mail:
International Monetary Fund, Publication Services
P.O. Box 92780, Washington, DC 20090, USA
Tel.: (202) 623-7430 Fax: (202) 623-7201
E-mail: publications@imf.org
www.imfbookstore.org
www.elibrary.imf.org

CONTENTS

Figures

ASSUMPTIONS AND CONVENTIONS

A number of assumptions have been adopted for the projections presented in the *World Economic Outlook* (WEO). It has been assumed that real effective exchange rates remained constant at their average levels during January 14 to February 11, 2019, except for those for the currencies participating in the European exchange rate mechanism II (ERM II), which are assumed to have remained constant in nominal terms relative to the euro; that established policies of national authorities will be maintained (for specific assumptions about fiscal and monetary policies for selected economies, see Box A1 in the Statistical Appendix); that the average price of oil will be $59.16 a barrel in 2019 and $59.02 a barrel in 2020 and will remain unchanged in real terms over the medium term; that the six-month London interbank offered rate (LIBOR) on US dollar deposits will average 3.2 percent in 2019 and 3.8 percent in 2020; that the three-month euro deposit rate will average –0.3 percent in 2019 and –0.2 in 2020; and that the six-month Japanese yen deposit rate will yield, on average, 0.0 percent in 2019 and 2020, respectively. These are, of course, working hypotheses rather than forecasts, and the uncertainties surrounding them add to the margin of error that would, in any event, be involved in the projections. The estimates and projections are based on statistical information available through March 29, 2019.

The following conventions are used throughout the WEO:

. . . to indicate that data are not available or not applicable;

– between years or months (for example, 2018-19 or January–June) to indicate the years or months covered, including the beginning and ending years or months; and

/ between years or months (for example, 2018/19) to indicate a fiscal or financial year.

"Billion" means a thousand million; "trillion" means a thousand billion.

"Basis points" refers to hundredths of 1 percentage point (for example, 25 basis points are equivalent to ¼ of 1 percentage point).

Data refer to calendar years, except in the case of a few countries that use fiscal years. Please refer to Table F in the Statistical Appendix, which lists the economies with exceptional reporting periods for national accounts and government finance data for each country.

For some countries, the figures for 2018 and earlier are based on estimates rather than actual outturns. Please refer to Table G in the Statistical Appendix, which lists the latest actual outturns for the indicators in the national accounts, prices, government finance, and balance of payments indicators for each country.

What is new in this publication:

- *FYR Macedonia* is now called *North Macedonia*.
- In February 2019, *Zimbabwe* adopted a new local currency unit, the RTGS dollar, which has become the official unit of account. Efforts are underway to revise and update all national accounts series to the new RTGS dollar. Current data are based on IMF staff estimates of price and exchange rate developments in US (and RTGS) dollars. Staff estimates of US dollar values may differ from authorities' estimates.

In the tables and figures, the following conventions apply:

- If no source is listed on tables and figures, data are drawn from the WEO database.
- When countries are not listed alphabetically, they are ordered on the basis of economic size.
- Minor discrepancies between sums of constituent figures and totals shown reflect rounding.

As used in this report, the terms "country" and "economy" do not in all cases refer to a territorial entity that is a state as understood by international law and practice. As used here, the term also covers some territorial entities that are not states but for which statistical data are maintained on a separate and independent basis.

Composite data are provided for various groups of countries organized according to economic characteristics or region. Unless noted otherwise, country group composites represent calculations based on 90 percent or more of the weighted group data.

The boundaries, colors, denominations, and any other information shown on the maps do not imply, on the part of the IMF, any judgment on the legal status of any territory or any endorsement or acceptance of such boundaries.

FURTHER INFORMATION

Corrections and Revisions

The data and analysis appearing in the *World Economic Outlook* (WEO) are compiled by the IMF staff at the time of publication. Every effort is made to ensure their timeliness, accuracy, and completeness. When errors are discovered, corrections and revisions are incorporated into the digital editions available from the IMF website and on the IMF eLibrary (see below). All substantive changes are listed in the online table of contents.

Print and Digital Editions

Print

Print copies of this WEO can be ordered from the IMF bookstore at imfbk.st/25771.

Digital

Multiple digital editions of the WEO, including ePub, enhanced PDF, Mobi, and HTML, are available on the IMF eLibrary at www.elibrary.imf.org/APR19WEO.

Download a free PDF of the report and data sets for each of the charts therein from the IMF website at www.imf.org/publications/weo or scan the QR code below to access the *World Economic Outlook* web page directly:

Copyright and Reuse

Information on the terms and conditions for reusing the contents of this publication are at www.imf.org/external/terms.htm.

DATA

This version of the *World Economic Outlook* (WEO) is available in full through the IMF eLibrary (www.elibrary.imf.org) and the IMF website (www.imf.org). Accompanying the publication on the IMF website is a larger compilation of data from the WEO database than is included in the report itself, including files containing the series most frequently requested by readers. These files may be downloaded for use in a variety of software packages.

The data appearing in the WEO are compiled by the IMF staff at the time of the WEO exercises. The historical data and projections are based on the information gathered by the IMF country desk officers in the context of their missions to IMF member countries and through their ongoing analysis of the evolving situation in each country. Historical data are updated on a continual basis as more information becomes available, and structural breaks in data are often adjusted to produce smooth series with the use of splicing and other techniques. IMF staff estimates continue to serve as proxies for historical series when complete information is unavailable. As a result, WEO data can differ from those in other sources with official data, including the IMF's International Financial Statistics.

The WEO data and metadata provided are "as is" and "as available," and every effort is made to ensure their timeliness, accuracy, and completeness, but these cannot be guaranteed. When errors are discovered, there is a concerted effort to correct them as appropriate and feasible. Corrections and revisions made after publication are incorporated into the electronic editions available from the IMF eLibrary (www.elibrary.imf.org) and on the IMF website (www.imf.org). All substantive changes are listed in detail in the online tables of contents.

For details on the terms and conditions for usage of the WEO database, please refer to the IMF Copyright and Usage website (www.imf.org/external/terms.htm).

Inquiries about the content of the WEO and the WEO database should be sent by mail, fax, or online forum (telephone inquiries cannot be accepted):

World Economic Studies Division
Research Department
International Monetary Fund
700 19th Street, NW
Washington, DC 20431, USA
Fax: (202) 623-6343
Online Forum: www.imf.org/weoforum

PREFACE

The analysis and projections contained in the *World Economic Outlook* are integral elements of the IMF's surveillance of economic developments and policies in its member countries, of developments in international financial markets, and of the global economic system. The survey of prospects and policies is the product of a comprehensive interdepartmental review of world economic developments, which draws primarily on information the IMF staff gathers through its consultations with member countries. These consultations are carried out in particular by the IMF's area departments—namely, the African Department, Asia and Pacific Department, European Department, Middle East and Central Asia Department, and Western Hemisphere Department—together with the Strategy, Policy, and Review Department; the Monetary and Capital Markets Department; and the Fiscal Affairs Department.

The analysis in this report was coordinated in the Research Department under the general direction of Gita Gopinath, Economic Counsellor and Director of Research. The project was directed by Gian Maria Milesi-Ferretti, Deputy Director, Research Department and Oya Celasun, Division Chief, Research Department; and Helge Berger, Assistant Director, Research Department and Head of the IMF's Spillover Task Force.

The primary contributors to this report were Christian Bogmans, Wenjie Chen, Federico Diez, Allan Dizioli, Romain Duval, Johannes Eugster, Benjamin Hunt, Florence Jaumotte, Callum Jones, Toh Kuan, Weicheng Lian, Margaux MacDonald, Akito Matsumoto, Malhar Nabar, Natalija Novta, Andrea Pescatori, Roberto Piazza, Rafael Portillo, Evgenia Pugacheva, Carolina Villegas-Sánchez, Yannick Timmer, and Petia Topalova.

Other contributors include Michal Andrle, Gavin Asdorian, Carlos Caceres, Luisa Calixto, Diego Cerdeiro, Kyun Suk Chang, Mai Chi Dao, Pankhuri Dutt, Angela Espiritu, Rebecca Eyassu, Jiayue Fan, Chanpheng Fizzarotti, Swarnali Ahmed Hannan, Mandy Hemmati, Ava Yeabin Hong, Christopher Johns, Lama Kiyasseh, Zsóka Kóczán, Jungjin Lee, Nan Li, Rui Mano, Sergii Meleshchuk, Cynthia Nyanchama Nyakeri, Emory Oakes, Ilse Peirtsegaele, Adrian Robles Villamil, Marika Santoro, Susie Xiaohui Sun, Ariana Tayebi, Nicholas Tong, Menexenia Tsaroucha, Shan Wang, Julia Xueliang Wang, Jilun Xing, Yuan Zeng, Qiaoqiao Zhang, Huiyuan Zhao, Caroline Chenqi Zhou, and Jillian Zirnhelt.

Joseph Procopio from the Communications Department led the editorial team for the report, with production and editorial support from Christine Ebrahimzadeh, and editorial assistance from James Unwin, Lucy Scott Morales, and Vector Talent Resources.

The analysis has benefited from comments and suggestions by staff members from other IMF departments, as well as by Executive Directors following their discussion of the report on March 21, 2019. However, both projections and policy considerations are those of the IMF staff and should not be attributed to Executive Directors or to their national authorities.

FOREWORD

One year ago economic activity was accelerating in almost all regions of the world and the global economy was projected to grow at 3.9 percent in 2018 and 2019. One year later, much has changed: the escalation of US–China trade tensions, macroeconomic stress in Argentina and Turkey, disruptions to the auto sector in Germany, tighter credit policies in China, and financial tightening alongside the normalization of monetary policy in the larger advanced economies have all contributed to a significantly weakened global expansion, especially in the second half of 2018. With this weakness expected to persist into the first half of 2019, the *World Economic Outlook* (WEO) projects a decline in growth in 2019 for 70 percent of the global economy. Global growth, which peaked at close to 4 percent in 2017, softened to 3.6 percent in 2018, and is projected to decline further to 3.3 percent in 2019. Although a 3.3 percent global expansion is still reasonable, the outlook for many countries is very challenging, with considerable uncertainties in the short term, especially as advanced economy growth rates converge toward their modest long-term potential.

While 2019 started out on a weak footing, a pickup is expected in the second half of the year. This pickup is supported by significant policy accommodation by major economies, made possible by the absence of inflationary pressures despite closing output gaps. The US Federal Reserve, in response to rising global risks, paused interest rate increases and signaled no increases for the rest of the year. The European Central Bank, the Bank of Japan, and the Bank of England have all shifted to a more accommodative stance. China has ramped up its fiscal and monetary stimulus to counter the negative effect of trade tariffs. Furthermore, the outlook for US–China trade tensions has improved as the prospects of a trade agreement take shape.

These policy responses have helped reverse the tightening of financial conditions to varying degrees across countries. Emerging markets have experienced a resumption in portfolio flows, a decline in sovereign borrowing costs, and a strengthening of their currencies relative to the dollar. While the improvement in financial markets has been rapid, those in the real economy have yet to materialize. Measures of industrial production and investment remain weak for most advanced and emerging economies, and global trade has yet to recover.

With improvements expected in the second half of 2019, global economic growth in 2020 is projected to return to 3.6 percent. This return is predicated on a rebound in Argentina and Turkey and some improvement in a set of other stressed emerging market and developing economies, and therefore subject to considerable uncertainty. Beyond 2020 growth will stabilize at around 3½ percent, bolstered mainly by growth in China and India and their increasing weights in world income. Growth in advanced economies will continue to slow gradually as the impact of US fiscal stimulus fades and growth tends toward the modest potential for the group, given ageing trends and low productivity growth. Growth in emerging market and developing economies will stabilize at around 5 percent, though with considerable variance between countries as subdued commodity prices and civil strife weaken prospects for some.

While the overall outlook remains benign, there are many downside risks. There is an uneasy truce on trade policy, as tensions could flare up again and play out in other areas (such as the auto industry) with large disruptions to global supply chains. Growth in China may surprise on the downside, and the risks surrounding Brexit remain heightened. In the face of significant financial vulnerabilities associated with large private and public sector debt in several countries, including sovereign-bank doom loop risks (for example, in Italy), there could be a rapid change in financial conditions owing to, for example, a risk-off episode or a no-deal Brexit.

With weak expansion projected for important parts of the world, a realization of these downside risks could dramatically worsen the outlook. This would take place at a time when conventional monetary and fiscal space is limited as a policy response. It is therefore imperative that costly policy mistakes are avoided. Policymakers need to work cooperatively to help ensure that policy uncertainty doesn't weaken investment. Fiscal policy will need to manage trade-offs between supporting demand and ensuring that public debt remains on a sustainable path, and the optimal mix will depend on country-specific circumstances. Financial sector policies must address vulnerabilities proactively by deploying macroprudential tools. Low-income commodity exporters should diversify away from commodities given the subdued outlook for commodity prices. Monetary policy should remain data dependent, be well communicated, and ensure that inflation expectations remain anchored.

Across all economies, the imperative is to take actions that boost potential output, improve inclusiveness, and strengthen resilience. A social dialogue across all stakeholders to address inequality and political discontent will benefit economies. There is a need for greater multilateral cooperation to resolve trade conflicts, to address climate change and risks from cybersecurity, and to improve the effectiveness of international taxation.

This issue of the WEO also tackles three major developments that need to be addressed to enhance long-term growth. The first is rising inequality, the second is weak investment, and the third is rising protectionism in trade. Chapter 2 investigates the evolution of corporate market power (as measured by markups) and its ability to explain several macro phenomena, including weak investment and the declining labor shares that help fuel inequality. The finding is that the aggregate increase in markups since 2000 has been modest and, consequently, the implications for the macroeconomy relatively modest. There is, however, significant heterogeneity, with the aggregate increase driven mainly by a more substantial increase in markups by a small number of firms that are the more productive and innovative firms. The increase in aggregate market power therefore appears to be, as of now, less a phenomenon of poor competition and more one of winner-takes-most dynamics, where markups compensate in part for investment in intangible assets. However, going forward this market dominance could lead to unfair advantages that weaken market entry and competition and, more significantly, dampen investment and innovation. It is therefore important to cut barriers to market entry and reform and strengthen competition law to better align with the new economy.

Chapter 3 highlights the benefits for investment of reducing trade barriers. Over the past three decades, the relative price of machinery and equipment has fallen in all countries, driven both by higher productivity in the capital-goods-producing sector and increased trade integration. This decline has supported the rise in real investment rates in machinery and equipment, benefiting developing countries. Rising trade tensions could reverse these price declines and damage investment at a time when investment is already weak, which only further emphasizes the need to quickly resolve trade disagreements.

The final chapter of the WEO examines the link between bilateral trade tariffs and trade imbalances. US–China trade frictions have brought a focus on the question of whether bilateral trade imbalances can (or should) be addressed using bilateral trade measures. This chapter demonstrates that the link between the two is precarious. Bilateral trade balances since the mid-1990s have reflected mostly aggregate macroeconomic forces known to determine aggregate trade balances at the country level and have had much less to do with bilateral tariffs. Targeting bilateral trade balances will likely only lead to trade diversion, with limited impact on country-level balances. The findings of this chapter help explain why, despite the tariff measures, the US trade deficit is the largest it has been since 2008. The chapter also establishes that the negative impact of tariffs on output is significantly higher today than in 1995 owing to the bigger role of global supply chains in world trade.

This is a delicate year for the global economy. If the downside risks do not materialize and the policy support put in place is effective, then global growth will return to 3.6 percent in 2020. If, however, any of the major risks materialize, then the expected recoveries in stressed economies, export-dependent economies, and highly indebted economies may not occur. In that case, policymakers will need to adjust. Depending on circumstances, this may require synchronized, country-specific policy stimulus across economies, complemented by accommodative monetary policy. Synchronization can make fiscal stimulus more effective through signaling effects that raise household and business confidence, and through the mitigation of leakages via imports. Finally, adequate resources for multilateral institutions remain essential to retain an effective global safety net, which would help stabilize the global economy.

Gita Gopinath
Economic Counsellor

A Weakening Expansion

After strong growth in 2017 and early 2018, global economic activity slowed notably in the second half of last year, reflecting a confluence of factors affecting major economies. China's growth declined following a combination of needed regulatory tightening to rein in shadow banking and an increase in trade tensions with the United States. The euro area economy lost more momentum than expected as consumer and business confidence weakened and car production in Germany was disrupted by the introduction of new emission standards; investment dropped in Italy as sovereign spreads widened; and external demand, especially from emerging Asia, softened. Elsewhere, natural disasters hurt activity in Japan. Trade tensions increasingly took a toll on business confidence and, so, financial market sentiment worsened, with financial conditions tightening for vulnerable emerging markets in the spring of 2018 and then in advanced economies later in the year, weighing on global demand. Conditions have eased in 2019 as the US Federal Reserve signaled a more accommodative monetary policy stance and markets became more optimistic about a US–China trade deal, but they remain slightly more restrictive than in the fall.

Figure 1. Half-Yearly Growth Rates
(Annualized semiannual percent change)

Global growth is expected to level off in the first half of 2019 and firm up after that.

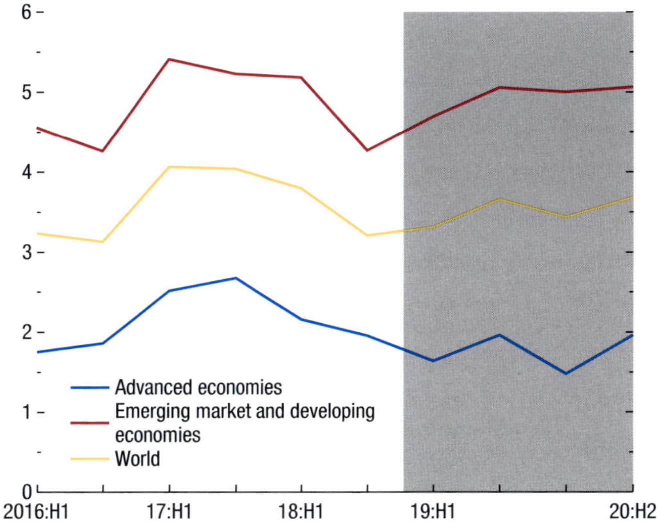

Source: IMF staff estimates.

Global Growth Is Set to Moderate in the Near Term, Then Pick Up Modestly

As a result of these developments, global growth is now projected to slow from 3.6 percent in 2018 to 3.3 percent in 2019, before returning to 3.6 percent in 2020. Growth for 2018 was revised down by 0.1 percentage point relative to the October 2018 *World Economic Outlook* (WEO), reflecting weakness in the second half of the year, and the forecasts for 2019 and 2020 are now marked down by 0.4 percentage point and 0.1 percentage point, respectively. The current forecast envisages that global growth will level off in the first half of 2019 and firm up after that (Figure 1). The projected pickup in the second half of 2019 is predicated on an ongoing buildup of policy stimulus in China, recent improvements in global financial market sentiment, the waning of some temporary drags on growth in the euro area, and a gradual stabilization of conditions in stressed emerging market economies, including Argentina and Turkey. Improved momentum for emerging market and developing economies is projected to continue into 2020, primarily reflecting developments in economies currently experiencing macroeconomic distress—a forecast subject to notable uncertainty. By contrast, activity in advanced economies is projected to continue to slow gradually as the impact of US fiscal stimulus fades and growth tends toward the modest potential for the group.

Beyond 2020, global growth is set to plateau at about 3.6 percent over the medium term, sustained by the increase in the relative size of economies, such as those of China and India, which are projected to have robust growth by comparison to slower-growing advanced and emerging market economies (even though Chinese growth will eventually moderate). As noted in previous WEO reports, tepid labor productivity growth and slowing expansion of the labor force amid population aging will drag advanced economy growth lower over the projection horizon.

Growth across emerging market and developing economies is projected to stabilize slightly below 5 percent, though with variations by region and country. The baseline outlook for emerging Asia remains favorable, with China's growth projected to slow gradually toward sustainable levels and convergence in frontier economies toward higher income levels. For other regions, the outlook is complicated by a combination of structural bottlenecks, slower advanced economy growth and, in some cases, high debt and tighter financial conditions. These factors, alongside subdued commodity prices and civil strife or conflict in some cases, contribute to subdued medium-term prospects for Latin America; the Middle East, North Africa, and Pakistan region; and parts of sub-Saharan Africa. In particular, convergence prospects are bleak for some 41 emerging market and developing economies, accounting for close to 10 percent of global GDP in purchasing-power-parity terms and with total population close to 1 billion, where per capita incomes are projected to fall further behind those in advanced economies over the next five years.

Risks Are Tilted to the Downside

While global growth could surprise favorably if trade differences are resolved quickly so that business confidence rebounds and investor sentiment strengthens further, the balance of risks to the outlook remains on the downside. A further escalation of trade tensions and the associated increases in policy uncertainty could further weaken growth. The potential remains for sharp deterioration in market sentiment, which would imply portfolio reallocations away from risk assets, wider spreads over safe haven securities, and generally tighter financial conditions, especially for vulnerable economies. Possible triggers for such an episode include a no-deal Brexit withdrawal of the United Kingdom from the European Union; persistently weak economic data pointing to a protracted global growth slowdown; and prolonged fiscal uncertainty and elevated yields in Italy—particularly if coupled with a deeper recession—with possible adverse spillovers for other euro area economies. A rapid reassessment by markets of the monetary policy stance in the United States could also tighten global financial conditions. Over the medium term, climate change and political discord in the context of rising inequality are key risks that could lower global potential output, with particularly severe implications for some vulnerable countries.

Policy Priorities

Amid waning global growth momentum and limited policy space to combat downturns, avoiding policy missteps that could harm economic activity needs to be the main priority. Macroeconomic and financial policy should aim to prevent further deceleration where output could fall below potential and facilitate a soft landing where policy support needs to be withdrawn. At the national level, this requires monetary policy to ensure that inflation remains on track toward the central bank's target (or if it is close to target, that it stabilizes there) and that inflation expectations remain anchored. It requires fiscal policy to manage trade-offs between supporting demand and making sure that public debt stays on a sustainable path. Where fiscal consolidation is needed and monetary policy is constrained, its pace should be calibrated to secure stability while avoiding harming near-term growth and depleting programs that protect the vulnerable. If the current slowdown turns out to be more severe and protracted than expected in the baseline, macroeconomic policies should become more accommodative, particularly where output remains below potential and financial stability is not at risk. Across all economies, the imperative is to take actions that boost potential output growth, improve inclusiveness, and strengthen resilience. At the multilateral level, the main priority is for countries to resolve trade disagreements cooperatively, without raising distortionary barriers that would further destabilize a slowing global economy.

CHAPTER 1 GLOBAL PROSPECTS AND POLICIES

Recent Developments: Global Expansion Loses Steam

Following a broad-based upswing in cyclical growth that lasted nearly two years, the global economic expansion decelerated in the second half of 2018. Activity softened amid an increase in trade tensions and tariff hikes between the United States and China, a decline in business confidence, a tightening of financial conditions, and higher policy uncertainty across many economies. Against this global backdrop, a combination of country- and sector-specific factors further reduced momentum. After peaking at close to 4 percent in 2017, global growth remained strong, at 3.8 percent in the first half of 2018, but dropped to 3.2 percent in the second half of the year.

Emerging Market and Developing Economies

In China, necessary domestic regulatory tightening to rein in debt, constrain shadow financial intermediation, and place growth on a sustainable footing contributed to slower domestic investment, particularly in infrastructure. Spending on durable consumption goods also softened, with automobile sales declining in 2018 following the expiration of incentive programs for car purchases. These developments contributed to slower momentum over the year, with further pressure from diminishing export orders as US tariff actions began to take hold in the second half of the year. As a result, China's growth declined from 6.8 percent in the first half of 2018 to 6.0 percent in the second half of the year. The resulting weakening in import demand appeared to have impacts on trading partner exports in Asia and Europe.

Elsewhere across emerging market economies, activity moderated as worsening global financial market sentiment in the second half of 2018 compounded country-specific factors. Needed policy tightening to reduce financial and macroeconomic imbalances took effect in Argentina and Turkey; sentiment weakened and sovereign spreads rose in Mexico, following the incoming administration's cancellation of a planned airport for the capital and backtracking on energy and education reforms; and geopolitical tensions contributed to weaker activity in the Middle East.

Advanced Economies

The euro area slowed more than expected as a combination of factors weighed on activity across countries, including (1) weakening consumer and business sentiment; (2) delays associated with the introduction of new fuel emission standards for diesel-powered vehicles in Germany; (3) fiscal policy uncertainty, elevated sovereign spreads, and softening investment in Italy; and (4) street protests that disrupted retail sales and weighed on consumption spending in France. Growing concerns about a no-deal Brexit also likely weighed on investment spending within the euro area. Following a notable uptick in 2017, euro area economies' exports softened considerably, in part because of weak intra-euro-area trade, which exacerbated poor sentiment across the currency area.

Elsewhere in advanced economies, activity weakened in Japan, largely due to natural disasters in the third quarter. One exception to the broader pattern was that momentum in the United States remained robust amid a tight labor market and strong consumption growth, but investment appeared to soften in the second half of the year.

A common influence on sentiment across advanced and emerging market and developing economies has been high policy uncertainty in the wake of policy actions and difficulties in reaching agreement on contentious issues. The extended truce in the US–China trade dispute has provided a welcome respite in an otherwise turbulent policy backdrop that included Brexit negotiations, discussions over the Italian budget, changes in Mexican policy direction under the new administration, the US federal government shutdown, and US policy on Iran.

Softening Industrial Production, Slower Trade

Amid high policy uncertainty and weakening prospects for global demand, industrial production decelerated (Figure 1.1), particularly for capital goods. The slowdown was broad based, notably across advanced economies, except the United States. While a cyclical slowdown in countries thought to be operating above potential was to be expected, the downturn was larger and appeared related to a souring of market sentiment, in part because of trade tensions. Global trade growth has slowed sharply from its peak in late 2017, with US imports from China

Figure 1.1. Global Activity Indicators

(Three-month moving average; year-over-year percent change, unless noted otherwise)

Indicators of global activity have generally softened since the second half of 2018.

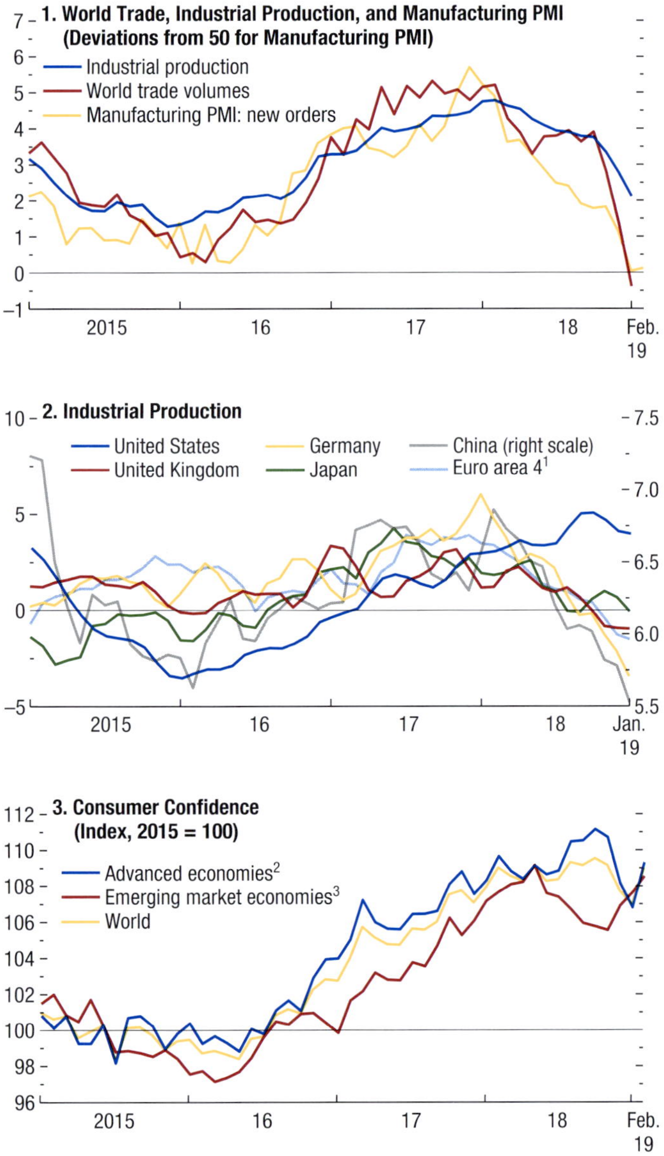

Sources: CPB Netherlands Bureau for Economic Policy Analysis; Haver Analytics; Markit Economics; and IMF staff calculations.
Note: CC = consumer confidence; PMI = purchasing managers' index.
[1]Euro area 4 comprises France, Italy, the Netherlands, and Spain.
[2]Australia, Canada (PMI only), Czech Republic, Denmark, euro area, Hong Kong SAR (CC only), Israel, Japan, Korea, New Zealand (PMI only), Norway (CC only), Singapore (PMI only), Sweden (CC only), Switzerland, Taiwan Province of China, United Kingdom, United States.
[3]Argentina (CC only), Brazil, China, Colombia (CC only), Hungary, India (PMI only), Indonesia, Latvia (CC only), Malaysia (PMI only), Mexico (PMI only), Philippines (CC only), Poland, Russia, South Africa, Thailand (CC only), Turkey, Ukraine (CC only).

Figure 1.2. Trade Indicators

(Year-over-year percent change)

Global trade growth has slowed sharply from its peak in late 2017. Following some front-loading, US imports from China subject to new US tariffs declined or stalled toward the end of the year.

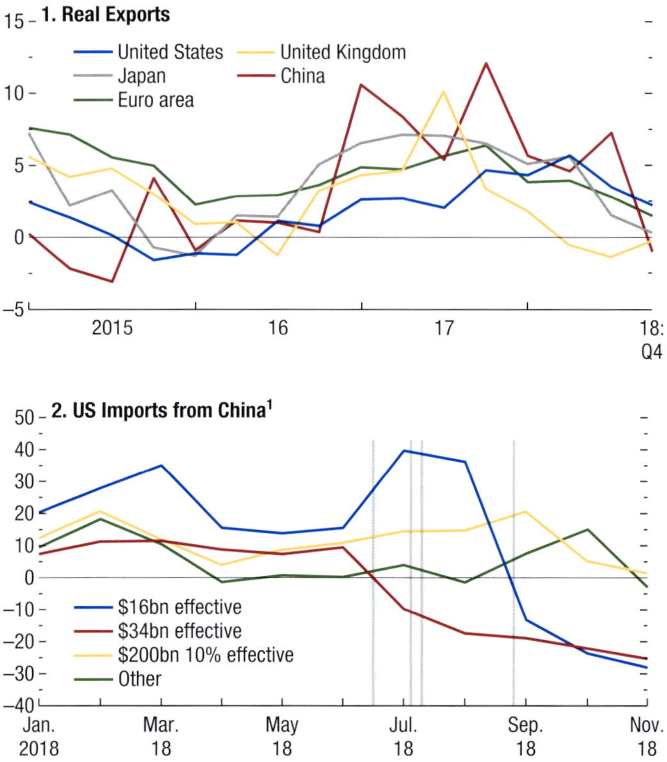

Source: IMF staff calculations.
[1]The vertical bars correspond to the timing of tariff increases: $50bn list announced June 15, 2018; $34bn effective (of $50bn list) July 6, 2018, and $16bn effective (of $50bn list) August 23, 2018; $200bn list announced July 10, 2018, with 10 percent tariff on $200bn effective September 24, 2018. The series show the evolution of US imports of goods in the various tariff lists. bn = billion.

subject to new US tariffs declining or stalling toward the end of the year (following some front-loading ahead of tariff hikes; Figure 1.2). Weak expectations of future activity seen in purchasing managers' indexes point to a continuation of the slow momentum this year.

Lower Commodity Prices, Subdued Inflation Pressure

Global energy prices declined by 17 percent between the reference periods for the October 2018 and current *World Economic Outlook* (WEO) as oil prices dropped from a four-year peak of $81 a barrel in October to $61 in February (Figure 1.3). While supply influences dominated initially—notably a temporary waiver in US sanctions on Iranian oil exports to certain countries and record-high US crude oil production—weakening global growth added downward pressure on prices toward the end of 2018. Since the beginning of this year, oil prices have recovered somewhat thanks to production cuts by oil-exporting countries. Prices of base metals have increased by 7.6 percent since August as a result of supply disruption in some metal markets more than offsetting subdued global demand.

Consumer price inflation remained muted across advanced economies, given the drop in commodity prices (Figure 1.4). For most countries in this group, core inflation is well below central bank targets despite the pickup in domestic demand in the past two years; in the United States and United Kingdom, it is close to 2 percent. Although wage growth has been picking up across most advanced economies, notably in the United States and United Kingdom, it is still sluggish despite lower unemployment rates and diminished labor market slack. With wage growth broadly in line with labor productivity growth, unit labor costs continue to be restrained (Box 1.1). Consistent with subdued overall price and wage pressures, and possibly reinforced by the slowing growth momentum, inflation expectations remain contained across advanced economies, and, in many cases, have softened recently.

Among emerging market economies, core inflation has remained below 2 percent in China as activity has moderated. In other cases, inflation pressure has eased toward the lower bound of the central bank's target range with the drop in commodity prices (Indonesia) and slowdown in food inflation (India). For some economies, currency depreciations have passed through to higher domestic prices, partially offsetting downward pressure from lower commodity prices.

Financial Conditions Are Marginally Tighter than in the Fall; Localized Pressures Continue

Following a notable tightening of financial conditions in late 2018, market sentiment rebounded in early 2019. Signs of slowing global growth, moderately less buoyant corporate earnings, and market concerns about the pace of Federal Reserve policy tightening weighed on sentiment at the end of 2018. Prospects for a disorderly exit of the United Kingdom from the European Union (a "no-deal Brexit") and news about macroeconomic stimulus and liquidity support in China have also influenced market movements since October. More recently, a shift toward more accommodative monetary policy stances by major central banks (including a pause in interest rate hikes by the Federal Reserve) and the outcome of US–China trade negotiations have supported a rebound in sentiment.

Figure 1.3. Commodity Prices
(Deflated using US consumer price index; index, 2014 = 100)

Commodity prices have been volatile in recent months, reflecting shifting supply influences against a backdrop of subdued demand.

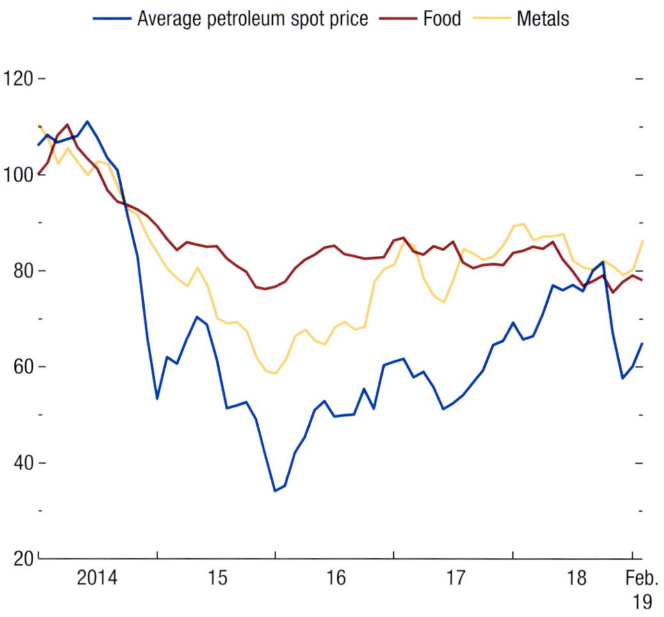

Sources: IMF, Primary Commodity Price System; and IMF staff calculations.

Financial conditions in advanced economies have eased since the start of the year, after tightening sharply in the final months of 2018 on equity price declines and higher risk spreads. As of early March, conditions were slightly tighter than in October (Figure 1.5; Figure 1.2 of the April 2019 *Global Financial Stability Report* (GFSR)), but, in most cases, still accommodative. This is especially the case in the United States, where bond yields dropped as investors reassessed the outlook for monetary policy normalization. The change in tone of communications by major central banks has been an important contributor to the easing of financial conditions since early 2019. In January, communication by the US Federal Reserve suggested a patient and flexible approach to policy normalization, and at the March meeting of the Federal Open Market Committee, it signaled a pause in its interest rate hikes for this year (see the April 2019 GFSR). The European Central Bank, which ended its net asset purchases in December, announced in March a new round of targeted bank financing and further postponed a rise in policy rates to at least the end of this year. The Bank of England and Bank of Japan have increasingly taken more cautious views on the outlook. Consistent with this shift in tone,

Figure 1.4. Global Inflation

(Three-month moving average; annualized percent change, unless noted otherwise)

Consumer price inflation remained muted across advanced economies, given the drop in commodity prices. For some emerging market economies, currency depreciations have passed through to higher domestic prices, partially offsetting downward pressure from lower commodity prices.

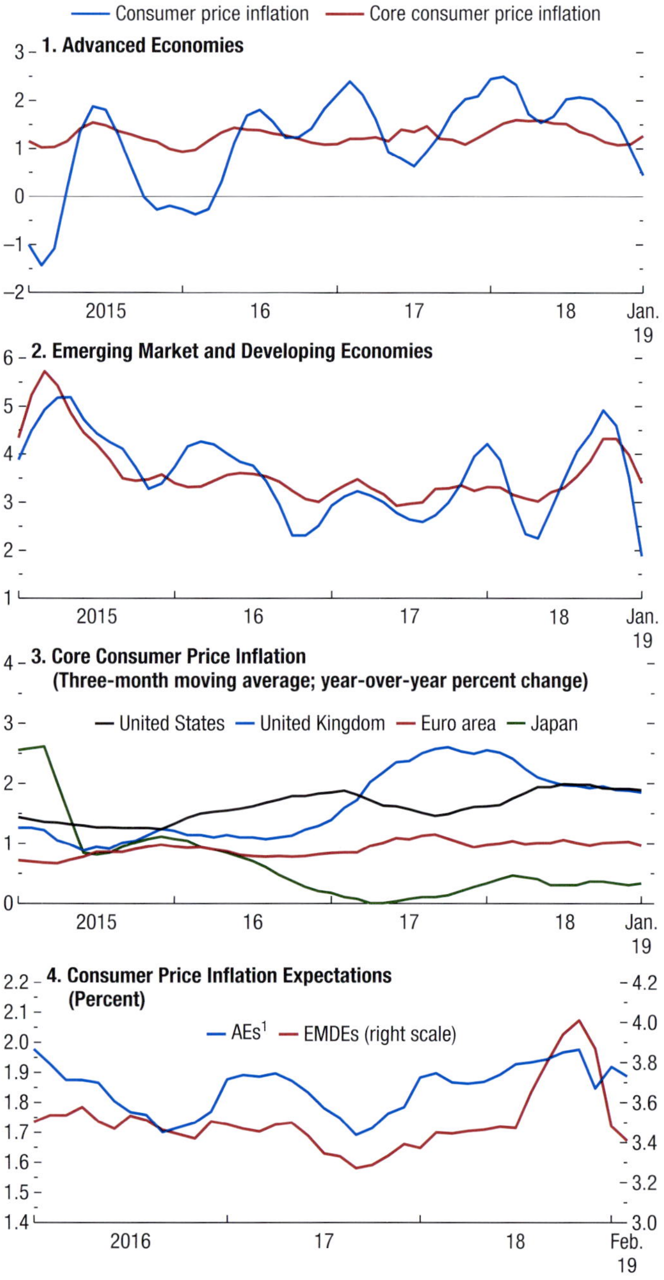

Sources: Consensus Economics; Haver Analytics; and IMF staff calculations.
Note: AEs = advanced economies (AUT, BEL, CAN, CHE, CZE, DEU, DNK, ESP, EST, FIN, FRA, GBR, GRC, HKG, IRL, ISR, ITA, JPN, KOR, LTU, LUX, LVA, NLD, NOR, PRT, SGP, SVK, SVN, SWE, TWN, USA); Emerging market and developing countries comprise BGR, BRA, CHL, CHN, COL, HUN, IDN, IND, MEX, MYS, PER, PHL, POL, ROU, RUS, THA, TUR, ZAF. Country list uses International Organization for Standardization (ISO) country codes.
[1]AEs include AUS; exclude LUX.

Figure 1.5. Advanced Economies: Monetary and Financial Market Conditions

(Percent, unless noted otherwise)

Financial conditions in advanced economies have eased since the start of the year, after tightening sharply in the final months of 2018.

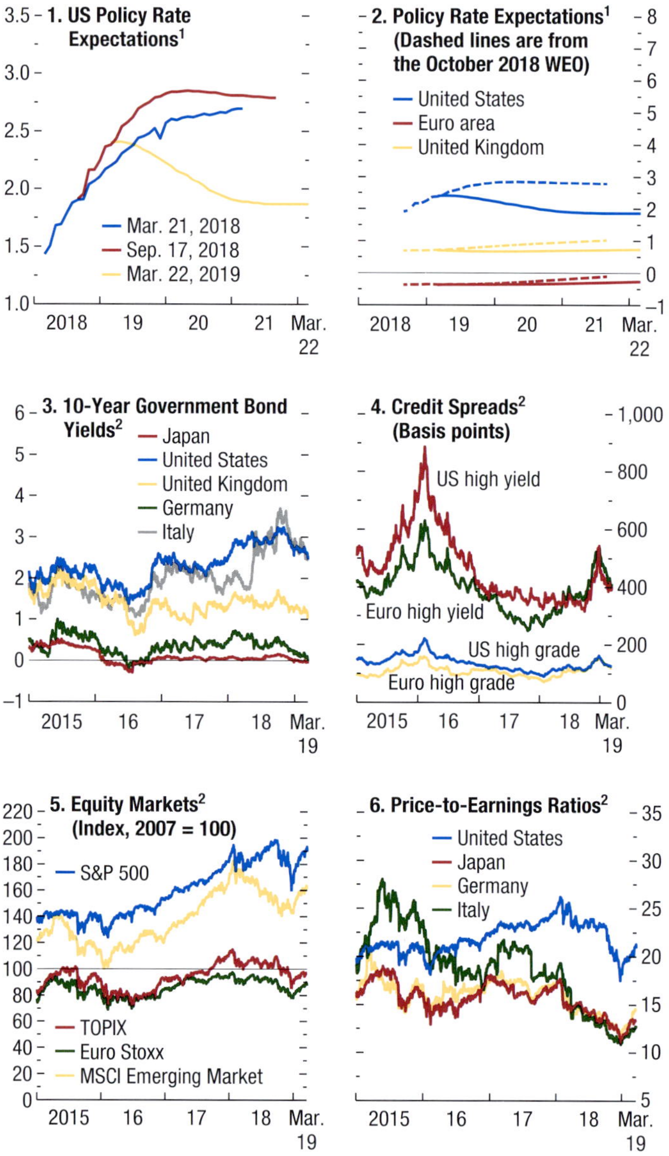

Sources: Bloomberg Finance L.P.; Haver Analytics; Thomson Reuters Datastream; and IMF staff calculations.
Note: MSCI = Morgan Stanley Capital International; S&P = Standard & Poor's; TOPIX = Tokyo Stock Price Index; WEO = *World Economic Outlook*.
[1]Expectations are based on the federal funds rate futures for the United States, the sterling overnight interbank average rate for the United Kingdom, and the euro interbank offered forward rate for the euro area; updated March 22, 2019.
[2]Data are through March 22, 2019.

advanced economy sovereign securities (in particular, 10-year US Treasury notes, German bunds, UK gilts) have priced in a lower path for future policy rates and are generally 40–80 basis points below the peaks of early November 2018. Italian spreads over German bunds, about 250 basis points as of late March, have declined from their late-October/early-November peaks, but remain elevated. Riskier asset classes have generally benefited from improved sentiment at the start of 2019. Equity markets in the United States and Europe have regained footing after the sharp sell-off at the end of 2018, while high-yield corporate spreads—which had decompressed significantly in December—have narrowed since, but still remain wider than in October.

Financial conditions in emerging markets improved in early 2019 but remain somewhat tighter than in October (Figure 1.6). Country-specific economic fundamentals and political factors continued to drive differentiation across economies in the group. Central banks in many emerging market economies (Chile, Indonesia, Mexico, Philippines, South Africa) have lifted policy rates since October because of concerns that inflation may rise following the increase in oil prices in 2018 and, for some countries, pass-through from previous currency depreciation. In China, the central bank provided liquidity support and reduced reserve requirements for all banks as growth moderated. Long-term sovereign yields and spreads over advanced economies are broadly back to October levels. In Mexico, concerns over policy reversals under the new administration led to a notable widening of the sovereign spread during November and December, but it has since narrowed. In Brazil, spreads have declined since October amid optimism about the prospects of pension reform under the new government. Following ongoing adjustments to rein in financial imbalances in Argentina and Turkey, spreads for both have declined somewhat but remain elevated. In line with improving risk sentiment this year, emerging market equity indexes have recovered some of the ground lost in late 2018 and are now broadly at or have surpassed the levels of October in most cases (Figure 1.7).

Exchange rates: With regard to major currencies, as of late March, the US dollar was back to its September 2018 level: the late-2018 appreciation reversed following a shift in market expectations about the pace and extent of monetary policy tightening (Figure 1.8, panel 1). The euro depreciated by about 3 percent over this period, on weaker-than-expected macroeconomic data and concerns about Italy. The yen appreciated modestly, and the pound strengthened by about 3 percent on shifting expectations of the outcome

Figure 1.6. Emerging Market Economies: Interest Rates and Spreads

Financial conditions in emerging market economies improved in early 2019, with differentiation across economies based on country-specific fundamentals.

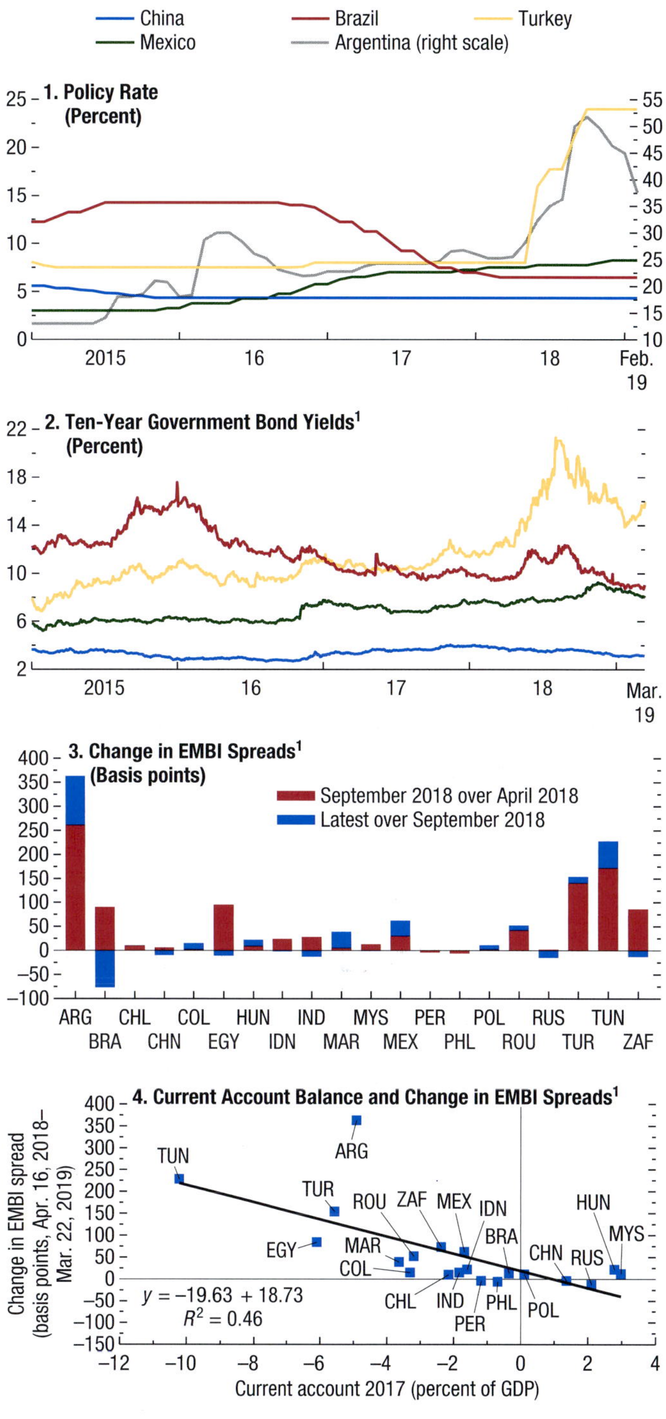

Sources: Haver Analytics; IMF, *International Financial Statistics*; Thomson Reuters Datastream; and IMF staff calculations.
Note: EMBI = J.P. Morgan Emerging Markets Bond Index. Data labels use International Organization for Standardization (ISO) country codes.
[1]Financial market data are through March 22, 2019.

Figure 1.7. Emerging Market Economies: Equity Markets and Credit

Emerging market equity indexes have recovered some of the ground lost in late 2018.

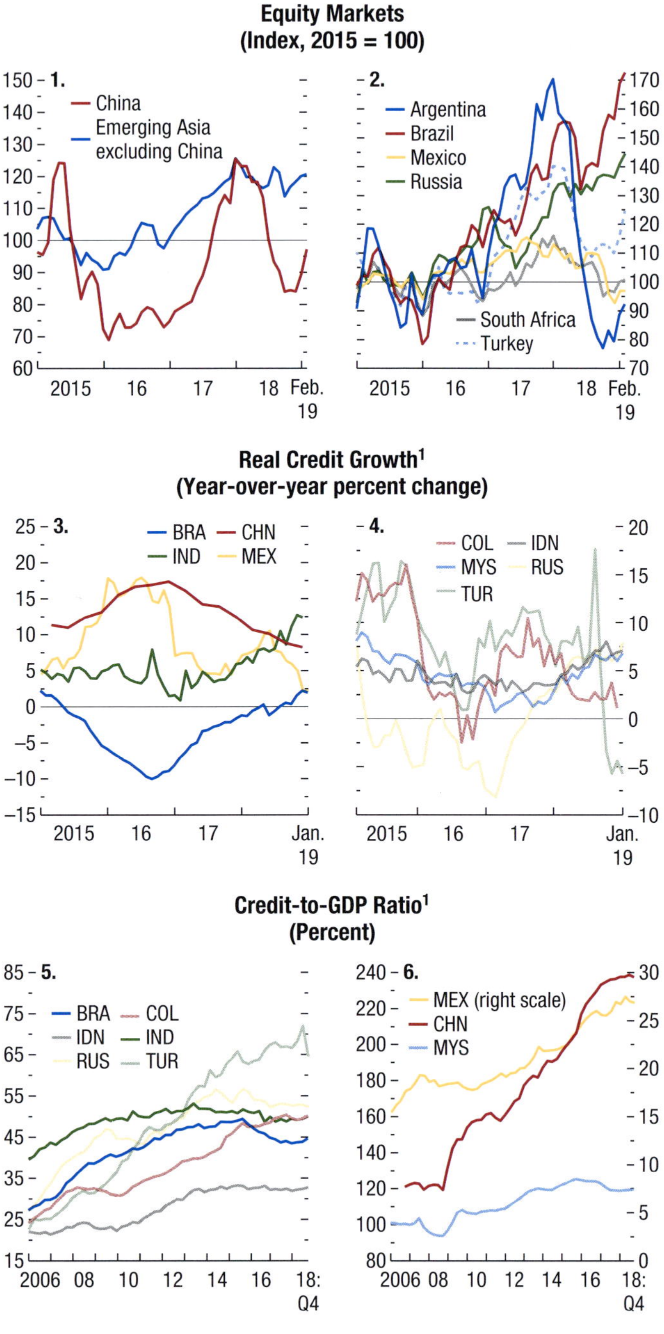

Sources: Bloomberg Finance L.P.; Haver Analytics; IMF, *International Financial Statistics* (IFS); Thomson Reuters Datastream; and IMF staff calculations.
Note: Data labels use International Organization for Standardization (ISO) country codes.
[1]Credit is other depository corporations' claims on the private sector (from IFS), except in the case of Brazil, for which private sector credit is from the Monetary Policy and Financial System Credit Operations published by Banco Central do Brasil, and China, for which credit is total social financing after adjusting for local government debt swaps.

Figure 1.8. Real Effective Exchange Rate Changes, September 2018–March 2019
(Percent)

Following a shift in market expectations about the pace and extent of US monetary policy tightening, the late-2018 appreciation of the dollar reversed and emerging market currencies generally strengthened.

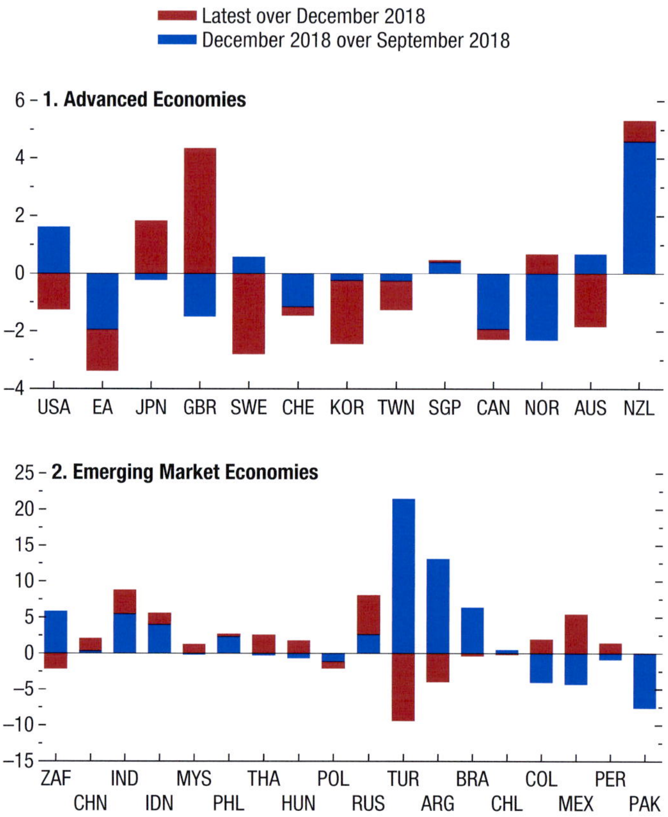

Source: IMF staff calculations.
Note: EA = euro area. Data labels use International Organization for Standardization (ISO) country codes. Latest data available are for March 22, 2019.

of Brexit negotiations. Emerging market currencies generally strengthened, helped by the pause in interest rate hikes by the Federal Reserve and by the truce in the US–China trade dispute (Figure 1.8, panel 2). This includes currencies that had come under more severe pressure in previous months—primarily the Argentine peso and the Turkish lira, but also the Brazilian real and the South African rand—as well as the Indian rupee and the Russian ruble. Most other Asian currencies also appreciated, with the Chinese renminbi strengthening by about 2 percent.

Capital flows: Improved market sentiment toward emerging markets was reflected in a stabilization and subsequent recovery in portfolio flows, which had dropped sharply in the second and third quarters of

Figure 1.9. Emerging Market Economies: Capital Flows

Investors increased allocations to emerging market bond and equity funds in early 2019.

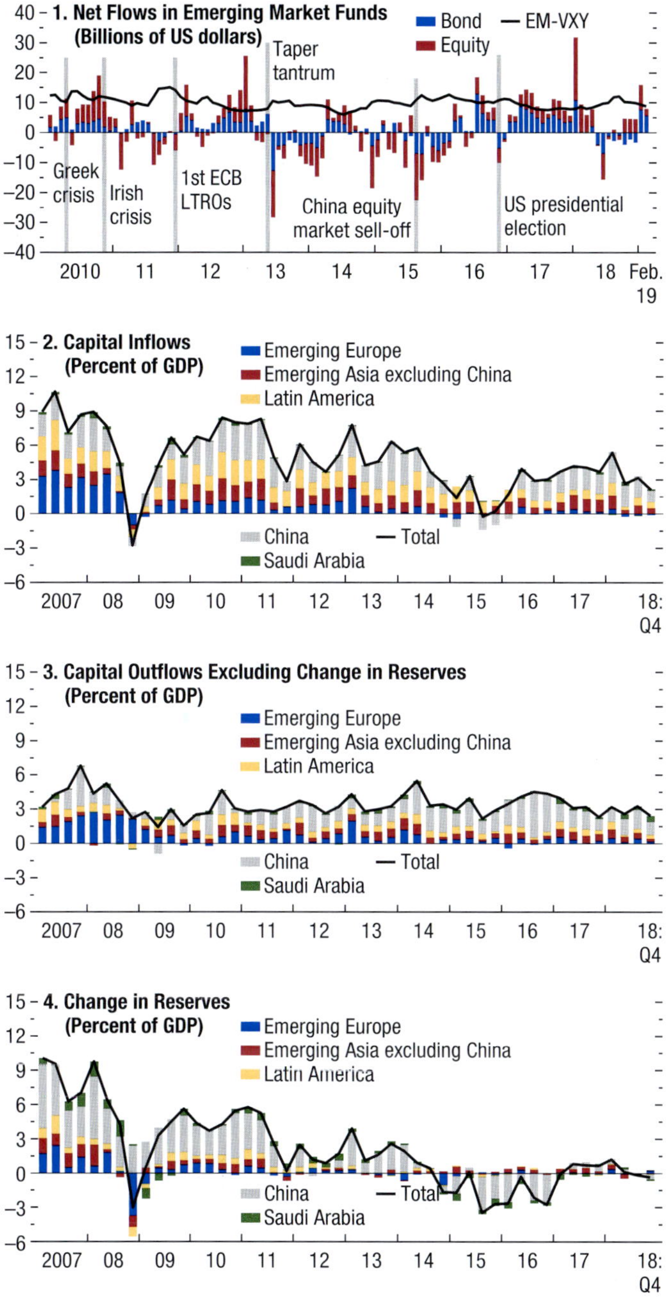

Sources: EPFR Global; Haver Analytics; IMF, *International Financial Statistics*; Thomson Reuters Datastream; and IMF staff calculations.
Note: Capital inflows are net purchases of domestic assets by nonresidents. Capital outflows are net purchases of foreign assets by domestic residents. Emerging Asia excluding China comprises India, Indonesia, Malaysia, the Philippines, and Thailand; emerging Europe comprises Poland, Romania, Russia, and Turkey; Latin America comprises Brazil, Chile, Colombia, Mexico, and Peru. ECB = European Central Bank; EM-VXY = J.P. Morgan Emerging Market Volatility Index; LTROs = long-term refinancing operations.

Figure 1.10. Half-Yearly Growth Forecasts
(Annualized semiannual percent change)

The global outlook envisages a stabilization of growth in the first half of 2019 followed by a gradual recovery.

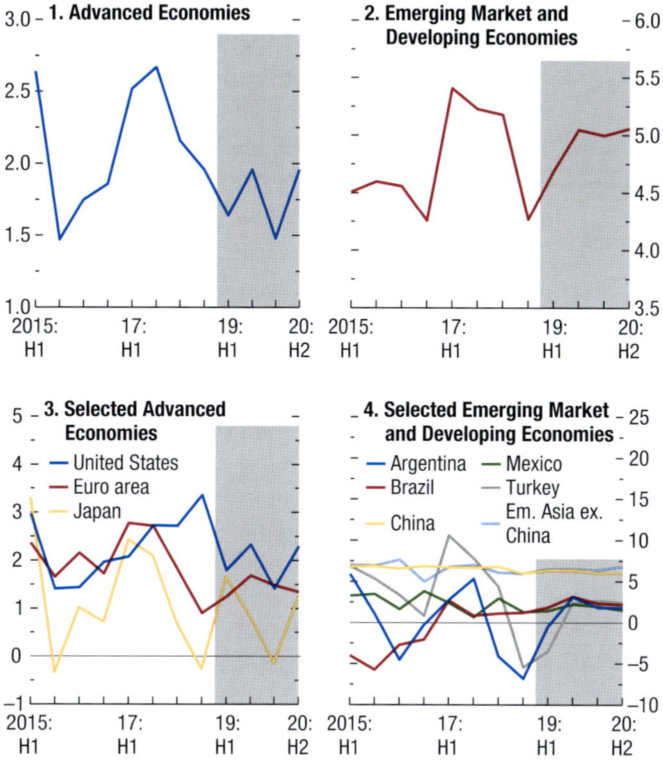

Source: IMF staff estimates.
Note: Em. Asia ex. China = emerging and developing Asia excluding China.

2018. The recovery was particularly notable in early 2019 as investors increased allocations to emerging market bond and equity funds (Figure 1.9).

The Forecast

Near-Term Moderation, Then a Modest Pickup

Industrial production figures and surveys of purchasing managers suggest that the slower momentum in global growth during the second half of 2018 is likely to continue in early 2019. The forecast envisages a stabilization of growth in the first half of the year and a gradual recovery thereafter (Figure 1.10).

Reflecting the slowdown in activity in the latter half of 2018 and the first half of 2019, global growth is set to moderate from 3.6 percent in 2018 to 3.3 percent in 2019, and then to return to 3.6 percent in 2020. The forecast for 2019 is 0.4 percentage point lower than in the October 2018 WEO, while the forecast for 2020 is 0.1 percentage point lower (Table 1.1).

Table 1.1. Overview of the *World Economic Outlook* Projections

(Percent change, unless noted otherwise)

		Projections		Difference from January 2019 *WEO Update*[1]		Difference from October 2018 WEO[1]	
	2018	2019	2020	2019	2020	2019	2020
World Output	**3.6**	**3.3**	**3.6**	**–0.2**	**0.0**	**–0.4**	**–0.1**
Advanced Economies	**2.2**	**1.8**	**1.7**	**–0.2**	**0.0**	**–0.3**	**0.0**
United States	2.9	2.3	1.9	–0.2	0.1	–0.2	0.1
Euro Area	1.8	1.3	1.5	–0.3	–0.2	–0.6	–0.2
Germany	1.5	0.8	1.4	–0.5	–0.2	–1.1	–0.2
France	1.5	1.3	1.4	–0.2	–0.2	–0.3	–0.2
Italy	0.9	0.1	0.9	–0.5	0.0	–0.9	0.0
Spain	2.5	2.1	1.9	–0.1	0.0	–0.1	0.0
Japan	0.8	1.0	0.5	–0.1	0.0	0.1	0.2
United Kingdom	1.4	1.2	1.4	–0.3	–0.2	–0.3	–0.1
Canada	1.8	1.5	1.9	–0.4	0.0	–0.5	0.1
Other Advanced Economies[2]	2.6	2.2	2.5	–0.3	0.0	–0.3	0.0
Emerging Market and Developing Economies	**4.5**	**4.4**	**4.8**	**–0.1**	**–0.1**	**–0.3**	**–0.1**
Commonwealth of Independent States	2.8	2.2	2.3	0.0	0.0	–0.2	–0.1
Russia	2.3	1.6	1.7	0.0	0.0	–0.2	–0.1
Excluding Russia	3.9	3.5	3.7	–0.2	0.0	–0.1	0.0
Emerging and Developing Asia	6.4	6.3	6.3	0.0	–0.1	0.0	–0.1
China	6.6	6.3	6.1	0.1	–0.1	0.1	–0.1
India[3]	7.1	7.3	7.5	–0.2	–0.2	–0.1	–0.2
ASEAN-5[4]	5.2	5.1	5.2	0.0	0.0	–0.1	0.0
Emerging and Developing Europe	3.6	0.8	2.8	0.1	0.4	–1.2	0.0
Latin America and the Caribbean	1.0	1.4	2.4	–0.6	–0.1	–0.8	–0.3
Brazil	1.1	2.1	2.5	–0.4	0.3	–0.3	0.2
Mexico	2.0	1.6	1.9	–0.5	–0.3	–0.9	–0.8
Middle East, North Africa, Afghanistan, and Pakistan	1.8	1.5	3.2	–0.9	0.2	–1.2	0.2
Saudi Arabia	2.2	1.8	2.1	0.0	0.0	–0.6	0.2
Sub-Saharan Africa	3.0	3.5	3.7	0.0	0.1	–0.3	–0.2
Nigeria	1.9	2.1	2.5	0.1	0.3	–0.2	0.0
South Africa	0.8	1.2	1.5	–0.2	–0.2	–0.2	–0.2
Memorandum							
European Union	2.1	1.6	1.7	–0.3	–0.1	–0.4	–0.1
Low-Income Developing Countries	4.6	5.0	5.1	–0.1	0.0	–0.2	–0.2
Middle East and North Africa	1.4	1.3	3.2	–0.9	0.3	–1.2	0.3
World Growth Based on Market Exchange Rates	3.1	2.7	2.9	–0.3	0.0	–0.4	0.0
World Trade Volume (goods and services)	**3.8**	**3.4**	**3.9**	**–0.6**	**–0.1**	**–0.6**	**–0.2**
Imports							
Advanced Economies	3.3	3.0	3.2	–1.1	–0.1	–1.0	–0.3
Emerging Market and Developing Economies	5.6	4.6	5.3	–0.5	–0.3	–0.2	–0.2
Exports							
Advanced Economies	3.1	2.7	3.1	–0.2	–0.3	–0.4	–0.3
Emerging Market and Developing Economies	4.3	4.0	4.8	–0.5	0.0	–0.8	0.0
Commodity Prices (US dollars)							
Oil[5]	29.4	–13.4	–0.2	0.7	0.2	–12.5	4.2
Nonfuel (average based on world commodity export weights)[6]	1.6	–0.2	1.1	2.5	–0.1	0.5	0.8
Consumer Prices							
Advanced Economies	2.0	1.6	2.1	–0.1	0.1	–0.3	0.1
Emerging Market and Developing Economies[7]	4.8	4.9	4.7	–0.2	0.1	–0.3	0.1
London Interbank Offered Rate (percent)							
On US Dollar Deposits (six month)	2.5	3.2	3.8	0.0	0.0	–0.2	–0.1
On Euro Deposits (three month)	–0.3	–0.3	–0.2	0.0	–0.2	–0.1	–0.3
On Japanese Yen Deposits (six month)	0.0	0.0	0.0	0.0	–0.1	–0.1	–0.1

Note: Real effective exchange rates are assumed to remain constant at the levels prevailing during January 14–February 11, 2019. Economies are listed on the basis of economic size. The aggregated quarterly data are seasonally adjusted. WEO = *World Economic Outlook.*

[1]Difference based on rounded figures for the current, January 2019 *World Economic Outlook Update*, and October 2018 *World Economic Outlook* forecasts. The differences are also adjusted to include Argentina's consumer prices since the July 2018 Update.

[2]Excludes the Group of Seven (Canada, France, Germany, Italy, Japan, United Kingdom, United States) and euro area countries.

[3]For India, data and forecasts are presented on a fiscal year basis and GDP from 2011 onward is based on GDP at market prices with fiscal year 2011/12 as a base year.

[4]Indonesia, Malaysia, Philippines, Thailand, Vietnam.

Table 1.1 *(continued)*

	Year over Year				Q4 over Q4[8]			
			Projections				Projections	
	2017	2018	2019	2020	2017	2018	2019	2020
World Output	**3.8**	**3.6**	**3.3**	**3.6**	**4.0**	**3.4**	**3.5**	**3.6**
Advanced Economies	**2.4**	**2.2**	**1.8**	**1.7**	**2.6**	**2.0**	**1.8**	**1.8**
United States	2.2	2.9	2.3	1.9	2.5	3.0	2.2	1.7
Euro Area	2.4	1.8	1.3	1.5	2.7	1.1	1.6	1.4
Germany	2.5	1.5	0.8	1.4	2.8	0.6	1.4	1.3
France	2.2	1.5	1.3	1.4	2.8	0.9	1.6	1.3
Italy	1.6	0.9	0.1	0.9	1.7	0.0	0.6	0.8
Spain	3.0	2.5	2.1	1.9	3.1	2.4	1.9	1.7
Japan	1.9	0.8	1.0	0.5	2.4	0.3	0.3	1.4
United Kingdom	1.8	1.4	1.2	1.4	1.6	1.4	1.0	1.5
Canada	3.0	1.8	1.5	1.9	2.9	1.6	1.8	1.8
Other Advanced Economies[2]	2.9	2.6	2.2	2.5	2.9	2.4	2.4	2.7
Emerging Market and Developing Economies	**4.8**	**4.5**	**4.4**	**4.8**	**5.2**	**4.7**	**4.9**	**5.0**
Commonwealth of Independent States	2.4	2.8	2.2	2.3	1.5	3.4	1.6	2.0
Russia	1.6	2.3	1.6	1.7	1.0	3.4	1.2	1.7
Excluding Russia	4.1	3.9	3.5	3.7	. . .	. . .	. . .	. . .
Emerging and Developing Asia	6.6	6.4	6.3	6.3	6.8	6.3	6.4	6.3
China	6.8	6.6	6.3	6.1	6.7	6.4	6.3	6.0
India[3]	7.2	7.1	7.3	7.5	8.1	6.8	7.2	7.6
ASEAN-5[4]	5.4	5.2	5.1	5.2	5.4	5.1	5.3	5.3
Emerging and Developing Europe	6.0	3.6	0.8	2.8	6.2	0.7	2.1	2.9
Latin America and the Caribbean	1.2	1.0	1.4	2.4	1.3	0.3	2.0	2.2
Brazil	1.1	1.1	2.1	2.5	2.2	1.1	2.8	2.2
Mexico	2.1	2.0	1.6	1.9	1.5	1.7	2.0	1.6
Middle East, North Africa, Afghanistan, and Pakistan	2.2	1.8	1.5	3.2	. . .	. . .	. . .	. . .
Saudi Arabia	–0.7	2.2	1.8	2.1	–1.4	4.0	1.0	2.1
Sub-Saharan Africa	2.9	3.0	3.5	3.7	. . .	. . .	. . .	. . .
Nigeria	0.8	1.9	2.1	2.5	. . .	. . .	. . .	. . .
South Africa	1.4	0.8	1.2	1.5	2.2	0.2	1.0	1.8
Memorandum								
European Union	2.7	2.1	1.6	1.7	2.8	1.6	1.7	1.7
Low-Income Developing Countries	4.9	4.6	5.0	5.1	. . .	. . .	. . .	. . .
Middle East and North Africa	1.8	1.4	1.3	3.2	. . .	. . .	. . .	. . .
World Growth Based on Market Exchange Rates	3.2	3.1	2.7	2.9	3.3	2.8	2.8	2.8
World Trade Volume (goods and services)	**5.4**	**3.8**	**3.4**	**3.9**	**. . .**	**. . .**	**. . .**	**. . .**
Imports								
Advanced Economies	4.3	3.3	3.0	3.2	. . .	. . .	. . .	. . .
Emerging Market and Developing Economies	7.5	5.6	4.6	5.3	. . .	. . .	. . .	. . .
Exports								
Advanced Economies	4.4	3.1	2.7	3.1	. . .	. . .	. . .	. . .
Emerging Market and Developing Economies	7.2	4.3	4.0	4.8	. . .	. . .	. . .	. . .
Commodity Prices (US dollars)								
Oil[5]	23.3	29.4	–13.4	–0.2	19.6	9.5	–7.5	–1.3
Nonfuel (average based on world commodity export weights)[6]	6.4	1.6	–0.2	1.1	3.5	–1.9	3.6	0.9
Consumer Prices								
Advanced Economies	1.7	2.0	1.6	2.1	1.7	1.9	1.9	1.9
Emerging Market and Developing Economies[7]	4.3	4.8	4.9	4.7	3.7	4.3	4.0	3.9
London Interbank Offered Rate (percent)								
On US Dollar Deposits (six month)	1.5	2.5	3.2	3.8	. . .	. . .	. . .	. . .
On Euro Deposits (three month)	–0.3	–0.3	–0.3	–0.2	. . .	. . .	. . .	. . .
On Japanese Yen Deposits (six month)	0.0	0.0	0.0	0.0	. . .	. . .	. . .	. . .

[5]Simple average of prices of UK Brent, Dubai Fateh, and West Texas Intermediate crude oil. The average price of oil in US dollars a barrel was $68.33 in 2018; the assumed price, based on futures markets, is $59.16 in 2019 and $59.02 in 2020.

[6]Starting with the January 2019 WEO *Update*, the IMF commodity price index and its sub-indices have been updated and have expanded coverage. The nonfuel commodity forecast revisions compare current projections with October 2018 projections, however, due to methodological and coverage changes, comparability is limited.

[7]Excludes Venezuela. See country-specific note for Venezuela in the "Country Notes" section of the Statistical Appendix.

[8]For World Output, the quarterly estimates and projections account for approximately 90 percent of annual world output at purchasing-power-parity weights. For Emerging Market and Developing Economies, the quarterly estimates and projections account for approximately 80 percent of annual emerging market and developing economies' output at purchasing-power-parity weights.

Figure 1.11. Forecast Assumptions: Fiscal Indicators

(Percent of GDP)

Fiscal policy is assumed to be expansionary across advanced economies in 2019 and expected to turn contractionary in 2020 as the US stimulus starts going into reverse. Across the emerging market and developing economy group, fiscal policy is assumed to be expansionary in 2019 (in part reflecting a projected fiscal stimulus in China to offset some of the negative effects of higher tariffs), before turning contractionary in 2020.

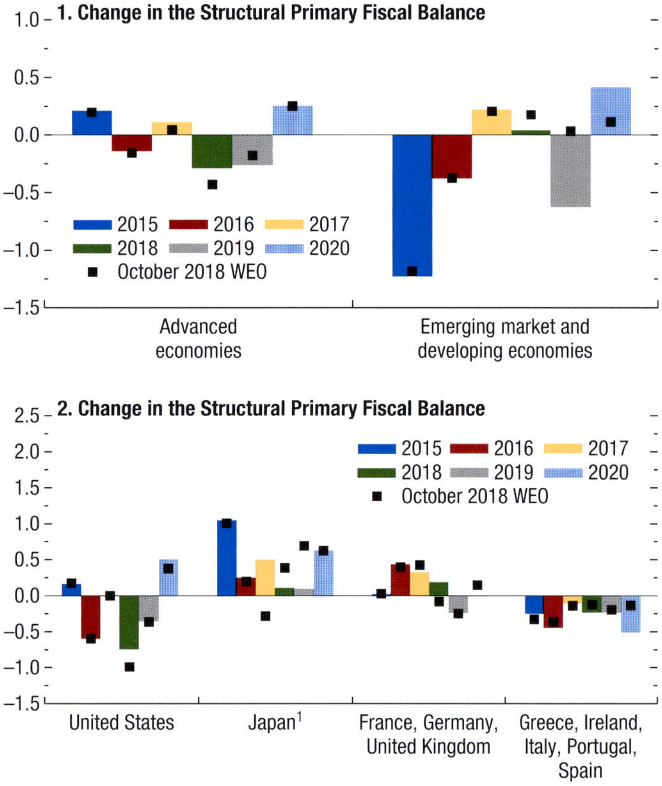

Source: IMF staff estimates.
Note: WEO = *World Economic Outlook.*
[1]Japan's latest figures reflect comprehensive methodological revisions adopted in December 2016.

Figure 1.12. Commodity Price Assumptions and Terms-of-Trade Windfall Gains and Losses

(Percent of GDP, unless noted otherwise)

Based on oil futures contracts, average oil prices are projected at $54.1 in 2019, rising to $55.2 in 2020. Metal prices are expected to decline 6.0 percent year over year in 2019 and inch down a further 0.8 percent in 2020. Food prices are projected to decline 2.6 percent year over year in 2019 before increasing by 1.7 percent in 2020.

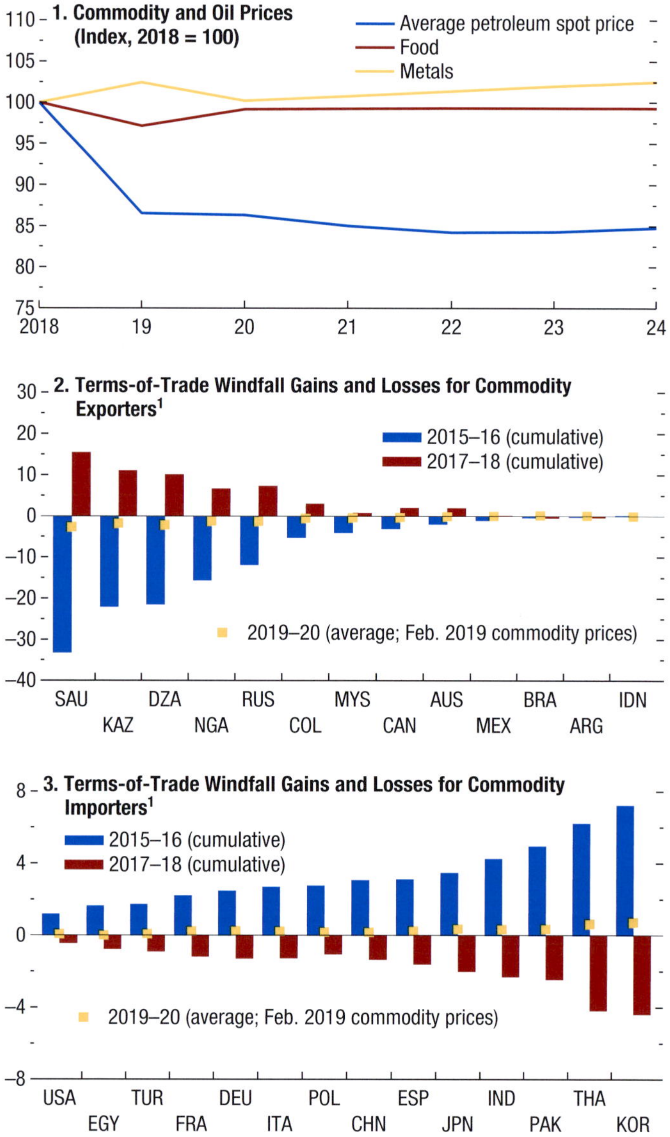

Sources: IMF, Primary Commodity Price System; and IMF staff estimates.
Note: Data labels use International Organization for Standardization (ISO) country codes.
[1]Gains (losses) for 2019–20 are simple averages of annual incremental gains (losses) for 2019 and 2020. The windfall is an estimate of the change in disposable income arising from commodity price changes. The windfall gain in year *t* for a country exporting *x* US dollars of commodity *A* and importing *m* US dollars of commodity *B* in year $t - 1$ is defined as $(\Delta p_t^A x_{t-1} - \Delta p_t^B m_{t-1}) / Y_{t-1}$, in which Δp_t^A and Δp_t^B are the percentage changes in the prices of *A* and *B* between year $t - 1$ and year *t*, and *Y* is GDP in year $t - 1$ in US dollars. See also Gruss (2014).

Beyond 2020, global growth is projected to plateau at about 3.6 percent over the medium term, similarly to the medium-term forecast of the October 2018 WEO. The assumptions for trade, fiscal, and monetary policies as well as commodity prices, which underpin this baseline forecast, are outlined in Box 1.2 (see also Figures 1.11 and 1.12). Importantly, tariffs on $200 billion of US imports from China are assumed to stay at 10 percent (whereas in the October 2018 WEO and the January 2019 WEO *Update* they had been assumed to rise to 25 percent as of March 1, 2019).

The global growth forecast reflects a combination of waning cyclical forces and a return to tepid potential growth in advanced economies; a precarious recovery in emerging market and developing economies, driven to a great extent by economies currently experiencing severe macroeconomic distress; and complex factors that shape the prospects for potential growth in both groups.

Waning Cyclical Forces in Advanced Economies

Growth in advanced economies is projected to slow from 2.2 percent in 2018 to 1.8 percent in 2019 and 1.7 percent in 2020. The estimated growth rate for 2018 and the projection for 2019, respectively, are 0.2 percentage point and 0.3 percentage point lower than in the October 2018 WEO, mostly reflecting downward revisions for the euro area.

The projected slowdown in advanced economies in 2019 accounts for over two-thirds of the expected deceleration in global growth relative to 2018. With output gaps estimated as being closed for most economies in the group (indeed some are operating above their estimated potential in a context of historically low unemployment rates), the cyclical upsurge is set to retreat toward more modest potential rates of growth.

The retreat in part reflects the anticipated negative effects of the tariff increases enacted in 2018. A second notable aspect of the advanced economy growth profile is that the temporary boost to US and trading partner growth from the sizable US fiscal stimulus is expected to diminish during 2019 (and particularly in 2020 as some of its provisions start to reverse). But beyond these two features already incorporated into the previous forecast, the waning of cyclical forces appears more rapid than expected, triggered by additional developments in particular economies during the second half of 2018.

Growth in the euro area is set to moderate from 1.8 percent in 2018 to 1.3 percent in 2019 (0.6 percentage point lower than projected in October) and 1.5 percent in 2020. Although growth is expected to recover in the first half of 2019 as some of the temporary factors that held activity back dissipate, carryover from the weakness in the second half of 2018 is expected to hold the 2019 growth rate down. Growth rates have been marked down for many economies, notably *Germany* (due to soft private consumption, weak industrial production following the introduction of revised auto emission standards, and subdued foreign demand); *Italy* (due to weak domestic demand, as sovereign yields remain elevated); and *France* (due to the negative impact of street protests).

The baseline projection of about 1.2 percent and 1.4 percent growth in the *United Kingdom* in 2019–20 is surrounded by uncertainty. The downward revisions relative to the October 2018 WEO reflect the negative effect of prolonged uncertainty about the Brexit outcome, only partially offset by the positive impact from fiscal stimulus announced in the 2019 budget. This baseline projection assumes that a Brexit deal is reached in 2019 and that the United Kingdom transitions gradually to the new regime. However, as of mid-March, the form Brexit will ultimately take remained highly uncertain.

In the *United States*, growth is expected to decline to 2.3 percent in 2019 and soften further to 1.9 percent in 2020 with the unwinding of fiscal stimulus. The downward revision to 2019 growth reflects the impact of the government shutdown and somewhat lower fiscal spending than previously anticipated, while the modest upward revision for 2020 reflects a more accommodative stance of monetary policy than in the October forecast. Despite the downward revision, the projected pace of expansion for 2019 is above the US economy's estimated potential growth rate. Strong domestic demand growth will support higher imports and contribute to some widening of the current account deficit.

Japan's economy is set to grow by 1.0 percent in 2019 (0.1 percentage point higher than in the October WEO). This revision mainly reflects additional fiscal support this year, including measures to mitigate the effects of the planned consumption tax rate increase in October 2019. Growth is projected to moderate to 0.5 percent in 2020 (0.2 percentage point higher than in the October 2018 WEO, reflecting the effects of the aforementioned mitigating measures).

A Precarious Recovery in Emerging Market and Developing Economies

Global growth in 2019 is also weighed down by the emerging market and developing economy group, where growth is expected to tick down to 4.4 percent in 2019 (from 4.5 percent in 2018), 0.3 percentage point lower than in the October 2018 WEO. The decline in growth relative to 2018 reflects lower growth in China and the recession in Turkey, with an important carryover from weaker activity in late 2018, as well as a deepening contraction in Iran.

Conditions are projected to improve during 2019 as stimulus measures sustain activity in China and recession strains gradually ease in economies such as Argentina and Turkey. In 2020, growth is projected to rise to 4.8 percent, driven almost entirely by an expected

Figure 1.13. Growth Rate: Emerging Market and Developing Economies
(Percent)

The projected pickup in growth among emerging market and developing economies in 2020 is driven almost entirely by an expected strengthening of activity in economies currently in macroeconomic distress and some easing of strains in countries affected by conflict and geopolitical tensions.

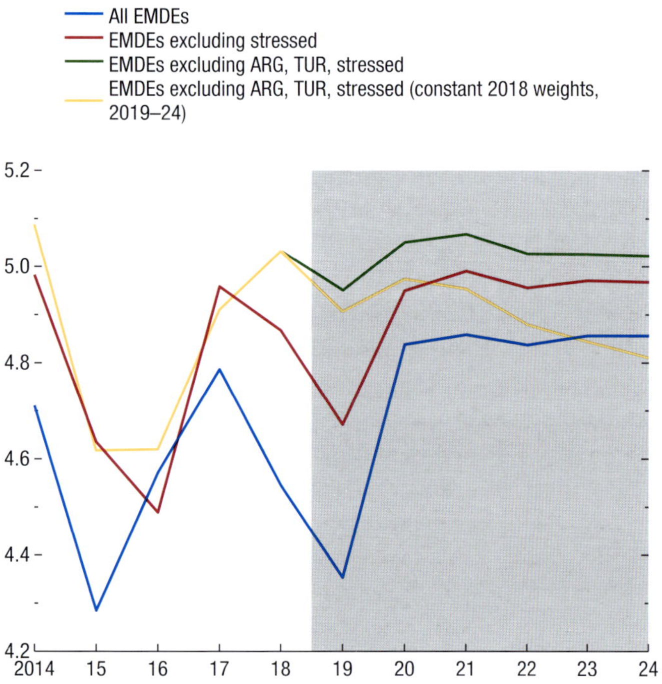

Source: IMF staff estimates.
Note: EMDEs = emerging market and developing economies; stressed = IRN, IRQ, LBY, SDN, SSD, UKR, VEN, YEM. Country list uses International Organization for Standardization (ISO) country codes.

strengthening of activity in these economies on the back of policy adjustment and some easing of strains in countries affected by conflict and geopolitical tensions (Figure 1.13). For the latter group of countries in particular, the forecast is subject to very significant uncertainty. With declining growth in advanced economies, the projected pickup in global growth in 2020 is entirely predicated on this projected improvement for the emerging market and developing economy group. Figure 1.13 also highlights the role played by the increasing weight of fast-growing economies, such as China and India, in supporting aggregate growth for emerging markets and developing economies as well as world growth.

Near-term prospects for emerging market and developing economies continue to be shaped by the interaction between country-specific fundamentals and a challenging external environment marked by the slowdown in advanced economies; trade tensions; expected gradual tightening of financial conditions consistent with some further removal of monetary policy accommodation in the United States; and, for commodity exporters, a generally subdued outlook for commodity prices (including oil prices, which are projected to remain below their 2018 average throughout the forecast horizon).

Growth in *emerging and developing Asia* is expected to dip to 6.3 percent in 2019 and 2020 (from 6.4 percent in 2018), with a marginal downward revision for 2020 relative to the October WEO. Economic growth in *China*, despite fiscal stimulus and no further increase in tariffs from the United States relative to those in force as of September 2018, is projected to slow on an annualized basis in 2019 and 2020. This reflects weaker underlying growth in 2018, especially in the second half, and the impact of lingering trade tensions with the United States. The projection for 2019 is slightly stronger than in the October 2018 WEO, reflecting the revised assumption on United States tariffs on Chinese exports, as described in Box 1.2, while the projection for 2020 is slightly weaker, as the underlying momentum in activity is more subdued. In *India*, growth is projected to pick up to 7.3 percent in 2019 and 7.5 percent in 2020, supported by the continued recovery of investment and robust consumption amid a more expansionary stance of monetary policy and some expected impetus from fiscal policy. Nevertheless, reflecting the recent revision to the national account statistics that indicated somewhat softer underlying momentum, growth forecasts have been revised downward compared with the October 2018 WEO by 0.1 percentage point for 2019 and 0.2 percentage point for 2020, respectively.

Activity in *emerging and developing Europe* in 2019 is expected to weaken more than previously anticipated, despite generally buoyant and higher-than-expected growth in several central and eastern European countries, before recovering in 2020. The sizable revision for the region is mostly due to a substantial projected contraction in *Turkey* in 2019, where the weakness in demand—following tighter external financing conditions and needed policy tightening—is expected to continue in early 2019 before a recovery takes hold in the second half of the year.

In *Latin America*, growth is projected to recover over the next two years, to 1.4 percent in 2019 and 2.4 percent in 2020. In *Brazil*, growth is projected to strengthen from 1.1 percent in 2018 to 2.1 percent in

2019 and 2.5 percent in 2020. In *Mexico,* growth is now forecast to remain below 2 percent in 2019–20, a markdown close to 1 percentage point for both years relative to October. These changes, in part, reflect shifts in perceptions about policy direction under new administrations in both countries. *Argentina*'s economy is projected to contract in the first half of 2019 as domestic demand slows with tighter policies to reduce imbalances, returning to growth in the second half of the year as real disposable income recovers and agricultural production rebounds after last year's drought. *Venezuela*'s economy is expected to contract by one-fourth in 2019, and a further 10 percent in 2020—a greater collapse than projected in the October 2018 WEO and one that generates a sizable drag on projected growth for the region and for the emerging market and developing economy group in both years.

Growth in the *Middle East, North Africa, Afghanistan, and Pakistan* region is expected to decline to 1.5 percent in 2019, before recovering to about 3.2 percent in 2020. The outlook for the region is weighed down by multiple factors, including slower oil GDP growth in *Saudi Arabia*; ongoing macroeconomic adjustment challenges in *Pakistan*; US sanctions in *Iran*; and civil tensions and conflict across several other economies, including Iraq, Syria, and Yemen, where recovery from the collapse associated with the war is now expected to be slower than previously anticipated.

In *sub-Saharan Africa,* growth is expected to pick up to 3.5 percent in 2019 and 3.7 percent in 2020 (from 3.0 percent in 2018). The projection is 0.3 percentage point and 0.2 percentage point lower for 2019 and 2020, respectively, than in the October 2018 WEO, reflecting downward revisions for *Angola* and *Nigeria* with the softening of oil prices. Growth in *South Africa* is expected to marginally improve from 0.8 percent in 2018 to 1.2 percent in 2019 and 1.5 percent in 2020, a 0.2 percentage point downward revision for both years relative to the October projections. The projected recovery reflects modestly reduced but continued policy uncertainty in the South African economy after the May 2019 elections.

Activity in the *Commonwealth of Independent States* is projected to expand about 2¼ percent in 2019–20, slightly lower than projected in the October 2018 WEO, as weaker oil prices weigh on *Russia's* growth prospects.

Modest Outlook for Medium-Term Growth

Beyond 2020, global growth is set to plateau at 3.6 percent over the medium term. For the advanced economy group, growth is projected to moderate further over the medium term as the underlying structural headwinds to potential output (namely, continued weak productivity growth and slowing labor force growth) increasingly assert influence on the path of output as the cyclical forces discussed above fade away. Growth for the emerging market and developing economy group is expected to broadly stabilize at its 2020 level for the outer years of the forecast horizon, but with important offsetting regional differences.

Specifically, for advanced economies, growth is projected to slow to 1.6 percent by 2022 and remain at that level thereafter. The productivity slowdown that set in before the 2008–09 global financial crisis (Adler and others 2017) is projected to abate somewhat, with a slight pickup in productivity expected over the medium term. Despite the apparent proliferation of digitalization and automation, their cumulative impact on productivity is expected to be modest over the forecast horizon—likely benefiting consumer welfare to a larger extent than labor productivity (Box 1.5 of the April 2018 WEO). Other developments potentially have less favorable implications for productivity. These include the retreat from global economic integration (projections for global trade volume growth have been marked down following the tariff increases of 2018).

The modest uptick expected in productivity is likely only partially to counteract the drag on potential output growth anticipated from slower labor force growth as the population ages. This is particularly relevant for Japan and southern Europe (see Chapter 2 of the April 2018 WEO for a discussion of the changes in labor force participation rates across advanced economies).

For emerging market and developing economies, growth is projected to stabilize at about 4.8 percent over the medium term. The combination of higher growth than in advanced economies and the group's rising weight in global GDP translates into a significant increase in emerging market and developing economies' share of global growth, from 76 percent in 2019 to about 85 percent in 2024.

The medium-term growth forecast incorporates continued strong investment growth in emerging market and developing economies, accounting for more than one-third of their GDP growth rate during the projection horizon (Figure 1.14). In turn, this robust investment path is predicated on a smooth trajectory for the drivers of capital spending; a gradual tightening in financial conditions (which is particularly relevant to the investment outlook in the emerging market and developing economy group, given the rapid buildup of

Figure 1.14. Contributions to GDP Growth
(Percent)

Over the forecast horizon, investment growth in emerging market and developing economies is projected to account for more than one-third of their GDP growth rate.

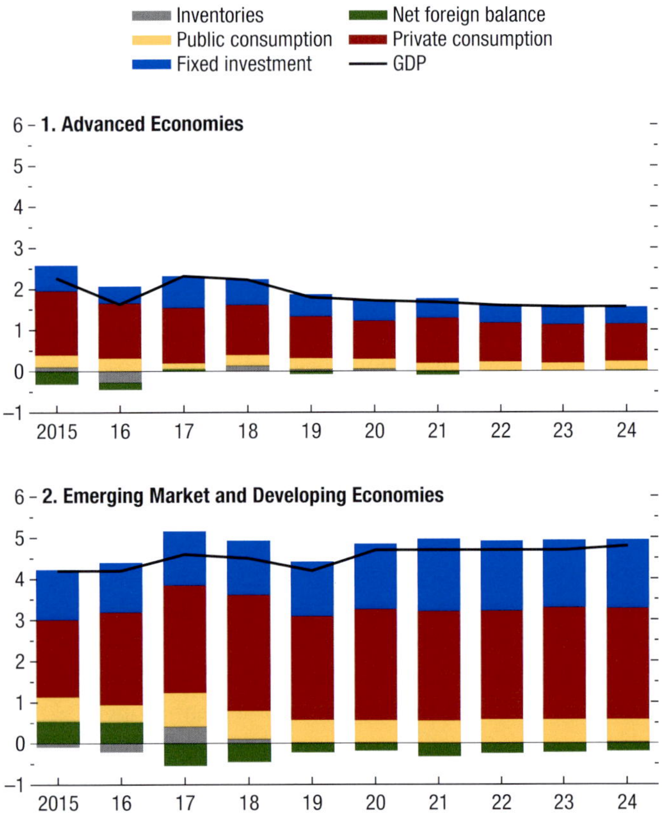

Source: IMF staff estimates.

leverage during years of low interest rates); quick resolution of trade disagreements and subsequent easing of trade tensions; and broader policy actions that help reduce uncertainty. Chapter 3 discusses how the retreat from trade integration threatens the long-standing downward trend in the relative price of capital goods and how this could weigh on the investment prospects of developing economies.

The medium-term growth forecast for emerging market and developing economies reflects important differences across regions. In emerging Asia, growth is expected to remain above 6 percent through the forecast horizon. Central to this smooth growth profile is a gradual slowdown in China to 5.5 percent by 2024 as internal rebalancing toward a private-consumption and services-based economy continues and regulatory tightening slows the accumulation of debt and associated vulnerabilities. Growth in India is expected to stabilize at just under 7¾ percent over the medium term, based on continued implementation of structural reforms and easing of infrastructure bottlenecks.

In Latin America, growth is projected to increase from 2.4 percent in 2020 to 2.8 percent over the medium term. Financial stabilization and recovery in Argentina, where growth is projected to strengthen to about 3½ percent over the medium term, contributes to that region's growth improvement. So is stable, though moderate, growth in Brazil and Mexico (in the range of 2¼–2¾ percent) as structural rigidities, subdued terms of trade, and fiscal imbalances (particularly for Brazil) weigh on the outlook.

Activity in emerging Europe is projected to pick up from the current post-global-financial-crisis low, with the region expected to grow just above 3 percent over the medium term. This improvement reflects primarily the forecast for Turkey, where activity is projected to gradually strengthen after the economy returns to positive annual growth in 2020. Over the medium term, Turkey's growth is projected to pick up to 3.5 percent as domestic demand recovers from the current sharp contraction that is reducing macroeconomic and financial imbalances. For other economies in the region with robust growth rates in recent years, such as Poland and Romania, growth is expected to moderate to about 3 percent over the medium term, reflecting the fading of stimulus from EU investment funds and accommodative policies.

The outlook for the Commonwealth of Independent States is for growth to stabilize at 2.4 percent over the medium term. This largely reflects sluggish growth in Russia of about 1½ percent over the medium term, weighed down by the modest outlook for oil prices and structural headwinds.

Prospects vary across sub-Saharan Africa, reflecting the heterogeneity of the economies, associated with disparities in the level of development, exposure to weather shocks, and commodity dependence. For the region as a whole, growth is projected to increase from 3.7 percent in 2020 to about 4 percent in 2024 (although for close to two-fifths of economies, the average growth rate over the medium term is projected to exceed 5 percent). Growth prospects for commodity exporters are weighed down by the soft outlook for commodity prices, including for Nigeria and Angola, where growth is expected to reach about 2.6 percent and 3.9 percent, respectively, in the medium term. In South Africa, growth is projected to stabilize at 1¾ percent over the medium term as structural bottlenecks continue to weigh on investment and productivity, and metal export prices are expected to remain subdued. Rising debt-service costs as financial conditions tighten globally and difficult adjustment processes to diversify production structures away from resource extraction are expected to weigh on growth in many economies across the region.

The medium-term outlook for the Middle East, North Africa, Afghanistan, and Pakistan region is largely shaped by the outlook for fuel prices, needed adjustment to correct macroeconomic imbalances in certain economies, and geopolitical tensions. Growth in Saudi Arabia is expected to stabilize at about 2¼–2½ percent over the medium term, as stronger non-oil growth is countered by the subdued outlook for oil prices and output. In Pakistan, in the absence of further adjustment policies, growth is projected to remain subdued at about 2.5 percent, with continued external and fiscal imbalances weighing on confidence. Elsewhere in the region, activity is weighed down by the expected impact of sanctions in Iran, civil strife in Syria and Yemen, and rising debt-service costs and tighter financial conditions in Lebanon.

Convergence prospects are bleak for some emerging market and developing economies. Across sub-Saharan Africa and the Middle East, North Africa, Afghanistan, and Pakistan region, 41 economies, accounting for close to 10 percent of global GDP in purchasing-power-parity terms and close to 1 billion in population, are projected to grow by less than advanced economies in per capita terms over the next five years, implying that their income levels are set to fall further behind those economies (Figure 1.15, panels 1 and 2). Panel 3 of Figure 1.15 documents the heterogeneity in per capita growth rates in sub-Saharan Africa, where the majority of countries is projected to grow at rates well above the weighted average for the region.

Inflation Outlook

The outlook for inflation largely mirrors the prospects for growth and commodity prices discussed above. Inflation is projected to remain broadly at current levels for the advanced economy group, while for the emerging market and developing economy group excluding Venezuela, it is set to resume its steady decline of the past decade after a temporary modest rise this year.

Consistent with the softer outlook for commodity prices and the expected moderation in growth,

Figure 1.15. Per Capita Real GDP Growth
(Percent, unless noted otherwise)

41 economies accounting for close to 10 percent of global GDP in purchasing-power-parity terms and close to 1 billion in population are projected to grow by less than advanced economies in per capita terms over the next five years. Some regions, such as sub-Saharan Africa, feature considerable heterogeneity in per capita growth rates.

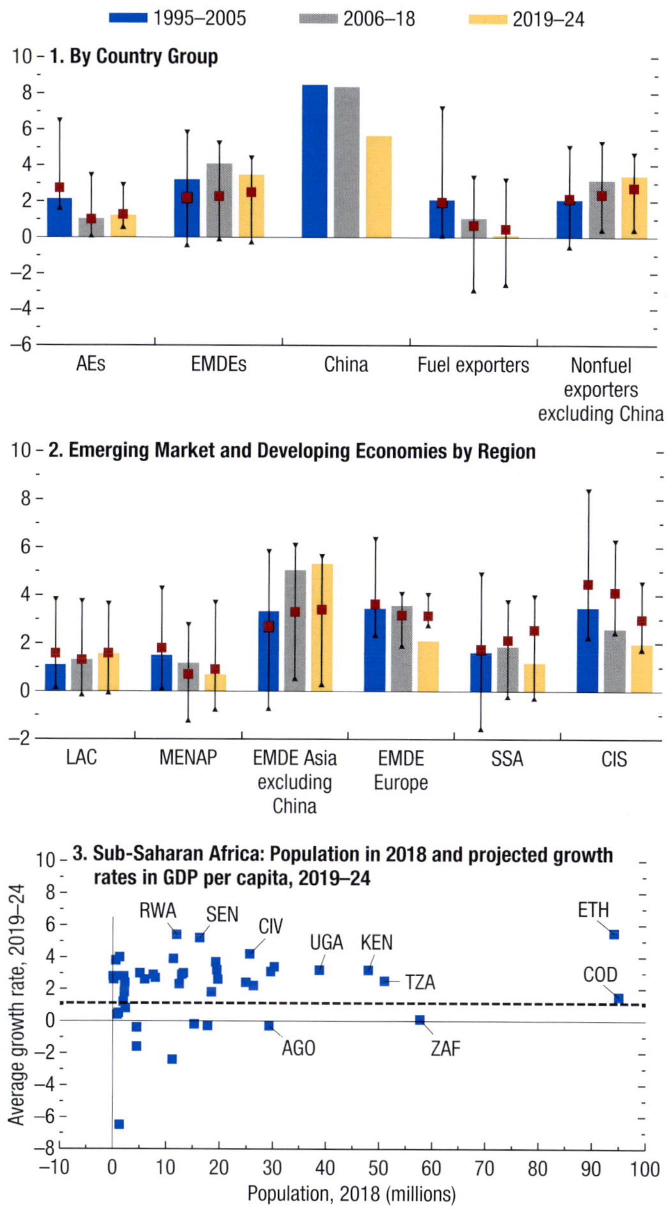

Source: IMF staff estimates.
Note: AEs = advanced economies; CIS = Commonwealth of Independent States; EMDE = emerging market and developing economy; LAC = Latin America and the Caribbean; MENAP = Middle East, North Africa, Afghanistan, and Pakistan; PPP = purchasing power parity; SSA = sub-Saharan Africa. Bars denote PPP GDP-weighted averages, red markers indicate the medians, and black markers denote the top and bottom deciles of per capita GDP growth in the country groups. The fuel and nonfuel exporter subgroups are defined in Table D of the Statistical Appendix and cover EMDEs only. Data labels use International Organization for Standardization (ISO) country codes. The dashed line in panel 3 shows the weighted average per capita growth rate in SSA over 2019–24.

inflation is expected to decline to 1.6 percent this year in advanced economies, from 2.0 percent in 2018. With the US economy operating above potential this year and next, core inflation is expected to exceed the medium-term target of 2.0 percent, and decline to target thereafter. In the euro area, core inflation is expected to gradually increase from 1.2 percent in 2018 to about 2 percent in 2022 as the economy is operating above potential. Japan's core inflation rate (excluding fresh food and energy) is projected to rise to 1.4 percent by the end of 2020 as the consumption tax rate is raised in October this year, softening back to about 1.3 percent in the medium term.

Inflation in emerging market and developing economies excluding Venezuela, while stable across most regions, is nonetheless expected to firm to 4.9 percent this year from 4.8 percent in 2018, reflecting developments in a few economies. These include a temporary boost to consumer price inflation from a higher value-added tax rate in Russia and a gradual pickup in price pressure in India because of relatively strong demand conditions and a modest increase in food inflation from a low base. Still-elevated inflation expectations as Argentina adjusts to a new anchoring regime under a revamped monetary and exchange rate framework is also a notable temporary effect. As they fade, and growth stabilizes across the emerging market and developing economy group, inflation is set to moderate to about 4 percent over the medium term.

External Sector Outlook

Trade Growth

Global trade growth slowed considerably in 2018. The slowdown reflects some payback in the first quarter from very high growth in late 2017 and, subsequently, the impact of increased trade tensions on spending on capital goods (which are heavily traded) and a more general slowdown in global activity. The forecast for 2019 is for some further slowdown, reflecting to an important extent the weakness in trade growth in late 2018, followed by some recovery in 2020. In subsequent years, trade growth is projected to continue at broadly the same pace as in 2018 as investment demand gradually recovers in emerging market and developing economies, offsetting the slowdown in capital spending in advanced economies projected for 2020 and beyond.

Current Account Positions

Global current account deficits and surpluses are estimated to have widened marginally in 2018 compared with the previous year. Higher oil prices have been the main driver of this widening: they are estimated to have boosted the current account balance of oil exporters by about 3½ percent of their GDP. Symmetrically, the current account deficits of some Asian net oil importers (such as India, Indonesia, and Pakistan) have widened, reflecting their higher oil import bills. Among major current account surplus and deficit countries and regions, the current account surplus of China declined considerably, to 0.4 percent of GDP, while the US current account deficit was unchanged at 2.3 percent, and the surplus of the euro area declined marginally to 3.0 percent.

Forecasts for 2019 and beyond indicate a gradual reduction in global current account deficits and surpluses, particularly after 2020 (Figure 1.16).[1] The surplus of oil exporters will fall, as average oil prices are projected to drop from their 2018 level, and the current account surpluses in the euro area, Japan, and other advanced Asian economies are projected to decline gradually. Among deficit countries, the current account balance of the United States is projected to widen in 2019–20—driven by expansionary fiscal policy—and to narrow again thereafter. The recently imposed trade measures by the United States and retaliatory actions by trading partners are expected to have limited impact on overall external imbalances (see Chapter 4 and the 2018 *External Sector Report* for a discussion of the relationship between trade costs and external imbalances).

As highlighted in the *External Sector Report*, many countries' current account imbalances in 2017 were too large in relation to country-specific norms consistent with underlying fundamentals and desirable policies. As shown in panel 1 of Figure 1.17, excess current account balances in 2018 are estimated to have declined, supported in many cases by real exchange rate movements. Medium-term projections suggest, on average, further movement of current account balances in the same direction (Figure 1.17, panel 2).[2] At the same time, given that changes in macroeconomic fundamentals relative to 2017 affect not only current

[1]Balance of payments data show a notable positive world current account discrepancy in recent years. This discrepancy is assumed to decline gradually during the forecast period, with projected global current account surpluses compressing more than global current account deficits.

[2]The change in the current account balance during 2018 is estimated to have offset, on average, about one-fifth of the 2017 current account gap; the change between 2017 and 2024 would offset less than half of the 2017 gap.

Figure 1.16. Global Current Account Balance
(Percent of world GDP)

Global current account deficits and surpluses are projected to gradually decline, particularly after 2020.

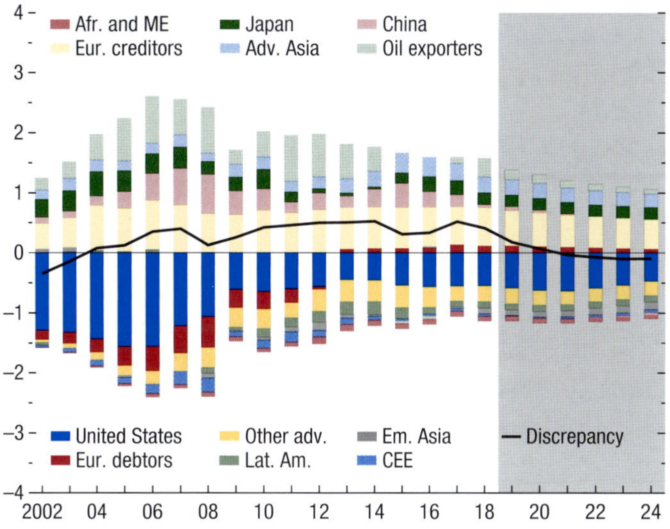

Source: IMF staff estimates.
Note: Adv. Asia = advanced Asia (Hong Kong SAR, Korea, Singapore, Taiwan Province of China); Afr. and ME = Africa and the Middle East (Democratic Republic of the Congo, Egypt, Ethiopia, Ghana, Jordan, Kenya, Lebanon, Morocco, South Africa, Sudan, Tanzania, Tunisia); CEE = central and eastern Europe (Belarus, Bulgaria, Croatia, Czech Republic, Hungary, Poland, Romania, Slovak Republic, Turkey, Ukraine); Em. Asia = emerging Asia (India, Indonesia, Pakistan, Philippines, Thailand, Vietnam); Eur. creditors = European creditors (Austria, Belgium, Denmark, Finland, Germany, Luxembourg, Netherlands, Norway, Sweden, Switzerland); Eur. debtors = European debtors (Cyprus, Greece, Ireland, Italy, Portugal, Spain, Slovenia); Lat. Am. = Latin America (Argentina, Brazil, Chile, Colombia, Mexico, Peru, Uruguay); Oil exporters = Algeria, Azerbaijan, Iran, Kazakhstan, Kuwait, Nigeria, Oman, Qatar, Russia, Saudi Arabia, United Arab Emirates, Venezuela; Other adv. = other advanced economies (Australia, Canada, France, Iceland, New Zealand, United Kingdom).

Figure 1.17. Current Account Balances in Relation to Economic Fundamentals

Excess current account balances in 2018 are estimated to have declined, supported in many cases by real exchange rate movements. Medium-term projections suggest, on average, further movement of current account balances in the same direction.

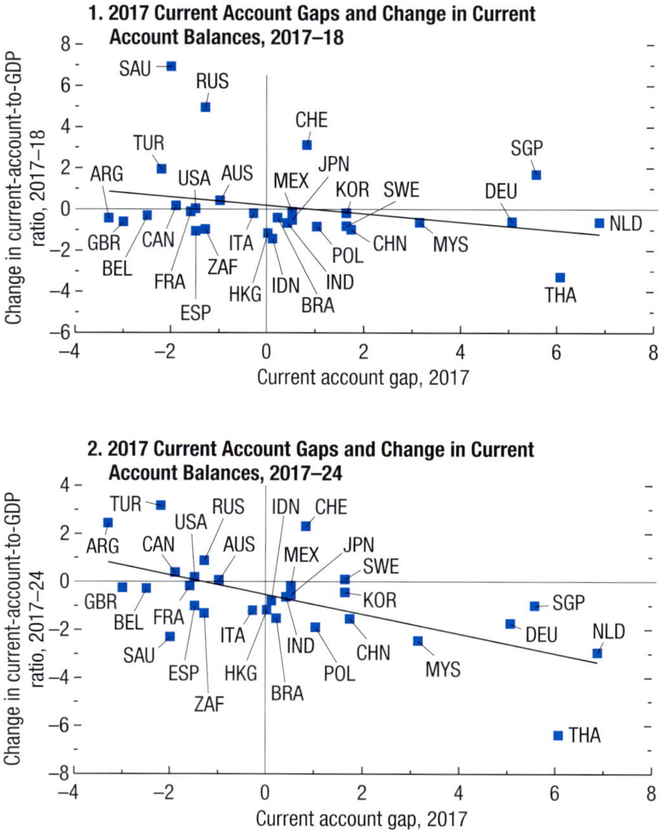

Source: IMF staff calculations.
Note: Data labels use International Organization for Standardization (ISO) country codes.

account balances but also their equilibrium values, the path of future excess imbalances cannot be precisely inferred from this exercise.[3]

International Investment Positions

Changes in international investment positions reflect both net financial flows and valuation changes arising from fluctuations in exchange rates and asset prices. Given that WEO projections assume broadly stable real effective exchange rates and limited variation in asset prices, changes in international investment positions are driven by projections for net external borrowing and lending (in line with the current account balance), with their ratios to domestic and world GDP affected by projected growth rates for individual countries and for the global economy as a whole.[4,5]

[3]For instance, an improvement in the terms of trade is typically associated with a more appreciated equilibrium exchange rate.

[4]WEO forecasts include projections of 10-year government bond yields, which would affect bond prices going forward, but the impact of those changes in bond prices on the valuation of external assets and liabilities is typically not included in international investment position forecasts.

[5]In addition to changes in exchange rates, the decline in global equity prices in late 2018 (compared with their levels at the end of 2017) implies deterioration of international investment positions at the end of 2018 in countries with significant net holdings of equity and foreign direct investment abroad and a corresponding improvement in positions for countries with net equity liabilities.

Figure 1.18. Net International Investment Position

Creditor and debtor positions as a share of world GDP are projected to widen slightly this year, and then to broadly stabilize as a share of world GDP over the forecast horizon.

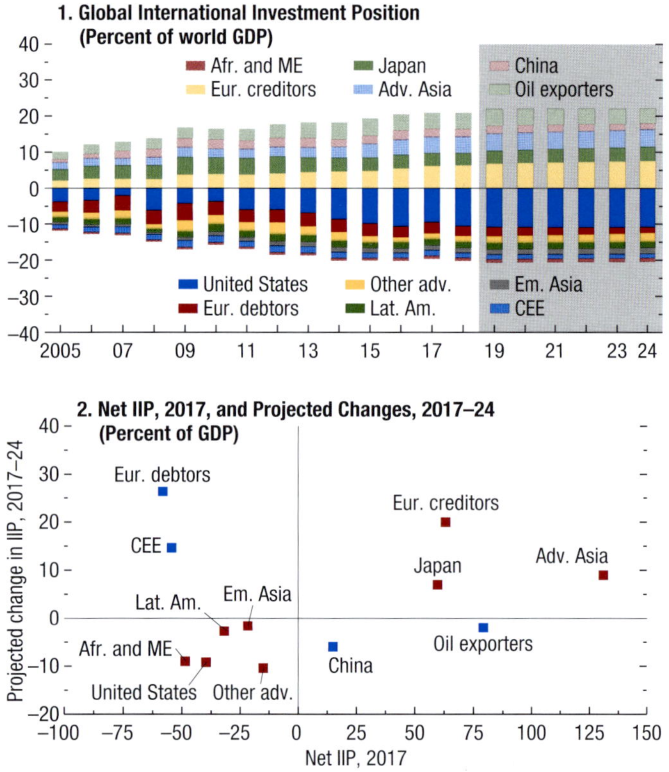

Source: IMF staff estimates.
Note: Adv. Asia = advanced Asia (Hong Kong SAR, Korea, Singapore, Taiwan Province of China); Afr. and ME = Africa and the Middle East (Democratic Republic of the Congo, Egypt, Ethiopia, Ghana, Jordan, Kenya, Lebanon, Morocco, South Africa, Sudan, Tanzania, Tunisia); CEE = central and eastern Europe (Belarus, Bulgaria, Croatia, Czech Republic, Hungary, Poland, Romania, Slovak Republic, Turkey, Ukraine); Em. Asia = emerging Asia (India, Indonesia, Pakistan, Philippines, Thailand, Vietnam); Eur. creditors = European creditors (Austria, Belgium, Denmark, Finland, Germany, Luxembourg, Netherlands, Norway, Sweden, Switzerland); Eur. debtors = European debtors (Cyprus, Greece, Ireland, Italy, Portugal, Spain, Slovenia); IIP = international investment position; Lat. Am. = Latin America (Argentina, Brazil, Chile, Colombia, Mexico, Peru, Uruguay); Oil exporters = Algeria, Azerbaijan, Iran, Kazakhstan, Kuwait, Nigeria, Oman, Qatar, Russia, Saudi Arabia, United Arab Emirates, Venezuela; Other adv. = other advanced economies (Australia, Canada, France, Iceland, New Zealand, United Kingdom).

As panel 1 of Figure 1.18 shows, creditor and debtor positions as a share of world GDP are projected to widen slightly this year, and then to broadly stabilize as a share of world GDP over the forecast horizon. On the creditor side, the growing creditor positions of a group of European advanced economies, a result of large projected current account surpluses, is offset by some reduction in the creditor position of China and oil exporters. On the debtor side, the debtor position of the United States increases initially and then stabilizes with the forecast reduction in its current account deficit as the fiscal stimulus is withdrawn, while the position of euro area debtor countries further improves significantly.

Similar trends are highlighted in panel 2 of Figure 1.18, which shows projected changes in net international investment positions as a percentage of domestic GDP across countries and regions between 2017 and 2024, the last year of the WEO projection horizon. The net creditor position of advanced European economies is projected to be above 80 percent of GDP and of Japan to exceed 65 percent, while the net creditor position of China would decline to below 10 percent. The debtor position of the United States is projected to approach 50 percent of GDP, some 9 percentage points above the 2017 estimate, while the net international investment position of a group of euro area debtor countries, including Italy and Spain, is expected to improve by more than 25 percentage points of their collective GDP. By 2024, net foreign liabilities, at about 32 percent of their GDP, would be half what they were a decade earlier.

Implications of Imbalances

Sustained excess external imbalances in the world's key economies and policy actions that threaten to widen such imbalances pose risks to global stability. The fiscal easing under way in the United States is projected to increase the US current account deficit. This could aggravate trade tensions and result in a faster tightening of global financing conditions, with negative implications for emerging market economies, especially those with weak external positions. Over the medium term, widening debtor positions in key economies could constrain global growth and possibly result in sharp and disruptive currency and asset price adjustments (see also the 2018 *External Sector Report*).

As discussed in the "Policy Priorities" section, the US economy—which is already operating beyond full employment—should implement a medium-term plan to reverse the rising ratio of public debt, accompanied by fiscal measures to gradually boost domestic capacity. This would help ensure more sustainable growth dynamics and contain external imbalances. Stronger reliance on demand growth in some creditor countries, especially those, such as Germany, with the policy space to support it, would help facilitate domestic and global rebalancing while sustaining global growth over the medium term.

Risks: Skewed to the Downside

The outlook discussed in the preceding section envisages that global growth will stabilize in the first half of 2019 and recover gradually thereafter. If the ongoing trade truce between the United States and China is resolved with a rollback of tariff increases enacted in 2018, rising business confidence and financial sentiment could lift growth above this baseline forecast. Some optimism about a positive resolution of trade differences between the United States and China is indeed already reflected in market valuations. However, the possibility of further downward revisions is high, and the balance of risks remains skewed to the downside. Key sources of downside risk to the global outlook include:

Trade tensions: Global trade, investment, and output remain under threat from ongoing trade tensions. The November 30, 2018, signing of the US-Mexico-Canada Agreement to replace the North American Free Trade Agreement; the extension past March 1, 2019, of the truce between the United States and China on tariff increases; and the announced reduction in Chinese tariffs on US car imports are steps in the right direction. However, final outcomes remain subject to a negotiation process in the case of the US–China dispute and domestic ratification processes for the US-Mexico-Canada Agreement. In addition, a proposal to raise tariffs on all imported cars and car parts remains under consideration in the United States. Failure to resolve differences and a resulting increase in tariff barriers above and beyond what is incorporated into the forecast would lead to higher costs of imported intermediate and capital goods and higher final goods prices for consumers. Beyond these direct impacts, higher trade policy uncertainty and concerns of escalation and retaliation would reduce business investment, disrupt supply chains, and slow productivity growth. The resulting depressed outlook for corporate profitability could dent financial market sentiment and further dampen growth (see Scenario Box 1 of the October 2018 WEO).

Downside risks in systemic economies: The global growth profile is shaped by projections of a recovery in the euro area as one-off factors dissipate, avoidance of a no-deal Brexit, some firming of growth in China as stimulus measures take effect, and a gradual softening of growth in the United States as fiscal stimulus fades. The materialization of risks in these economies would lower global growth directly and through real and financial spillovers.

In Europe, a protracted period of elevated yields in Italy would put further stress on Italian banks, weigh on economic activity, and worsen debt dynamics. Other Europe-specific factors that could give rise to broader risk aversion and a widespread increase in risk spreads include the rising possibility of a no-deal Brexit and European Parliamentary election outcomes that delay or reverse progress on strengthening the euro area architecture. More generally, a no-deal Brexit that severely disrupts supply chains and raises trade costs could potentially have large and long-lasting negative impacts on the economies of the United Kingdom and the European Union (see Scenario Box 1).

In the United States, the market-implied path of expected policy rates remains below the Federal Open Market Committee's projections, raising the possibility of a market reassessment of the expected policy path if US economic data remain strong. This could result in higher US interest rates, renewed dollar appreciation, and tighter financial conditions for emerging market and developing economies with balance sheet vulnerabilities (in the form of elevated currency and maturity mismatches). As discussed in the April 2019 GFSR, the US credit cycle is at an advanced stage, with a rising share of lower-rated issuers in the corporate bond market and a growing volume of covenant-lite loans extended to highly indebted companies that offer limited protection for investors in the event of a default. If US growth were to weaken, such financial fragilities could amplify and prolong the slowdown by leading to debt-service difficulties in highly leveraged companies, credit rating downgrades, and rising rollover risks, with further negative feedback effects on corporate spending.

In China, the authorities have responded to the slowdown in 2018 by limiting the extent of financial regulatory tightening, injecting liquidity through cuts in bank reserve requirements, and reducing the personal income tax and value-added tax for small and medium enterprises. Nevertheless, if trade tensions fail to ease, activity may fall short of expectations. Furthermore, excessive stimulus to support near-term growth through a loosening of credit standards, or a resurgence of shadow banking activity and off-budget infrastructure spending, would heighten financial vulnerabilities,

Figure 1.19. Policy Uncertainty and Trade Tensions
(Index)

Global economic policy uncertainty remains elevated, notwithstanding a decline in US trade policy uncertainty.

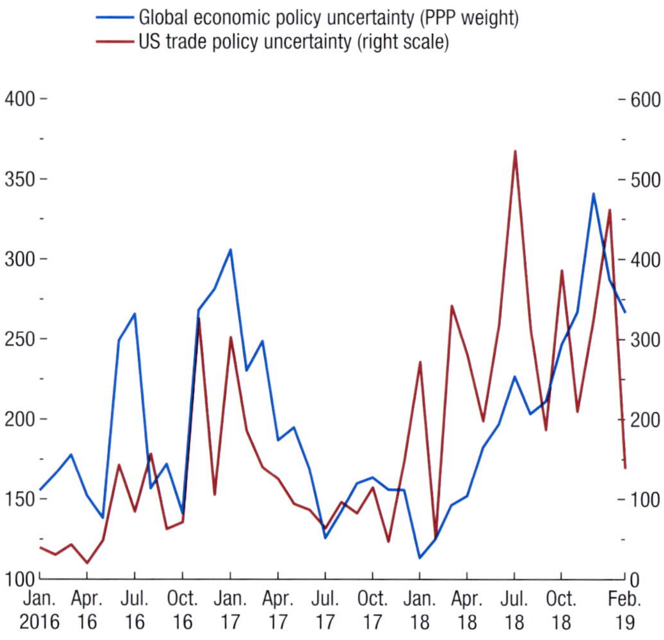

Source: Baker, Bloom, and Davis (2016).
Note: The Baker-Bloom-Davis index of Global Economic Policy Uncertainty (GEPU) is a GDP-weighted average of national EPU indices for 20 countries: Australia, Brazil, Canada, Chile, China, France, Germany, Greece, India, Ireland, Italy, Japan, Korea, Mexico, the Netherlands, Russia, Spain, Sweden, the United Kingdom, and the United States. Mean of global economic policy uncertainty index from 1997 to 2015 = 100; mean of US trade policy uncertainty index from 1985 to 2010 = 100. PPP = purchasing power parity.

Figure 1.20. Geopolitical Risk Index
(Index)

High geopolitical risk complicates the outlook.

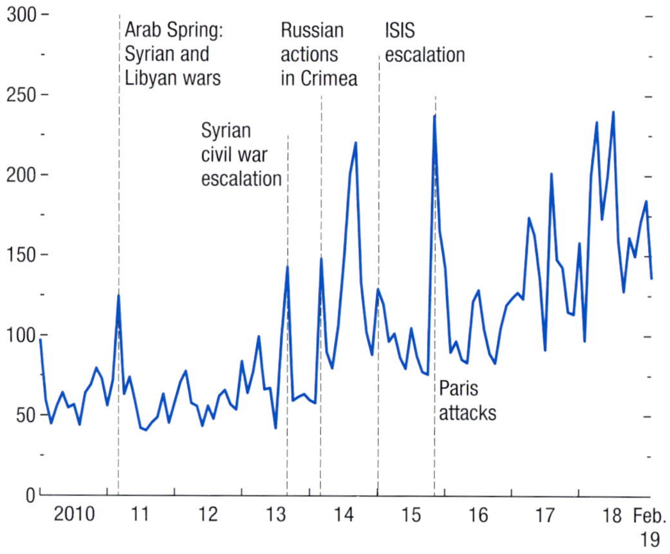

Source: Caldara and Iacoviello (2018).
Note: ISIS = Islamic State. The Caldara and Iacoviello Geopolitical Risk index reflects automated text-search results of the electronic archives of 11 national and international newspapers. The index is calculated by counting the number of articles related to geopolitical risk in each newspaper for each month (as a share of the total number of news articles), and normalized to average a value of 100 in the 2000–09 decade.

reduce future policy space, and raise downside risks to medium-term growth.

Other financial vulnerabilities: Cyberattacks on financial infrastructure are another source of risk because they can severely disrupt cross-border payment systems and the flow of goods and services. As noted in the April 2019 GFSR, wide-ranging reversals of postcrisis regulatory reform or a continuation of still relatively accommodative financial conditions could foster additional financial vulnerabilities, especially if financial intermediaries intensify their search for returns in an environment of slower global growth.

Political uncertainty: A host of other potential factors add downside risk to global investment and growth. These include policy uncertainty about the agenda of new administrations or surrounding elections, geopolitical conflict in the Middle East, and tensions in east Asia (Figures 1.19 and 1.20; see also see Box 1.5 of the October 2018 WEO). These risk factors in isolation may not have a strong impact on investment and growth beyond the countries directly affected, but a sequence of such events—combined with trade tensions and tighter global financial conditions—could have outsize effects on sentiment that reverberate on a broader scale.

Medium-term risks: Risks of a somewhat slower-moving nature with serious implications for the medium- and long-term outlook include pervasive effects of climate change and a decline in trust with regard to establishment institutions and political parties. The Intergovernmental Panel on Climate Change (IPCC) reported in October 2018 that, at current rates of increase, global warming could reach 1.5°C above preindustrial levels between 2030 and 2052, bringing with it extremes of temperature, precipitation, and drought. Such extremes would have devastating humanitarian effects and inflict severe, persistent output losses across a broad range of economies

(Chapter 3 of the October 2017 WEO). The warning from the IPCC comes amid substantial distrust of establishment institutions and mainstream political parties—a distrust often born of rising inequality and entrenched beliefs that existing economic arrangements do not work for all. The accompanying polarization of views and growing appeal of extreme policy platforms imperil the medium-term outlook by making it difficult to implement structural reforms for boosting potential output growth and strengthening resilience, including against climate-related risks.

Fan chart analysis: Fan chart analysis—based on equity and commodity market data and the dispersion of inflation and term spread projections of private forecasters—shows a downward shift in the balance of risks relative to the April 2018 WEO (Figure 1.21). The worsening profile mostly reflects the anticipated drag associated with the risk of oil prices rebounding sharply from their recent rapid drop. As discussed in the April 2019 GFSR, growth-at-risk analysis suggests slightly higher near-term downside risks to global financial stability compared with those in the October 2018 report and continued elevated risks to medium-term growth.

Policy Priorities: Enhance Resilience, Raise Medium-Term Growth Prospects

The modest projected pickup in global economic growth next year relies to an important extent on the easing of macroeconomic strains in currently stressed emerging market and developing economies and on avoiding a sharp slowdown in advanced economies. In this context, avoiding policy missteps that could harm economic activity should be the main priority. Macroeconomic and financial policy should aim to guard against further deceleration where output may fall below potential and to ensure a soft landing where policy support needs to be withdrawn. At the national level, monetary policy should aim to keep inflation on track toward the central bank's target (and, where it is on target, to ensure that it stabilizes there) and to keep inflation expectations anchored. Fiscal policy will need to manage trade-offs between supporting demand and ensuring that public debt remains on a sustainable path. In particular, where fiscal consolidation is needed, policy should calibrate its pace to secure stability without suppressing near-term growth and harming programs that protect the vulnerable (see the April 2019 *Fiscal Monitor*). Financial sector policies can

Figure 1.21. Risks to the Global Outlook

The balance of risks to the outlook has shifted downward relative to the April 2018 *World Economic Outlook*.

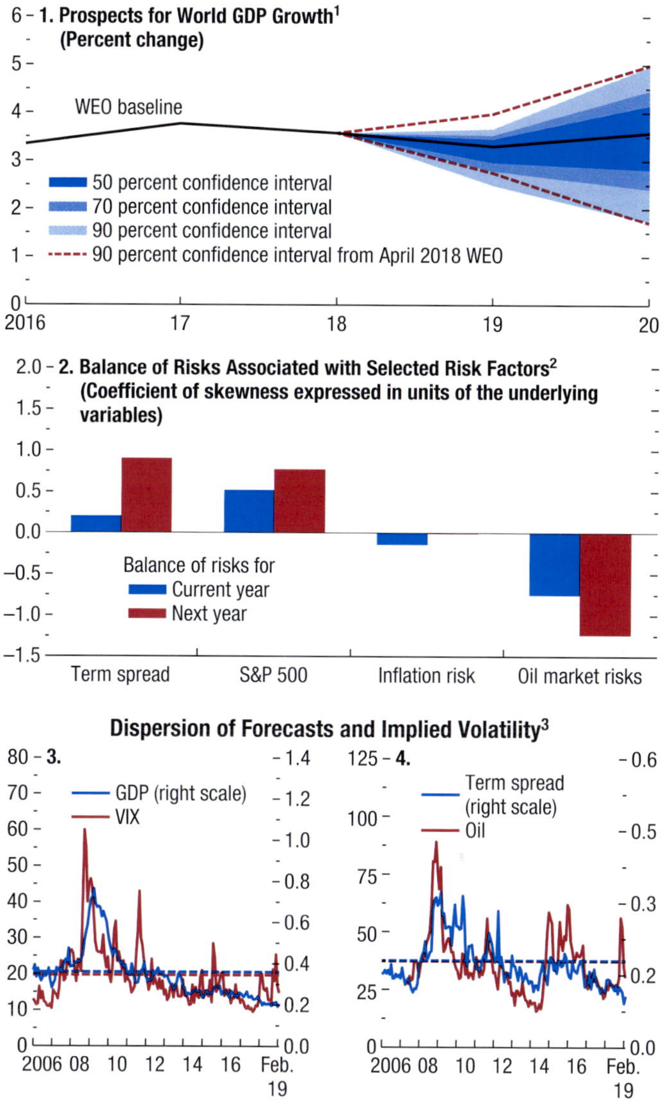

Sources: Bloomberg Finance L.P.; Chicago Board Options Exchange (CBOE); Consensus Economics; Haver Analytics; and IMF staff estimates.

[1]The fan chart shows the uncertainty around the April 2019 *World Economic Outlook* (WEO) central forecast with 50, 70, and 90 percent confidence intervals. As shown, the 70 percent confidence interval includes the 50 percent interval, and the 90 percent confidence interval includes the 50 and 70 percent intervals. See Appendix 1.2 of the April 2009 WEO for details. The 90 percent intervals for the current-year and one-year-ahead forecasts from the April 2018 WEO are shown.

[2]The bars depict the coefficient of skewness expressed in units of the underlying variables. The values for inflation risks and oil market risks enter with the opposite sign since they represent downside risks to growth.

[3]GDP measures the purchasing-power-parity-weighted average dispersion of GDP growth forecasts for the Group of Seven economies (Canada, France, Germany, Italy, Japan, United Kingdom, United States), Brazil, China, India, and Mexico. VIX is the CBOE Standard & Poor's (S&P) 500 Implied Volatility Index. Term spread measures the average dispersion of term spreads implicit in interest rate forecasts for Germany, Japan, the United Kingdom, and the United States. Oil is the CBOE crude oil volatility index. Forecasts are from Consensus Economics surveys. Dashed lines represent the average values from 2000 to the present.

complement these efforts by securing the strength of balance sheets and address vulnerabilities proactively by deploying macroprudential tools, such as countercyclical capital buffers or targeted sectoral capital buffers (or higher risk weights and provisions on such exposures) and developing, where needed, borrower-based tools to mitigate risks stemming from high debt vulnerabilities. This will enhance resilience to a potentially more volatile environment in global asset markets (as discussed in greater detail in the April 2019 GFSR).

If the current slowdown turns more severe and protracted than envisaged in the baseline, the macroeconomic policy stance should become more accommodative, particularly where output already is or could fall below potential and where there is policy space. If fiscal policy is on a consolidation path and monetary policy is constrained, its pace would have to slow to ensure adequate support for near-term demand. Where a weaker outlook and worsening market sentiment reinforce each other, the need for clear communication and cooperative efforts to tackle unresolved issues—such as the US–China trade dispute and Brexit—will become even more pressing.

Beyond 2020, the forecast of broadly stable growth at 3.6 percent, despite major subregions and key economies slowing over the medium term, relies to an important extent on weights shifting toward those with relatively higher growth rates. Boosting medium-term growth prospects remains a priority for most advanced economies. A policy priority for several emerging market and developing economies continues to be a stronger revenue base for needed social and infrastructure spending. Sustained poverty reduction and increased inclusiveness, as well as debt sustainability, depend on it. A second cross-cutting theme is the need to ensure that the gains benefit all segments of society through adequate social spending on education, health, and safety net policies that protect the vulnerable. (Box 1.3 documents a related set of challenges stemming from persistent spatial disparities in labor market outcomes and productivity within countries.)

Advanced Economies—Policy Priorities

Among *advanced economies*, consumer price inflation generally remains below target, and wage pressures are relatively subdued (although picking up in a few cases). Monetary policy should stay accommodative in these economies until inflation starts showing clear signs of rising toward central banks' targets. With monetary policy trained on countercyclical demand management, fiscal policy should emphasize measures that boost potential output and raise inclusiveness, while maintaining public finances on a sustainable path. In the absence of a major deceleration of growth, countries where public debt is high should pursue gradual fiscal consolidation that avoids sharp drags on growth and secures adequate social insurance for the vulnerable. If there are clear signs of a substantially deeper and more protracted slowdown, monetary and fiscal policy would need to become more accommodative. Further safeguarding financial systems—including through raising bank capital and liquidity buffers, enhancing macroprudential oversight of nonbank financial institutions, developing macroprudential tools as needed, and avoiding a rollback of postcrisis regulatory reforms—remains vital in the context of continued monetary policy accommodation.

The modest medium-term outlook for the group (potential output growth rates are estimated in the range of 0.5–1.5 percent for most advanced economies) calls for measures to raise labor force participation rates and productivity growth. These include public investment (coupled with incentives to raise private spending as needed) in infrastructure, lifelong learning and workforce skills, and research and development. Protecting dynamism—by ensuring that competition policy frameworks facilitate new firm entry and curb incumbents' abuse of market power—remains vital when a few big firms are cornering increasingly larger market shares across technology, retail, financial services, and other sectors in many advanced economies (Chapter 2 documents trends in market power across advanced economies and their macroeconomic implications).

In the *United States*, even though output is already above potential, the Federal Reserve's patient approach to normalization is appropriate, considering the uncertainty around the baseline and muted inflation. The path of the policy interest rate should depend on incoming data, the economic outlook, and risks. Under the WEO baseline projection, labor markets are expected to tighten further and wage growth to pick up, likely warranting a further rate hike in the second half of the year. Rapid tightening could weaken inflation expectations and activity, while delayed tightening could contribute to financial vulnerabilities and a sharper downturn down the road. The 2017 tax overhaul and subsequent increases in spending have widened the fiscal deficit and added to an already unsustainable US public debt profile. Fiscal policy should focus on raising the revenue-to-GDP ratio, with greater reliance on indirect taxes to counteract the anticipated rise in aging-related spending. Regarding financial sector policies, the current risk-based approach to regulation, supervision, and resolution should be preserved (and strengthened in the case of nonbank financial institutions) to counteract vulnerability from weaker corporate credit underwriting standards, rising corporate leverage, and emerging cybersecurity threats. Improving medium-term growth prospects will require incentivizing greater labor force participation and enhancing workforce skills.

In the *United Kingdom*, despite the historically low unemployment rate and a recent pickup in wage growth, the uncertainty surrounding Brexit negotiations calls for a cautious, data-dependent monetary response. Similarly, the envisaged pace of fiscal consolidation, anchored by the objective of narrowing the cyclically adjusted public sector deficit to below 2 percent of GDP by 2020–21, should be adjusted if growth slows materially. Structural reforms should focus on improving infrastructure quality and boosting the basic skills of high school graduates, and labor market policies should ensure a smooth redeployment of workers to expanding sectors from those negatively affected after Brexit.

In the *euro area*, core inflation continues to remain well below target and wage growth relatively sluggish despite labor markets tightening in many economies in the currency zone. Monetary policy should continue to remain accommodative. In this regard, the forward guidance from the European Central Bank that it will reinvest maturing securities until well after the first interest rate hikes is welcome. Fiscal space varies across the currency area. In some countries (France, Italy, Spain), buffers should be rebuilt gradually to avoid reigniting adverse feedback spirals between sovereign and bank risks and to secure stability. In Germany, where growth has been slowing, the available fiscal space can be used to increase public investment in physical and human capital or reduce the labor tax wedge—measures that would boost potential output and help with external rebalancing. Prompt adoption of these measures is essential if the current weakness in activity persists. If a severe downside scenario were to materialize in the euro area, available monetary policy tools could be complemented with fiscal easing by countries that have appropriate fiscal space and financing conditions. A synchronized fiscal response, albeit appropriately differentiated across member countries, can strengthen the area-wide impact. Completing the banking union and continuing the cleanup of balance sheets remain vital for strengthening credit intermediation in some economies. Structural reform priorities vary according to country-specific needs. In France, efforts to reduce corporate administrative burdens, promote innovation, and strengthen competition in the services sector would complement steps taken to improve labor market flexibility and boost potential growth. In Italy, measures to decentralize wage bargaining would help align wages and labor productivity, thereby enhancing labor market flexibility and boosting employment growth. In Spain, efforts to reduce labor market duality would support job creation and incentivize private investment.

In *Japan*, sustained monetary accommodation will be necessary to lift inflation expectations and progress toward the central bank's target. Fiscal policy should be geared toward ensuring long-term fiscal sustainability while protecting growth. The coupling of the planned October increase in the consumption tax rate with fiscal measures to support near-term activity is welcome. A sustainable debt trajectory calls for further gradual and steady increases in the consumption tax rate and reforms of the social security framework. The success of the broad Abenomics agenda of reflating the economy depends crucially on also lifting productivity growth and wage inflation, for which reducing labor market duality to increase productivity of nonregular workers remains vital. Durably counteracting the aging-induced decline in labor force growth will require, among other initiatives, further raising female labor force supply and encouraging more use of foreign labor.

Emerging Market and Developing Economies—Policy Priorities

The variation in performance across *emerging market and developing economies* in the recent past in a context of volatile external conditions has highlighted the importance of policy frameworks oriented toward securing growth prospects and strengthening resilience. Monetary policy should focus on anchoring inflation expectations where inflation remains high or recent currency depreciations threaten pass-through to domestic prices. Where expectations are well anchored, monetary policy can support domestic activity as needed (see Chapter 3 of the October 2018 WEO).

Tighter external financial conditions can expose vulnerabilities related to high public debt as well as balance sheet maturity and currency mismatches accumulated during years of ultralow interest rates (see Box 1.1 of the April 2019 *Fiscal Monitor* for an analysis of the fiscal implications of potentially tighter financial conditions in emerging market economies). Fiscal policy should ensure that debt ratios remain sustainable, which would also contain borrowing costs and create space to combat downturns. Improving the targeting of subsidies, rationalizing recurrent expenditures, and mobilizing revenue can help preserve capital outlays needed to boost potential growth and the social spending that improves inclusion. In some cases, macroprudential regulatory and supervisory frameworks will have to be strengthened to deal with high private debt burdens, rein in excess credit growth, and contain balance sheet currency and maturity mismatches. Exchange rate flexibility can complement these policies by helping to buffer shocks. It can also help prevent persistent misalignments of relative prices that lead to resource misallocation and the buildup of financial imbalances. Across all economies, reforms to ensure sustainable, inclusive growth remain essential, particularly given that the medium-term prospects for per capita growth are relatively subdued for many economies in this group.

In *China*, the economy's reliance on credit has declined somewhat following regulatory efforts to rein in shadow banking and control the buildup of debt. Despite recent weaker momentum stemming from trade tensions, policies should stay focused on deleveraging and rebalancing the economy away from a growth model based on credit-fueled investment toward one that is more sustainable and led by private consumption. Reducing leverage in the economy will require continued scaling back of widespread implicit guarantees on debt, early recognition and disposal of distressed assets, and fostering more market-based credit allocation that better aligns risk-adjusted returns with borrowing costs. Building on the recent increases in the private consumption share of GDP (up close to 40 percent in 2017 from 35 percent in 2012), continued rebalancing will require a more progressive tax code; higher spending on health, education, and social transfers; and reduced barriers to labor mobility. Enhancing productivity growth will require reducing the footprint of state-owned enterprises and further reducing barriers to entry in certain sectors, such as telecommunications and banking. To avoid a sharp near-term growth slowdown that could derail the overarching reform agenda, some centrally financed on-budget fiscal expansion in 2019 may be appropriate. It should avoid large-scale infrastructure stimulus and instead emphasize targeted transfers to low-income households so as to lower poverty and inequality (Box 1.2 of the April 2019 *Fiscal Monitor*).

In *India*, continued implementation of structural and financial sector reforms with efforts to reduce public debt remain essential to secure the economy's growth prospects. In the near term, continued fiscal consolidation is needed to bring down India's elevated public debt. This should be supported by strengthening goods and services tax compliance and further reducing subsidies. Important steps have been taken to strengthen financial sector balance sheets, including through accelerated resolution of nonperforming assets under a simplified bankruptcy framework. These efforts should be reinforced by enhancing governance of public sector banks. Reforms to hiring and dismissal regulations would help incentivize job creation and absorb the country's large demographic dividend; efforts should also be enhanced on land reform to facilitate and expedite infrastructure development.

In *Argentina*, projections for growth have been revised upward, and higher nominal wages and rising inflation expectations are expected to generate more persistent inflationary pressures in 2019 than projected in the October 2018 WEO. Downside risks to the economy remain sizable, the materialization of which could lead to a shift in investor preferences away from peso assets and put pressure on the currency and the capital account. Against this backdrop, continued implementation of the stabilization plan under the IMF-supported economic reform program is crucial to shore up investor confidence and restore sustainable growth that lifts living standards for all segments of society. To this end, meeting the primary fiscal balance target of zero in 2019 and 1 percent of GDP in 2020 is essential to bring down financing needs and avoid reigniting liquidity pressures. Continued achievement of monetary targets will be crucial to re-anchoring inflation expectations and rebuilding central bank credibility. Complementing these efforts to stabilize the economy in the near term, a resumption of the structural reform agenda will help lift the economy's medium-term growth prospects.

In *Brazil*, the main priority is to contain rising public debt while ensuring that needed social spending remains intact. The spending cap introduced in 2016, which envisages a 0.5 percent of GDP a year improvement in the primary fiscal balance, is a step in the right direction toward facilitating fiscal consolidation. However, more up-front adjustment is needed, particularly cuts to the public wage bill and pension reforms to curb rising outlays—while protecting vital social programs for the vulnerable. With inflation still close to target, monetary policy can stay accommodative to support aggregate demand as needed. Building on recent reforms to labor and subsidized credit markets, efforts to improve infrastructure and the efficiency of financial intermediation would help lift productivity and boost medium-term growth prospects.

In *Mexico*, where sovereign spreads have widened significantly since October, it is essential to avoid delaying needed structural reforms, as this would create additional uncertainty detrimental to private investment and employment growth. Sticking with the medium-term fiscal consolidation plan (and possibly aiming for an even larger reduction in the deficit) would stabilize the public debt, lift confidence, and create space both to respond to shocks and to accommodate aging-related spending needs. Provided inflation remains subdued and expectations well anchored, monetary policy can stay accommodative with scope to cut rates if needed.

In *Turkey*, the New Economic Program provides a framework to deal with complex issues in the economy. Against this backdrop, a comprehensive and credible policy mix is needed to secure macroeconomic stability. The pace of fiscal consolidation should be appropriately calibrated given the subdued outlook and—in a context of high inflation and elevated inflation expectations—the limited scope for monetary policy to support activity. Steps to rationalize spending channeled through public-private partnerships and more transparency in this area would help underpin the fiscal anchor. Greater transparency about financial balance sheet health, and further strengthening balance sheets where needed, would be helpful in addressing lingering uncertainties, as would additional efforts to address nonfinancial corporate sector stress, including debt vulnerabilities.

In *Russia*, the recent revision of the fiscal rule delivered a procyclical positive fiscal impulse and could weaken policy credibility. Further fiscal consolidation will be needed over the medium term to ensure sustainability. The central bank policy rate has been raised above the neutral rate following higher inflation pressure in the second half of 2018. Accordingly, provided inflation does not rise, there is room to provide monetary support should activity weaken in the near term. Building on efforts to strengthen financial stability (including closure of weak banks and reforms to the resolution framework), the structure and governance of the banking system should be geared toward enhancing efficiency of credit intermediation. In addition, continued efforts to improve property rights and governance, reform labor markets, and invest in infrastructure would boost private investment and productivity growth and support convergence toward advanced economy income.

In *South Africa*, gradual fiscal consolidation will be needed to stabilize the public debt. Public wage savings should be given priority to preserve vital social outlays for the vulnerable and fund productive investment to boost potential growth. Transfers to public entities should be contingent on downsizing and eliminating wasteful spending. The fiscal consolidation could also be supported by expanding the tax base and through strengthening tax administration and effective anti-tax-avoidance provisions that reduce profit shifting. Structural reforms, particularly to product and labor markets, would foster an environment conducive to expanding private investment, job creation, and productivity growth.

Low-income developing countries share many of the policy priorities of the emerging market economy group, especially in raising resilience to volatile external conditions. Several low-income "frontier" economies have seen external financing conditions tighten sharply in recent months. Priorities include strengthening monetary and macroprudential policy frameworks while preserving exchange rate flexibility. Public debt stocks have increased rapidly in this group during a period of low interest rates. As financial conditions turn less accommodative, rollover risks may increase, and wider sovereign spreads may spill into higher borrowing costs for firms and households. Fiscal policy should be geared toward containing the buildup of debt while protecting measures that help the vulnerable and support progress toward the Sustainable Development Goals. This would require broadening the revenue base; strengthening tax administration; eliminating wasteful subsidies; and prioritizing spending initiatives on infrastructure, health, education, and poverty reduction.

While gradual fiscal consolidation is a priority shared across the group of low-income developing countries, *commodity-exporting developing economies* face additional pressure from the subdued outlook for commodity prices. Reorienting spending toward infrastructure and social outlays, together with boosting domestic revenue mobilization by broadening the tax base and strengthening revenue administration, are crucial in this regard. Beyond placing public finances on a sustainable footing, an overarching priority for this group is to diversify away from dependence on resource extraction and refining. While country circumstances differ, common policy areas help achieve this broad goal. These include sound macroeconomic management, ensuring broad-based labor force participation by lifting education quality and worker skills, reducing infrastructure shortfalls, boosting financial development and inclusion, and incentivizing the entry of firms and private investment (by strengthening property rights, contract enforcement, and reducing barriers to trade).

Low-income developing countries have also borne the brunt of climate change and potent natural disasters. Lowering the fallout from these events will require adaptation strategies that invest in climate-smart infrastructure, incorporate appropriate technologies and zoning regulations, and deploy well-targeted social safety nets.

Multilateral Policies

Since early 2018, trade actions by the United States and retaliation by trading partners have taken an increasing toll on sentiment. Policymakers should cooperate to address the sources of dissatisfaction with the rule-based trading system, reduce trade costs, and resolve disagreements without raising tariff and nontariff barriers. Doing so would avoid injecting further destabilizing dynamics into a slowing global economy. Beyond trade, fostering closer cooperation on a range of issues would help broaden the gains from global economic integration. The agenda includes completing the postcrisis financial regulatory reforms, strengthening the global financial safety net to reduce the need for countries to self-insure against external shocks, tackling international taxation issues and minimizing cross-border avenues for tax evasion, and promoting mitigation of and adaptation to climate change.

Trade: Cross-border integration through trade openness has been a critical source of productivity growth, knowledge diffusion, and welfare gains for countries at all income levels (see, for example, Chapter 2 of the October 2016 WEO for estimates of welfare gains from trade and Chapter 3 of this WEO on the role of trade integration in lowering capital goods prices and boosting investment globally over the past three decades). Unwinding the trade-restrictive measures implemented so far, reducing trade costs further, and resolving disagreements durably within the rule-based multilateral trade system could therefore reignite a major driver of global productivity growth. This would be supported by modernizing the World Trade Organization (WTO) rules and commitments to address areas of growing relevance, such as services and e-commerce and subsidies and technology transfer—and ensuring that existing rules are applied and enforced, for example, by urgently resolving the impasse over the WTO's Appellate Body. Well-designed and ambitious regional arrangements—such as the Comprehensive and Progressive Agreement for Trans-Pacific Partnership and the EU-Japan Economic Partnership Agreement—can also help. More generally, there is a need to enhance the governance of trade. For example, the idea that all countries need to participate in all negotiations is being revisited; this could allow those countries that wish to move further and faster to do so, while keeping new agreements inside the WTO and open to all WTO members.

Global financial stability: Global cooperation is needed to safeguard the significant gains achieved over the past decade in strengthening the financial system and to resist pressure to roll back portions of the reform. The reform agenda should be fully implemented. Examples include implementing the leverage ratio and net stable funding ratio; devising effective resolution frameworks and enhancing supervisory intensity for globally important financial institutions, especially across borders; bolstering the tools and policymaking capabilities of macroprudential entities; and mitigating systemic risk from nonbank financial institutions through continued vigilance on the regulatory perimeter and filling data gaps. Coordinated and collective action is needed to confront emerging risks, such as those arising from the growing importance of central counterparties and the potential for cybersecurity breaches, and to combat cross-border money laundering and the financing of terrorism. These would also help limit the withdrawal of correspondent banking relationships, which are vital to low-income countries' access to international payment systems. In addition, an adequately financed global safety net can protect economies with robust fundamentals that may otherwise be vulnerable to cross-border contagion and spillovers when downside risks to the global outlook are elevated.

Taxation: With the rise of multinational enterprises, international tax competition has made it increasingly difficult for governments to collect revenues needed to finance their budgets. Multilateral cooperation is needed to reinforce existing efforts aimed at tackling tax evasion and avoidance and mitigation of tax competition, such as through the Organisation for Economic Co-operation and Development–Group of Twenty Base Erosion and Profit Shifting initiative (see Box 1.3 of the April 2019 *Fiscal Monitor*).

Longer-term challenges: Multilateral cooperation is indispensable for tackling longer-term issues that imperil the sustainability and inclusiveness of global growth. Curbing greenhouse gas emissions and containing the associated consequences of rising global temperatures and devastating climate events are a global imperative (see Chapter 3 of the October 2017 WEO on the macroeconomic impact of weather shocks and IMF 2019 for a discussion of fiscal policy options for implementing climate change mitigation and adaptation strategies). By adding to migrant flows, climate-related events compound an already-complex situation of refugee flight from conflict areas, often to countries already under severe strain. International migration will become increasingly important, too, as many advanced economies confront the challenges of their aging populations. International cooperation would create opportunities to streamline the integration of migrants—and so help to maximize the labor supply and productivity benefits they bring to destination countries, and to support remittance flows that lessen the burden on source countries. Finally, a truly global effort is also needed to curb corruption, which is undermining faith in government and institutions in many countries (see the April 2019 *Fiscal Monitor*).

Scenario Box 1.1. A No-Deal Brexit

The IMF's Global Integrated Monetary and Fiscal model is used to explore the economic implications of the United Kingdom's withdrawal from the European Union without a free trade deal in the second quarter of 2019. Two scenarios are presented, providing a range of possible outcomes. Both scenarios include measures already in place or announced that seek to lower the short-term impact, including temporary exemption of a large share of UK imports (from both the European Union and countries outside the European Union) from tariffs in the event of no-deal, and temporary recognition regimes for some financial services. Differences between the two scenarios illustrate some of the uncertainty about the impact of a no-deal Brexit. Scenario A assumes no border disruptions and a relatively small increase in UK sovereign and corporate spreads. Scenario B incorporates significant border disruptions that increase import costs for UK firms and households (and to a lesser extent for the European Union) and a more severe tightening in financial conditions. Both scenarios are compared to the April 2019 *World Economic Outlook* (WEO) baseline, which assumes that the United Kingdom leaves the European Union's customs union and single market and reaches a broad free trade agreement with the European Union, with a gradual transition to the new regime.

There are several common assumptions behind the two scenarios:

Trade costs with European Union (tariffs): Under a no-deal Brexit, UK exports to the European Union revert to being subject to the World Trade Organization's Most Favored Nation (MFN) rules, with tariffs increasing by mid-2019 as a result (see Scenario Table 1 for a comparison of some of the assumptions in the current baseline and in the no-deal Brexit scenarios). Imports from the European Union not subject to the temporary tariff regime also revert to MFN rules in mid-2019, while those subject to the regime revert in mid-2020.

Trade costs with European Union (nontariff barriers): The scenarios assume an increase in nontariff trade costs, reflecting the emergence of a customs and regulatory border between the United Kingdom and the European Union, including the loss of passporting rights for the United Kingdom's financial sector. Most of the increase in nontariff costs on the EU side takes place in the first year, with the exemption of nontariff barriers on some services, such as certain financial sector activities and transport, which increase in the second year. On the UK side, there is a gradual three-year transition, reflecting the United Kingdom's stated approach to prioritize continuity by temporarily recognizing EU standards in multiple areas. Overall, the reduction in nontariff barriers gained from the United Kingdom's EU membership—about 20 percent in tariff-equivalent terms—is eventually reversed.[1]

Trade costs with countries outside the European Union: The United Kingdom loses most third-country free trade agreements currently in place through its EU membership (covering about 15 percent of all UK trade). UK exports to those countries revert to MFN rules for two years starting in mid-2019, while UK imports do so either in mid-2019 or in mid-2020, depending on whether the temporary tariff regime

[1]IMF (2018). The box does not assume additional disruptions in the financial sector beyond the loss of passporting rights, which is modeled as a barrier to services trade.

Scenario Table 1. Trade Assumptions in the Baseline, Scenario A, and Scenario B

		The WEO Baseline	No-Deal Scenarios: A	No-Deal Scenarios: B
Trade arrangements	Trade with third countries	The United Kingdom retains access to existing agreements between EU and third countries	The United Kingdom sets tariffs unilaterally to zero on 87 percent of its imports from mid-2019 to mid-2020; the United Kingdom loses access to most existing agreements, secures new agreements by 2021	
	Trade with the European Union	No tariff increases; nontariff barriers gradually increase by 10 percent in tariff equivalent terms	Tariffs increase by 4 percent in mid-2019 (mid-2020 for UK imports subject to temporary tariff regime); nontariff barriers increase gradually by an additional 14 percent (in tariff equivalent terms) relative to baseline	
Border disruption		No	No	Yes
Tightening of financial conditions		No	Small	More severe

Scenario Box 1 *(continued)*

applies. The scenarios assume new trade agreements are secured after two years, and on terms similar to those currently in place.

Stricter immigration policies: Both scenarios assume a reduction in the net migration flow from the European Union to the United Kingdom of 25,000 people per year until 2030, in line with the UK government's intention to reduce net immigration. For simplicity, it is assumed that the net flow of migrants to the European Union increases by a similar amount.

The scenarios differ in the extent of border disruptions and in the reaction of financial markets following no deal:

Border disruption: To illustrate the possible contribution of border disruptions to a no-deal Brexit, Scenario A makes the simplifying assumption that no such disruptions take place. Under Scenario B instead, delays in the customs-clearing process arise despite the preparatory measures, raising import costs for firms and households in the United Kingdom, and to a lesser extent in the European Union. The trade disruptions in that scenario are estimated to cause in the first and second year, respectively, a decline in UK GDP of 1.4 percent and 0.8 percent and a decline in EU GDP of 0.2 percent and 0.1 percent.[2]

Financial conditions: The simulations include additional effects coming from a tightening of financial conditions, lasting through the second half of 2020, due to greater uncertainty, a decline in confidence, or both. The tightening is small in Scenario A, with UK sovereign spreads increasing by 12.5 basis points and UK corporate spreads increasing by 20 basis points, and no tightening of financial conditions in the European Union or the rest of the world. Given the border disruption costs, the tightening is more severe in Scenario B, with UK sovereign and corporate spreads increasing by 100 basis points and 150 basis points, respectively.[3] Corporate spreads would increase temporarily by 25 basis points in the European Union, and by 15 basis points in the rest of the world.

Regarding the scope for a policy response, it is assumed that monetary policy in the United Kingdom is eased according to a Taylor-type reaction function, while the euro area is unable to ease conventional monetary policy further due to the lower bound constraint on nominal interest rates. Should additional unconventional monetary policy measures be implemented, the decline in EU GDP would be smaller in the short to medium term than what is simulated here.[4] The scenarios also assume some automatic fiscal stabilization, which is reflected in an increase in the overall government deficit in both the United Kingdom and the European Union in the short to medium term.

Before turning to the results, it is worth stressing that the simulations do not reflect the full effects from Brexit, as some of these effects are already in the current baseline. In addition, the range of possible effects provided by the two alternative scenarios captures some, but not all, of the uncertainty about the timing and magnitude of the channels associated with a no-deal Brexit, as well as possible policy responses. The assumed increase in nontariff barriers could be considerably smaller, and the outcome more benign, if the two sides recognize existing product standards, at least temporarily. The extent of the border disruption and the tightening of financial conditions are also very uncertain, as is the degree to which financial sector output would decline in the long term due to the loss of passporting rights. The simulations do not include additional effects on productivity from higher trade costs, which could similarly weigh on long-term output, nor do they include possible effects stemming from capital outflows and additional pressures on the exchange rate.[5]

[2]The loss in GDP assumes there will be delays in the processing of imports from the European Union during the first month of the new regime (equivalent to 8 percent of UK imports). For comparison, the assumed effect from this channel is about half the effect assumed in the disorderly "no deal, no transition" scenario by the Bank of England (Bank of England 2018).

[3]The calibration of this layer is based on estimates according to which the Brexit vote outcome contributed about 100 basis points to corporate spreads in the United Kingdom (ECB 2017). The observed increase in spreads was smaller, as the Brexit vote effect was offset in part by accommodative monetary policy and supportive global macro conditions.

[4]The monetary policy response in the remaining regions follows a Taylor-type reaction function, except for Japan, which is also constrained by the lower bound on nominal interest rates. The latter does not play any role in the simulations given the small impact on that country.

[5]The simulations feature a small, temporary real depreciation of the pound, mainly due to an accommodative monetary policy. Effects on output from capital outflows are unclear. On one hand, a more depreciated exchange rate would support external competitiveness. On the other hand, there could be a negative shock on UK households' wealth, especially if financial conditions tighten further..

Scenario Box 1 *(continued)*

Scenario Figure 1. Real GDP in Brexit Scenario

(Percent deviation from control, unless noted otherwise)

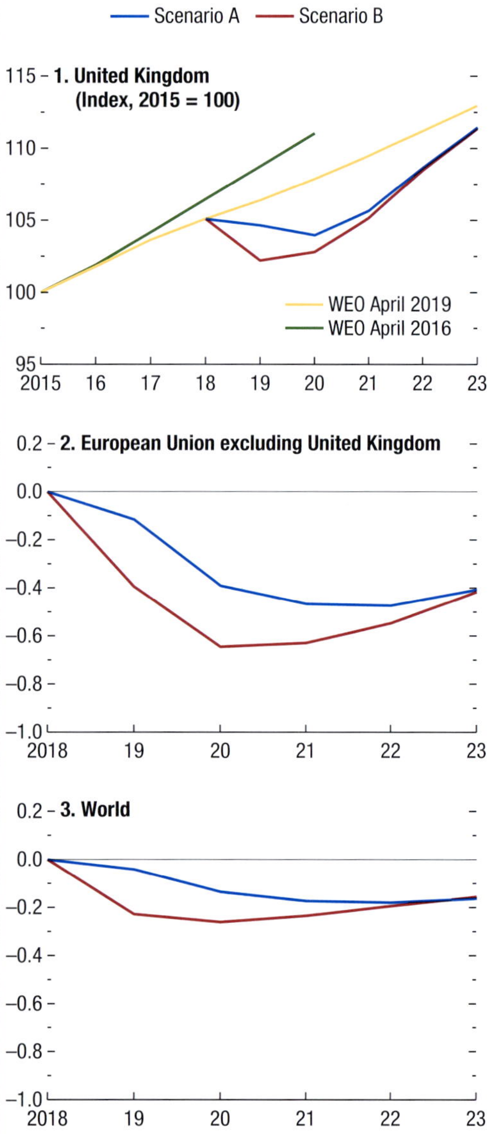

Source: IMF staff estimates.
Note: WEO = *World Economic Outlook.*

The simulations are shown in Scenario Figure 1. Panel 1 plots the paths for UK GDP implied by the two alternative scenarios—the current (April 2019 WEO) baseline, and the WEO baseline from April 2016 (before the Brexit vote)—to help illustrate the effects of Brexit already present in the current baseline. Results for the European Union and the world in panels 2 and 3 are shown, instead, as deviations from the current baseline. Under Scenario A, the increase in trade barriers has an immediate negative impact on UK foreign and domestic demand. The more gradual approach on the UK side eases transition costs by limiting the increase in import costs in the short term. Other channels—modest financial tightening and stricter immigration policies—add little to the short-to-medium-term dynamics. The total negative effect on UK GDP (the difference between the yellow and blue line in panel 1) is about 3.5 percent by 2021. As UK monetary policy stays accommodative and wages and prices adjust, households and firms gradually replace imports with domestic production, and the economy recovers somewhat in the medium term. The decline in UK demand and the gradual increase in trade costs also lead to a decline in activity in the European Union, with a 0.5 percent decrease in GDP by 2021. The aggregate EU effects mask important heterogeneity across countries, given varying degrees of exposures to the United Kingdom.[6] Effects on other regions are negligible. The decline in the United Kingdom and the European Union accounts for most of the decrease in global GDP (0.2 percent over the same period).

The long-term effects of a no-deal Brexit relative to the current WEO baseline are the same in both alternative scenarios (shown in Scenario Figure 2) and reflect two channels. First, higher tariffs and nontariff barriers significantly reduce the returns to capital in the United Kingdom and the European Union. Consequently, firms' desired capital stock falls, reducing potential output in the long term. The impact, not surprisingly, is much larger in the United Kingdom. Second, stricter immigration policies reduce the size of the labor force in the United Kingdom and expand the size of the labor force in the European Union. In combination, these effects lower UK potential output

[6] A country-specific analysis is beyond the scope of this box.

Scenario Box 1 *(continued)*

by almost 3 percent in the long term, relative to the current baseline. In the case of the European Union, the decline in potential output is about 0.3 percent. The long-term effect on output in other regions is negligible, whereas global GDP is down by 0.1 percent in the long term.

Comparison with Other Studies

Other studies have typically focused on the long-term impact of Brexit relative to staying in the European Union, with negative effects on output estimated at 3 percent to 10 percent. The long-term results presented here are in the middle of the range, once the effects that are in the current baseline—a long-term loss of 3 percent of GDP according to IMF (2018)—are included.[7]

[7]Other studies have estimated the prior gains to the United Kingdom from joining the European Union, with most papers focusing on the impact on trade flows and showing a wide range of estimates. When mapped into output effects, and depending on the approach, the benefits range from 3 percent to 20 percent (HM Treasury 2016).

Scenario Figure 2. Brexit Long-Term Real GDP Effects

(Percent deviation from April 2019 WEO baseline)

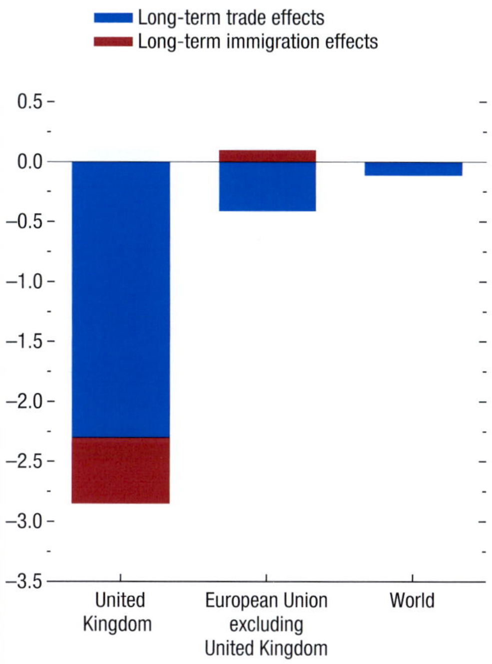

Source: IMF staff estimates.
Note: WEO = *World Economic Outlook.*

Box 1.1. Labor Market Dynamics in Selected Advanced Economies

During the 2017–18 cyclical upsurge in global growth, labor markets tightened in advanced economies, such as Germany, Japan, the United Kingdom, and the United States. Headline unemployment rates declined (in some cases from levels already approaching historical lows); rates of involuntary part-time employment dropped; and labor force participation rates rose (Figure 1.1.1).

Consistent with the decline in headline unemployment and diminishing latent slack in the form of involuntary part-time employment, nominal wage growth picked up in these economies. (Chapter 2 of the October 2017 *World Economic Outlook* discusses the importance of these cyclical factors in accounting for subdued wage growth in advanced economies after the 2008–09 global financial crisis.) Wage growth in these economies has recovered some of the lost ground, but it is still below averages seen before the crisis.

The continued sluggishness in wage growth can largely be accounted for by productivity growth being far weaker than it was before the crisis. Nominal wage growth has been broadly in line with labor productivity growth in these economies, and there is scant evidence of unit labor costs (the ratio of nominal wages to labor productivity) rising in a sustained manner—as seen in panel 3 of Figure 1.1.1. As such, pass-through from rising wage growth to consumer price inflation has been limited so far, even after a sustained period of declining unemployment.

The authors of this box are Weicheng Lian and Yuan Zeng.

Box 1.1 *(continued)*

Figure 1.1.1. Labor Market Dynamics in Selected Advanced Economies
(Percent)

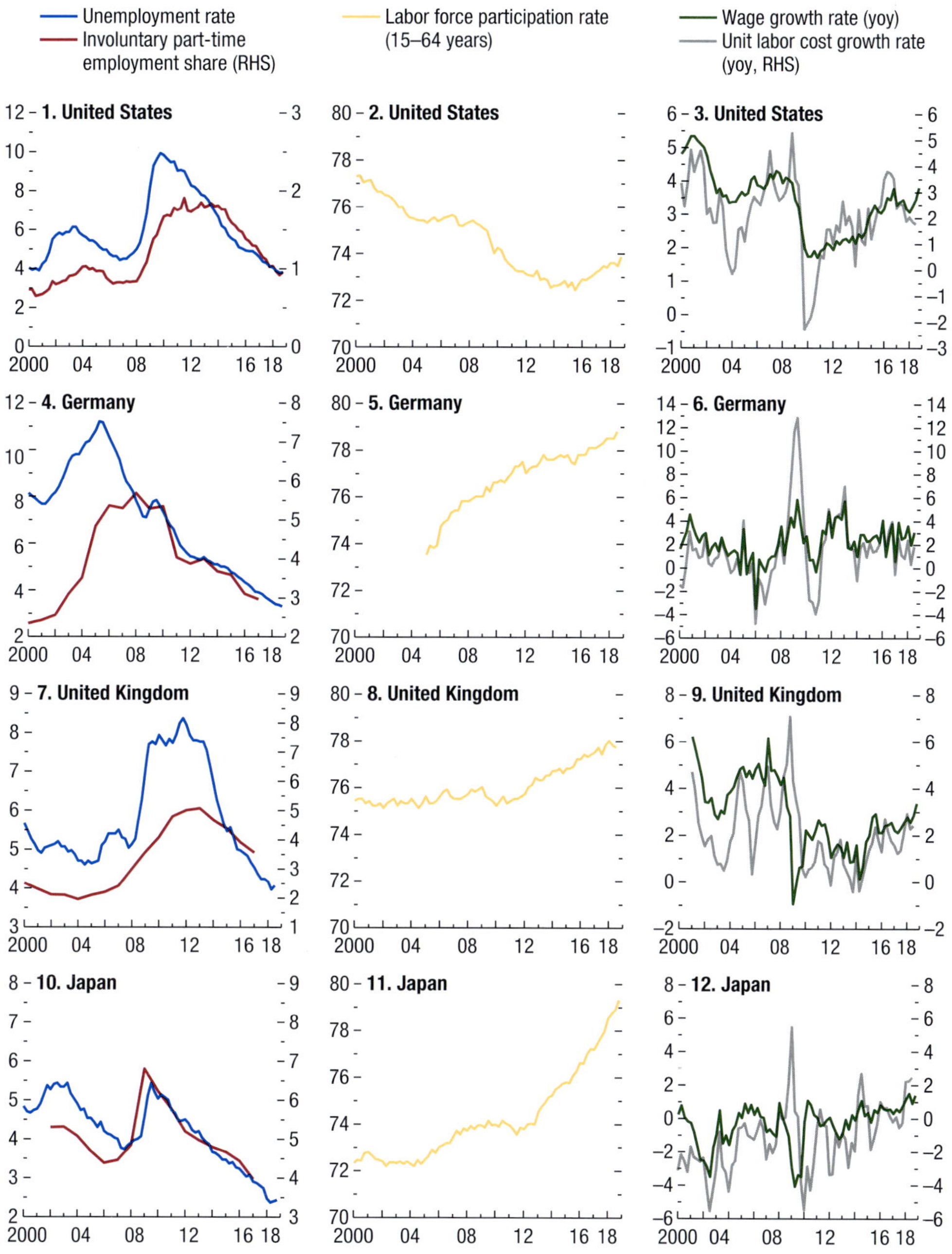

Sources: Haver Analytics; national authorities; Organisation for Economic Co-operation and Development; and IMF staff calculations.
Note: RHS = right scale; yoy = year over year.

Box 1.2. Global Growth Forecast: Assumptions on Policies, Financial Conditions, and Commodity Prices

The global forecast rests on the following key assumptions on policies, financial conditions, and commodity prices:

- *Tariffs*: The tariffs imposed by the United States as of September 2018 and retaliatory measures by trading partners are factored into the baseline forecast. For US actions, besides tariffs on solar panels, washing machines, aluminum, and steel announced in the first half of 2018, these include a 25 percent tariff on \$50 billion in imports from China (July and August 2018) and a 10 percent tariff on an additional \$200 billion in imports from China (September 2018). In light of recent developments in the US–China negotiations, tariffs on \$200 billion of US imports from China are assumed to stay at 10 percent (whereas in the October 2018 *World Economic Outlook* (WEO) and the January 2019 WEO *Update* they had been assumed to rise to 25 percent as of March 1, 2019). Also incorporated in the baseline forecast is China's response to the September 2018 US action, which included tariffs of 5–10 percent on \$60 billion in imports from the United States.
- *Fiscal policy*: Fiscal policy is assumed to be expansionary across advanced economies in 2019 and expected to turn contractionary in 2020 as the US stimulus starts unwinding. Similarly, fiscal policy is assumed to be expansionary across the emerging market and developing economy group in 2019 (in part reflecting a projected fiscal stimulus in China to offset some of the negative effects of higher tariffs), before turning contractionary in 2020 (Figure 1.11).
- *Monetary policy*: The US federal funds rate is expected to increase to about 2.75 percent by the end of 2019, with one hike projected this year. Policy rates are assumed to remain at close to zero in Japan through 2020 and negative in the euro area until mid-2020.
- *Financial conditions*: The baseline forecast assumes a gradual tightening of global financial conditions with the relative intensity varying across economies, based on underlying economic and political fundamentals.
- *Commodity prices*: Based on oil futures contracts, average oil prices are projected at \$59.2 in 2019 and \$59.0 in 2020 (down from \$68.8 and \$65.7, respectively, in the October 2018 WEO). Oil prices are expected to remain in that range, reaching about \$60 a barrel by 2023 (broadly unchanged from the October 2018 WEO forecast), consistent with subdued medium-term demand prospects and offsetting production adjustments that avoid large excess supply. Metal prices are expected to increase 2.4 percent year over year in 2019 and decline by 2.2 percent in 2020 (compared with a decrease of 3.6 percent followed by a slight pickup of 0.4 percent in the October WEO). Price forecasts of most major agricultural commodities have been revised down. Food prices are projected to decline 2.9 percent year over year in 2019 before increasing 2.1 percent in 2020 (compared with the projected increases of 1.7 percent and 0.3 percent in the October 2018 WEO).

Box 1.3. Worlds Apart? Within-Country Regional Disparities

Regional and urban–rural disparities in income, labor market outcomes, and productivity have attracted a lot of attention in recent years. There is concern that, coupled with a slow recovery from the global financial crisis, persistent and rising spatial disparity may have contributed to widening income inequality and growing disillusionment with globalization.

Regional disparities may not necessarily call for policy intervention. If spatial inequality results from regional specialization based on comparative advantage (for instance due to natural endowments) or returns to scale in production (due to complementarities and agglomeration economies), spatial inequality in output may be the flip side of efficient resource allocation. Over time, regional incomes should converge as labor and capital reallocate in response to interregional factor price differentials.

However, in some cases, regions fail to converge in this way. Many countries have regions with chronic problems. Regional disparities could remain persistently large because of market failures: when there are difficulties starting new centers of activity, coordination failure can follow, and obstacles to factor mobility can limit their reallocation.

Large, persistent disparities impose costs on the people and places left behind and on booming areas. These can have political economy implications, reduce trust, and increase political polarization. Although it is only one component of income inequality across individuals and households, this dimension has been studied much less and may have added significance when spatial and regional divisions align with political and ethnic tensions.

Large Disparities

Within-country disparities in per capita GDP are large (Figure 1.3.1, panels 1 and 2).[1] While regional disparities in the per capita GDP of emerging markets

Figure 1.3.1. Regional Disparities in GDP per Capita

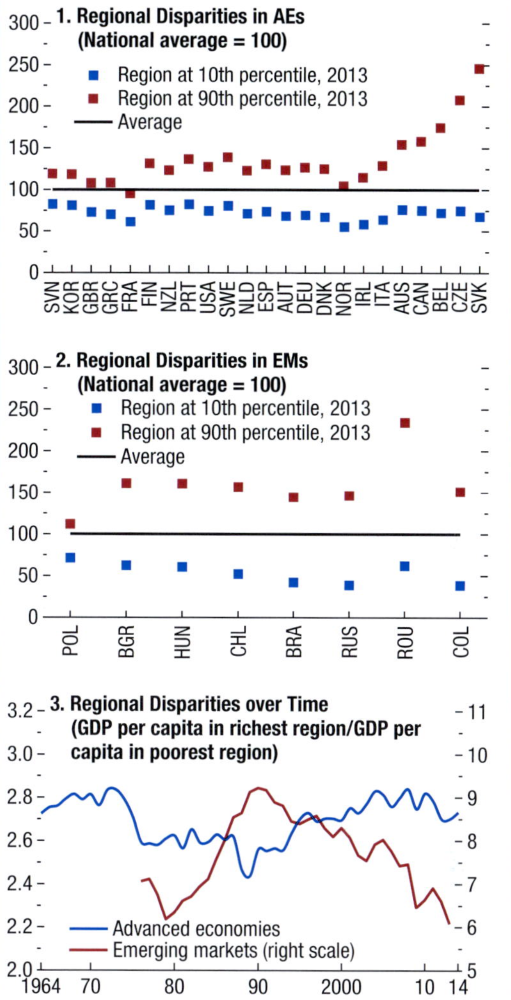

Sources: Gennaioli and others (2014); Organisation for Economic Co-operation and Development Regional Database; and IMF staff calculations.
Note: Panels 1 and 2 refer to 2013 (the most recent year with wide cross-country coverage), constant PPP GDP per capita. Panel 3 is based on a balanced subset of eight advanced economies and eight emerging markets for which longer time series are available. Recent patterns are very similar for a larger set of countries with shorter time series. Overseas territories are included. AEs = advanced economies; EMs = emerging markets; PPP = purchasing power parity.

The author of this box is Zsoka Koczan.

[1]The Organisation for Economic Co-operation and Development regional database relies on national purchasing-power-parity (PPP) deflators because subnational PPP deflators are not widely available. The lack of region-specific PPP deflators may lead to overestimation of within-country income differentials (as poorer regions likely also have lower prices; see, for instance, Aten and Heston 2005). Rich and poor regions also exhibit systematic differences alongside other dimensions, such as labor market indicators, educational attainment, and even health outcomes.

Box 1.3 *(continued)*

are more pronounced than in advanced economies, these ranges have been shrinking since the early 1990s, following a rise before that. In contrast, advanced economies experienced shrinking disparities and within-country convergence until the 1980s, but divergence since. This pattern is widely documented for the United States,[2] where the increase in spatial disparity has been particularly marked.

Regional differences in per capita GDP also appear to be very persistent. A region's relative position compared with the country average is closely correlated with its relative position even 10 years ago: the 10-year lag of normalized GDP per capita at the regional level still predicts about three-quarters of the variation in normalized regional per capita GDP today.

Obstacles to Mobility?

Such persistence may raise concerns about adjustment mechanisms. With free mobility of labor, workers in regions with high unemployment or low average wages would choose to migrate to regions with low unemployment and a higher average wage, and thereby over time eliminate the differential in unemployment and wages.

However, wages may not be responsive enough to labor market conditions, leading to excessive swings in unemployment in response to shocks. Liquidity constraints may force workers who become unemployed to leave the region rather than borrow and wait for the upturn, leading to excessive labor outmigration. Conversely, large fixed costs of migration may prevent the unemployed or those with fewer skills from moving. The behavior of house prices may affect the mobility of homeowners.

The differential impacts of globalization and automation across sectors, occupations, and geographic areas could also result in different regional effects of global forces. In the context of such diverse regional economies experiencing localized shocks, country-level policies may then be ineffective.[3]

Declining mobility has received a lot of attention in the United States, where interstate mobility is at a historic low. However, that fits with the broad decline of within-country migration in advanced economies.[4] Migration is also highly selective. Those with more education and the employed are more likely to move than those with less education or who are unemployed. This could suggest that falling dynamism may be one of the factors underlying the recent increase in regional disparities in advanced economies.

[2]See Berry and Glaeser (2005); Moretti (2011); Ganong and Shoag (2017); Giannone (2017); Austin, Glaeser, and Summers (2018); Economic Innovation Group (2018); Hendrickson, Muro, and Galston (2018); and Nunn, Parsons, and Shambaugh (2018).

[3]See Leichenko and Silva (2004); Chiquiar (2008); Kandilov (2009); Autor, Dorn, and Hanson (2013); Hakobyan and McLaren (2016); and Partridge and others (2017). See also Chapter 2 of the April 2018 *World Economic Outlook*.

[4]It has increased in emerging markets, on average, though from very low levels.

Special Feature: Commodity Market Developments and Forecasts

Energy prices have decreased since the release of the October 2018 World Economic Outlook *(WEO), mostly driven by lower oil prices. After surging to their highest point since 2014 because of concerns over US sanctions against Iran, oil prices fell to their lowest point since the second half of 2017 following record US oil production growth, the prospects for weaker global economic growth, and temporary waivers for imports of Iranian oil. In response to falling prices, oil exporters agreed to cut production, providing some price support. While a growth slowdown in China and trade tensions put downward pressure on metal prices in 2018, metal prices recovered on fiscal stimulus in China, improved global market sentiment, and supply disruptions in some metal markets. Prices of agricultural goods have increased somewhat as news of weaker global income growth and excess supply conditions in some grain markets were more than offset by a recovery of world sugar prices and excess demand for animal protein sources. This special feature also includes an in-depth analysis of the relationship between commodity prices and economic activity.*

The IMF's Primary Commodity Price Index declined by 6.9 percent between August 2018 and February 2019, the reference periods for the October 2018 and current WEO, respectively (Figure 1.SF.1, panel 1). Amid high volatility, energy prices drove that decline, falling sharply by 17.0 percent, while base metal prices increased as trade tensions and weaker economic activity in China were more than offset by supply disruptions. Food prices increased by 1.9 percent as exceptional yields in some grain markets were more than offset by higher prices for meat and a rebound in sugar prices. Oil prices increased to more than $80 a barrel in early October, attaining their highest level since November 2014 as US sanctions against oil imports from Iran loomed.[1] In the last months of 2018, however, oil prices declined sharply thanks to record production growth in the United States and the issuance of waivers for most of the countries that import oil from Iran. In response to that slump, Organization of the Petroleum Exporting Countries (OPEC) and non-OPEC oil exporters agreed to cut production. Coal prices decreased as China's economy grew at its slowest pace since 1990, while natural gas prices fluctuated widely, driven by changing weather conditions, especially in North America.

Oil Price Roller Coaster

In early October, oil prices surpassed $80, their highest level since November 2014, ahead of US sanctions against Iran's oil sector that took effect in November. However, the US administration issued waivers that allowed several major importing countries to continue importing crude oil from Iran. In addition, US crude oil production averaged 10.9 million barrels a day (mbd) in 2018, an increase of 1.6 mbd over the previous year (exceeding expectations by 0.3 mbd since the October WEO) and the largest growth in its history.[2] Canada, Iraq, Russia, and Saudi Arabia also produced at high levels. As a result, oil prices fell sharply between early October and the end of November. On December 7, 2018, OPEC and non-OPEC (including Russia) countries agreed to cut their crude oil production by 0.8 mbd and 0.4 mbd, respectively, from their October 2018 level, starting in January 2019 for an initial six-month period. Oil producers' cuts, coupled with unplanned outages supported oil prices, which rebounded to above $60 in February. Natural gas spot prices declined sharply in response to ample supply following a volatile start of the winter because of changing weather conditions; long-term natural gas contract prices declined in tandem with medium-term oil price futures. Coal prices have decreased, prompted by lower Chinese economic activity as well as lower oil prices.

As of February, oil futures contracts indicated that Brent prices will stay at about $60 for the next five years. (Figure 1.SF.1, panel 2). Baseline assumptions, also based on futures prices, suggest average annual prices of $59.2 a barrel in 2019—a decrease of 13.4 percent from the 2018 average—and $59.0 a barrel in 2020 for the IMF's average petroleum spot prices. On the demand side, lower oil prices are offsetting underlying oil demand from weaker global economic growth—the International Energy Agency expects oil demand

The authors of this special feature are Christian Bogmans, Lama Kiyasseh, Akito Matsumoto, Andrea Pescatori (team leader), and Julia Xueliang Wang, with research assistance from Lama Kiyasseh and Julia Xueliang Wang.

[1]Oil price in this document refers to the IMF average petroleum spot price, which is based on UK Brent, Dubai, and West Texas Intermediate, equally weighted, unless specified otherwise.

[2]In September 2018, the Energy Information Agency expected an increase in US oil production of 1.3 mbd.

Figure 1.SF.1. Commodity Market Developments

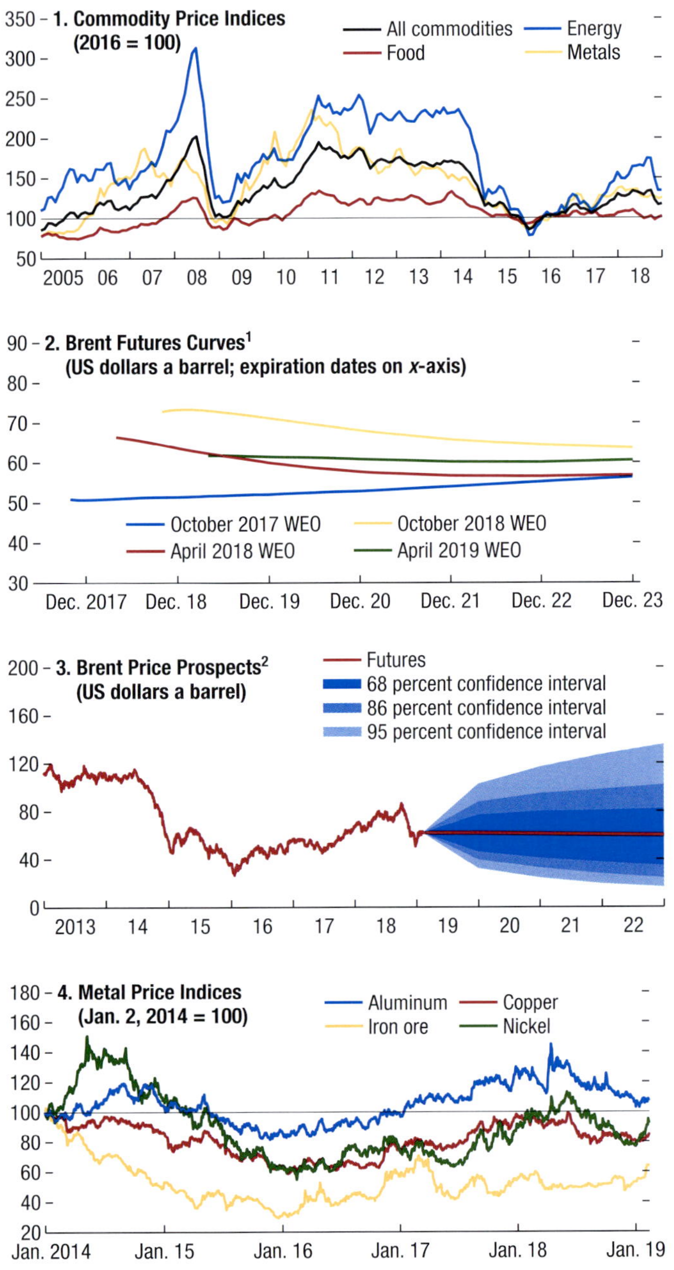

Sources: Bloomberg Finance L.P.; IMF, Primary Commodity Price System; Thomson Reuters Datastream; and IMF staff estimates.
Note: WEO = *World Economic Outlook.*
[1]WEO futures prices are baseline assumptions for each WEO and are derived from future prices. October 2018 WEO prices are based on February 7, 2019, closing.
[2]Derived from prices of futures options on February 7, 2019.

to grow by 1.3 mbd and 1.4 mbd in 2018 and 2019, respectively, a 0.1 mbd downward revision for both years (relative to the October WEO). On the supply side, since the beginning of 2019, mandatory production cuts by Canada and the supply cuts by OPEC and non-OPEC countries, including involuntary outages in Venezuela, are gradually slowing oil output growth.

Although risks are balanced, substantial uncertainty around the baseline oil price projections remains because of high policy uncertainty (Figure 1.SF.1, panel 3). Upside risks to prices in the short term include geopolitical events in Middle East, civil unrest in Venezuela, a tougher US stance against Iran and Venezuela, and slower-than-expected US production growth. Downside risks include stronger-than-expected US production and noncompliance among OPEC and non-OPEC countries. Trade tensions and other risks to global growth can also further affect global activity and its prospects, in turn reducing oil demand.

Metal Prices Rebounded

Metal prices increased 7.6 percent between August 2018 and February 2019. By the end of 2018, the IMF annual base metals price index had reached its lowest point in 16 months due to weakening growth, notably in China, and global trade tensions. However, metal prices rebounded since then, driven by the expectation of fiscal stimulus in China and improved global market sentiment—coupled with a sharp increase in iron ore prices due to the Brumadinho dam disaster (Brazil).

Iron ore prices increased 28.8 percent between August 2018 and February 2019 amid supply disruptions from the world's top iron ore miners, including a derailment of a BHP iron ore train on November 5, a fire at a Rio Tinto's export terminal on January 10, and the collapse of Brumadinho dam at Vale SA's mine on January 25. The dam collapse will have ramifications for the industry, which could experience a prolonged halt of operations at some iron ore mines and a slowdown of new projects. (Figure 1.SF.1, panel 4). Copper prices increased 4.1 percent on US–China trade optimism and market deficit for both concentrate and refined copper. Aluminum fell 9.2 percent, following the lifting of US sanctions on the giant Russian aluminum producer Rusal and improved prospects for removal of the production embargo by the Brazilian Federal government on Hydro's Alunorte (the world's largest alumina refinery) in the second half of 2019. Nickel, a key input for stainless steel and batteries in electric vehicles, dropped 5.4 percent between August and February 2019 on stronger-than-expected production from Indonesia and the Philippines. Zinc, which is used mainly to galvanize steel, increased 7.8 percent from August to February 2019 on persistent supply tightness, partly due to the ongoing environmental clampdown in China, the world's largest producer of zinc. Cobalt saw the deepest fall in prices of all metals during the reference period, declining by 49.3 percent due to rising supply from the Democratic Republic of the Congo.

The IMF annual base metal price index is projected to increase by 2.4 percent in 2019 (relative to its average in 2018) and decrease by 2.2 percent per year in 2020. Upside risks to the outlook are higher-than-expected metals demand from China and supply shortages as a result of more stringent environmental regulations in major metal-producing countries. Downside risks stem from a faster moderation in global economic growth and a further slowdown of the Chinese economy (the biggest world metal consumer).

Food Prices Increased Slightly

Trade tensions, weak emerging market currencies, and exceptionally strong US grain yields constituted the primary drags on global food prices in the first three quarters of 2018. Since then, prices have been less volatile. The IMF's food and beverage price index has increased slightly, by 1.9 percent, as news of weaker global economic activity and excess supply in markets, such as those for wheat and cotton, was outweighed by excess demand for animal protein sources and a recovery of world sugar prices from multiyear lows.

Wheat prices decreased by 15.8 percent between August 2018 and February 2019 as a competitive Russian ruble supported Russian exports. Absent news on harvests from major producing countries and in anticipation of lower trade tensions, a reversal of yields to the mean, and normalization of US dollar strength, prices of corn and soybeans have slowly moved up, increasing by 4.4 percent and 5.6 percent, respectively, between August 2018 and February 2019.

Poultry prices increased, by 3.9 percent, because of strong consumer demand. World sugar prices jumped by 23.7 percent, in part due to expectations of lower output in 2019 from top producers Brazil and India. Following weaker-than-expected demand and given ample stocks in China, the price of cotton declined by 14.2 percent between August 2018 and February 2019, even as hot weather took a toll on global cotton crops.

Food prices are projected to decrease by 2.9 percent a year in 2019 and then increase by 2.1 percent in 2020. Weather disruptions are an upside risk to the forecast. On February 14, 2019, the US National Oceanic and Atmospheric Administration announced that weak El Niño climate conditions have taken effect and are expected to continue into spring, which could have local impacts on crops. A resolution of the trade conflict between the United States—the world's largest food exporter—and China is another source of upside potential for prices.

Commodity Prices and Economic Activity

Introduction

What do commodity prices tell us about economic activity? This special feature analyzes the bountiful and rich information embedded in the prices of the many commodities traded in major commodity markets around the world and shows how this information is useful to nowcast or even forecast global economic activity.[3]

There are at least two major reasons commodity prices are useful indicators of global economic activity. First, even in a world where services take the spotlight, commodities still represent about 17 percent of global trade and are fundamental production inputs.[4] A change in global economic activity will therefore be reflected in the global demand for commodities (Barsky and Kilian 2004; Alquist, Bhattarai, and Coibion forthcoming). Second, commodities are storable, so, like those of financial assets, their prices reflect both current and expected *future* demand and supply conditions. Given that many commodities are regularly traded in liquid and deep markets, their prices can swiftly move in response to changes in market tightness, including news and changes in sentiment about global economic conditions.

In practice, it is not easy to infer economic activity from commodity prices. The presence of commodity supply shocks and commodity-specific demand factors is, in fact, a prominent confounding influence[5] and

[3]Nowcasting is a statistical model that exploits real-time data to provide a timely estimate of major economic activity indicators (such as GDP) that are usually released by statistical agencies with a delay.

[4]Industrial commodities (metals and raw agricultural materials) are essential inputs for the manufacturing sector. Energy commodities, because they are crucial to the transportation and petrochemical sectors and to power generation, indirectly affect the entire global production system. And food and beverage commodities, usually affected by income, underpin the food chain.

[5]For example, extreme weather conditions can substantially affect crop output and demand for natural gas.

Figure 1.SF.2. Commodity Cycles and Economic Activity

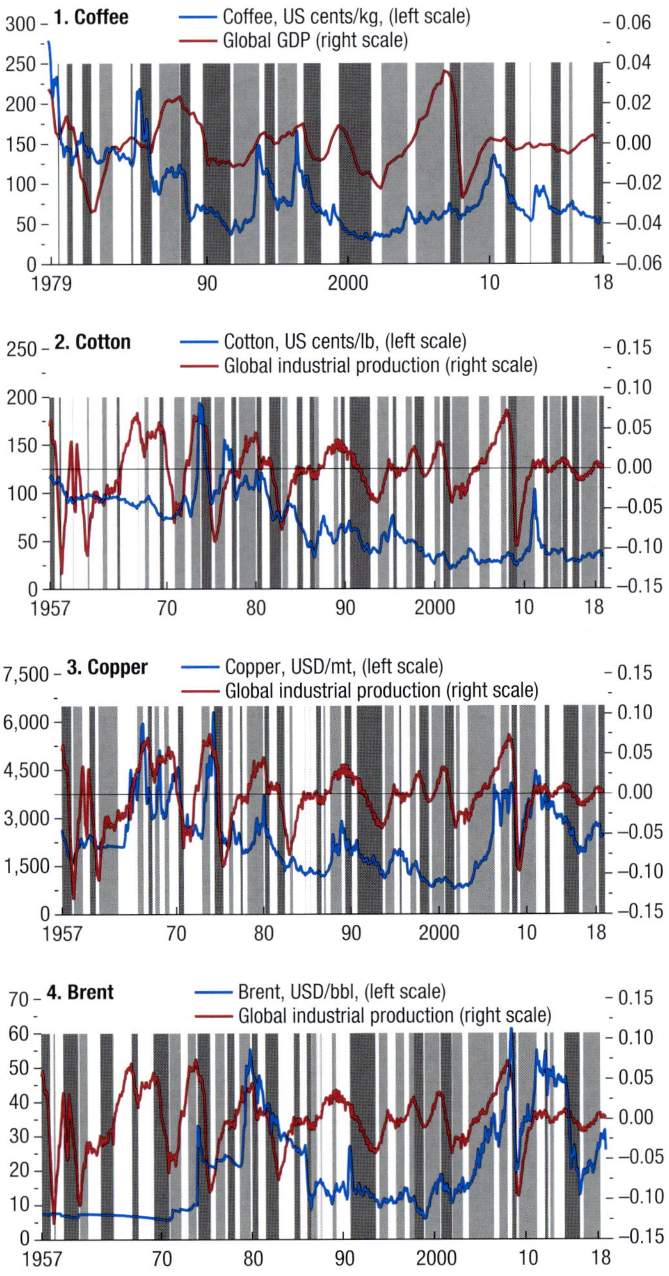

Sources: IMF, Primary Commodity Price System; Organisation for Economic Co-operation and Development (OECD); and IMF staff calculations.
Note: Peaks and troughs are identified using the Harding and Pagan's (2002) business cycle dating procedure. Global industrial production (IP) is spliced back using OECD IP (1975/79) and US IP (<1975). Dark (light) shaded areas represent synchronized contractions (expansions) in both economic activity and the selected commodity price. White shaded areas represent asynchronized movements. bbl = barrel; kg = kilogram; lb = pound; mt = metric ton; USD = US dollar.

even perhaps a reason for reverse causality—especially in the case of oil—potentially introducing an element of countercyclicality (Hamilton 1996, 2003). To tackle this problem, the analysis is split into two parts. The first identifies commodity price cycles and provides insights into the cyclical synchronization between commodity prices and economic activity. The second part exploits comovement among commodity prices to isolate global demand factors from other confounding influences and then tests whether the extracted global factors have nowcasting and predictive power for economic activity.

Cyclicality and Comovement of Commodity Prices

This section identifies commodity price cycles and looks, across a broad set of commodity prices, at commodities with the highest pair-wise synchronization with economic activity (that is, *bellwethers*). It also derives a commodity-market-wide synchronization measure.

The methodology to identify periods of *contraction* and *expansion* follows the business-cycle-dating procedure of Harding and Pagan (2002).[6] This procedure is applied to an unbalanced panel, starting in 1957, of 57 (real) commodity price series that fall into four broad categories: energy, metals, food and beverages, and raw agricultural materials.[7] The same procedure is also applied to detrended global industrial production and GDP.[8] (Figure 1.SF.2 presents four examples.)

[6]Drawing on Cashin, McDermott, and Scott (2002), the Harding and Pagan (2002) methodology is used to identify peaks and troughs in the time path of real commodity prices. A candidate turning point is identified as a local maximum or minimum if the price in that month is either greater or less than the price in the two months before and the two months after. The sequence of resulting candidate turning points is then required to alternate between peaks and troughs. Furthermore, each phase defined by the turning points (expansion or contraction) must be at least 12 months long. (This commodity-price-cycle-dating algorithm is an adaptation of the business-cycle-dating algorithm set out by Bry and Boschan (1971) and later popularized by Harding and Pagan (2002). An advantage of using a Bry and Boschan–type algorithm to date commodity price cycles is that it provides a tractable means of applying an objective cycle-dating rule to a large data set.)

[7]All commodity price series are monthly averages of prices from the IMF's Primary Commodity Price System and are denominated in US dollars and divided by US consumer price inflation. Prices are not prefiltered, given that most commodities do not show a clear trend. The academic literature still debates whether commodity prices, in general, have a trend. Grilli and Yang (1988) argues that commodity prices have a downward tendency; more recently, Jacks (2013) and Stuermer (2018) found a modest upward trend. Results are mostly unchanged if a linear trend is removed.

[8]A Hodrick-Prescott filter with a very low lambda is used to extract a stable trend from global industrial production and GDP. Quarterly GDP data have been interpolated monthly. Although the dating algorithm can handle nonstationarity, some statistics that

Table 1.SF.1. Commodity Price Cycle Descriptive Statistics

	Duration (Months)		Amplitude (Log difference, percent)		Sharpness (Log difference, percent)	
	Expansion	Contraction	Expansion	Contraction	Expansion	Contraction
Energy	20	24	64.72	62.81	3.37	3.01
Base Metals	18	24	55.19	57.98	3.05	2.41
Food and Beverages	16	20	45.25	49.60	2.80	2.33
Agricultural Raw Materials	18	22	43.27	46.70	2.46	2.00

Sources: IMF, Primary Commodity Price System; and IMF staff calculations.
Note: Price cycles are identified using the Harding and Pagan (2002) methodology. Duration measures the average length (in months) of a price phase (expansion or contraction). Amplitude measures the average price change (in percentage terms) from trough to peak in case of an expansion, and from peak to trough in case of a contraction. Sharpness measures the average price increase per month (in percentage terms) experienced during an expansion, and the average price decline during a contraction. All statistics are calculated by averaging over all commodities in a particular group.

Most commodities show asymmetric phases characterized by longer and dull contractions punctuated by sharp expansions (Table 1.SF.1).[9] Energy commodities stand out because they have the longest and sharpest phases; a full energy cycle tends to last slightly less than four years. Overall, however, the characterization of cycles is quite similar across commodity groups and appears to be in line with a long-standing body of literature that highlights the interaction of commodity supply shocks with storage demand as an important driver of commodity price movements (Deaton and Laroque 1992; Cashin, McDermott, and Scott 2002).

Supply shocks, especially when inventory stocks or spare production capacity is low, tend to cause spikes in prices, but a large array of literature also stresses the role of demand factors (Barsky and Kilian 2004; Alquist, Bhattarai, and Coibion forthcoming—among many). It is therefore interesting to calculate the synchronization of phases (or technically, *concordance*) between commodity prices and economic activity.[10]

With few exceptions, agricultural prices, especially food prices, are, on average, only modestly in sync with economic activity (Figure 1.SF.3). Bellwethers of global industrial production are mostly base metals (such as zinc, copper, and tin) and, to a lesser extent, energy and fertilizers. Propane shows the highest synchronization with global industrial production, but its time series and the time series for natural gas start only in 1992 and hence are shorter than for most other commodities—suggesting a possible increase in synchronization between commodities and economic activity over the past few decades, which is also consistent with the findings of the factor analysis in the next section. Interestingly, some raw agricultural materials, such as cotton, have relatively high synchronization with global industrial production while, in general, food and beverages, relative to other commodities, are more synchronized to global GDP than to industrial production. This is because income, rather than production, plays a more relevant role in their demand (an example is arabica coffee).[11]

Periods of sizable movement in economic activity (booms or busts) should increase comovement, and therefore synchronization, among all commodities. Most commodities, not only bellwethers, should move in sync with global industrial production or GDP. Accordingly, it is useful to derive a metric that calculates the share of commodities that are in the expansion (contraction) phase—that is, a commodity-wide concordance.[12] This metric should be related to global economic activity, with turning points (periods of maximum or minimum synchronization among commodity prices) falling within expansionary or contractionary phases of global activity. The commodity-wide concordance should, thus, be indicative of how much global demand factors, relative to supply or

compare stationary and nonstationary series (for example, concordance) can be misleading.

[9]Online Annex 1.SF.1 (available at www.imf/en/Publications/WEO) shows cyclical properties for each individual commodity price series and tests different sets of parameters for the dating algorithm that impose longer minimum durations for phases and cycles.

[10]Technically, the synchronization metric used is the *concordance*, which calculates the share of time two series that are in the same phase (Harding and Pagan 2002). Concordance is bounded between 0 and 1; two independent random walks have a concordance of 0.5.

[11]As expected, the metals that are less in sync with economic activity are precious metals, such as gold and silver, and those that have not always been freely traded in spot markets, such as iron ore (before 2009), because both buyers and suppliers seek long-term security in a market with little output growth. Uranium is not freely traded because of its unique applications and geopolitical sensitivity.

[12]A value of 1 (–1) means that all commodity prices are expanding (contracting) simultaneously—perfect synchronization—while a value of 0 implies that half of commodity prices are in the same phase, lowest synchronization.

Figure 1.SF.3. Synchronization with Economic Activity

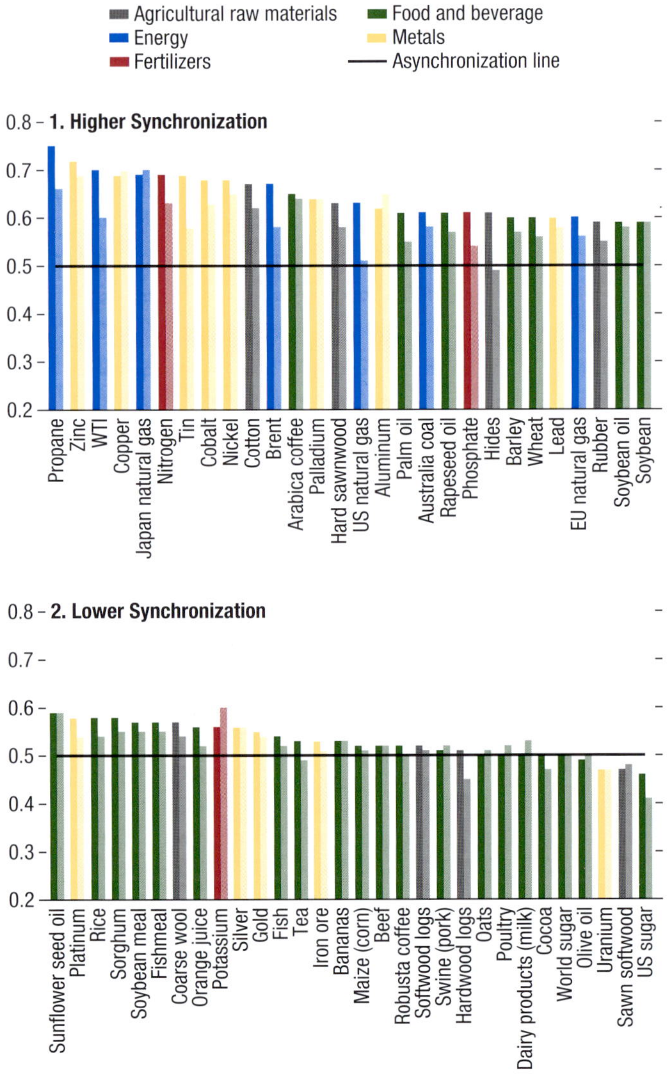

Sources: IMF, Primary Commodity Price System; Organisation for Economic Co-operation and Development; and IMF staff calculations.
Note: Bars represent the synchronization of a given commodity with de-trended global industrial production (IP) (darker bars) and GDP (lighter bars). Synchronization is defined as the concordance between the price cycle of a given commodity and the business cycle (de-trended GDP or IP) where phases of expansions and contractions are identified using Harding and Pagan's (2002) procedure. Concordance calculates the share of time two series are in the same phase; a concordance above 0.5 denotes a positive synchronization. WTI = West Texas Intermediate.

Figure 1.SF.4. Commodity-Wide Synchronization
(Percent)

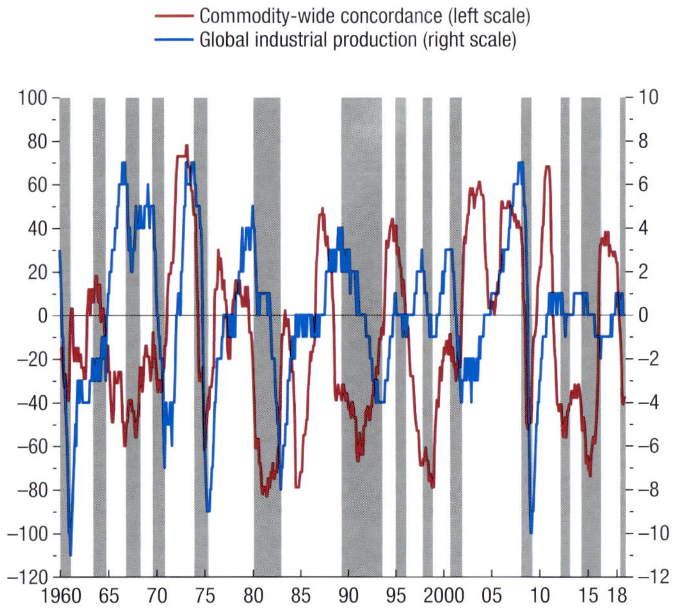

Sources: IMF, Primary Commodity Price System; Organisation for Economic Co-operation and Development (OECD); and IMF staff calculations.
Note: Global industrial production (IP) is spliced back using OECD IP (1975–79) and US IP (<1975). Shading represents contractions in the IP variable. Commodity-wide concordance is the share of commodities in expansion (contraction).

commodity-specific demand factors, are driving commodity prices in a given period.

Figure 1.SF.4 shows that commodity-wide concordance anticipates turning points of economic activity, given that it typically peaks (or troughs) when activity is expanding or contracting most. This is a promising result, highlighting the presence of common latent factor(s) related to global activity that drive commodity prices. The next section will try to exploit this insight to nowcast and forecast movements in the global business cycle using commodity prices.

Do Commodity Prices Help Nowcast and Forecast Global Economic Activity?

To isolate movements in commodity prices that are driven by global economic activity, a factor model is estimated at monthly frequency using principal components (Stock and Watson 2002; West and Wong 2014; Delle Chiaie, Ferrara, and Giannone 2018).[13]

[13]The approach in Delle Chiaie, Ferrara, and Giannone (2018) that allows for group-specific factors gives slightly inferior results.

Given that supply- and commodity-specific demand shocks make commodity prices diverge, estimating latent factors that cause commodity prices to comove should help construct a proxy for global economic activity.[14] Following this logic, the higher the number of commodities used, the better the identification of global demand factors. In practice, however, it may be preferable to exclude commodities, such as gold and silver, that behave more like financial assets or those that are too closely related, such as soybean meal and soybean oil (Kilian and Zhou 2018).[15]

The first two extracted factors explain about 20 percent of the variance in commodity price monthly changes. The relevance of the remaining factors drops off quickly and is not statistically related to economic activity.[16] Figure 1.SF.5 plots the first and second latent factors extracted jointly with (demeaned) global GDP growth, cumulated over time. Even though the first and second factors are contemporaneously orthogonal by construction, when cumulated, they show a positive correlation, 0.67. The first factor is a *global factor;* the second represents a negative demand shift for agricultural products relative to energy and metals and is therefore a *relative-price factor*.[17] Given that the relative-price factor helps account for movements in agricultural prices, first factors are extracted by first splitting the sample into agricultural and nonagricultural (energy and metals) commodities. Interestingly, the global factor and the relative-price factor are very well approximated by a linear combination of the two first factors of the split subsamples.[18] The relative-price factor, however, has a negative sign on the first factor of the agriculture subsample. The relationship between the global factor and global GDP is visually quite striking (Figure 1.SF.5), but the relative-price factor also seems to move with GDP during some sharp downturns (by leading them) and subsequent recoveries.[19]

Because the first release of global industrial production lags by two months and that of GDP lags by one quarter, they are often substantially revised, so it is useful to test whether latent factors can help nowcast global activity. To do so, global industrial production and GDP are regressed on their own lagged value

Figure 1.SF.5. Latent Factors and Economic Activity

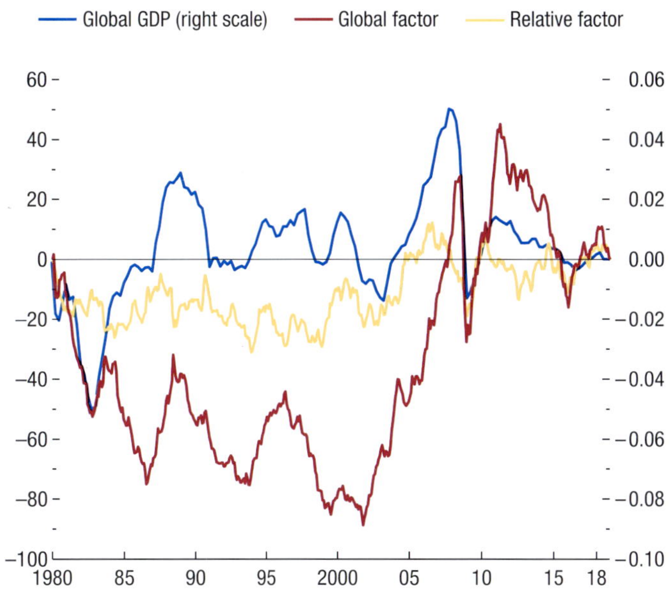

Sources: IMF, Primary Commodity Price System; and IMF staff calculations.
Note: First and second principal components are cumulated; log difference in global GDP is de-meaned and cumulated.

[14]The idea that global demand causes comovement in commodity prices is clearly not novel. For example, Barsky and Kilian (2004) interprets the strong comovement of the real price of oil and a real price index of industrial raw materials and metals in the early 1970s as evidence of a common demand component in both prices. More generally, a large body of literature is based on a range of different models and data that finds most of the fluctuations in (especially industrial) commodity prices are driven by shifts in aggregate demand (see, for example, Barsky and Kilian 2004; Kilian 2009; Nakov and Pescatori 2010; Kilian and Murphy 2014; Alquist, Bhattarai, and Coibion forthcoming; and Delle Chiaie, Ferrara, and Giannone 2018, among others).

[14]Interestingly, Pindyck and Rotemberg (1990) notes how seemingly uncorrelated commodities (whose cross-price elasticities of demand and supply are close to zero) show excess comovement, which suggests the presence of a latent global (possibly heteroscedastic) factor that affects all prices at the same time.

[15]To estimate the latent factors, the log differences of prices (divided by the US consumer price index) have been *z*-scored. The use of log-detrended or log differences is less relevant for the estimation (Kilian and Zhou 2018).

[16]This is in line with Stock and Watson (2002). That study uses a different set of indicators to show that the first two factors are the most informative and have the highest predictive content.

[17]This can be seen by inspecting the factor loadings, available on request.

[18]A regression of the global (relative-price) factor on the first factors extracted from the agriculture and nonagriculture samples separately yields an R-squared of 0.99 (0.88).

[19]The (negative of the) first factor in levels mimics movements in the US dollar real effective exchange rate (REER), which is not a surprise, given that the dollar is the numerator for all commodity prices in the sample. This association is, however, much weaker at higher frequencies, such as monthly changes, and weakens further when, to construct the REER, noncommodity currencies are excluded because, as is well known, they move inversely with the price of the commodity exported (Chen and Rogoff 2003). Introducing the US dollar REER into the nowcasting and forecasting exercise does not alter the results.

Table 1.SF.2. Global Industrial Production Nowcast

	Benchmark	Specification 1	Specification 2	Specification 3
RMSE	0.55%	0.54%	0.53%	0.54%
Ratio	1	0.99	0.97	0.98

Sources: IMF, Primary Commodity Price System; and IMF staff calculations.
Note: Sample period = January 1980 to December 2018. Benchmark = autoregressive process with the optimal lag based on Bayesian information criterion; Specification 1 = first principal component; Specification 2 = first two principal components; Specification 3 = first principal components of agricultural and nonagricultural commodities. Optimal lag of independent variables added based on Bayesian information criterion for all specifications. RMSE = root mean square error; Ratio = relative RMSE, RMSE divided by benchmark RMSE.

and latent factors and on one period of their own lag. Whether the introduction of the latent factors statistically improves the nowcast estimate of the economic activity indicator (industrial production or GDP) is tested, and the results are compared with a *benchmark* autoregressive (AR)(p) process (following Stock and Watson 2002). Varying specifications are tried: only the global factor is used (specification 1); the global and relative factors are introduced together (specification 2); the sample is split into agricultural and nonagricultural commodities and the respective first factors are used (specification 3). All specifications can include their own lags, optimally chosen.

Results shown in Table 1.SF.2 indicate that for industrial production, at monthly frequency, introducing the global factor and the relative-price factor increases the ability to nowcast industrial production relative to the benchmark AR(p) process—in which the number of lags, p, is determined optimally. Because monthly industrial production growth is quite volatile, nowcasting yields modest improvements. More striking is its ability to nowcast GDP (Table 1.SF.3). The improvement in the root mean square error relative to the AR(p) benchmark is already 10 percent with only the global factor from one month of commodity price information. The improvement increases to 15 percent when the quarter is completed. The R-squared is also high, at about 0.48.[20] Interestingly, commodity prices are mostly informative during periods of high economic volatility, when the AR(p) process fails the most (Figure 1.SF.6). Results are similar when using the two first factors extracted from the agricultural and nonagricultural group taken separately.

Factor lags are also significant, so it is possible to test whether commodity prices also help predict global activity. Forecast evaluations are based on the out-of-sample forecast performance. Given data for industrial production, GDP, and estimated principal components, each specification is first estimated using the sample period 1980–98 and then recursively reestimated to forecast for 2000–18.[21] For each period, the model forecasts for next period's one-month-ahead and three-month-ahead industrial

[20]Regression results are available upon request. It is also worth noting that predictability declines when using global GDP (industrial production) at market exchange rates, probably because of the greater relevance of services in advanced economies.

[21]Each model is reestimated with the addition of new data (recursive scheme). Models using principal components have a fixed lag length, but the optimal lag length of the AR model is chosen each time, using Bayesian information criteria or Akaike information criteria.

Table 1.SF.3. Global GDP Nowcast

	Metric	Benchmark	Specification 1	Specification 2	Specification 3
One Month Information	RMSE	0.42%	0.38%	0.37%	0.38%
	Ratio	1	0.90	0.90	0.90
Two Months Information	RMSE	0.42%	0.36%	0.36%	0.36%
	Ratio	1	0.87	0.86	0.86
Quarter Information	RMSE	0.42%	0.36%	0.35%	0.35%
	Ratio	1	0.86	0.84	0.85

Sources: IMF, Primary Commodity Price System; and IMF staff calculations.
Note: Sample period = 1980:Q1 to 2018:Q3. Benchmark = autoregressive process with the optimal lag based on Bayesian information criterion; Specification 1 = first principal component; Specification 2 = first two principal components; Specification 3 = first principal components of agricultural and nonagricultural commodities. One-period lagged dependent variable is added in all specifications. Information is available one, two, or three months into the quarter. RMSE = root mean square error; Ratio = relative RMSE, RMSE divided by benchmark RMSE.

Figure 1.SF.6. Global Real GDP Growth Nowcast: Actual versus Fitted Value
(Percent, quarter-over-quarter)

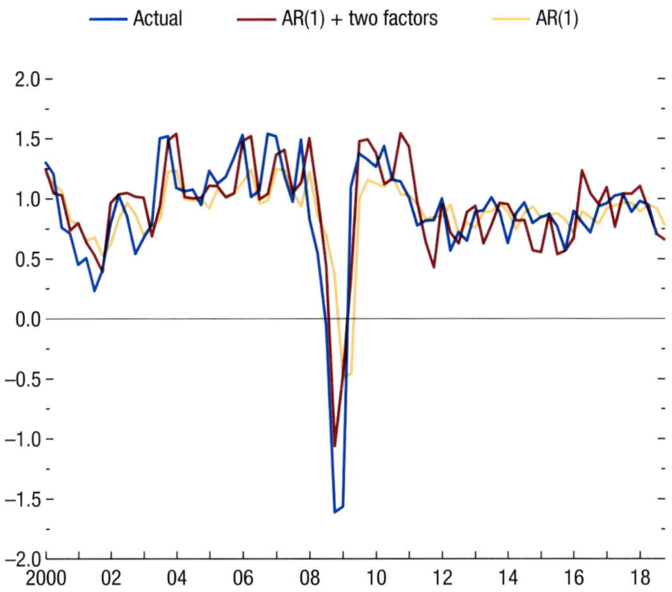

Sources: IMF, Primary Commodity Price System; and IMF staff calculations.
Note: AR = autoregressive process; two factors = first two principal components. Regressions are based on quarterly data from 1980:Q1 to 2018:Q3.

production growth.[22] The forecast performance is based on the root mean squared forecast error.

Results in Table 1.SF.4 show that all specifications improve the one-month-ahead global industrial production forecast (relative to the benchmark): specification (2), which uses both the global and relative factors, does best and improves the forecast by 10 percent.

The one-quarter-ahead GDP forecast is also improved, but only as price information in the quarter becomes available.[23] In practice, global GDP data may not be available in the next two quarters. For example, in May, first-quarter world GDP is not available, whereas data for April commodity prices are. This timeliness is why commodity prices are useful to forecast GDP growth for the next quarter. As months pass, the forecasting performance improves because commodity price movements more accurately reflect the current quarter. When the full quarter is available, the root mean squared forecast error of the next-quarter GDP is improved by almost 10 percent relative to the benchmark.

In conclusion, there is a wealth of information embedded in commodity prices that can be very useful for taking the pulse of global economic activity. Once idiosyncratic factors are eliminated, major movements in prices of base metals, and, to some extent, energy and agricultural products, can tell us a lot about the state of the global economy, especially when economic activity takes place during significant fluctuations—when the need for forecasting and nowcasting is most compelling.

[22]After running the forecast through entire periods, several forecast performance measures are calculated. These include the root mean squared prediction errors between model forecasts and actual growth, mean absolute prediction errors, bias (mean prediction error), and efficiency (the correlation between prediction error and prediction). Results are available on request.

[23]The specification is tested when price data for the first, both first and second, and all three month(s) of the quarter are available.

Table 1.SF.4. Forecasting Global Industrial Production and GDP

		Metric	Benchmark	Specification 1	Specification 2	Specification 3
IP	Month	RMSE	0.55%	0.50%	0.49%	0.50%
		Ratio	1	0.92	0.90	0.92
GDP	One Month Information	RMSE	0.51%	0.50%	0.51%	0.51%
		Ratio	1	0.99	1.00	1.00
	Two Months Information	RMSE	0.51%	0.48%	0.48%	0.48%
		Ratio	1	0.95	0.95	0.95
	Quarter Information	RMSE	0.51%	0.46%	0.46%	0.46%
		Ratio	1	0.91	0.91	0.90

Sources: IMF, Primary Commodity Price System; and IMF staff calculations.
Note: Benchmark = autoregressive process with the optimal lag based on Bayesian information criterion; Specification 1 = first principal component; Specification 2 = first two principal components; Specification 3 = first principal components of agricultural and nonagricultural commodities. One-period lagged dependent variable is added in all specifications for IP. Information is available one, two, or three months into the quarter. IP = industrial production; RMSE = root mean square error; Ratio = relative RMSE, RMSE divided by benchmark RMSE.

Annex Table 1.1.1. European Economies: Real GDP, Consumer Prices, Current Account Balance, and Unemployment

(Annual percent change, unless noted otherwise)

	Real GDP			Consumer Prices[1]			Current Account Balance[2]			Unemployment[3]		
		Projections			Projections			Projections			Projections	
	2018	2019	2020	2018	2019	2020	2018	2019	2020	2018	2019	2020
Europe	**2.2**	**1.2**	**1.8**	**3.2**	**2.9**	**2.8**	**2.2**	**2.2**	**2.1**	...	...	...
Advanced Europe	**1.8**	**1.3**	**1.6**	**1.9**	**1.4**	**1.6**	**2.7**	**2.6**	**2.5**	**7.1**	**7.0**	**6.9**
Euro Area[4,5]	1.8	1.3	1.5	1.8	1.3	1.6	3.0	2.9	2.8	8.2	8.0	7.7
Germany	1.5	0.8	1.4	1.9	1.3	1.7	7.4	7.1	6.8	3.4	3.4	3.3
France	1.5	1.3	1.4	2.1	1.3	1.5	–0.7	–0.4	0.0	9.1	8.8	8.4
Italy	0.9	0.1	0.9	1.2	0.8	1.2	2.6	2.9	2.6	10.6	10.7	10.5
Spain	2.5	2.1	1.9	1.7	1.2	1.6	0.8	0.8	0.8	15.3	14.2	14.1
Netherlands	2.5	1.8	1.7	1.6	2.3	1.6	9.8	9.3	8.9	3.8	3.7	3.6
Belgium	1.4	1.3	1.4	2.3	1.9	1.6	0.4	0.3	0.5	5.9	5.9	5.9
Austria	2.7	2.0	1.7	2.1	1.8	2.0	2.3	2.0	1.9	4.9	5.1	5.0
Greece	2.1	2.4	2.2	0.8	1.1	1.4	–3.4	–2.7	–2.6	19.6	18.5	17.5
Portugal	2.1	1.7	1.5	1.2	1.0	1.7	–0.6	–0.4	–0.5	7.1	6.8	6.3
Ireland	6.8	4.1	3.4	0.7	1.2	1.5	10.0	9.1	8.3	5.7	5.3	5.0
Finland	2.4	1.9	1.7	1.2	1.3	1.5	–0.5	0.1	0.4	7.5	7.2	7.1
Slovak Republic	4.1	3.7	3.5	2.5	2.4	2.2	–2.0	–1.0	–0.7	6.6	6.1	6.0
Lithuania	3.4	2.9	2.6	2.5	2.3	2.3	1.4	1.1	0.6	6.3	6.3	6.2
Slovenia	4.5	3.4	2.8	1.7	1.4	1.6	6.5	4.4	3.4	5.3	4.8	4.9
Luxembourg	3.0	2.7	2.8	2.0	1.6	1.9	5.2	5.0	5.0	5.0	5.0	5.0
Latvia	4.8	3.2	3.1	2.6	2.4	2.4	–1.0	–1.4	–1.7	7.4	7.3	7.3
Estonia	3.9	3.0	2.9	3.4	3.0	2.8	1.7	1.5	1.1	5.4	4.7	3.5
Cyprus	3.9	3.5	3.3	0.8	0.5	1.6	–5.6	–7.3	–6.5	8.4	7.0	6.0
Malta	6.4	5.2	4.4	1.7	1.8	1.9	10.1	9.3	8.8	4.0	4.1	4.3
United Kingdom	1.4	1.2	1.4	2.5	1.8	2.0	–3.9	–4.2	–4.0	4.1	4.2	4.4
Switzerland	2.5	1.1	1.5	0.9	0.8	0.9	9.8	9.0	9.0	2.6	2.8	2.8
Sweden	2.3	1.2	1.8	2.0	1.9	1.7	2.0	2.4	2.5	6.3	6.3	6.3
Norway	1.4	2.0	1.9	2.8	1.9	1.7	8.1	7.4	7.2	3.9	3.7	3.7
Czech Republic	2.9	2.9	2.7	2.2	2.3	2.0	0.2	–0.6	–0.8	2.5	3.1	3.2
Denmark	1.2	1.7	1.8	0.7	1.1	1.3	6.0	5.5	5.1	5.0	4.9	4.9
Iceland	4.6	1.7	2.9	2.7	2.8	2.5	2.9	0.8	1.1	2.7	3.3	3.6
San Marino	1.1	0.8	0.7	1.6	1.6	1.7	0.4	0.4	0.2	8.0	8.1	8.1
Emerging and Developing Europe[6]	**3.6**	**0.8**	**2.8**	**8.7**	**9.0**	**7.5**	**–2.2**	**–0.9**	**–1.4**	...	...	...
Turkey	2.6	–2.5	2.5	16.3	17.5	14.1	–3.6	0.7	–0.4	11.0	12.7	11.4
Poland	5.1	3.8	3.1	1.6	2.0	1.9	–0.7	–1.1	–1.5	3.8	3.6	3.5
Romania	4.1	3.1	3.0	4.6	3.3	3.0	–4.6	–5.2	–4.8	4.2	4.8	4.9
Hungary	4.9	3.6	2.7	2.8	3.2	3.1	0.5	0.5	0.6	3.7	3.5	3.4
Bulgaria[5]	3.2	3.3	3.0	2.6	2.4	2.3	3.9	1.9	1.3	5.2	5.0	5.0
Serbia	4.4	3.5	4.0	2.0	2.0	2.5	–5.2	–5.5	–5.0	13.7	13.4	13.2
Croatia	2.7	2.6	2.5	1.5	1.5	1.6	2.9	2.1	1.6	10.0	9.0	8.0

Note: Data for some countries are based on fiscal years. Please refer to Table F in the Statistical Appendix for a list of economies with exceptional reporting periods.
[1]Movements in consumer prices are shown as annual averages. Year-end to year-end changes can be found in Tables A6 and A7 in the Statistical Appendix.
[2]Percent of GDP.
[3]Percent. National definitions of unemployment may differ.
[4]Current account position corrected for reporting discrepancies in intra-area transactions.
[5]Based on Eurostat's harmonized index of consumer prices except for Slovenia.
[6]Includes Albania, Bosnia and Herzegovina, Kosovo, Montenegro, and North Macedonia.

Annex Table 1.1.2. Asian and Pacific Economies: Real GDP, Consumer Prices, Current Account Balance, and Unemployment

(Annual percent change, unless noted otherwise)

	Real GDP			Consumer Prices[1]			Current Account Balance[2]			Unemployment[3]		
		Projections			Projections			Projections			Projections	
	2018	2019	2020	2018	2019	2020	2018	2019	2020	2018	2019	2020
Asia	**5.5**	**5.4**	**5.4**	**2.4**	**2.5**	**2.8**	**1.2**	**1.2**	**1.1**	**. . .**	**. . .**	**. . .**
Advanced Asia	**1.8**	**1.7**	**1.7**	**1.3**	**1.3**	**1.6**	**3.9**	**3.9**	**3.9**	**3.2**	**3.1**	**3.1**
Japan	0.8	1.0	0.5	1.0	1.1	1.5	3.5	3.5	3.6	2.4	2.4	2.4
Korea	2.7	2.6	2.8	1.5	1.4	1.6	4.7	4.6	4.5	3.8	4.0	3.9
Australia	2.8	2.1	2.8	2.0	2.0	2.3	–2.1	–2.1	–2.1	5.3	4.8	4.8
Taiwan Province of China	2.6	2.5	2.5	1.5	1.1	1.2	11.6	11.4	10.7	3.8	3.7	3.7
Singapore	3.2	2.3	2.4	0.4	1.3	1.4	17.7	17.6	17.1	2.1	2.0	2.0
Hong Kong SAR	3.0	2.7	3.0	2.4	2.4	2.5	3.5	3.2	3.4	2.8	2.8	2.8
New Zealand	3.0	2.5	2.9	1.6	2.0	1.9	–4.0	–4.4	–4.3	4.2	4.4	4.4
Macao SAR	4.7	4.3	4.2	3.0	2.5	2.7	35.0	37.4	38.7	1.8	1.8	1.8
Emerging and Developing Asia	**6.4**	**6.3**	**6.3**	**2.6**	**2.8**	**3.1**	**–0.1**	**–0.1**	**–0.2**	**. . .**	**. . .**	**. . .**
China	6.6	6.3	6.1	2.1	2.3	2.5	0.4	0.4	0.3	3.8	3.8	3.8
India[4]	7.1	7.3	7.5	3.5	3.9	4.2	–2.5	–2.5	–2.4	. . .	. . .	. . .
ASEAN-5	**5.2**	**5.1**	**5.2**	**2.8**	**2.8**	**3.0**	**0.6**	**0.6**	**0.4**	**. . .**	**. . .**	**. . .**
Indonesia	5.2	5.2	5.2	3.2	3.3	3.6	–3.0	–2.7	–2.6	5.3	5.2	5.0
Thailand	4.1	3.5	3.5	1.1	1.0	1.3	7.7	7.1	6.3	1.2	1.2	1.2
Malaysia	4.7	4.7	4.8	1.0	2.0	2.6	2.3	2.1	2.1	3.3	3.3	3.3
Philippines	6.2	6.5	6.6	5.2	3.8	3.3	–2.6	–2.2	–1.8	5.3	5.5	5.4
Vietnam	7.1	6.5	6.5	3.5	3.1	3.3	3.0	3.1	2.6	2.2	2.2	2.2
Other Emerging and Developing Asia[5]	**5.3**	**6.3**	**6.2**	**4.5**	**4.6**	**5.3**	**–3.3**	**–2.8**	**–2.8**	**. . .**	**. . .**	**. . .**
Memorandum												
Emerging Asia[6]	**6.5**	**6.3**	**6.3**	**2.6**	**2.8**	**3.0**	**0.0**	**0.0**	**–0.1**	**. . .**	**. . .**	**. . .**

Note: Data for some countries are based on fiscal years. Please refer to Table F in the Statistical Appendix for a list of economies with exceptional reporting periods.
[1]Movements in consumer prices are shown as annual averages. Year-end to year-end changes can be found in Tables A6 and A7 in the Statistical Appendix.
[2]Percent of GDP.
[3]Percent. National definitions of unemployment may differ.
[4]See country-specific note for India in the "Country Notes" section of the Statistical Appendix.
[5]Other Emerging and Developing Asia comprises Bangladesh, Bhutan, Brunei Darussalam, Cambodia, Fiji, Kiribati, Lao P.D.R., Maldives, Marshall Islands, Micronesia, Mongolia, Myanmar, Nauru, Nepal, Palau, Papua New Guinea, Samoa, Solomon Islands, Sri Lanka, Timor-Leste, Tonga, Tuvalu, and Vanuatu.
[6]Emerging Asia comprises the ASEAN-5 (Indonesia, Malaysia, Philippines, Thailand, Vietnam) economies, China, and India.

Annex Table 1.1.3. Western Hemisphere Economies: Real GDP, Consumer Prices, Current Account Balance, and Unemployment

(Annual percent change, unless noted otherwise)

	Real GDP			Consumer Prices[1]			Current Account Balance[2]			Unemployment[3]		
		Projections			Projections			Projections			Projections	
	2018	2019	2020	2018	2019	2020	2018	2019	2020	2018	2019	2020
North America	**2.7**	**2.2**	**1.9**	**2.7**	**2.2**	**2.7**	**–2.3**	**–2.4**	**–2.6**	...	...	...
United States	2.9	2.3	1.9	2.4	2.0	2.7	–2.3	–2.4	–2.6	3.9	3.8	3.7
Canada	1.8	1.5	1.9	2.2	1.7	1.9	–2.6	–3.1	–2.8	5.8	5.9	6.0
Mexico	2.0	1.6	1.9	4.9	3.8	3.1	–1.8	–1.7	–1.9	3.3	3.5	3.6
Puerto Rico[4]	–2.3	–1.1	–0.7	2.5	0.3	1.3	...	...	...	11.0	11.0	11.2
South America[5]	**0.4**	**1.1**	**2.4**	**7.1**	**8.1**	**6.1**	**–1.8**	**–1.9**	**–1.9**	...	...	...
Brazil	1.1	2.1	2.5	3.7	3.6	4.1	–0.8	–1.7	–1.6	12.3	11.4	10.2
Argentina	–2.5	–1.2	2.2	34.3	43.7	23.2	–5.4	–2.0	–2.5	9.2	9.9	9.9
Colombia	2.7	3.5	3.6	3.2	3.4	3.2	–3.8	–3.9	–3.8	9.7	9.7	9.5
Venezuela	–18.0	–25.0	–10.0	929,789.5	10,000,000	10,000,000	6.0	1.4	–1.9	35.0	44.3	47.9
Chile	4.0	3.4	3.2	2.3	2.3	3.0	–3.1	–3.2	–2.8	6.9	6.5	6.2
Peru	4.0	3.9	4.0	1.3	2.4	2.0	–1.5	–1.4	–1.5	6.7	6.6	6.5
Ecuador	1.1	–0.5	0.2	–0.2	0.6	1.2	–0.7	0.4	1.4	3.7	4.3	4.7
Bolivia	4.3	4.0	3.9	2.3	2.3	3.6	–4.7	–5.2	–5.1	4.0	4.0	4.0
Uruguay	2.1	1.9	3.0	7.6	7.6	7.2	–0.6	–0.8	–1.2	8.0	8.1	7.9
Paraguay	3.7	3.5	4.0	4.0	3.6	4.0	0.5	–0.8	0.4	5.6	5.7	5.8
Central America[6]	**2.7**	**3.2**	**3.5**	**2.6**	**2.7**	**3.0**	**–3.6**	**–2.9**	**–2.7**	...	...	...
Caribbean[7]	**4.7**	**3.6**	**3.7**	**3.7**	**2.4**	**4.3**	**–2.3**	**–2.3**	**–2.0**	...	...	...
Memorandum												
Latin America and the Caribbean[8]	1.0	1.4	2.4	6.2	6.5	5.1	–1.9	–1.9	–2.0	...	...	...
East Caribbean Currency Union[9]	2.1	4.0	3.1	1.3	1.6	2.0	–10.5	–9.6	–9.4	...	...	...

Note: Data for some countries are based on fiscal years. Please refer to Table F in the Statistical Appendix for a list of economies with exceptional reporting periods.

[1]Movements in consumer prices are shown as annual averages. Aggregates exclude Venezuela. Year-end to year-end changes can be found in Tables A6 and A7 in the Statistical Appendix.

[2]Percent of GDP.

[3]Percent. National definitions of unemployment may differ.

[4]Puerto Rico is a territory of the United States but its statistical data are maintained on a separate and independent basis.

[5]Includes Guyana and Suriname. See country-specific notes for Argentina and Venezuela in the "Country Notes" section of the Statistical Appendix.

[6]Central America comprises Belize, Costa Rica, El Salvador, Guatemala, Honduras, Nicaragua, and Panama.

[7]The Caribbean comprises Antigua and Barbuda, Aruba, The Bahamas, Barbados, Dominica, Dominican Republic, Grenada, Haiti, Jamaica, St. Kitts and Nevis, St. Lucia, St. Vincent and the Grenadines, and Trinidad and Tobago.

[8]Latin America and the Caribbean comprises Mexico and economies from the Caribbean, Central America, and South America. See country-specific notes for Argentina and Venezuela in the "Country Notes" section of the Statistical Appendix.

[9]Eastern Caribbean Currency Union comprises Antigua and Barbuda, Dominica, Grenada, St. Kitts and Nevis, St. Lucia, and St. Vincent and the Grenadines as well as Anguilla and Montserrat, which are not IMF members.

Annex Table 1.1.4. Commonwealth of Independent States Economies: Real GDP, Consumer Prices, Current Account Balance, and Unemployment

(Annual percent change, unless noted otherwise)

	Real GDP			Consumer Prices[1]			Current Account Balance[2]			Unemployment[3]		
		Projections			Projections			Projections			Projections	
	2018	2019	2020	2018	2019	2020	2018	2019	2020	2018	2019	2020
Commonwealth of Independent States[4]	**2.8**	**2.2**	**2.3**	**4.5**	**5.7**	**5.0**	**5.0**	**3.8**	**3.4**	**. . .**	**. . .**	**. . .**
Net Energy Exporters	**2.7**	**2.1**	**2.2**	**4.0**	**5.7**	**5.0**	**6.2**	**4.9**	**4.4**	**. . .**	**. . .**	**. . .**
Russia	2.3	1.6	1.7	2.9	5.0	4.5	7.0	5.7	5.1	4.8	4.8	4.7
Kazakhstan	4.1	3.2	3.2	6.0	5.5	5.0	0.6	0.1	0.6	5.0	5.0	5.0
Uzbekistan	5.0	5.0	5.5	17.9	16.5	11.9	–7.8	–5.6	–4.7	. . .	. . .	. . .
Azerbaijan	1.4	3.4	3.1	2.3	2.5	2.5	12.6	11.7	13.3	5.0	5.0	5.0
Turkmenistan	6.2	6.3	6.0	13.6	13.0	9.0	3.1	–2.3	–3.2	. . .	. . .	. . .
Net Energy Importers	**3.6**	**2.8**	**3.1**	**7.6**	**6.2**	**5.3**	**–4.3**	**–4.0**	**–3.4**	**. . .**	**. . .**	**. . .**
Ukraine	3.3	2.7	3.0	10.9	8.0	5.9	–3.7	–2.5	–2.4	9.0	8.5	8.1
Belarus	3.0	1.8	2.2	4.9	5.0	5.0	–2.3	–4.0	–2.3	0.8	0.8	0.8
Georgia	4.7	4.6	5.0	2.6	2.5	3.0	–7.9	–8.0	–7.8	. . .	. . .	. . .
Armenia	5.0	4.6	4.5	2.5	2.1	3.0	–6.2	–4.6	–4.3	18.1	17.9	17.7
Tajikistan	7.0	5.0	4.5	3.8	6.7	6.2	–5.3	–7.0	–6.8	. . .	. . .	. . .
Kyrgyz Republic	3.5	3.8	3.4	1.5	2.2	4.9	–9.8	–10.9	–8.6	6.8	6.8	6.8
Moldova	4.0	3.5	3.8	3.1	3.3	5.1	–9.9	–7.7	–8.0	4.1	4.0	4.0
Memorandum												
Caucasus and Central Asia[5]	4.2	4.1	4.1	8.2	7.8	6.4	0.5	–0.5	–0.1	. . .	. . .	. . .
Low-Income CIS Countries[6]	5.0	4.8	5.1	11.9	11.3	9.0	–7.8	–6.6	–6.0	. . .	. . .	. . .
Net Energy Exporters Excluding Russia	4.1	4.0	4.1	9.0	8.4	6.7	1.6	0.5	0.8	. . .	. . .	. . .

Note: Data for some countries are based on fiscal years. Please refer to Table F in the Statistical Appendix for a list of economies with exceptional reporting periods.
[1]Movements in consumer prices are shown as annual averages. Year-end to year-end changes can be found in Table A7 in the Statistical Appendix.
[2]Percent of GDP.
[3]Percent. National definitions of unemployment may differ.
[4]Georgia, Turkmenistan, and Ukraine, which are not members of the Commonwealth of Independent States (CIS), are included in this group for reasons of geography and similarity in economic structure.
[5]Caucasus and Central Asia comprises Armenia, Azerbaijan, Georgia, Kazakhstan, the Kyrgyz Republic, Tajikistan, Turkmenistan, and Uzbekistan.
[6]Low-Income CIS countries comprise Armenia, Georgia, the Kyrgyz Republic, Moldova, Tajikistan, and Uzbekistan.

Annex Table 1.1.5. Middle East, North African Economies, Afghanistan, and Pakistan: Real GDP, Consumer Prices, Current Account Balance, and Unemployment

(Annual percent change, unless noted otherwise)

	Real GDP			Consumer Prices[1]			Current Account Balance[2]			Unemployment[3]		
		Projections			Projections			Projections			Projections	
	2018	2019	2020	2018	2019	2020	2018	2019	2020	2018	2019	2020
Middle East, North Africa, Afghanistan, and Pakistan	**1.8**	**1.5**	**3.2**	**10.4**	**9.7**	**9.3**	**2.3**	**–0.9**	**–0.7**	**. . .**	**. . .**	**. . .**
Oil Exporters[4]	**0.6**	**0.4**	**2.8**	**9.2**	**9.0**	**8.8**	**5.3**	**0.9**	**1.0**	**. . .**	**. . .**	**. . .**
Saudi Arabia	2.2	1.8	2.1	2.5	–0.7	2.2	8.3	3.5	2.8	. . .	. . .	. . .
Iran	–3.9	–6.0	0.2	31.2	37.2	31.0	4.3	–0.4	–0.6	13.9	15.4	16.1
United Arab Emirates	1.7	2.8	3.3	3.1	2.1	2.1	6.6	5.9	5.1	. . .	. . .	. . .
Algeria	2.1	2.3	1.8	4.3	5.6	6.7	–9.1	–12.5	–9.3	11.7	12.6	13.7
Iraq	0.6	2.8	8.1	0.4	2.0	2.0	4.9	–6.7	–2.9	. . .	. . .	. . .
Qatar	2.2	2.6	3.2	0.2	0.1	3.7	9.3	4.6	4.1	. . .	. . .	. . .
Kuwait	1.7	2.5	2.9	0.7	2.5	2.7	12.7	7.4	8.0	1.3	1.3	1.3
Oil Importers[5]	**4.2**	**3.6**	**4.0**	**12.8**	**11.0**	**10.2**	**–6.5**	**–6.1**	**–5.3**	**. . .**	**. . .**	**. . .**
Egypt	5.3	5.5	5.9	20.9	14.5	12.3	–2.4	–2.4	–1.7	10.9	9.6	8.3
Pakistan	5.2	2.9	2.8	3.9	7.6	7.0	–6.1	–5.2	–4.3	6.1	6.1	6.2
Morocco	3.1	3.2	3.8	1.9	1.4	2.0	–4.5	–4.1	–3.5	9.8	9.2	8.9
Sudan	–2.1	–2.3	–1.3	63.3	49.6	58.1	–11.5	–9.9	–10.0	19.5	21.4	20.9
Tunisia	2.5	2.7	3.2	7.3	7.5	5.6	–11.2	–10.1	–9.1	15.6	. . .	. . .
Lebanon	0.2	1.3	2.0	6.1	2.0	2.3	–27.0	–28.2	–28.4	. . .	. . .	. . .
Jordan	2.0	2.2	2.4	4.5	2.0	2.5	–7.4	–8.2	–8.0	18.3	. . .	. . .
Memorandum												
Middle East and North Africa	1.4	1.3	3.2	11.4	10.0	9.6	3.1	–0.5	–0.4	. . .	. . .	. . .
Israel[6]	3.3	3.3	3.3	0.8	0.9	1.7	1.9	1.7	1.4	4.0	4.0	4.0
Maghreb[7]	3.4	2.8	2.5	5.1	5.2	5.7	–6.8	–8.3	–7.4	. . .	. . .	. . .
Mashreq[8]	4.8	5.0	5.5	18.8	13.0	11.1	–7.0	–6.8	–6.1	. . .	. . .	. . .

Note: Data for some countries are based on fiscal years. Please refer to Table F in the Statistical Appendix for a list of economies with exceptional reporting periods.
[1]Movements in consumer prices are shown as annual averages. Year-end to year-end changes can be found in Tables A6 and A7 in the Statistical Appendix.
[2]Percent of GDP.
[3]Percent. National definitions of unemployment may differ.
[4]Includes Bahrain, Libya, Oman, and Yemen.
[5]Includes Afghanistan, Djibouti, Mauritania, and Somalia. Excludes Syria because of the uncertain political situation.
[6]Israel, which is not a member of the economic region, is included for reasons of geography but is not included in the regional aggregates.
[7]The Maghreb comprises Algeria, Libya, Mauritania, Morocco, and Tunisia.
[8]The Mashreq comprises Egypt, Jordan, and Lebanon. Syria is excluded because of the uncertain political situation.

Annex Table 1.1.6. Sub-Saharan African Economies: Real GDP, Consumer Prices, Current Account Balance, and Unemployment

(Annual percent change, unless noted otherwise)

	Real GDP			Consumer Prices[1]			Current Account Balance[2]			Unemployment[3]		
		Projections			Projections			Projections			Projections	
	2018	2019	2020	2018	2019	2020	2018	2019	2020	2018	2019	2020
Sub-Saharan Africa	**3.0**	**3.5**	**3.7**	**8.5**	**8.1**	**7.4**	**–2.6**	**–3.7**	**–3.7**	**. . .**	**. . .**	**. . .**
Oil Exporters[4]	**1.3**	**2.0**	**2.6**	**12.9**	**11.8**	**10.9**	**1.5**	**–1.2**	**–0.6**	**. . .**	**. . .**	**. . .**
Nigeria	1.9	2.1	2.5	12.1	11.7	11.7	2.1	–0.4	–0.2	22.6	. . .	. . .
Angola	–1.7	0.4	2.9	19.6	17.5	11.1	1.3	–3.8	–1.9	. . .	. . .	. . .
Gabon	1.2	3.1	3.9	4.8	3.0	2.5	–1.9	–3.6	–1.2	. . .	. . .	. . .
Chad	3.1	4.5	6.0	2.5	2.9	3.0	–4.8	–6.1	–4.3	. . .	. . .	. . .
Republic of Congo	0.8	5.4	1.5	1.2	1.5	1.8	5.5	4.7	5.9	. . .	. . .	. . .
Middle-Income Countries[5]	**2.7**	**3.4**	**3.3**	**4.6**	**5.1**	**5.3**	**–3.2**	**–3.2**	**–3.5**	**. . .**	**. . .**	**. . .**
South Africa	0.8	1.2	1.5	4.6	5.0	5.4	–3.4	–3.4	–3.7	27.1	27.5	27.8
Ghana	5.6	8.8	5.8	9.8	9.1	8.4	–3.2	–3.0	–3.5	. . .	. . .	. . .
Côte d'Ivoire	7.4	7.5	7.2	0.3	2.0	2.0	–3.4	–3.0	–2.8	. . .	. . .	. . .
Cameroon	4.0	4.3	4.7	0.9	1.2	1.5	–4.0	–3.7	–3.4	. . .	. . .	. . .
Zambia	3.5	3.1	2.9	7.0	10.7	12.0	–5.0	–2.9	–2.7	. . .	. . .	. . .
Senegal	6.2	6.9	7.5	0.5	1.3	1.5	–7.2	–7.3	–10.2	. . .	. . .	. . .
Low-Income Countries[6]	**5.9**	**5.3**	**5.7**	**7.7**	**7.4**	**5.7**	**–6.8**	**–7.3**	**–7.8**	**. . .**	**. . .**	**. . .**
Ethiopia	7.7	7.7	7.5	13.8	9.3	8.0	–6.5	–6.0	–5.4	. . .	. . .	. . .
Kenya	6.0	5.8	5.9	4.7	4.4	5.0	–5.4	–5.0	–4.9	. . .	. . .	. . .
Tanzania	6.6	4.0	4.2	3.5	3.5	4.5	–3.7	–3.9	–4.2	. . .	. . .	. . .
Uganda	6.2	6.3	6.2	2.6	3.6	4.4	–6.8	–8.2	–9.1	. . .	. . .	. . .
Madagascar	5.2	5.2	5.3	7.3	6.7	6.3	0.3	–1.4	–3.5	. . .	. . .	. . .
Democratic Republic of the Congo	3.9	4.3	4.4	29.3	8.4	6.7	–0.5	–1.8	–2.9	. . .	. . .	. . .
Memorandum												
Sub-Saharan Africa Excluding South Sudan	3.1	3.4	3.7	8.2	8.1	7.4	–2.6	–3.7	–3.7	. . .	. . .	. . .

Note: Data for some countries are based on fiscal years. Please refer to Table F in the Statistical Appendix for a list of economies with exceptional reporting periods.
[1]Movements in consumer prices are shown as annual averages. Year-end to year-end changes can be found in Table A7 in the Statistical Appendix.
[2]Percent of GDP.
[3]Percent. National definitions of unemployment may differ.
[4]Includes Equatorial Guinea and South Sudan.
[5]Includes Botswana, Cabo Verde, Eswatini, Lesotho, Mauritius, Namibia, and Seychelles.
[6]Includes Benin, Burkina Faso, Burundi, the Central African Republic, Comoros, Eritrea, The Gambia, Guinea, Guinea-Bissau, Liberia, Malawi, Mali, Mozambique, Niger, Rwanda, São Tomé and Príncipe, Sierra Leone, Togo, and Zimbabwe.

Annex Table 1.1.7. Summary of World Real per Capita Output

(Annual percent change; in international currency at purchasing power parity)

	Average 2001–10	2011	2012	2013	2014	2015	2016	2017	2018	Projections 2019	2020	2024
World	**2.4**	**3.0**	**2.0**	**2.2**	**2.3**	**2.1**	**2.1**	**2.5**	**2.4**	**2.1**	**2.4**	**2.5**
Advanced Economies	**1.1**	**1.2**	**0.7**	**0.9**	**1.6**	**1.7**	**1.2**	**1.9**	**1.8**	**1.3**	**1.3**	**1.2**
United States	0.8	0.8	1.5	1.1	1.7	2.1	0.8	1.6	2.2	1.6	1.2	0.9
Euro Area[1]	0.8	1.3	–1.1	–0.5	1.1	1.7	1.7	2.3	1.7	1.0	1.4	1.2
Germany	1.0	3.7	0.5	0.3	1.8	0.6	1.3	2.1	1.2	0.7	1.4	1.3
France	0.6	1.7	–0.2	0.1	0.4	0.7	0.9	1.9	1.4	0.8	1.0	1.1
Italy	–0.2	0.2	–3.2	–2.3	–0.3	0.9	1.3	1.7	1.1	–0.3	0.9	0.7
Spain	0.8	–1.4	–3.0	–1.3	1.7	3.8	3.2	3.0	2.4	1.7	1.4	1.3
Japan	0.6	–0.3	1.7	2.2	0.5	1.3	0.6	2.1	1.0	1.2	0.8	1.0
United Kingdom	1.0	0.8	0.8	1.4	2.2	1.5	1.0	1.2	0.7	0.6	0.8	1.1
Canada	0.8	2.1	0.7	1.3	1.8	–0.1	0.1	1.7	0.4	0.2	1.0	0.7
Other Advanced Economies[2]	2.6	2.5	1.3	1.6	2.2	1.4	1.6	2.2	1.9	1.5	1.8	1.7
Emerging Market and Developing Economies	**4.6**	**4.9**	**3.6**	**3.6**	**3.2**	**2.8**	**3.1**	**3.3**	**3.2**	**3.0**	**3.5**	**3.6**
Commonwealth of Independent States (CIS)	5.3	4.6	3.2	2.0	1.3	–2.5	0.4	1.9	2.4	1.8	2.0	2.2
Russia	5.1	5.0	3.6	1.7	0.6	–2.6	0.2	1.6	2.4	1.7	1.8	1.8
CIS Excluding Russia	6.7	4.6	2.6	3.3	2.5	–1.7	1.2	3.3	3.1	2.7	2.9	3.3
Emerging and Developing Asia	7.2	6.7	5.9	5.9	5.8	5.7	5.7	5.6	5.5	5.4	5.4	5.3
China	9.9	9.0	7.4	7.3	6.7	6.4	6.1	6.2	6.2	5.9	5.8	5.5
India[3]	5.9	5.2	4.1	5.0	6.0	6.6	6.8	5.8	5.7	5.9	6.1	6.3
ASEAN-5[4]	3.7	3.1	4.7	3.7	3.3	3.6	3.8	4.2	4.1	3.9	4.0	4.1
Emerging and Developing Europe	3.5	6.2	2.1	4.3	3.5	4.3	2.9	5.6	3.0	0.2	2.3	2.6
Latin America and the Caribbean	1.9	3.4	1.7	1.7	0.2	–0.9	–1.8	0.1	0.1	0.4	1.6	2.0
Brazil	2.5	3.1	1.0	2.1	–0.3	–4.4	–4.1	0.3	0.4	1.3	1.8	1.7
Mexico	0.2	2.4	2.4	0.2	1.7	2.2	1.9	1.0	1.0	0.7	1.0	1.9
Middle East, North Africa, Afghanistan, and Pakistan	1.8	3.8	0.6	–0.1	0.0	0.4	2.9	–0.4	–0.2	–0.5	1.2	0.8
Saudi Arabia	0.3	6.8	2.5	–0.1	1.1	3.3	–0.7	–3.2	0.2	–0.2	0.1	0.3
Sub-Saharan Africa	2.9	2.5	1.6	2.5	2.4	0.5	–1.3	0.2	0.4	0.9	1.1	1.3
Nigeria	6.0	2.1	1.5	2.6	3.5	–0.1	–4.2	–1.9	–0.8	–0.6	–0.2	–0.2
South Africa	2.2	1.8	0.7	1.0	0.3	–0.4	–1.2	–0.2	–1.3	–0.4	–0.1	0.2
Memorandum												
European Union	1.2	1.5	–0.6	0.1	1.6	2.0	1.8	2.5	1.9	1.3	1.5	1.4
Low-Income Developing Countries	3.8	3.6	1.7	3.7	3.7	2.2	1.2	2.6	2.4	2.7	2.9	3.1

Note: Data for some countries are based on fiscal years. Please refer to Table F in the Statistical Appendix for a list of economies with exceptional reporting periods.
[1]Data calculated as the sum of individual euro area countries.
[2]Excludes the Group of Seven (Canada, France, Germany, Italy, Japan, United Kingdom, United States) and euro area countries.
[3]See country-specific note for India in the "Country Notes" section of the Statistical Appendix.
[4]Indonesia, Malaysia, Philippines, Thailand, Vietnam.

References

Adler, Gustavo, Romain Duval, Davide Furceri, Sinem Kilic Celik, Ksenia Koloskova, and Marcos Poplawski-Ribeiro. 2017. "Gone with the Headwinds: Global Productivity." IMF Staff Discussion Note 17/04, International Monetary Fund, Washington, DC.

Alquist, Ron, Saroj Bhattarai, and Olivier Coibion. 2014. "Commodity-Price Comovement and Global Economic Activity." NBER Working Paper 20003, National Bureau of Economic Research, Cambridge, MA.

———. Forthcoming. "Commodity-Price Comovement and Global Economic Activity." *Journal of Monetary Economics.*

Aten, Bettina, and Alan Heston. 2005. "Regional Output Differences in International Perspective." In *Spatial Inequality and Development*, edited by Ravi Kanbur and Anthony J. Venables. New York: Oxford University Press.

Austin, Benjamin, Edward Glaeser, and Lawrence H. Summers. 2018. "Saving the Heartland: Place-Based Policies in 21st Century America." *Brookings Papers on Economic Activity* (March 8).

Autor, David H., David Dorn, and Gordon H. Hanson. 2013. "The China Syndrome: Local Labor Market Effects of Import Competition in the United States." *American Economic Review* 103 (6): 2121–168.

Baker, Scott, Nicholas Bloom, and Steven J. Davis. 2016. "Measuring Economic Policy Uncertainty." *Quarterly Journal of Economics* 131 (4): 1593–636.

Bank of England. 2018. "EU Withdrawal Scenarios and Monetary and Financial Stability."

Barsky, Robert B., and Lutz Kilian. 2004. "Oil and the Macroeconomy since the 1970s." *Journal of Economic Perspectives* 18 (4): 115–34.

Berry, Christopher R., and Edward Glaeser. 2005. "The Divergence of Human Capital Levels across Cities." NBER Working Paper 11617, National Bureau of Economic Research, Cambridge, MA.

Bry, Gerhard, and Charlotte Boschan. 1971. "Interpretation and Analysis of Time-Series Scatters." *American Statistician* 25 (2): 29–33.

Caldara, Dario, and Matteo Iacoviello. 2018. "Measuring Geopolitical Risk." International Finance Discussion Papers 1222, Board of Governors of the Federal Reserve System.

Cashin, Paul, Christopher McDermott, and Alasdair Scott. 2002. "Booms and Slumps in World Commodity Prices." *Journal of Development Economics* 69 (1): 277–96.

Chiquiar, Daniel. 2008. "Globalization, Regional Wage Differentials, and the Stolper-Samuelson Theorem: Evidence from Mexico." *Journal of International Economics* 74: 70–93.

Deaton, Angus, and Guy Laroque. 1992. "On the Behavior of Commodity Prices." *Review of Economic Studies* 59 (1): 1–23.

Delle Chiaie, Simona, Laurent Ferrara, and Domenico Giannone. 2018. "Common Factors of Commodity Prices." CEPR Discussion Paper 12767, Center for Economic Policy Research, Washington, DC.

Economic Innovation Group. 2018. "From Great Recession to Great Reshuffling: Charting a Decade of Change Across American Communities." https://eig.org/wp-content/uploads/2018/10/2018-DCI.pdf.

European Central Bank (ECB). 2017. "Assessing the Decoupling of Economic Policy Uncertainty and Financial Conditions," Special Feature in *ECB Financial Stability Review*, May 2017.

Ganong, Peter, and Daniel Shoag. 2017. "Why Has Regional Income Convergence Declined?" *Journal of Urban Economics* 102: 76–90.

Gennaioli, Nicola, Rafael LaPorta, Florencio Lopez de Silanes, and Andrei Shleifer. 2014. "Growth in Regions." *Journal of Economic Growth* 19 (3): 259–309.

Giannone, Elisa. 2017. *Skilled-Biased Technical Change and Regional Convergence.* Chicago: University of Chicago.

Grilli, Enzo, and Maw Cheng Yang. 1988. "Primary Commodity Prices, Manufactured Goods Prices, and the Terms of Trade of Developing Countries: What the Long Run Shows." *World Bank Economic Review* 2 (1): 1–47.

Gruss, Bertrand. 2014. "After the Boom-Commodity Prices and Economic Growth in Latin America and the Caribbean." IMF Working Paper 14/154, International Monetary Fund, Washington, DC.

Hakobyan, Shushanik, and John McLaren. 2016. "Looking for Local Labor Market Effects of NAFTA." *Review of Economics and Statistics* 98 (4): 728–41.

Hamilton, James. 1996. "This Is What Happened to the Oil Price-Macroeconomy Relationship." *Journal of Monetary Economics* 38 (2): 215–20.

———. 2003. "What Is an Oil Shock?" *Journal of Econometrics* 113 (2): 363–98.

Harding, Don, and Adrian Pagan. 2002. "Dissecting the Cycle: A Methodological Investigation." *Journal of Monetary Economics* 49 (2): 365–81.

Hendrickson, Clara, Mark Muro, and William A. Galston. 2018. *Strategies for Left-Behind Places.* Washington, DC: Brookings Institution.

HM Treasury. 2016. "HM Treasury analysis: the long-term economic impact of EU membership and the alternatives"

International Monetary Fund (IMF). 2018. "United Kingdom: Selected Issues." IMF Country Report 18/317, Washington, DC.

International Monetary Fund (IMF). 2019. "Fiscal Policies for Implementing Paris Climate Strategies." Washington, DC.

Jacks, David S. 2013. "From Boom to Bust: A Typology of Real Commodity Prices in the Long Run." *Cliometrica* 1–20.

Kandilov, Ivan T. 2009. "Do Exporters Pay Higher Wages? Plant-Level Evidence from an Export Refund Policy in Chile." *World Bank Economic Review* 23 (2): 269–94.

Kilian, Lutz. 2009. Not All Oil Price Shocks Are Alike: Disentangling Demand and Supply Shocks in the Crude Oil Market." *American Economic Review* 99 (3): 1053–69.

Kilian, Lutz, and Daniel P. Murphy. 2014. "The Role of Inventories and Speculative Trading in the Global Market for Crude Oil." *Journal of Applied Econometrics* 29 (3): 454–78.

Kilian, Lutz, and Xiaoqing Zhou. 2018. "Modeling Fluctuations in the Global Demand for Commodities." *Journal of International Money and Finance* 88: 54–78.

Leichenko, Robin, and Julie Silva. 2004. "International Trade, Employment, and Earnings: Evidence from US Rural Counties." *Regional Studies* 38 (4): 355–74.

Moretti, Enrico. 2011. "Local Labor Markets." In *Handbook of Labor Economics*, edited by O. Ashenfelter and D. E. Card, 1237–313. Amsterdam: Elsevier.

Nakov, Anton, and Andrea Pescatori. 2010. "Oil and the Great Moderation." *Economic Journal* 120 (543): 131–56.

Nunn, Ryan, Jana Parsons, and Jay Shambaugh. 2018. "The Geography of Prosperity." The Hamilton Project, Brookings Institution, Washington, DC.

Partridge, Mark D., Dan S. Rickman, M. Rose Olfert, and Ying Tan. 2017. "International Trade and Local Labor Markets: Do Foreign and Domestic Shocks Affect Regions Differently?" *Journal of Economic Geography* 17 (2): 375–409.

Pindyck, Robert, and Julio Rotemberg. 1990. "The Excess Comovement of Commodity Prices." *Economic Journal* 100 (December): 1173–189.

Stock, James H., and Mark W. Watson. 2002. "Forecasting Using Principal Components from a Large Number of Predictors." *Journal of the American Statistical Association* 97 (460): 1167–179.

Stuermer, Martin. 2018. "150 Years of Boom and Bust: What Drives Mineral Commodity Prices?" *Macroeconomic Dynamics* 22 (3): 702–17.

West, Kenneth D., and Ka-Fu Wong. 2014. "A Factor Model for Co-Movements of Commodity Prices." *Journal of International Money and Finance* 42: 289–309.

CHAPTER 2

THE RISE OF CORPORATE MARKET POWER AND ITS MACROECONOMIC EFFECTS

This chapter investigates whether corporate market power has increased and, if so, what the macroeconomic implications are. The three main takeaways from a broad analysis of cross-country firm-level patterns are that (1) market power has increased moderately across advanced economies, as indicated by firms' price markups over marginal costs rising by close to 8 percent since 2000, but not in emerging market economies; (2) the increase has been fairly widespread across advanced economies and industries, but within them, it has been concentrated among a small fraction of dynamic—more productive and innovative—firms; and (3) although the overall macroeconomic implications have been modest so far, further increases in the market power of these already-powerful firms could weaken investment, deter innovation, reduce labor income shares, and make it more difficult for monetary policy to stabilize output. Even as rising corporate market power seems, so far, more reflective of "winner-takes-most" by more productive and innovative firms than of weaker pro-competition policies, its challenging macroeconomic implications call for reforms that keep future market competition strong.

Introduction

Public debate about rising corporate power is mounting. Heightened interest has unfolded amid the rise of corporate giants, such as in the tech industry, and because of broader, often worrisome macroeconomic trends in advanced economies over the past three decades. As shown in Figure 2.1, these trends include (1) sluggish investment despite falling borrowing costs and rising expected returns from investment, as captured by the ratio of the market value of firms to the book value of their capital stock (so-called Tobin's Q); (2) a growing disconnect between a roughly stable rate of return on productive capital and a falling rate of return on safer assets, such as the bonds of governments and the healthiest firms; (3) a widening gap between financial and productive wealth; and (4) falling labor income shares and rising income inequality. A fifth trend is the well-documented slowdown in productivity growth (Adler and others 2017).

Could rising market power be one factor behind slowing trend growth and growing inequality? Other drivers that may account for one or several of the five macroeconomic trends listed above have been put forward. Examples include a slowing pace of major inventions or long lags before these pay off; protracted weak demand, as featured in Chapter 4 of the April 2015 *World Economic Outlook* (WEO); mismeasured (underreported) intangible capital; falling investment prices (Chapter 3 of the April 2017 WEO); growing demand for safe assets; and weaker worker bargaining power. Unlike these drivers, however, rising corporate market power can, in principle, contribute to all five trends simultaneously (Stiglitz 2015; Caballero, Farhi, and Gourinchas 2017; De Loecker and Eeckhout 2017; Eggertsson, Robbins, and Wold 2018). Increased market power would be expected to lead firms to invest less in physical and other forms of capital than would be optimal (trend 1), which would weaken productivity growth (trend 5) without necessarily reducing returns on capital, even if returns on risk-free assets were to decline for other reasons (trend 2). In parallel, the value of shareholders' assets would grow faster than the sheer value of their productive capital (trend 3), and workers' share of total income would mechanically fall (trend 4).

At the same time, neither the rise of market power itself nor its macroeconomic implications have been firmly established. Broad market concentration is generally not a good gauge of market power; it is hard to measure and can be misleading. Better, more direct measures, such as price markups—the ratio of a good's price to the marginal cost of producing it—are not readily available and, so far, they have been studied mostly for the small subset of listed firms (De Loecker and Eeckhout 2017, 2018; Díez, Leigh, and Tambunlertchai 2018). A full picture of market power trends

The authors of this chapter are Wenjie Chen, Federico Díez (lead), Romain Duval (lead), Callum Jones, and Carolina Villegas-Sánchez, with contributions from Mai Chi Dao, Jiayue Fan, Christopher Johns, and Nan Li, and supported by Luisa Calixto, Rebecca Eyassu, and Ariana Tayebi.

Figure 2.1. Worrisome Macroeconomic Trends

Increased market power could, in principle, be a factor behind several important macroeconomic trends of the past decades.

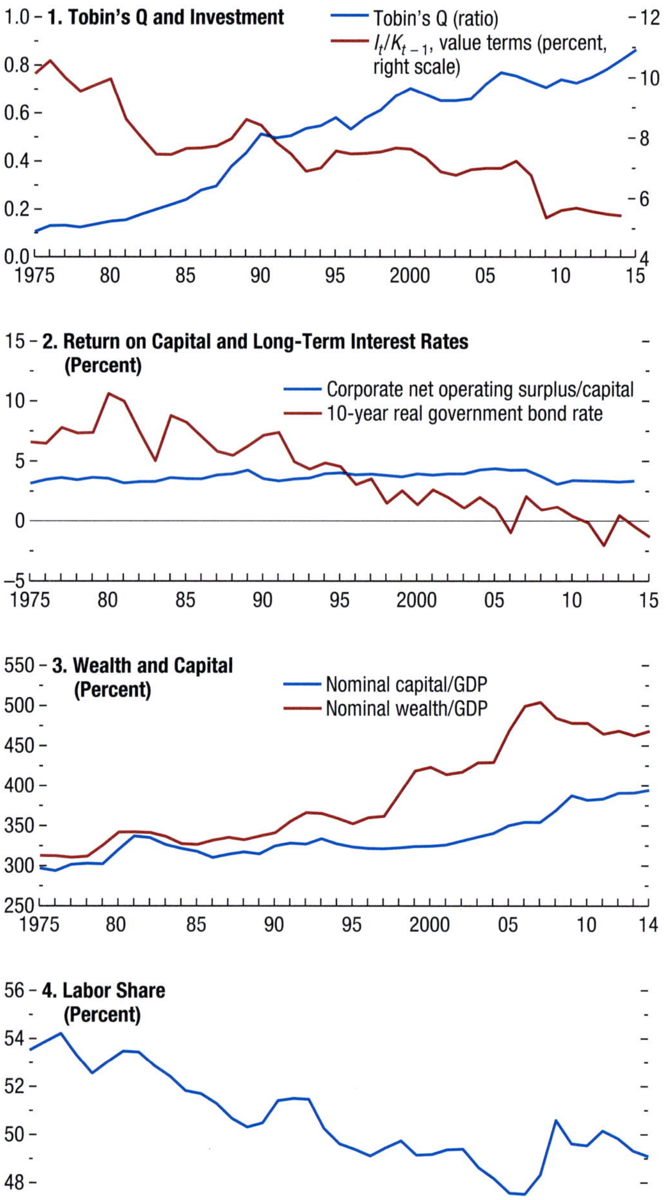

Sources: Organisation for Economic Co-operation and Development; Penn World Table 9.0; United Nations; World Inequality Database; and IMF staff calculations.
Note: Aggregate series are advanced economy medians. Tobin's Q is defined as equity value/net worth (current prices). Investments are cumulated into capital stocks using asset-specific geometric depreciation rates using the perpetual inventory method. See Online Annex Table 2.1.2 for a list of countries used in median calculations.

across the broader economy is needed to gauge the macroeconomic implications for aggregate investment, labor income shares, and the effectiveness of monetary policy, to use these as examples. Even rising economy-wide markups need not imply declining competition if they merely enable firms to recoup the growing fixed costs—or reward them for the higher risks—associated with large investments in intangible assets, such as research and development or information technology systems.

The drivers of any possible rise in market power have also yet to be uncovered. This matters because different drivers could call for very different policy remedies. At one extreme, rising market power could be the outcome of *greater* competition and winner-takes-most dynamics in the digital age. For example, in many industries, the rising importance of economies of scale and scope, network effects, managerial and technical skills, and specific intangible assets—such as patents, proprietary information technology systems, and large consumer databases—may help the most dynamic firms achieve market dominance. Inasmuch as such firms have higher markups and profit shares, any increase in competition that benefits them could result in higher aggregate markups and profit shares (Van Reenen 2018). At the other extreme, rising market power could reflect an increase in anticompetitive product market regulations or weaker antitrust enforcement (Gutiérrez and Philippon 2018).

To explore these issues, this chapter looks at close to 1 million firms covering large swaths of the economy across 27 countries—about two-thirds of which are advanced economies and one-third (mostly central and eastern European) are emerging market economies. The aim is to gauge market power trends over the past two decades, assess their macroeconomic implications, and—more tentatively—shed some preliminary light on their underlying drivers.[1] The chapter tackles the following questions:

- Has corporate market power increased globally? How do trends in market power differ across country income groups, countries, industries, and firms?
- What might be the drivers of rising market power? Can the data reveal the possible roles of changes in the structure of product markets—associated with

[1]The countries included in the analysis are Austria, Belgium, Bulgaria, the Czech Republic, Denmark, Estonia, Finland, France, Germany, Greece, Hungary, Ireland, Italy, Japan, Korea, Latvia, the Netherlands, Poland, Portugal, Romania, Russia, the Slovak Republic, Slovenia, Spain, Turkey, the United Kingdom, and the United States.

the rise of the digital economy or other factors—and of a policy-driven weakening of competition?

- What is the impact of market power on growth and income distribution? How does it affect the drivers of growth, such as investment and innovation, as well as labor income shares?
- What are the policy implications? Should measures be taken to strengthen market competition and, if so, which would be effective? Are there also macroeconomic policy implications of rising market power, such as for monetary policy?

In tackling these questions, the chapter reaches the following conclusions:

- There has been a moderate rise in corporate market power across advanced economies. Economy-wide markups increased by close to 8 percent, on average, across firms during the 2000–15 sample period, alongside rising profits and market concentration. By contrast, markups remained broadly stable in emerging markets, possibly reflecting limited country coverage and the fact that market competition was weaker than in advanced economies to start with.
- Markup increases have been fairly broad based across countries and industries—taking place in almost all advanced economies and nearly two-thirds of country-industry pairs. The magnitude of this rise has varied across countries—it is larger in the United States than across the European Union, for example—and industries; it is essentially concentrated in nonmanufacturing industries.
- A key contributor almost everywhere is the increase in markups charged by a small fraction of firms. Most of these firms are rather small, but the larger ones in the group account for the vast majority of the group's total revenue. High-markup firms also perform better than others—their productivity is higher and they are more likely to invest in intangible assets, such as patents and software. In the United States, these firms also gained market share during 2000–15, contributing to the larger increase in aggregate markups compared with other countries—and consistent with a (productivity-enhancing) growth of high-productivity, high-markup firms at the expense of those with low productivity and low markups.
- This tentatively suggests that changes in the structure of product markets have underpinned at least some of the overall rise in market power. One such change would be the winner-takes-most outcome achieved by the most productive and innovative firms, rooted in part in specific intangible assets (technological, managerial, or other); network effects; and economies of scale. The rather broad-based nature of increasing markups across countries and industries, and the role played by a small fraction of firms in most cases, also hint at such common forces—more than a policy-driven weakening of competition. At the same time, weak pro-competition policies can magnify winner-takes-most dynamics, and firms that have so far achieved market dominance primarily through innovative products and business practices may attempt to entrench their positions by erecting barriers to entry.
- The impact of rising markups on economic growth has been rather modest so far, but it could grow increasingly negative if the market power of high-markup firms—in particular—rises further. Higher markups have been associated with somewhat weaker investment, despite higher profits and Tobin's Q; empirical estimates suggest that because of this, output would be about 1 percent higher today in the average advanced economy if markups had not increased since 2000—ignoring such factors as technological or organizational improvements that may have enabled some firms to raise their markups over time. Through this investment channel, rising market power may have also slightly reduced the natural (real) rate of interest, thereby making the effective lower bound on policy interest rates more binding. Effects on innovation are more ambiguous; the analysis suggests that they may have been marginally positive so far, but would turn increasingly negative if high-markup firms further increase their market power.
- Higher markups may not only reduce firms' own capital and output, but may also spill over to other domestic and foreign firms through supply-chain links. Empirical evidence suggests that higher markups across foreign suppliers have been associated with slightly lower output among emerging market firms that purchase their inputs in less competitive markets.
- There is also evidence that rising market power throughout 2000–15 reduced labor shares of income, by a minimum of 0.2 percentage point—about 10 percent of the overall decline—across

advanced economies. This lower-bound estimate includes only the impact of rising markups *within* firms and ignores the effect of reallocation of resources *between* firms, which is an additional factor in countries where high-markup, low-labor-share firms have gained market share from those with low markups and high labor shares. Also ignored is the possible contribution of the uneven rise in market power across firms to rising wage inequality between firms—which has contributed to the overall rise in wage inequality in some advanced economies—as well as to wealth inequality.

- With mounting risks of adverse growth and income distribution effects from rising corporate market power, policymakers should keep future market competition strong. Helpful reforms would include cutting domestic barriers to entry in nonmanufacturing industries, liberalizing trade and foreign direct investment, adjusting competition policy frameworks to deal with emerging issues as needed, easing obstacles to technological catchup by lagging firms, and shifting the burden of corporate taxation onto economic rent.

The next section examines trends in market power across countries, industries, and firms, and attempts to explain what may lie behind them. The section that follows analyzes the implications for growth and income distribution, focusing on investment, innovation, and labor shares. It also explores whether rising market power affected inflation, interest rates, and the dynamics of output in advanced economies after the 2008–09 global financial crisis. The main takeaways and policy implications are discussed in the conclusion.

The Rise of Corporate Market Power

Measuring market power is challenging. This chapter considers two main alternatives. The first, and most common, is the ability of firms to charge prices that exceed their marginal cost of production. Under this definition, a firm's market power can be measured through its markup, defined as the ratio of price to marginal cost. This is the main measure used throughout the chapter. A second possible definition is the ability of firms to obtain extraordinary profits—so-called economic rents. A frequently used indicator here is an (operational) profitability measure, such as the ratio of operating earnings to sales; this is an empirical measure of the Lerner index, which also relates closely to a firm's markup.[2] These have limitations: markups can be estimated from often available firm-level data, but might overestimate market power in the presence of fixed costs, as these need to be recouped through markups if firms are to avoid incurring losses; Lerner indices are easy to compute, but hard to measure accurately and, like all measures of profitability, they can be volatile. As a complement, measures of market concentration are also computed, focusing, in particular, on the share of top firms in the total sales of a particular industry. These should be interpreted with great caution; they require identifying the appropriate market and can be misleading—for example, *stronger* competition may lead to larger, more productive firms gaining market share over their less productive, smaller counterparts, resulting in *higher*, not lower, concentration. For these reasons, markup indicators, rather than market concentration measures, are used in the empirical analysis of this chapter.

How has corporate market power evolved over the past two decades? To answer this question, the chapter uses firm-level data covering 27 countries—16 advanced economies and 11 emerging market economies—since 2000.[3] The raw data, which include information on publicly listed and privately held firms, typically cover at least 40 percent of total output reported in official sources in a given country and year. They have been found to be reasonably representative of the full population of firms in most of the countries considered (Kalemli-Özcan and others 2015). The final data set obtained after cleaning the raw data includes more than 900,000 distinct firms. Markups and Lerner indices are computed for each firm—and then aggregated up to industry or country level for parts of the analysis; concentration indices are computed for narrowly defined (four-digit NACE (Nomenclature statistique des activités économiques dans les Communauté européenne)) industries in each country. Building on these three measures, the analysis

[2]Markups and Lerner indices are closely related in theory; their empirical measures, however, are very different. Following De Loecker and Warzynski (2012), markups are measured as the ratio of a firm's output elasticity of a variable input to the share of that input in total revenue. By contrast, the empirical Lerner measure focuses on overall, not marginal, operational profitability and, as such, it captures the wedge between prices and average—not marginal—costs. As a result, there is no reason to expect both measures to be correlated a priori.

[3]The definition of advanced economies used in the empirical work of this chapter follows the WEO classification in 2000 (the first year in the data set, which extends to 2015). For details on the data, see Online Annex 2.1. All annexes are available at www.imf.org/en/Publications/WEO.

begins by establishing a series of facts on the recent dynamics of corporate market power across countries, industries, and firms.

Aggregate Market Power Trends

All available indicators point to a moderate increase in aggregate market power since 2000. Across the 27 sample countries, the (firm-revenue-weighted) average markup increased by 6 percent during 2000–15, a modest yet steady increase (Figure 2.2, panel 1).[4] At the same time, while more volatile than markups, average profitability, as measured by the Lerner index, also increased throughout the sample period (Figure 2.2, panel 2). This accompanying rise in profitability suggests that the increase in markups goes beyond a mere technological change—such as higher fixed costs from larger intangible investments needed for firms to be competitive.[5] Finally, to a lesser extent, market concentration has also increased (Figure 2.2, panel 3).

While the increase in market power has been fairly broad based, its magnitude—focusing hereafter on markups—has varied across countries and industries. First, the rise is strongly concentrated among advanced economies, whose average markup rose by about 7.7 percent throughout 2000–15, versus only 1.8 percent for the group of emerging market economies—mostly in central and eastern Europe—covered by the data (Figure 2.3).[6] There is substantial variation, as well, in the rise in markups across advanced economies, with

[4]This is a substantially smaller number than the increase found in recent studies that focus only on listed firms (De Loecker and Eeckhout 2017, 2018; Díez, Leigh, and Tambunlertchai 2018). In level terms, the (firm-revenue-weighted) average markup shows an increase from about 1.28—corresponding to a markup of the price over marginal cost of 28 percent—in 2000 to 1.36 in 2015. Qualitatively similar, but quantitatively smaller, increases are obtained when considering cost-weighted average markups. However, given the estimation technique employed, these point estimates are identified only up to a constant and should therefore be seen as illustrative. See De Loecker and Warzynski (2012) for details.

[5]The correlation between changes in markups and profits across firms is statistically significant at the 1 percent confidence level. Additional analysis also finds that the increase in markups remains essentially unchanged after accounting for the role of overhead costs; this further suggests that the rise in markups reflects more than just the need to recoup higher fixed costs.

[6]This comparison refers to the differential *increases* in market power—the focus of this chapter—across country income groups, not to differences in markup *levels* and the level of competition in general. Considering only listed firms, but a broader sample of countries and a longer period, Díez, Leigh, and Tambunlertchai (2018) also find much smaller increases in markups in emerging market than in advanced economies.

Figure 2.2. Evolution of Market Power

All measures point toward a moderate increase in market power over time: higher markups, higher profitability, and, to a lesser extent, higher concentration.

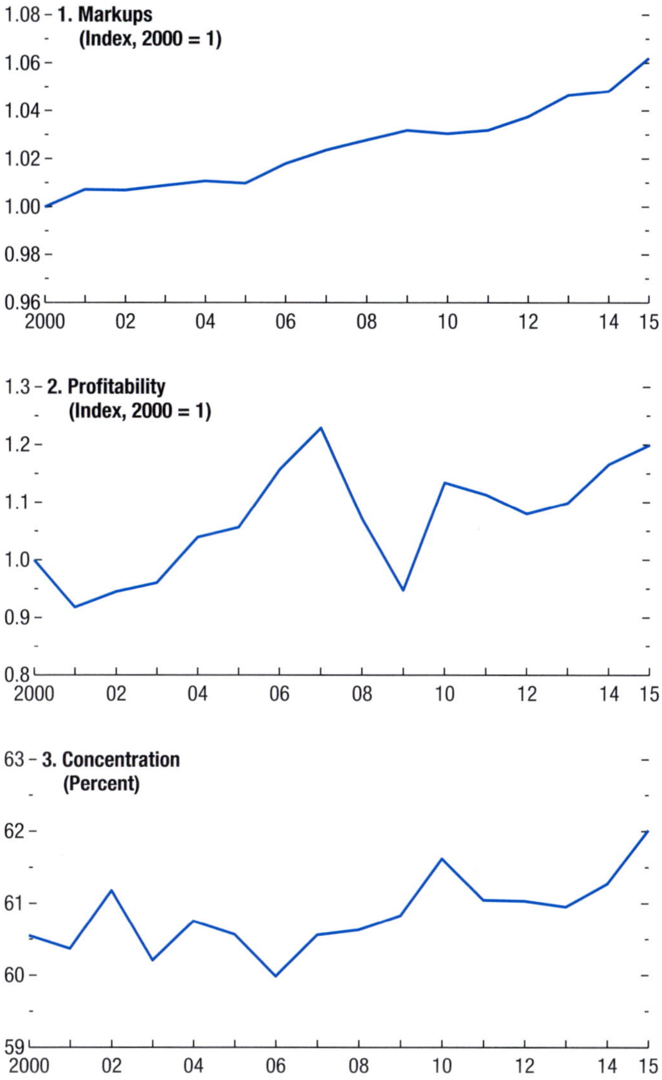

Sources: Orbis; and IMF staff calculations.
Note: Markup calculations are based on the approach of De Loecker and Warzynski (2012) using the Orbis database. Panel 1 plots year fixed effects from regressions of markups that also include country fixed effects to account for entry and exit to/from the sample. Regressions are weighted by firms' operating revenue. The measure of profitability used in the figure is the Lerner index, computed as the weighted average of firms' ratio of earnings before taxes to revenue. Concentration is computed as the ratio of sales of top four to top 20 firms within each country-sector bin. To aggregate, simple averages are taken across sectors within a country, and then the median across countries, to obtain the plotted line. See Online Annex Table 2.1.2 for a list of countries used in the calculations.

Figure 2.3. Markup Increases, by Country Income Group
(Percent change, cumulative 2000–15)

Markup increases are concentrated in advanced economies; markups in the selected emerging markets covered by the analysis have risen only slightly.

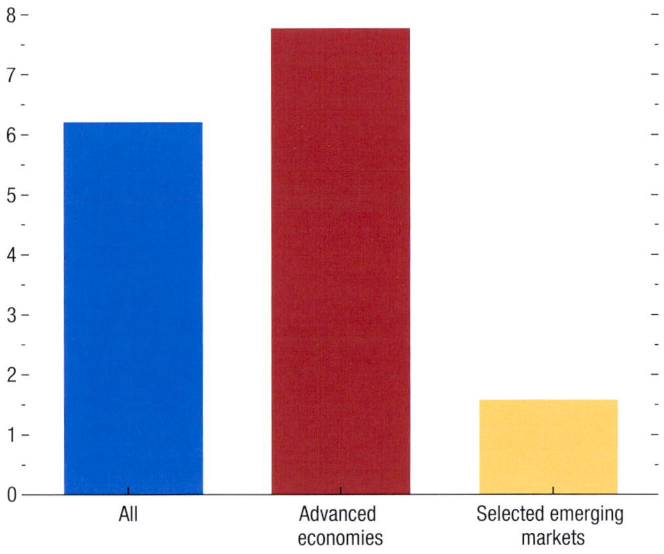

Sources: Orbis; and IMF staff calculations.
Note: Figure uses the 2000 *World Economic Outlook* definition for advanced economies. Markups weighted by firms' operating revenue.

Figure 2.4. Decomposition of Markup Increases
(Percent)

Two-thirds of the overall markup increase can be accounted for by incumbent firms (intensive margin) and the remainder by the net entry of new firms (extensive margin). Among incumbents, the rise in markups reflects primarily an increase within firms rather than reallocation of market shares away from low-markup toward high-markup firms.

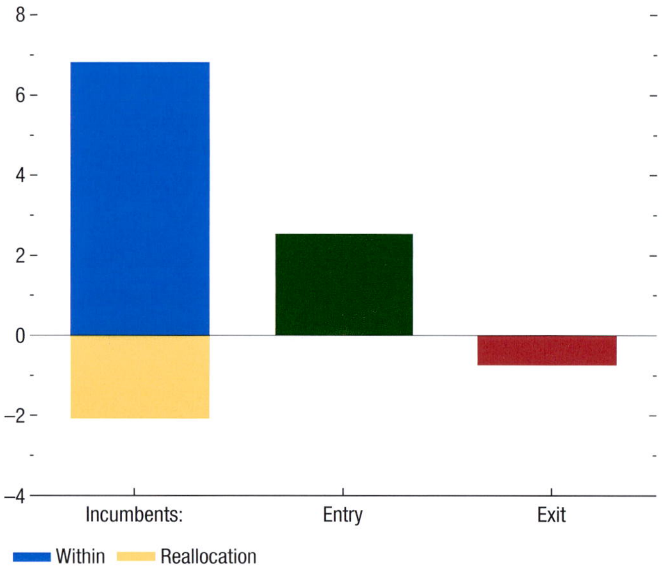

Sources: Orbis; and IMF staff calculations.
Note: The bars plot the change in overall markups explained by each component, after applying a Melitz-Polanec decomposition to the markup changes between 2000 and 2015. See Online Annex 2.2.C for details on the decomposition.

significantly larger increases in the United States (twice as large as in the average advanced economy). Although markup increases have also been rather broad based across industries, trends differ: nearly two-thirds of the country-industry pairs in the sample show markup increases, with the largest among nonmanufacturing industries and in industries that use digital technologies most intensively.[7] The average markup across manufacturing industries has been mostly flat.

With some exceptions, the rise in aggregate markups reflects mostly higher markups within incumbent firms and, to a lesser extent, the entry of new firms with higher markups, rather than a greater market share of high-markup incumbents. Over the full sample, markup increases within incumbent firms accounted for the full increase in the aggregate markup (the large positive "within" component, shown in blue in Figure 2.4), whereas high-markup incumbents did not increase their relative size (negative "reallocation" component). One noticeable exception is the United States, for which the reallocation component accounted for about 80 percent of the rise in the aggregate markup.[8] New firms entering the market with high markups also contributed about one-third of the overall rise in markups across advanced economies (the "entry" component in Figure 2.4).

Rise in Markups across Firms Is Highly Uneven

Markups have increased significantly in only a small fraction of incumbent firms—they are the dominant force behind the higher aggregate markups in most economies. Firms in the top decile of the markup distribution increased their (weighted) average markup

[7]Intensity of digital usage is constructed based on Organisation for Economic Co-operation and Development estimates; for details, see Online Annex 2.2 and Calligaris, Criscuolo, and Marcolin (2018), which also finds larger markup increases among digital-intensive firms than among other firms.

[8]The analysis results from applying a so-called Melitz-Polanec decomposition (see Online Annex 2.2). The large "between" component found for the United States is in line with recent evidence; see Baqaee and Farhi (2017) and De Loecker, Eeckhout, and Unger (2018).

by more than 30 percent, while the remaining nine deciles report a (weighted) average increase of just 2 percent (Figure 2.5, panel 1). This means that any analysis of the drivers and macroeconomic implications of the overall rise in corporate market power must pay particular attention to this small fraction of firms in the top decile of the markup distribution.

These high-markup firms are typically found in every broad economic sector and vary in size. In terms of revenue, the most-represented sectors in the top decile are information and communication, financial and insurance activities, manufacturing, and utilities. After accounting for the fact that some sectors have more firms than others, in general, the likelihood that a firm be in the top decile is above (the cross-sector) average in information and communication, finance and insurance activities, and utilities, while it is below average in construction, manufacturing, and wholesale and retail trade.

High-markup firms vary in size, but they tend to perform better than others. Most of these firms are rather small—in the bottom half of the size (revenue) distribution—but the larger ones in the group account for the vast majority of the group's total revenue (Figure 2.5, panel 2).[9] As regards performance, the top 10 percent of firms in the markup distribution are, on average, about 50 percent more profitable, more than 30 percent more productive, and more than 30 percent more intensive in their use of intangible assets than the other 90 percent (Figure 2.5, panel 3).

To sum up, there has been a moderate rise in corporate market power since 2000 across advanced economies, but not across the emerging markets covered by the analysis. Although increases have varied in magnitude across advanced economies and industries, in most cases, the main driving force was the ability of a small fraction of high-markup firms to strengthen their market power—and also gain market share in some countries, such as the United States. These firms were typically more dynamic than others, tentatively suggesting that changes in the structure of product markets—such as the winner-takes-most dynamics benefiting the most productive and innovative firms, rooted in part in specific intangible assets—are behind at least some of the overall rise in market power.

[9]For further details on the relationship between markups and size, see Díez, Fan, and Villegas-Sánchez (forthcoming).

Figure 2.5. Disconnect between Firms in the Top Decile and the Rest

Markup increases have been largely concentrated in the top 10 percent of the markup distribution; most of these firms are small, but the larger ones account for most of the group's revenue; firms in the top decile tend to be more profitable, more productive, and make relatively more intensive use of intangibles than other firms.

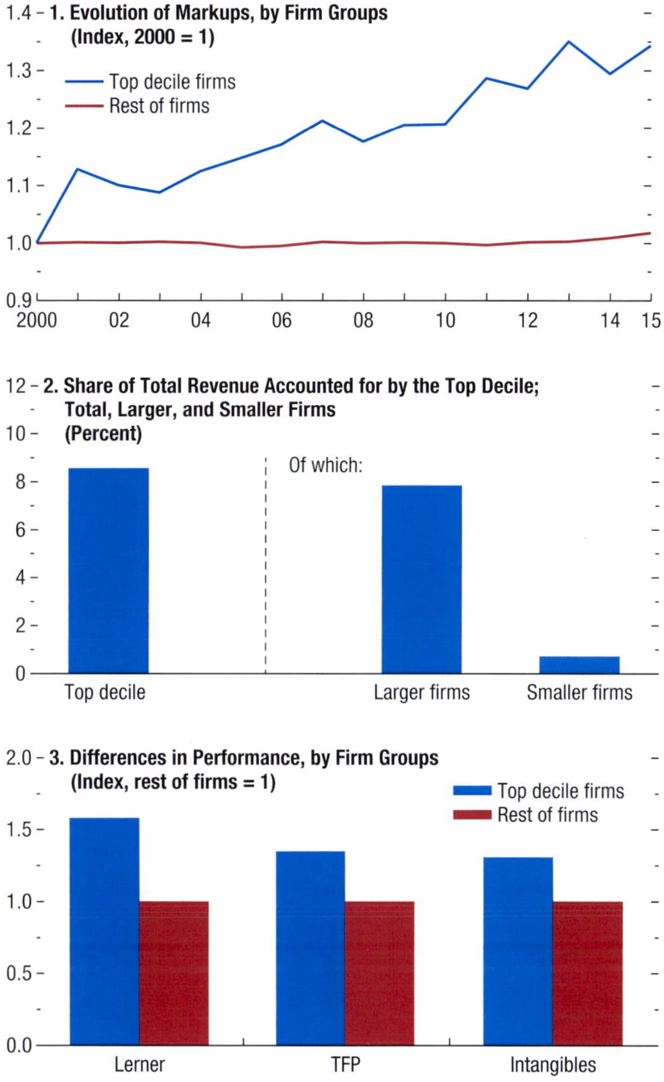

Sources: Orbis; and IMF staff calculations.
Note: Firms are sorted by their average markups over the sample period into two groups: top decile and the rest. Panel 1 plots, for each group, year fixed effects from regressions of markups that also include country fixed effects to account for entry and exit to/from the sample. The regressions are weighted by firms' operating revenue. The bars in panel 2 show the share of total revenue accounted for by firms in the top decile as a whole (left bar); the larger firms within the top decile (10 percent largest firms within top decile, middle bar); smaller firms within the top decile (90 percent smallest firms within top decile, right bar). Each bar in panel 3 plots the average value of the Lerner index/TFP/intangibles ratio for the firms in the top decile of the markup distribution and for the other firms. The values for the rest of the firms were normalized to one. TFP = total factor productivity.

Macroeconomic Implications of Rising Market Power

What are the implications of rising market power for growth and the distribution of income? To assess the former, this section examines the impact of rising markups on key firm- and industry-level drivers of growth, namely innovation (as proxied by individual patents) and physical capital investment. This analysis relies on cross-country firm- and industry-level regressions that include a rich set of fixed effects and account for other potential drivers of innovation and investment. In an attempt to identify the causal effect of rising markups on these outcomes, markups are lagged and instrumental variable strategies are pursued—using as instruments markups in other firms in the same country and industry. A similar approach then explores whether markup increases have contributed to the downward trend in the labor share of income—the share of national income paid in wages, including benefits, to workers—in recent decades. This matters for income distribution, given that capital ownership tends to be concentrated among top incomes (Wolff 2010).

The empirical exploration of the growth impact of markup increases is complemented by the use of a dynamic stochastic general equilibrium model that also sheds light on implications for inflation, interest rates, and monetary policy in the euro area and in the United States. There are other macroeconomic trends of the past two decades that coincide with rising markups. Box 2.1 shows that rising corporate saving across advanced economies is closely linked to greater concentration in corporate sales and assets and to increased markups. Other trends that could reflect in part rising markups, but are not directly explored here, include declining business and labor market dynamism and rising wage inequality, among others.[10]

Innovation

Market power has ambiguous effects on firms' decisions to innovate, reflecting two opposing forces.[11] On one hand, firms need to expect some degree of market power (and profitability) to invest in innovative products and processes. On the other hand, greater competition—that is, less market power—incentivizes firms to try to escape their competitors through innovation. A synthetic view of these two forces argues for a hump-shaped relationship: starting from low levels, stronger market power will first increase innovation but, beyond a certain point, additional market power will weaken the desire to innovate.[12]

The empirical analysis explores whether there is a hump-shaped relationship between market power and innovation at both industry and firm levels across the full sample of 27 countries. Innovation is measured by (various alternative indicators of) firms' patenting activity and is linked to market power, measured either by firm-level markups or industry-level average markups and Lerner indices. The analysis consists of a (Poisson) regression in which the number of patents depends on the lagged (logarithm of the) markup and its square, controlling for a rich set of fixed effects and using instrumental variable techniques to address potential reverse causality—that is, innovation may affect markups. Specifically, all firm-level regressions control for firm size, firm fixed effects, and alternatively (four-digit NACE) country-industry-year fixed effects or country-year and industry-year fixed effects. These fixed effects ensure that results are not driven by other, omitted drivers—for example, consumer demand. To address reverse causality concerns, besides lagged markup values, some specifications use, as an instrumental variable, the median markup of all firms (except that of the firm being instrumented) in a given country-industry-year. The industry-level regressions use the lagged (logarithm of the) markup or the Lerner index and country-year and industry-year fixed effects (see Online Annex 2.3A for further details).

There is strong and robust evidence that higher markups increase patents at both industry and firm levels when markup levels are low, but have the opposite effect when markups are high. At the industry level, more than 80 percent of the observations were located before the turning point (the red line in Figure 2.6) over the sample period, implying that, for most country-industry pairs, higher markups led to more innovation.[13] However, the fraction of observations located beyond the turning point increased from roughly 15 percent in

[10]For a more detailed description of these trends and the possible contribution of rising markups, see Davis and others (2007); De Loecker and Eeckhout (2017); Van Reenen (2018); and Autor and others (2017a, 2017b).

[11]See, for example, Shapiro (2012) for a review of the literature on competition and innovation.

[12]This hypothesis, which goes back at least to Scherer (1967) and Kamien and Schwartz (1976), was further modeled and tested on British firm data by Aghion and others (2005).

[13]Comparable results are obtained when using, as a measure of market power, the Lerner index rather than the markup, with almost 85 percent of observations located before the turning point.

Figure 2.6. Patents and Markups: A Hump-Shaped Relationship

There is a hump-shaped relationship between markups and patents. Starting from low markup levels, an increase leads to more patents. Beyond the red line, further markup increases lead, instead, to fewer patents.

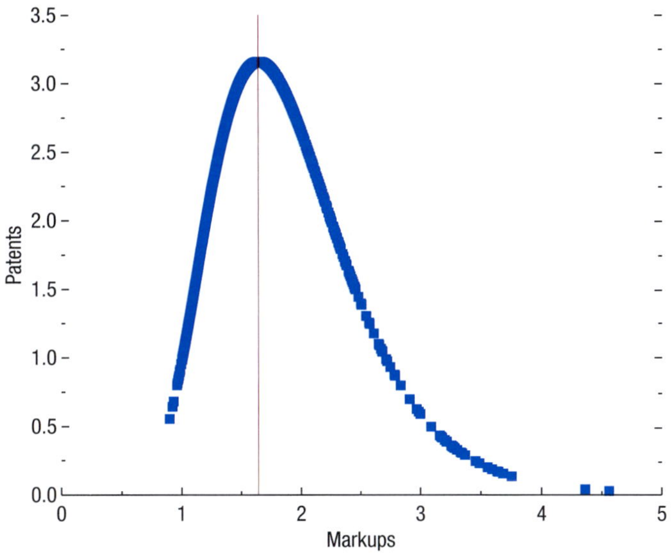

Sources: Orbis; PATSTAT (Worldwide Patent Statistical database); and IMF staff calculations.
Note: The figure plots the effects of markups on the predicted average number of patents by country-sector. Predicted patents normalized to 1 for markups = 1.

Figure 2.7. Implied Relationship between Higher Markups and Patents
(Percent change in patents)

Past overall increases in markups are estimated to have had a marginally positive effect on patents. However, if markups continue to rise at the same rate, patents are predicted to fall, mostly driven by firms in the top decile of the markup distribution.

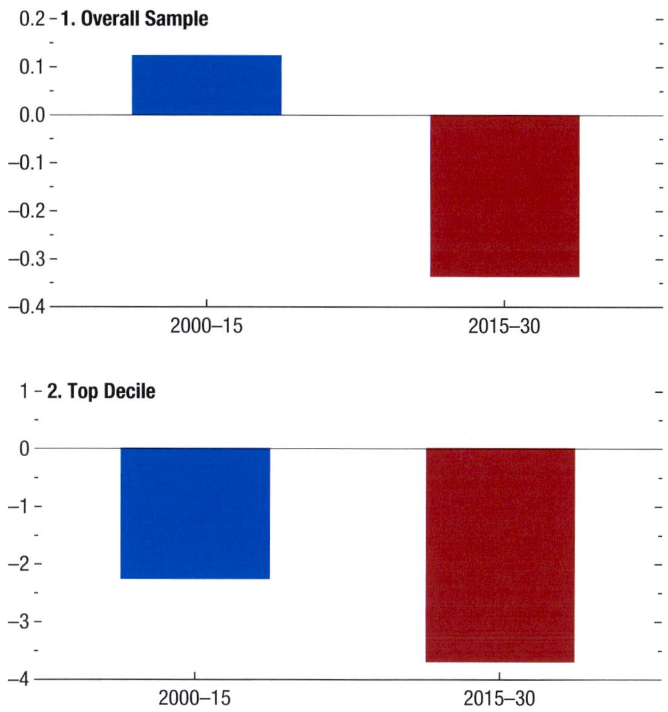

Sources: Orbis; PATSTAT (Worldwide Patent Statistical database); and IMF staff calculations.
Note: The 2000–15 bars show the implied predicted percent change in patents resulting from the markup increase in 2000–15, weighted by operating revenue. The 2015–30 bars show the implied predicted change if markups increase in 2015–30 at the same rate as in 2000–15. Panel 1 makes use of the whole sample; panel 2 uses information only from the top decile of the markup distribution.

2000 to 21 percent in 2015. A similar pattern emerges at the firm level. Under this approach, the share of firms located beyond the turning point is still small, at about 7.5 percent in 2015, implying that past markup increases may have been associated with higher innovation for most firms. However, that share increased by 50 percent during the sample period.

The analysis implies that, while the overall impact of rising market power on the pace of innovation may have been marginally positive so far, it could become increasingly negative if high-markup firms—in particular—further strengthen their market power in the future. Firms in the top decile of the markup distribution are (on average) already beyond the turning point of the estimated hump-shaped firm-level relationship. This is a potential cause for concern, given that those are the firms whose markups have risen sharply over the past two decades. As an example, if across the sample, markups rose as much during 2015–30 as they did during 2000–15, the predicted patent stock of high-markup firms would be almost 4 percent lower than if markups were stable, and the overall patent stock would be more than 0.3 percent lower, taking the empirical estimates at face value (Figure 2.7).

Investment

Private fixed investment has declined by about 25 percent, on average, across advanced economies since the global financial crisis, compared with its precrisis trend (Chapter 2 of the October 2018 WEO). This has happened despite a large and persistent fall in borrowing costs, higher rates of corporate profit, and higher expected returns on capital (Tobin's Q). Although weak economic growth since the crisis has played a role (Chapter 4 of the April 2015 WEO), other possible factors include credit constraints or

Figure 2.8. Markups and Physical Capital Investment
(Percentage point change in investment rate)

For the overall sample, the average increase in firms' markups is associated with a 0.4 percentage point decrease in the physical capital investment rate. For the firms in the top decile of the markup distribution, the (larger) average increase in firms' markups is associated with a decrease in the investment rate of 2 percentage points.

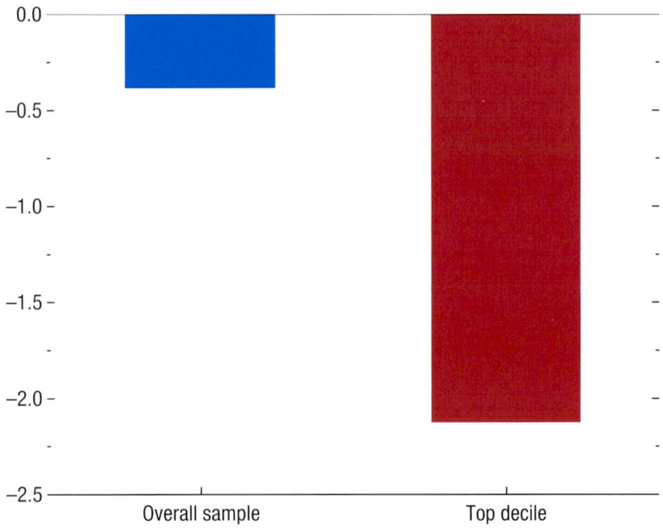

Sources: Orbis; and IMF staff calculations.
Note: Average changes in markups across firms are weighted by operating revenue.

shifts in the composition of investment toward (possibly undermeasured) intangibles, but also increased market power (Gutiérrez and Philippon 2017).[14] As a firm's market power increases, it can—at any given marginal cost—increase its profits by charging a higher price and reducing its output. This, in turn, leads the firm to reduce its demand for capital and, therefore, its investment.[15] Over the long term, inasmuch as the return on capital and labor supply remain unchanged, firms' lower desired output will also translate into a lower capital-to-output ratio. However, only a few studies explore empirically the link between markups and investment, and they focus primarily on the United States and publicly listed firms.[16]

Empirical analysis finds that rising markups have contributed to some reduction in firms' physical capital investment since the early 2000s. Cross-country firm-level analysis is performed for the same set of countries and firms used in the previous subsection. A firm's net investment rate in tangible assets is explained by its lagged markup, controlling for other firm-level drivers of investment and the rich set of fixed effects considered in the innovation analysis.[17,18] Similar instrumental variable techniques are also used to address risks of reverse causality and omitted variable bias. The main finding is that a 10 percentage point increase in a firm's markup is associated with a statistically significant 0.6 percentage point decrease in its physical capital investment rate. Figure 2.8 illustrates that, for the overall sample, the average increase in firms' markups since 2000 is associated with a 0.4 percentage point decrease in the investment rate, whereas for the sample of top decile firms, the average increase in markups is associated with a 2 percentage point decrease in the investment rate.

The results imply that if markups had remained stable since 2000, the overall capital stock today would be about 3 percent, and output about 1 percent, above current levels in the average advanced economy. The broad country- and firm-level coverage of the data set used in the analysis makes it possible to gauge the implications of higher markups for *aggregate* investment, capital, and output. Specifically, the path of each firm's net tangible asset stock during 2000–15 is simulated under a (counterfactual) scenario in which the firm's markup is set at its 2000 level—or, for new firms, its initial level—using the estimated impact on investment shown in Figure 2.8. The calculated capital gaps between the actual and counterfactual scenarios can then be aggregated to obtain an aggregate estimate of the capital shortfall for each economy. For the group of advanced economies in the sample, this exercise yields a 3 percent larger physical capital stock in 2015 in the average advanced economy under constant markups; that would have translated into an output gain of about 1 percent, assuming an elasticity of

[14]See more details on the possible drivers of low investment in Gutiérrez and Philippon (2017); Hall (2017); Crouzet and Eberly (2018); and Chapters 4 and 2, respectively, of the April 2015 and October 2018 WEOs.

[15]Online Annex 2.3C provides a more detailed discussion of the mechanism through which higher market power reduces investment in the short term and the capital-to-output ratio over the long term.

[16]See Gutiérrez and Philippon (2017); De Loecker, Eeckhout, and Unger (2018); Díez, Leigh, and Tambunlertchai (2018); and Eggertsson, Robbins, and Wold (2018).

[17]The net investment rate in tangible assets is calculated as the ratio of the change in the stock of tangible assets to value added. For more details, see Online Annex 2.3B.

[18]One difference from the innovation analysis is that the relationship between investment and markups is assumed to be monotonic, in line with investment theory. Additional (unreported) analysis could not find robust evidence of a nonlinear (for example, hump-shaped) relationship.

output to capital of about one-third.[19] However, these estimates do not factor in (growth-enhancing) technological or organizational improvements that may have enabled firms to raise their markups in the first place. Furthermore, it reflects only a *within*-firm effect—as a firm's markup increases, it tends to decrease its own physical investment rate—leaving aside any possible *between*-firm effect stemming from the reallocation of capital between firms with different markup levels. Additional analysis suggests that any such effects, however, have typically been small.[20]

Higher markups may not only reduce firms' own capital and output, but may also spill over to other firms through domestic and international supply-chain links. Adverse international spillovers may arise because domestic firms that raise their markups may reduce their demand for foreign inputs (demand channel) or raise the price of the goods they sell as inputs to foreign firms (input channel). These channels are analyzed by regressing a country-industry's (logarithm of) value added on the weighted average of its foreign buyers' markups (demand channel) and the weighted average of its foreign suppliers' markups (input channel), controlling for domestic firm links and a rich set of fixed effects (see Online Annex 2.3E for details). Weights reflect the importance, for each country-industry considered, of each foreign country-industry as a source of demand and as an input provider. The results point to moderate negative international spillovers of higher markups through the input channel. For example, for a hypothetical industry in an emerging market economy that imports 40 percent of its value added, a 10 percentage point markup increase across all its foreign suppliers is found to reduce output by 0.3 percent, all else equal.

The upshot of the analysis is that higher markups have been associated with somewhat lower investment and capital in advanced economies over the past two decades. This has been mostly driven by the small fraction of firms whose markups increased sharply. Higher markups in advanced economies may have also entailed mild adverse spillovers to emerging markets. Together with the mixed impact of higher markups on innovation—which the previous analysis suggests may be negligible so far, but would turn increasingly negative with increased market power of high-markup firms—these macroeconomic implications of rising market power should be a cause for policy concern.

Economic Slack, Interest Rates, and Inflation

By reducing investment, rising markups can generate economic slack that may offset their immediate inflationary effect and may also imply a trade-off for monetary policy. These issues are explored through an estimated dynamic stochastic general equilibrium model of the euro area and the United States (see Online Annex 2.3C for details). The model is calibrated to match the within-firm component of the observed trend in markups since 2000 in each of the two areas documented in the section titled "The Rise of Corporate Market Power." Considering only the within-firm rise in markups, rather than the total increase, aligns more closely with the model's setup and focus on rising market power *within* firms. Rising markups are modeled as a decline in the substitutability between the goods and services produced by different firms (Jones and Philippon 2016; Eggertsson, Robbins, and Wold 2018). In this setup, a sustained, unexpected rise in markups is inflationary as firms raise prices. There is an offsetting contractionary force, however: firms with greater market power face more inelastic demand for their products and cut output and investment to earn higher profits—as confirmed by the empirical analysis. These declines, and the resulting fall in employment, are magnified by the failure of wages and prices to adjust immediately, due to nominal rigidities.

Model simulations suggest that the trend rise in markups may have raised inflation somewhat, produced some slack, and slightly reduced natural interest rates in advanced economies, starting from at least the early 2000s. Under rising markups, inflation is higher and potential output growth is lower, and so the natural interest rate—the interest rate that arises absent wage and price rigidities—is also lower than it would be under stable markups. For the euro area and the United States as a group, the output gap might have been about 0.3 percentage point wider, inflation about 0.2 percentage point higher, and the natural interest rate about 10 basis points lower by 2015 than if

[19]This magnitude in the predicted loss in physical capital is somewhat below, but close to, that obtained when simulating the macroeconomic model of the next subsection. See also Gutiérrez, Jones, and Philippon (2019) for the US economy.

[20]See Online Annex 2.3B. In addition, to check whether this decrease in physical investment may have been replaced with increased investment in intangibles, as some suggest (Crouzet and Eberly 2018), the same empirical analysis is rerun with the net intangible asset investment rate as the dependent variable. The estimated relationship between markups and intangible investment is found to be economically insignificant.

Figure 2.9. Markup Increases, Investment, and the Natural Interest Rate
(Percentage point change; index, 2000 = 0)

The trend rise in markups since 2000 may be associated with a 0.1 percentage point reduction in the net investment rate and a 10 basis point reduction in the annual natural interest rate by 2015.

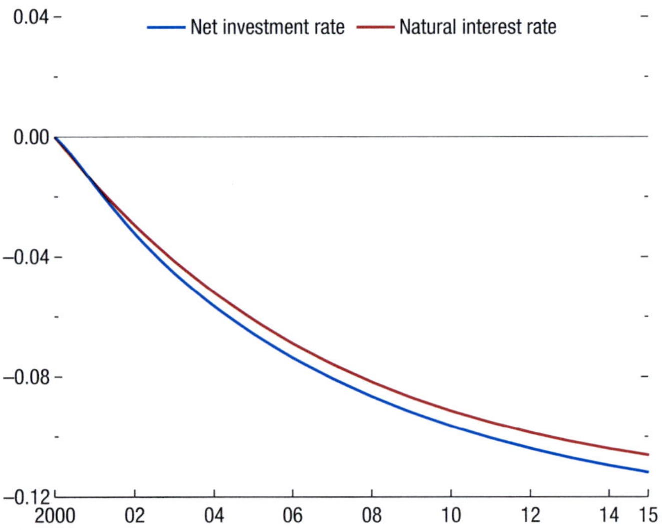

Source: IMF staff calculations.
Note: Interest rates are annualized.

markups had stayed at their 2000 level—all else equal; that is, abstracting from the impact of the 2008 financial crisis (Figure 2.9). The focus of the model-based analysis on weaker investment is qualitatively—and quantitatively—consistent with the empirical results, which highlight higher markups' harm on investment and their broadly neutral effect on innovation.

Because a trend rise in markups fosters some economic slack and slightly lowers the natural interest rate, it can deepen a recession when other macroeconomic shocks bring the policy interest rate down to its effective lower bound. Following the 2008 financial crisis, this may have either marginally amplified the recession, pushed central banks to rely even more on unconventional monetary policies, or both.

The impact of rising market power on the responsiveness of inflation to economic conditions—the so-called Phillips curve, which has flattened over the past two decades (Chapter 3 of the April 2013 WEO and Chapter 3 of the October 2016 WEO)—is less clear and depends on how firms (re)set prices, among other factors. On one hand, greater market power could weaken firms' incentives to keep prices close to those of their competitors for fear of losing market share; they might then be more inclined to adjust their prices after a shock, in which case inflation would become *more* responsive to economic conditions. On the other hand, if a firm incurs a cost from changing its price, it will adjust *less* frequently when it has more market power because its demand—and profit margin—is less sensitive to shocks. Model simulations suggest that in either case, the implied change in the responsiveness of inflation to economic conditions has been small, largely because the increase in markups has not been large enough to make a major difference, at least so far (Online Annex 2.3C).

Income Distribution

After remaining largely stable for decades, the share of national income paid to labor has fallen since the 1980s across many advanced economies, by an average of about 2 percentage points (Chapter 3 of the April 2017 WEO). The four most widely studied explanations for this decline are technological change, including the associated decline in the relative price of capital; globalization and offshoring; measurement difficulties associated with the rise of intangible capital or increased depreciation of physical capital; and weaker worker bargaining power.[21] In particular, Chapter 3 of the April 2017 WEO highlights the role of technology and globalization in reducing labor shares in advanced and emerging market and developing economies. A fifth possible driver, which has gained recent attention, could be increased corporate market power and the associated rise in economic rents accruing to firm owners (Barkai 2017; De Loecker, Eeckhout, and Unger 2018; Eggertsson, Robbins, and Wold 2018).

Empirical analysis finds that rising markups have compressed firms' labor income shares. Similar to the approach taken to explore the effects of higher markups on investment, cross-country firm-level regressions explain the labor share within each firm by its markup—instrumented to address endogeneity concerns (Online Annex 2.3D)—as well as firm-level control variables and a rich set of fixed effects. The results imply that an increase in markups of 10 percentage points is associated with a statistically significant 0.3 percentage point decrease in the labor share,

[21]Regarding the first three explanations, see Chapter 3 of the April 2017 WEO and references therein. Regarding labor market deregulation, worker bargaining power, and labor shares, see Ciminelli, Duval, and Furceri (2018) and its references.

measured as the ratio of the firm's wage bill to value added. Figure 2.10 illustrates that, for the overall sample, the average increase in firms' markups since 2000 is associated with a 0.2 percentage point decrease in the labor share, whereas for the sample of top decile firms, the average increase in markups is associated with a 1 percentage point decrease in the labor share.

Taken at face value, the empirical estimates imply that rising markups have accounted for at least 10 percent of the trend decline in the labor share in the average advanced economy. Without any markup increases since 2000, the average labor share across the sample of advanced economies might have been at least 0.2 percentage point higher today; this compares with an average fall in the labor share of about 2 percentage points over the past two decades. Because the underlying empirical analysis estimates only the labor share impact of rising markups *within* firms, it is likely to underestimate the overall effect on the aggregate labor share in countries where resource reallocation *between* firms also accounts for some of the rise in markups. In the United States, in particular, high-markup firms have gained market share at the expense of low-markup firms (see "The Rise of Corporate Market Power" section). Given that the former tend to have lower labor shares than the latter, the aggregate labor share falls through a composition effect—even leaving aside any markup increase and its labor share impact *within* those firms.[22] Indeed, when considering both the within- and between-firm components of the rise in markups in the empirical analysis—by removing the firm fixed effects from the regression—the estimated impact of markups on the labor share becomes larger. This tentatively suggests that the within-firm contribution may underestimate the overall impact of rising markups on the aggregate labor share (see Online Annex 2.3D for details).

Although analyzing the full income and wealth distribution implications of market power is beyond the scope of this chapter, the uneven rise in markups across firms that is documented here may have been accompanied by greater earnings inequality between workers. Recent evidence shows that earnings inequality between firms—as opposed to within firms—has been the main driver of the overall rise in earnings inequality in recent decades, at least in the United States (Song and others 2019). One factor, among others, might be that only a small fraction of high-pay workers has been able to capture a share of their firms' growing economic rents.

[22]Autor and others (2017a, 2017b) and Kehrig and Vincent (2018) find that this contribution of resource reallocation between firms overshadows that of rising markups within firms in accounting for the aggregate fall in the US labor share. Both studies link this large, between-firm component to the growing weight in the economy of high-productivity firms at the expense of those with low productivity—which tend to have lower markups and higher labor shares.

Figure 2.10. Markups and Labor Income Shares
(Percentage point change in labor shares)

For the overall sample, the average increase in firms' markups is associated with a 0.2 percentage point decrease in the labor share. For the firms in the top decile of the markup distribution, the average increase in firms' markups is associated with a decrease in the labor share of 1 percentage point.

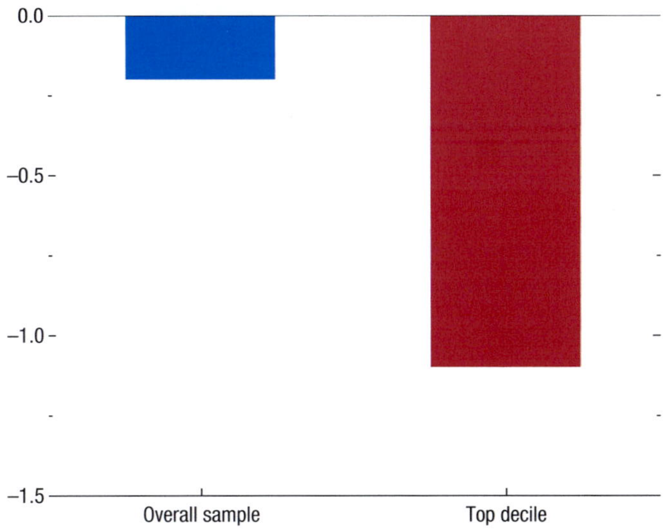

Sources: Orbis; and IMF staff calculations.
Note: Average changes in markups across firms are weighted by operating revenue.

Summary and Policy Implications

Over the past two decades, a generally moderate but broad-based rise in corporate market power has been observed across advanced economies, driven primarily by a small fraction of firms. The analysis in this chapter finds that the macroeconomic implications, including for the worrisome trends documented in Figure 2.1, have been rather modest so far. However, they would become increasingly negative if the market power of high-markup firms, in particular, were to continue to rise in the future—investment would weaken, innovation could slow, labor income shares would fall further, and monetary policymakers might find it even more difficult to stabilize output in the event of major downturns. Unlike in advanced economies, market power seems to have remained broadly stable in emerging market economies, possibly because of their greater distance to the technological frontier, smaller service sectors—where markup increases have been concentrated globally—and weaker competition to start with.

Several findings in this chapter tentatively suggest that technology-driven changes in the structure of many product markets have underpinned at least some of the rise in market power in advanced economies. First, the rather broad-based nature of the rise in markups across countries and industries, and the role played by a small fraction of firms in most cases, point to common underlying forces, rather than country- or industry-specific drivers related to antitrust policy or product market regulation.[23] Although markups increased more in the United States than in other countries, this also seems to reflect in part a growth-enhancing reallocation of resources away from low-markup, low-productivity firms toward high-markup, high-productivity counterparts. Second, and on a related note, in most countries and industries, only a small fraction of firms raised their markups, and these were typically the most dynamic—more productive and innovative—firms. This hints at winner-takes-most dynamics, rooted in part in specific intangible assets (technological, managerial, or other), network effects, and economies of scale in driving some of the overall rise in markups. Third, there is little direct evidence that pro-competition policies have weakened across advanced economies so far. On the contrary, tariff and nontariff barriers to trade and behind-the-border barriers have been vastly reduced across advanced economies and emerging market economies alike over the past three decades (see, for example, Koske and others 2015; and Duval and others 2018). These policies strengthened, rather than weakened, product market competition in manufacturing and service industries, although some firms may well have done better than others at seizing the opportunities that liberalization offered.

Other factors may have also played some role, however—possibly magnifying the impact of technological changes. Winner-takes-most outcomes and the associated increase in winners' market power may be more likely when competition policy fails to adapt or becomes less stringent, for example, when it comes to merger enforcement or exclusionary conduct by dominant firms.[24] Over the broad sample of firms analyzed in this chapter, the evidence shows that mergers and acquisitions have been followed by significantly higher markups (Box 2.2). That said, whether the loss to consumers from such increases has been typically more than offset by gains from cost and price reductions due to economies of scale and scope, or by other efficiency gains, is an open question that warrants investigation. Another related concern, and a lesson from economic history, is that firms that have, so far, achieved market dominance primarily through innovative products and business practices, may attempt to entrench their positions by erecting barriers to entry going forward—for example, potential competitors may find it hard to enter markets where incumbents' success is underpinned by hard-to-reproduce (or hard-to-buy) intangible assets, such as large proprietary consumer databases.[25]

The possibility of successful firms discouraging the entry and growth of competitors, and the increasingly negative association between rising market power within firms and key macroeconomic outcomes, such as investment or innovation documented in this

[23]For example, EU countries have undergone major product market deregulation since the early 1990s, and the combination of country-level and EU-level competition law and policy is widely seen as stringent in international comparison (Bergman and others 2010; Alemani and others 2013); yet the analysis above finds that markups and market concentration have increased across the European Union (see also Calligaris, Criscuolo, and Marcolin 2018; Bajgar and others, forthcoming).

[24]For example, debate is ongoing regarding the extent to which rising market concentration, markups, and profits in the United States might reflect a weakening of antitrust enforcement, notably starting with the revision in 1982 of the 1968 merger guidelines that discouraged increases in concentration only in already highly concentrated markets. Khan (2017) and Kwoka (2017) argue that these changes should be reconsidered, while Peltzman (2014) uncovers a rising concentration trend since then. So, too, do Grullon, Larkin, and Michaely (2018) and Gutiérrez and Philippon (2018), which highlight the implications of this rise in concentration for profits, market power, and the macroeconomy. By contrast, Rossi-Hansberg, Sarte, and Trachter (2018) cautions against the use of concentration data, especially at the national rather than local level. So does Shapiro (2019), which nevertheless identifies some scope for improvement in current US competition policy.

[25]For example, in a study of US firms, Bessen (2017) finds a significant role of proprietary information technology systems in entrenching market power. At the same time, rising barriers to entry may not *necessarily* lead to higher aggregate markups. This is because they enable less productive, lower-markup firms to survive more easily, which, all else equal, should lead to lower concentration and a possibly unchanged aggregate markup relative to an unchanged-barriers scenario (Edmond, Midrigan, and Xu 2018).

chapter, call for structural reforms to keep product market competition strong in the future. This need for reform applies particularly to nonmanufacturing industries. It is an agenda that remains unfinished in advanced economies, and even more so in emerging market economies, despite major deregulation in past decades. Regardless of the drivers of rising corporate market power, strengthening market contestability by cutting domestic regulatory barriers to entry (such as administrative burdens on start-ups or regulatory protections of incumbents) and further openness to trade and foreign direct investment would make markets more contestable by increasing the threat of entry and, so, help to spur growth (Chapter 3 of the April 2016 WEO; Duval and Furceri 2018). This is even more relevant for emerging markets than for advanced economies, given that emerging markets face larger barriers to domestic and foreign competition.[26]

Strong competition law and policy are key complements to product market deregulation—just as financial supervision is a key complement to financial liberalization. More research is needed to determine whether competition policies have contributed to rising market power and, if so, the possible remedies. Depending on the jurisdiction, a case might be made for strengthening some aspects of competition law and policy to ensure that they remain supportive of strong market contestability, firm entry, and rivalry—including in two-sided markets, such as digital platforms, which raise new challenges that may require guidelines for competition policy to be redrawn (Tirole 2017). In general, competition authorities should have ample resources to investigate mergers in detail and assess whether they will benefit consumers. Anticompetitive behavior may be deterred more effectively if competition authorities also have the ability to undertake market examinations and—when evidence of anticompetitive behavior is found—enforce strong remedies, including directing firms to divest assets if deemed necessary. An open question is whether authorities should have the power to investigate, and pay greater attention to, issues of potential loss of competition when a large incumbent firm acquires a small—but potentially large in the future—competitor, as has happened regularly in the high-tech sector. Figuring out the counterfactual—whether the small target could become a large competitor if not acquired—is difficult ex ante, calling for caution; the argument for such action will increase according to the size and persistence of the incumbent firm's market power. Finally, competition policy may also need to take a dynamic perspective: the larger and more persistent an industry's profits, the more likely there are barriers to entry, and the greater the need for close examination of the industry.

The concentration of markup increases among a small set of high-productivity firms suggests that easing obstacles to technological catch-up by lagging firms could also strengthen competition. Examples of helpful policies on this front include well-calibrated intellectual property rights that keep on incentivizing groundbreaking innovation without undermining technological diffusion,[27] and competition-neutral data governance regimes.

Finally, rising market power may further strengthen the case for corporate taxation reform. A regular corporate income tax system taxes not only the excess returns on capital derived from market power—so-called economic rents—but also normal returns.[28] An efficient corporate tax, however, would exempt normal returns and focus on economic rents only. This can be achieved through cash flow taxes, which allow investment to be expensed, or, alternatively, by providing some allowance for corporate equity (a deduction from regular corporate profit taxation equal to the normal return on equity). Innovation, which often generates economic rents, can be encouraged efficiently through incentives, such as research and development tax credits (Chapter 2 of the April 2016 *Fiscal Monitor*). The destination-based version of these taxes—which tax corporate income based on the location of final consumption, rather than the origin of profits—has the further advantage of being able to withstand profit shifting by multinational firms (Auerbach and others 2017). In this way, it also helps level the playing field between large firms—which are typically better equipped to shift profits across jurisdictions—and their smaller, current, or potential competitors.

[26]Product market regulations and barriers to trade and foreign direct investment remain comparatively more stringent, and competition policy enforcement weaker, in emerging market economies (Koske and others 2015; WB 2017).

[27]For example, this might require that intellectual property rights protect disruptive innovations better than those that are incremental (Acemoglu and Akcigit 2012). Also, patent pools—agreements between different firms to jointly market licenses of a group of individual patents they own regarding a particular technology—should be designed to facilitate, rather than hinder, the use of new technologies and firm entry (see, for example, Lerner and Tirole 2004).

[28]In the case of monopolies, achieving an efficient output level would also require combining high profit taxes with output subsidies (Paulsen and Adams 1987).

Box 2.1. The Comovement between Industry Concentration and Corporate Saving

The past two decades have witnessed a broad-based increase in corporate saving across major advanced economies (see, for example, Chen, Karabarbounis, and Neiman 2017; Dao and Maggi 2018).[1] This box presents new firm-level evidence that shows that the rise in the corporate saving rate is closely linked to increased concentration in corporate sales and assets—which has occurred alongside rising markups and profitability, as discussed in "The Rise of Corporate Market Power" section in Chapter 2.

Among publicly traded firms, the average saving rate across narrowly defined (four-digit NACE (Nomenclature statistique des activités économiques dans les Communauté européenne)) industries in Group of Seven (G7) countries appears to comove strongly over time with the average share of sales by the largest four firms in an industry, with a correlation coefficient of 0.8 (Figure 2.1.1).[2] Uncovering the drivers of this comovement could shed light on several issues, including the drivers of current account imbalances, whose dynamics largely reflect the evolution of corporate saving in advanced economies (IMF 2017).

Analysis using data for listed firms in the G7 countries reveals four key findings:

- Most of the increase in aggregate corporate saving reflects higher saving by incumbent firms rather than compositional changes driven by entry of new firms, exit, or market share reallocation among incumbent firms.
- Incumbent firms have been increasing their saving rates more in industries where concentration (or markups) has risen more (Figure 2.1.2), consistent with the time series correlation shown in Figure 2.1.1.[3]
- Rising pretax profits (gross operating surplus) as a share of corporate value added are the main source for this increase in corporate saving in concentrating industries. Despite their rising profitability, firms in industries with larger increases in concentration have not significantly raised their dividends or tax payments.[4]
- The within-firm rise in saving has been driven by large firms, with the top 1 percent (by size) showing the largest increases.

Figure 2.1.1. Comovement between Average Industry Concentration and Corporate Saving in Group of Seven Countries
(Percent)

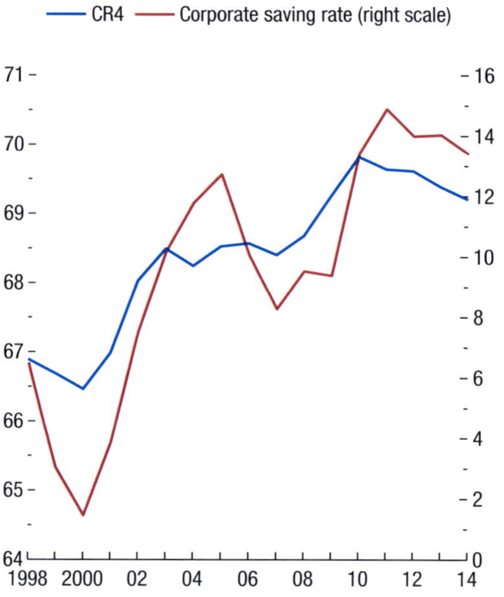

Sources: Thomson Reuters Worldscope; and IMF staff calculations.
Note: This figure reports the movements of the average firm's saving and average concentration (at four-digit industry level) across countries and industries. The set of countries includes Canada, France, Germany, Italy, Japan, the United Kingdom, and the United States. Utility and financial sectors are excluded due to regulation; agriculture and other services are excluded because of poor coverage. CR4 = total market share of the four largest firms in an industry.

The authors of this box are Mai Chi Dao and Nan Li, based on Dao and others (forthcoming).

[1]The corporate saving rate here refers to total gross saving (undistributed gross profits) as a share of gross value added.

[2]All the results presented here hold when the average firm markup is used as a measure of market concentration. Firm markups are defined and calculated in the same way as in the rest of the chapter.

[3]This finding is confirmed in a more detailed panel regression, which is estimated using Worldscope data for 1996–2014:
$$s_{ijct} = \beta_0 + \beta_1 CR4_{jt} + \beta_2 X_{ijct} + \gamma_{ct} + \delta_i + \varepsilon_{ijct},$$
where $s_{ijct} = \frac{Grosssavings}{Grossvalueadded}$ is the saving rate of firm i in industry j, country c, at time t; $CR4$ is market concentration, measured as the fraction of total sales (or assets) accrued to the four largest firms in an industry j; X_{ijct} is a vector of other firm-specific controls, such as age, and γ_{ct} and δ_i are country-year and firm fixed effects, respectively. Coefficient β_1 is found to be positive and statistically significant.

[4]Again, this finding is based on a similar regression specification, with profits, dividends, and tax payments (as a share of value added) as the dependent variables.

Box 2.1 *(continued)*

Figure 2.1.2. Change in Industry Concentration and Change in Saving Rates
(Percentage points)

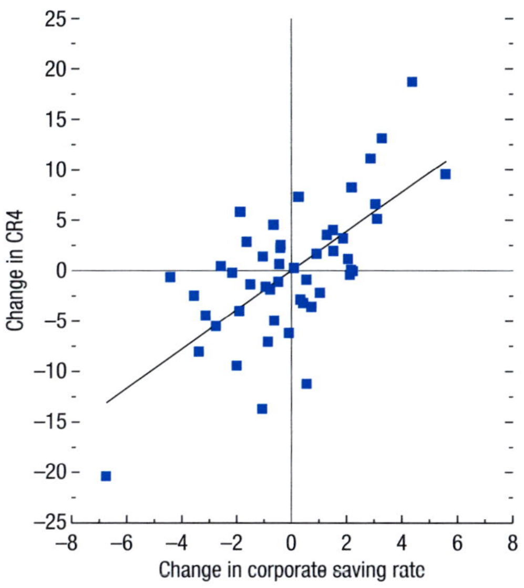

Sources: Thomson Reuters Worldscope; and IMF staff calculations.
Note: The distributions of concentration and saving rate changes were divided into 50 equally sized bins. Each point in the figure represents the average change in concentration within a bin (CR4 at four-digit industry level, absorbing country-industry fixed effects), plotted against the corresponding (bin) average change in saving rates (conditional on firm fixed effects). CR4 = total market share of the four largest firms in an industry.

The drivers of the relationship between rising concentration (or markups) and increasing corporate saving are not yet fully understood. One possible factor, explored in Dao and others (forthcoming), is the trend decline in global real interest rates (and corporate tax rates) over the past couple of decades. Given that larger firms are less financially constrained and able to leverage more, lower interest rates benefit them disproportionately. As a result, they are better able to exploit opportunities to invest in high-return projects (because, for example, of network effects or increasing returns to scale). When liquidity is constrained and firms must put away investment funds for future projects, larger firms save disproportionately more for these high-return projects.

Box 2.2. Effects of Mergers and Acquisitions on Market Power

Renewed debate about the economic welfare implications of mergers and acquisitions has preoccupied many economists and policymakers in recent years.[1] Mergers and acquisitions can enhance efficiency through economies of scale and scope, thereby reducing production costs and prices or improving product quality. At the same time, however, the consolidation of firms can leave an economy with fewer and larger firms that eventually use reduced competitive pressure to raise prices or offer consumers lower product variety or quality. This box investigates whether acquiring firms' price markups have increased following mergers and acquisitions across the large cross-country sample of firms considered in this chapter. To this end, the extensive firm-level data set on markups is combined with transaction-specific data on mergers and acquisitions.[2] The main finding from this box is that mergers and acquisitions are followed by markup increases by acquiring firms.[3]

The total number of worldwide mergers and acquisitions deals has grown steadily since 2000 (Figure 2.2.1). Among these, the value share of horizontal deals—those in which acquirer and target firms are in the same industry—has recovered to its pre–global financial crisis average of about one-third. The pickup in mergers and acquisitions activity raises the question of its economic effects.

Mergers and acquisitions have been generally accompanied by markup increases by acquiring firms. To assess the change in the markup of acquirers against that of nonacquirers, a simple ordinary least squares regression is run that explains the markup by a dummy variable that takes a value of 0 for all firms in 2000 and switches to 1 starting from the year of the mergers and acquisitions. To address the risk that the relationship between mergers and acquisitions and markups may be obscured by confounding factors, the analysis controls for firm and country-industry-year (four-digit NACE (Nomenclature statistique des activités économiques dans les Communauté européenne)) fixed effects, as well as for the firm's size (operating revenue), efficiency (total factor productivity), and profitability (earned income before interest and taxes divided by total assets). Standard errors are clustered at the firm level. The results show a sizable and statistically significant association between mergers and acquisitions and the subsequent change in a firm's markup, on the order of 1.1 percentage points, on average, and 1.2 percentage points for horizontal mergers and acquisitions (Figure 2.2.2, rows 1 and 2).

In a counterfactual exercise that attempts to control for unobserved factors that could drive a firm to seek a merger or acquisition and also increase its markups,

Figure 2.2.1. Total Number of Deals and Share of Horizontal Deals

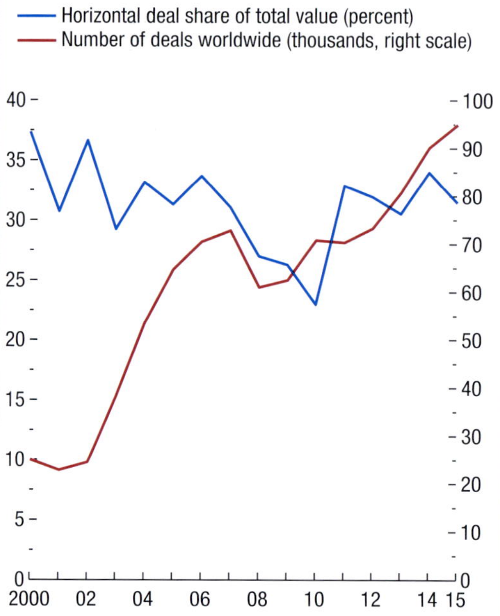

Sources: Zephyr; and IMF staff calculations.

The author of this box is Wenjie Chen.

[1]For recent examples regarding the United States, see Peltzman (2014); Khan (2017); Kwoka (2017); Grullon, Larkin, and Michaely (2018); Gutiérrez and Philippon (2018); and Shapiro (2019).

[2]The mergers and acquisitions data are collected by Zephyr and come from governmental regulatory filings, media reports, and reporting arrangements with investment banks. Therefore, the resulting data set on mergers and acquisitions theoretically includes data for the universe of mergers and acquisitions transactions. One shortcoming is the underreporting of deal values, which are missing for about one-half of reported transactions. Hence, while some descriptive statistics are included using existing deal values—bearing in mind the underreporting issue—the main empirical analysis in this box abstracts from using deal values.

[3]The analysis builds on, and is consistent with, recent research on firms in the United States. Blonigen and Pierce (2016) finds that mergers and acquisitions in the US manufacturing industry are associated with increases in average markups for the acquired plant; in addition, they find little evidence of increased plant-level productivity.

Box 2.2 *(continued)*

Figure 2.2.2. Impact of Mergers and Acquisitions on Acquirer Firm's Markups, by Deal Type
(Percentage points)

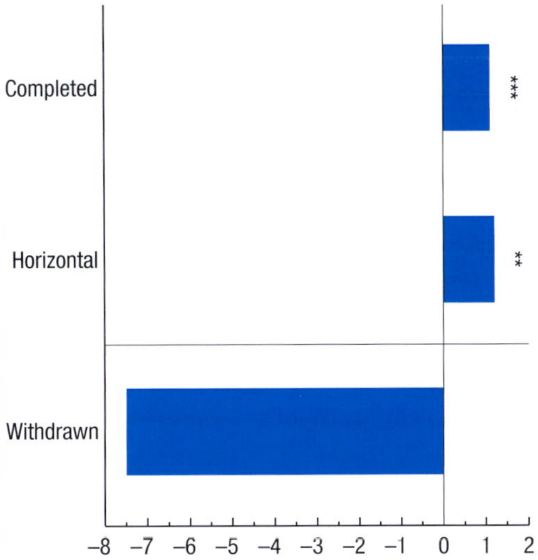

Sources: Orbis; Zephyr; and IMF staff calculations.
Note: ** and *** denote statistical significance at the 5 and 1 percent confidence levels, respectively.

the same regression estimation is performed using a sample of mergers and acquisitions deals that were announced but then aborted. This set of announced acquirers with ultimately withdrawn deals should share similar characteristics, observed and unobserved, with acquirers in completed deals. The result yields a (statistically insignificant) negative relationship between markups and the (counterfactual) post–mergers and acquisitions period, controlling for the same variables and including the same set of fixed effects as before. The sample size is much smaller for this set of counterfactual mergers and acquisitions, and there could be specific reasons behind the failure of these announced mergers and acquisitions that also negatively affect markup rates. Bearing these caveats in mind, the results suggest that when mergers and acquisitions are not completed, the markups of aspiring acquirers do not increase following the mergers and acquisitions announcement, while they do for firms that succeed in completing the deals.

More detailed analysis is required to establish a causal link between mergers and acquisitions activity and increasing markups, and to assess its impact on productivity and other measures of economic efficiency that can benefit consumers. Ultimately, a comparison of these two effects is needed before implications for welfare and competition policy can be drawn.

References

Acemoglu, Daron, and Ufuk Akcigit. 2012. "Intellectual Property Rights Policy, Competition and Innovation." *Journal of the European Economic Association* 10 (1): 1–42.

Ackerberg, Daniel, Kevin Caves, and Garth Frazer. 2015. "Identification Properties of Recent Production Function Estimators." *Econometrica* 83 (6): 2411–451.

Adler, Gustavo, Romain Duval, Davide Furceri, Sinem Kiliç Çelik, Ksenia Koloskova, and Marcos Poplawski-Ribeiro. 2017. "Gone with the Headwinds: Global Productivity." IMF Staff Discussion Note 17/04, International Monetary Fund, Washington, DC.

Aghion, Philippe, Nick Bloom, Richard Blundell, Rachel Griffith, and Peter Howitt. 2005. "Competition and Innovation: An Inverted-U Relationship." *Quarterly Journal of Economics* 120 (2): 701–28.

Alemani, Enrico, Caroline Klein, Isabell Koske, Cristiana Vitale, and Isabell Wanner. 2013. "New Indicators of Competition Law and Policy in 2013 for OECD and non-OECD Countries." OECD Economics Department Working Paper 1104, Organisation for Economic Co-operation and Development, Paris.

Auerbach, Alan, Michael Devereux, Michael Keene, and John Vella. 2017. "Destination-Based Cash Flow Taxation." Saïd Business School Research Paper 17/01, Oxford.

Autor, David, David Dorn, Lawrence F. Katz, Christina Patterson, and John Van Reenen, 2017a. "Concentrating on the Fall of the Labor Share." *American Economic Review* 107 (5): 180–85.

———. 2017b. "The Fall of the Labor Share and the Rise of Superstar Firms." NBER Working Paper 23396, National Bureau of Economic Research, Cambridge, MA.

Bajgar, Matej, Giuseppe Berlingieri, Sara Calligaris, Chiara Criscuolo, and Jonathan Timmis. Forthcoming. "Industry Concentration in Europe and North America." OECD Science, Technology and Industry Department Working Paper, Organisation for Economic Co-operation and Development, Paris.

Baqaee, David, and Emmanuel Farhi. 2017. "Productivity and Misallocation in General Equilibrium." NBER Working Paper 24007, National Bureau of Economic Research, Cambridge, MA.

Barkai, Simcha. 2017. "Declining Labor and Capital Shares." Unpublished.

Bergman, Mats, Malcom Coate, Maria Jakobsson, and Shawn Ulrik. 2010. "Comparing Merger Policies in the European Union and the United States." *Review of Industrial Organization* 36 (4): 305–31.

Bessen, James. 2017. "Information Technology and Industry Concentration." Boston University School of Law & Economics Paper 17–41, Boston, MA.

Blonigen, Bruce, and Justin Pierce. 2016. "Evidence for the Effects of Mergers on Market Power and Efficiency." NBER Working Paper 22750, National Bureau of Economic Research, Cambridge, MA.

Caballero, Ricardo J., Emmanuel Farhi, and Pierre-Olivier Gourinchas. 2017. "Rents, Technical Change, and Risk Premia Accounting for Secular Trends in Interest Rates, Returns on Capital, Earning Yields, and Factor Shares." *American Economic Review* 107 (5): 614–20.

Calligaris, Sara, Chiara Criscuolo, and Luca Marcolin. 2018. "Markups in the Digital Era." OECD Science, Technology and Industry Working Paper 18/10, Organisation for Economic Co-operation and Development, Paris.

Calvo, Guillermo. 1983. "Staggered Prices in a Utility-Maximizing Framework." *Journal of Monetary Economics* 12 (3): 383–98.

Chen, Peter, Loukas Karabarbounis, and Brent Neiman. 2017. "The Global Rise of Corporate Saving." *Journal of Monetary Economics* 89 (C): 1–19.

Ciminelli, Gabriele, Romain A. Duval, and Davide Furceri. 2018. "Employment Protection Deregulation and Labor Shares in Advanced Economies." IMF Working Paper 18/186, International Monetary Fund, Washington, DC.

Crouzet, Nicolas, and Janice Eberly. 2018. "Intangibles, Investment, and Efficiency." *American Economic Review, Papers and Proceedings* 108: 426–31.

Dao, Mai Chi, Isabel Hanisch, Callum Jones, and Nan Li. Forthcoming. "The Granularity of Corporate Saving." IMF Working Paper, International Monetary Fund, Washington, DC.

Dao, Mai Chi, and Chiara Maggi. 2018. "The Rise in Corporate Saving and Cash Holding in Advanced Economies: Aggregate and Firm Level Trends." IMF Working Paper 18/262, International Monetary Fund, Washington, DC.

Davis, Steven. J., John Haltiwanger, Ron Jarmin, and Javier Miranda. 2007: "Volatility and Dispersion in Business Growth Rates: Publicly Traded versus Privately Held Firms," in *NBER Macroeconomics Annual 2006* (21): 107–80. Cambridge, MA: MIT Press.

De Loecker, Jan, and Jan Eeckhout. 2017. "The Rise of Market Power and the Macroeconomic Implications." NBER Working Paper 23687, National Bureau of Economic Research, Cambridge, MA.

———. 2018. "Global Market Power." NBER Working Paper 24768, National Bureau of Economic Research, Cambridge, MA.

———, and Gabriel Unger. 2018. "The Rise of Market Power and the Macroeconomic Implications." Unpublished.

De Loecker, Jan, and Frederic Warzynski. 2012. "Markups and Firm-Level Export Status." *American Economic Review* 102 (6): 2437–471.

Díez, Federico, Jiayue Fan, and Carolina Villegas-Sánchez. Forthcoming. "Global Declining Competition." IMF Working Paper, International Monetary Fund, Washington, DC.

Díez, Federico, Daniel Leigh, and Suchanan Tambunlertchai. 2018. "Global Market Power and Its Macroeconomic Implications." IMF Working Paper 18/137, International Monetary Fund, Washington, DC.

Duval, Romain, and Davide Furceri. 2018. "The Effects of Labor and Product Market Reforms: The Role of Macroeconomic Conditions and Policies." *IMF Economic Review* 66 (1): 31–69.

———, Bingjie Hu, Joao Jalles, and Huy Nguyen. 2018. "A Narrative Database of Major Labor and Product Market Reforms in Advanced Economies." IMF Working Paper 18/19, International Monetary Fund, Washington, DC.

Edmond, Chris, Virgiliu Midrigan, and Daniel Yi Xu. 2018. "How Costly Are Markups?" NBER Working Paper 24800, National Bureau of Economic Research, Cambridge, MA.

Eggertsson, Gauti B., Jacob A. Robbins, and Ella Getz Wold. 2018. "Kaldor and Piketty's Facts: The Rise of Monopoly Power in the United States." NBER Working Paper 24287, National Bureau of Economic Research, Cambridge, MA.

Gal, Peter. 2013. "Measuring Total Factor Productivity at the Firm Level Using OECD-ORBIS." OECD Economics Department Working Paper 1049, Organisation for Economic Co-operation and Development, Paris.

Galí, Jordi. 2008. *Monetary Policy, Inflation, and the Business Cycle: An Introduction to the New Keynesian Framework*. Princeton, NJ: Princeton University Press.

Gopinath, Gita, Şebnem Kalemli-Özcan, Loukas Karabarbounis, and Carolina Villegas-Sánchez. 2017. "Capital Allocation and Productivity in South Europe." *Quarterly Journal of Economics* 132 (4): 1915–967.

Grullon, Gustavo, Yelena Larkin, and Roni Michaely. 2018. "Are US Industries Becoming More Concentrated?" Unpublished.

Gutiérrez, German, Callum Jones, and Thomas Philippon. 2019. "Entry Costs and the Macroeconomy." NBER Working Paper 25609, National Bureau of Economic Research, Cambridge, MA.

Gutiérrez, German, and Thomas Philippon. 2017. "Investment-less Growth: An Empirical Investigation." Brookings Papers on Economic Activity, Washington, DC.

———. 2018. "How EU Markets Became More Competitive than US Markets: A Study of Institutional Drift." NBER Working Paper 24700, National Bureau of Economic Research, Cambridge, MA.

Hall, Robert E. 2017. "The Anatomy of Stagnation in a Modern Economy." *Economica* 84 (333): 1–15.

Inklaar, Robert, and Marcel P. Timmer. 2014. "The Relative Price of Services." *Review of Income and Wealth* 60 (4): 727–46.

International Monetary Fund (IMF). 2017. *External Sector Report.* Washington, DC.

Jones, Callum, and Thomas Philippon. 2016. "The Secular Stagnation of Investment?" Unpublished.

Kalemli-Özcan, Şebnem, Bent Sorensen, Carolina Villegas-Sánchez, Vadym Volosovych, and Sevcan Yesiltas. 2015. "How to Construct Nationally Representative Firm Level Data from the ORBIS Global Database." NBER Working Paper 21558, National Bureau of Economic Research, Cambridge, MA.

Kamien, Morton, and Nancy Schwartz. 1976. "On the Degree of Rivalry for Maximum Innovative Activity." *Quarterly Journal of Economics* 90 (2): 245–60.

Kehrig, Matthias, and Nicolas Vincent. 2018. "The Micro-Level Anatomy of the Labor Share Decline." NBER Working Paper 25275, National Bureau of Economic Research, Cambridge, MA.

Khan, Lina. 2017. "Amazon's Antitrust Paradox." *Yale Law Journal* 126 (3): 710–804.

Koske, Isabell, Isabelle Wanner, Rosamaria Bitetti, and Omar Barbiero. 2015. "The 2013 Update of the OECD's Database on Product Market Regulation: Policy Insights for OECD and non-OECD Countries." OECD Economics Department Working Paper 1200, Organisation for Economic Co-operation and Development, Paris.

Kwoka, John. 2017. "US Antitrust and Competition Policy amid the New Merger Wave." Washington Center for Equitable Growth, Washington, DC.

Lerner, Josh, and Jean Tirole. 2004. "Efficient Patent Pools." *American Economic Review* 94 (3): 691–711.

Melitz, Marc J., and Sašo Polanec. 2015. "Dynamic Olley-Pakes Productivity Decomposition with Entry and Exit." *RAND Journal of Economics* 46 (2): 362–75.

Paulsen, Jim, and Roy Adams. 1987. "Optimal Taxation of a Monopoly." *National Tax Journal* 40 (1): 121–25.

Peltzman, Sam. 2014. "Industrial Concentration under the Rule of Reason." *Journal of Law and Economics,* 57 (S3): 101–20.

Rossi-Hansberg, Esteban, Pierre-Daniel Sarte, and Nicholas Trachter. 2018. "Diverging Trends in National and Local Concentration." CEPR Discussion Paper 13174, Center for Economic and Policy Research, Washington, DC.

Rotemberg, Julio. 1982. "Sticky Prices in the United States." *Journal of Political Economy* 90 (6): 1187–211.

Scherer, Fredrick. 1967. "Market Structure and the Employment of Scientists and Engineers." *American Economic Review* 57 (3): 524–31.

Shapiro, Carl. 2012. "Competition and Innovation: Did Arrow Hit the Bull's Eye?" in *The Rate and Direction of Inventive Activity Revisited*, edited by Josh Lerner and Scott Stern. Chicago: University of Chicago Press.

———. 2019. "Antitrust Policy in a Time of Populism." *International Journal of Industrial Organization*, in press, available online February 27, 2019.

Song, Jae, David Price, Fatih Guvenen, Nicholas Bloom, and Till Von Wachter. 2019. "Firming Up Inequality." *Quarterly Journal of Economics* 134 (1): 1–50.

Stiglitz, Joseph E. 2015. "New Theoretical Perspectives on the Distribution of Income and Wealth among Individuals: Part I—The Wealth Residual." NBER Working Paper 21189, National Bureau of Economic Research, Cambridge, MA.

Tirole, Jean. 2017. *Economics for the Common Good*, Chapter 14. Princeton, NJ: Princeton University Press.

Van Reenen, John. 2018. "Increasing Differences between Firms: Market Power and the Macroeconomy." CEPR Discussion Paper 1576, Center for Economic and Policy Research, Washington, DC.

Wolff, Edward. 2010. "Recent Trends in Household Wealth in the United States: Rising Debt and the Middle Class Squeeze: An Update to 2007." Levy Economics Institute Working Papers Series 159, Bard College, Annandale-on-Hudson, NY.

World Bank (WB). 2017. *A Step Ahead: Competition Policy for Shared Prosperity and Inclusive Growth.* Washington, DC: World Bank.

CHAPTER 3

THE PRICE OF CAPITAL GOODS: A DRIVER OF INVESTMENT UNDER THREAT?

Over the past three decades, the price of machinery and equipment has fallen dramatically relative to other prices in advanced and emerging market and developing economies alike. Could rising trade tensions, a slowing pace of trade integration, and sluggish productivity growth threaten this potential driver of investment going forward? This chapter sets out to answer this question by documenting key patterns in the price of capital goods, its drivers, and its impact on real investment rates. Worldwide, investment growth has slowed considerably since the global financial crisis of 2008–09. Yet, when compared with its levels in the early 1990s, real investment in machinery and equipment as a share of real GDP has increased significantly. The chapter finds that the decline in the relative price of tradable investment goods has provided sizable impetus to the rise in real investment rates in machinery and equipment over the past three decades. The broad-based decline in the relative price of machinery and equipment, in turn, has been driven by faster productivity growth in the capital-goods-producing sector and rising trade integration. Yet, emerging market and developing economies still face higher relative prices of tradable investment goods, consistent with their higher policy-induced trade costs and lower productivity in the tradable goods sector. Taken together, the chapter's findings provide an additional, often overlooked, argument in support of policies aimed at reducing trade barriers and reinvigorating international trade. The analysis also highlights the importance of continued technological progress to maintain the pace of decline in relative capital goods prices, which has provided an important tailwind to investment around the world.

Introduction

The investment needs of most emerging market and developing economies remain substantial. These economies still have only a small fraction of the capital available in advanced economies, even though their investment rates have increased significantly over the past three decades, with a near doubling of real investment rates in machinery and equipment (Figure 3.1, panels 1–2). Meeting the United Nations Sustainable Development Goals would require a sizable boost to investment in many low-income developing countries (Gaspar and others 2019). High investment rates have been a key reason for significantly higher growth in emerging market and developing economies than in advanced economies since the early 2000s, which has helped narrow income gaps. The assumption of continued strength in investment in emerging market and developing economies underpins the projection that they will grow faster than advanced economies in the medium term (Figure 3.1, panels 3–4).[1]

The capital deepening in emerging market and developing economies over the past three decades has coincided with sizable declines in the price of investment goods and, in particular, of tradable capital goods, such as machinery and equipment, relative to other prices in the economy (Figure 3.1, panels 5–6).[2] Economists have long hypothesized that the relative price of investment is one of the key drivers of investment rates and therefore economic development.[3] The decline in relative investment prices, in turn, is often attributed to faster

The authors of this chapter are Weicheng Lian, Natalija Novta, Evgenia Pugacheva, Yannick Timmer, and Petia Topalova (lead), with support from Jilun Xing and Candice Zhao, and contributions from Michal Andrle, Christian Bogmans, Lama Kiyasseh, Sergii Meleshchuk, and Rafael Portillo. The chapter benefited from comments and suggestions by Andrei Levchenko and Maurice Obstfeld.

[1]Advanced economies experienced a similar increase in real investment rates in machinery and equipment until the 2008 global financial crisis. For an analysis of the investment slump in these economies in the aftermath of the global financial crisis, see Chapter 3 of the April 2015 *World Economic Outlook* (WEO).

[2]In this chapter, the relative price of investment refers to the ratio of the price of investment to the price of consumption. All stylized patterns and findings are qualitatively similar if the price of investment is instead compared with the overall GDP price level. The capital deepening also occurred in the context of improved macroeconomic policy and institutional frameworks, a synchronized pickup in economic activity until the global financial crisis, and falling global real interest rates.

[3]See, for example, DeLong and Summers (1991, 1992, 1993); Sarel (1995); Collins and Williamson (2001); Hsieh and Klenow (2007); Armenter and Lahiri (2012); and Mutreja, Ravikumar, and Sposi (2018). The relative price of investment goods tends to be inversely related to investment or per capita growth (Jones 1994; Sarel 1995; Restuccia and Urrutia 2001), and high relative investment prices likely serve as a headwind to the structural transformation many low-income developing countries need to converge to advanced economies' income levels. High tariffs on imported equipment, part of many developing economies' import-substitution growth strategies in the 1970s and 1980s, have often been cited as an important impediment to development (Taylor 1998a; Sen 2002; Estevadeordal and Taylor 2013; Johri and Rahman 2017).

Figure 3.1. Capital Stock, Investment, and the Relative Price of Capital Goods
(Percent, unless noted otherwise)

Real investment-to-real GDP ratios increased substantially in emerging market and developing economies over the past three decades, but capital stocks per capita remain very low. The rise in real investment-to-real GDP ratios coincided with large declines in the price of machinery and equipment relative to the price of consumption, with production of machinery and equipment being strongly embedded in global value chains.

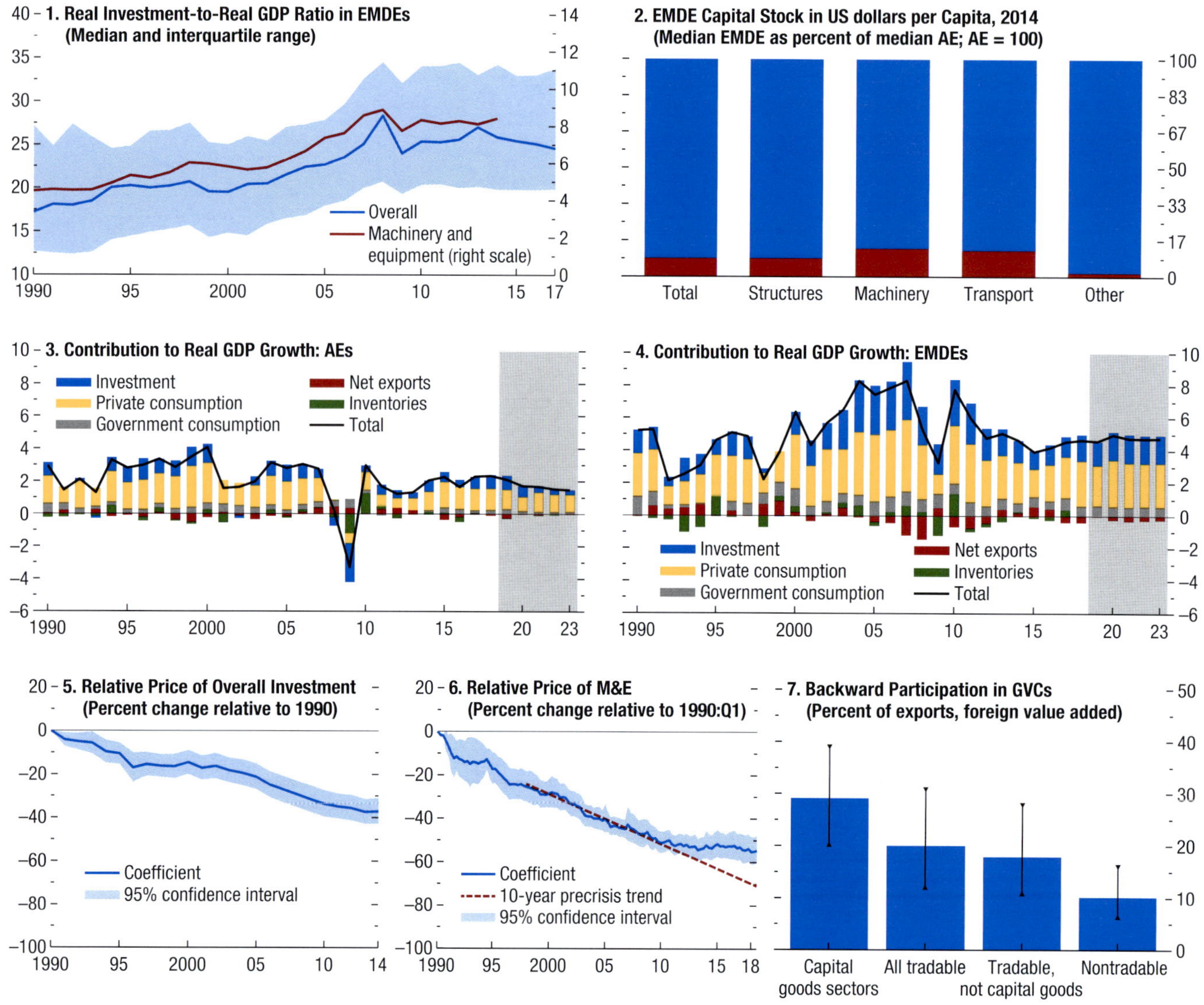

Sources: Eora Multi-Region Input-Output (MRIO) database; Haver Analytics; Penn World Table (PWT) 9.0; World Economic Outlook (WEO) database; and IMF staff calculations.
Note: Panel 1 shows the median and interquartile range of the overall real investment-to-GDP ratio (from WEO) and real investment in machinery and equipment to real GDP ratio (from PWT 9.0). Panels 3 and 4 show contributions to real GDP growth for advanced economies and emerging market and developing economies, respectively, based on WEO historical data and projections. In panels 5 and 6, the solid line plots year (quarter) fixed effects from a regression of log relative prices on year (quarter) fixed effects and country fixed effects to account for entry and exit during the sample period and level differences in the overall investment price relative to the price of consumption. Year (quarter) fixed effects are normalized to show percent change from the relative investment prices in 1990 (1990:Q1). Shaded areas indicate 95 percent confidence intervals. The relative price of investment is obtained by dividing the investment deflator by the consumption deflator. For further details, see Online Annex 3.1. The figure in panel 6 is based on quarterly data from select advanced economies, including: Australia, Canada, Germany, Hong Kong SAR, Italy, Norway, Portugal, Spain, United Kingdom, United States. Panel 7 depicts the median and interquartile range of the sector's backward global value chain participation (defined as the foreign value added in exports) across all economies in the Eora MRIO database deemed to have sufficient data quality at the sectoral level during 1995–2015. AEs = advanced economies; EMDEs = emerging market and developing economies; GVCs = global value chains; M&E = machinery and equipment.

growth in the productivity of sectors that produce capital goods than in sectors producing consumption goods and services, linked in part to advances in information technology. Efficiency gains from globalization and the associated specialization of production around the world have also supported the downward trend in capital goods prices because the production of machinery and equipment is strongly embedded in global value chains (Figure 3.1, panel 7). As emerging market and developing economies have become increasingly integrated into the world economy and have reduced barriers to trade, they have been able to benefit from, and contribute to, this engine of economic expansion, thus further reducing the relative prices of tradable capital goods.

Could this potential driver of investment come under threat going forward? The slowdown in global trade, the potential maturation of global value chains, and the waning pace of trade liberalization since the mid-2000s, as discussed in Chapter 2 of the October 2016 WEO, may limit further declines in the price of investment. Even more immediate is the threat from higher trade barriers in some advanced economies, which could jeopardize the benefits from free trade—taken for granted for so long in these economies. Hikes in tariffs and nontariff barriers could disrupt cross-border supply chains and, by making production less efficient, slow or even reverse the downward trend in capital goods prices. Even if not directly involved in the current trade tensions, many emerging market and developing economies stand to lose if the disputes escalate. As net importers of capital goods, they may face higher prices of machinery and equipment and, more broadly, diminished opportunities to benefit from the cross-border spread of knowledge and technology brought on by globalization (see Chapter 3 of the April 2018 WEO).

Sluggish productivity growth in advanced economies—a concern even before the global financial crisis—poses another threat to further declines in capital goods prices. Productivity in the world's leading capital-goods-producing economies has slowed further, with the global financial crisis leaving lasting scars on research and development spending and technology adoption (see Adler and others 2017 and Chapter 2 of the October 2018 WEO). Aging and the rise of market power in some of the main capital-goods-producing economies (see Chapter 2 of the April 2019 WEO) also cast a shadow on the innovation and continued technological advances that may be needed to spur further decline in the price of investment goods. The pace of decline in the relative price of machinery and equipment has already slowed considerably in advanced economies in the past decade, potentially exerting an additional drag on these economies' lackluster investment since the global financial crisis (Figure 3.1, panel 6).

With this backdrop in mind, the chapter examines several interrelated questions.[4]

- How have prices of investment goods evolved over time and across countries? Do lower-income countries face higher capital goods prices, in absolute terms and/or relative to other prices in the economy?
- What drives the price of tradable capital goods over time, and which factors explain differences across countries? How much have technological advances and trade integration contributed to the relative decline in the prices of machinery and equipment? To what extent are capital goods prices shaped by policy choices, particularly barriers to trade?
- How responsive is investment in machinery and equipment to the price of these assets? How much have changes in capital goods prices contributed to capital deepening over the past three decades?

The chapter's main findings are as follows:

- The relative price of tradable investment goods, namely machinery and equipment, has declined across advanced, emerging market, and developing economies over the past three decades. The declines have been significant and have been driven by faster productivity growth in capital goods production and deepening trade integration.
- Yet, the most recently available data on the price of comparable baskets of machinery and equipment across countries suggest that, in 2011, emerging market and developing economies faced higher machinery and equipment prices, both in absolute terms and especially relative to the price of consumption. The higher relative prices of machinery and equipment reflect these economies' lower relative efficiency in producing investment goods and tradable goods more broadly, and significantly higher trade costs, such as those arising from higher tariffs.
- Finally, model simulations and empirical evidence suggest that the relative price of investment goods is an important driver of real investment rates. There has been a slowdown in investment worldwide since the global financial crisis. Yet, over the past 30 years,

[4]In this chapter, unless otherwise noted, the terms tradable capital goods, tradable investment goods, and machinery and equipment are used interchangeably to denote tangible tradable investment goods—namely, machinery, equipment, and transportation capital goods.

real investment in machinery and equipment as a share of real GDP has increased significantly in both advanced as well as emerging market and developing economies. A nontrivial share of this increase can be attributed to the decline in the relative prices of machinery and equipment.

Taken together, the findings of this chapter provide an additional, often overlooked, argument in support of policies aimed at reducing trade costs and reinvigorating international trade. Many emerging market and developing economies still maintain trade barriers that raise the relative price of capital goods for domestic investors. An effort to remove these barriers would provide further impetus for investment in tradable capital goods and support the capital deepening needed in many of these economies, helping to counterbalance headwinds from abroad. Advanced economies, whose real investment—recent weakness notwithstanding—has been similarly supported by declining prices of capital goods, should also guard against protectionist measures that raise trade costs. For both groups of economies, reviving the process of trade liberalization, which has slowed down significantly since the mid-2000s, is vital for maintaining the pace of decline in relative capital goods prices. The impetus this would provide to real investment would come on top of the well-known welfare and productivity gains from international trade (for a discussion, see IMF/WB/WTO 2017).

The analysis in this chapter also highlights the importance of continued technological advances and innovation in capital goods production in advanced and emerging market and developing economies alike. Such advances, by lowering the relative price of investment goods, could generate dividends beyond their effect on aggregate productivity growth. As discussed in Adler and others (2017) and Chapter 2 of the April 2016 *Fiscal Monitor*, policies that stimulate research and development, entrepreneurship, and technology transfer, alongside continued investment in education and public infrastructure, can help.

The Price of Capital Goods: Key Patterns Over Time

Since the 1990s, capital goods prices relative to consumption prices have displayed two key patterns.[5]

First, the relative prices of the four main types of fixed capital assets—structures, machinery and equipment (excluding transportation), transportation equipment, and intellectual property products—have evolved quite differently (Figure 3.2, panels 1–4). According to data in the Penn World Table version 9.0 across 180 countries, the prices of machinery and equipment and transportation equipment have declined significantly since the early 1990s when compared with the consumption deflator.[6] On one hand, the relative price of machinery and equipment fell by about 60 percent in advanced and 40 percent in emerging market and developing economies. The price of residential and nonresidential structures, on the other hand, has more closely tracked consumption prices and, in advanced economies, has even increased since the mid-2000s in relative terms. The price of other investment, which consists mostly of intellectual property products, such as research and development and computer software and databases, has also come down, although more modestly than for tangible tradable investment goods. Finally, the dramatic decline in the relative prices of computing equipment (such as computer hardware, whose prices fell by 90 percent since 1990) and, to a lesser extent, communications equipment (whose prices fell by almost 60 percent), within the machinery and equipment asset type (Figure 3.2, panels 5–7), supports the hypothesis that advances in information technology have played an important role in driving down the relative price of investment.[7] Zooming in on the price of green capital goods, Box 3.1 documents large declines in the cost of installing and operating low-carbon electric generation capacity for some renewable energy sources over the past decade.

[5]See Online Annex 3.1 for country coverage, data sources, and variables definitions. All annexes are available at www.imf.org/en/Publications/WEO.

[6]The pace of decline in the relative price of tangible tradable capital goods accelerated significantly in the 1990s, especially for the emerging market and developing economy country group, as discussed in Online Annex 3.2. Recent data from 10 advanced economies suggest that the rate of decline in the relative price of machinery and equipment has slowed since the global financial crisis. Online Annex 3.2 provides additional stylized facts on the evolution of investment rates across types of fixed capital assets and country groups and the composition of investment across types of capital.

[7]Measuring changes in the prices of goods that undergo substantial quality improvements, such as computers, communications equipment, and so on, is a daunting task because of the difficulty of comparing products with very different attributes (Schreyer 2002). Statistical offices make substantial efforts to accurately reflect these changes in price indices, although methodologies likely differ significantly across countries. The chapter relies on the data provided by national authorities and compiled in Penn World Table 9.0.

Figure 3.2. Dynamics of Relative Prices across Types of Capital Goods and Broad Country Groups
(Percent change relative to 1990)

The decline in the relative price of investment was driven by a broad-based decline in the relative price of machinery and equipment. Within tangible tradable capital goods, computing and communications equipment experienced the largest price declines.

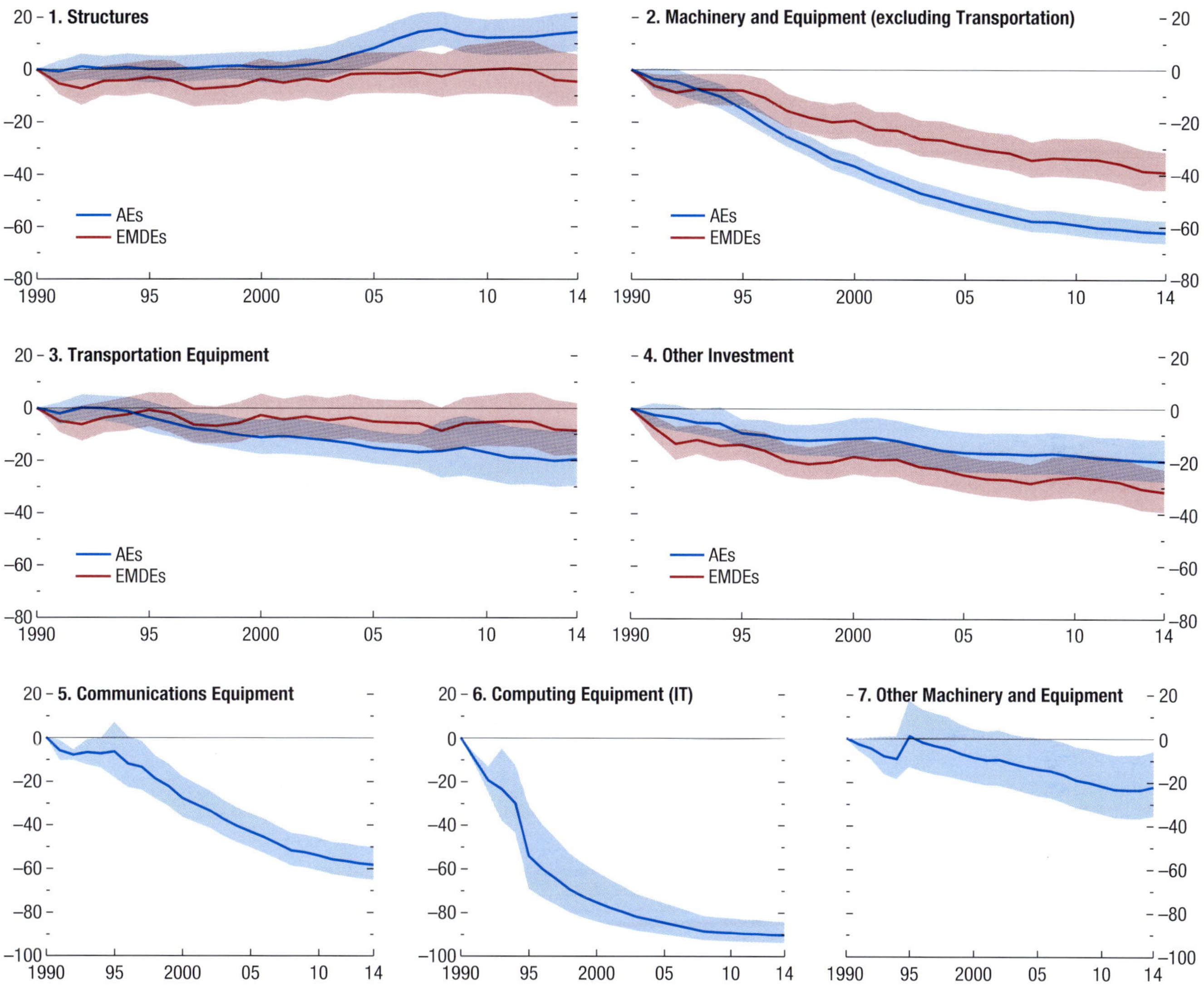

Sources: EU KLEMS; Penn World Table 9.0; World KLEMS; and IMF staff calculations.
Note: Panels 1–4 use data from the Penn World Table 9.0 capital detail file, while panels 5–7 use data from the EU and World KLEMS databases. The relative price of investment (for each type of capital good) is obtained by dividing the relevant investment deflator by the consumption deflator. The solid line plots year fixed effects from a regression of log relative prices on year fixed effects and country fixed effects to account for entry and exit during the sample period and level differences in relative prices. Year fixed effects are normalized to show percent change from the relative investment prices in 1990. Shaded areas indicate 95 percent confidence intervals. Other investment incudes intellectual property investment, such as research and development. AEs = advanced economies; EMDEs = emerging market and developing economies. IT = information technology.

Figure 3.3. Absolute and Relative Prices of Machinery and Equipment across Countries in 2011
(Ratio)

Relative to the price of consumption, the prices of machinery and equipment are significantly higher in emerging market and developing economies than in advanced economies. Lower-income countries also face marginally higher absolute prices of machinery and equipment.

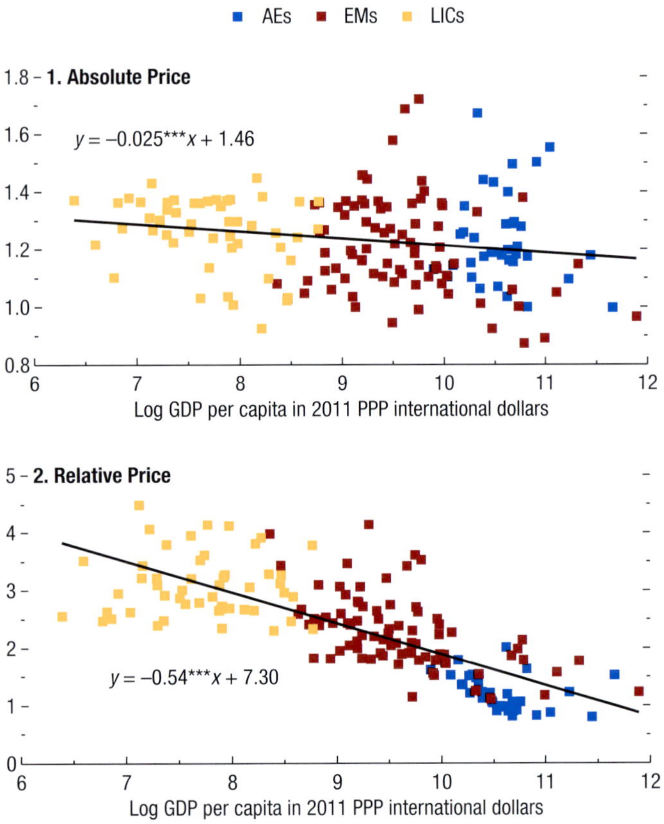

Sources: International Comparison Program (ICP) 2011; *World Economic Outlook*; and IMF staff calculations.
Note: The absolute price of machinery and equipment is the price level of machinery and equipment relative to its US level, derived by the ICP using a similar basket of products across countries. The relative price is the price of machinery and equipment relative to the price of consumption. See Online Annex 3.1 for a detailed description of country coverage, data sources, and methodology. AEs = advanced economies; EMs = emerging market economies; LICs = low-income countries; PPP = purchasing power parity. $^{***}p < 0.01$; $^{**}p < 0.05$; $^{*}p < 0.1$.

Second, the decline in the relative price of *tangible tradable* investment goods (namely, machinery and capital equipment and transportation equipment) is widespread. Compared with the early 1990s, by 2014, the price of machinery and equipment has declined relative to the consumption deflator in all advanced economies, 87 percent of emerging market economies, and 68 percent of low-income developing countries. In contrast, trends in the relative price of structures are very different across broad country groups.

Across Countries

Despite the broad-based decline in the relative price of tradable capital goods over time, the prices of these goods vary substantially across countries, especially relative to the price of consumption. According to the latest data from the International Comparison Program (ICP), which collects prices of comparable baskets of goods and services across countries, the absolute price of machinery and equipment in 2011 was inversely related to countries' development levels, with lower-income countries facing slightly higher prices than advanced economies. The same basket of machinery and equipment costs about 8 percent more in the median low-income country than in the median advanced economy. The difference between advanced economies and lower-income countries is particularly striking for the price of machinery and equipment relative to the countries' consumption price level, with the price in the median low-income country being 2.7 times the price in the median advanced economy (Figure 3.3).[8] Online price data from a global retailer of electronic goods, such as computers, cellular phones, and tablets, across a sample of 27 advanced and emerging market economies, reveal a similar pattern, as discussed in Box 3.2.

The dramatic and widespread changes in the relative prices of capital goods over the past three decades, against a backdrop of large cross-country differences in these relative prices at a particular point in time, raise a number of questions. How significant is the relative price of capital goods for countries' real investment rates? What are the drivers of the relative prices of tradable investment goods? What is required for the downward trend in these prices to continue? And, if the relative price of capital goods is indeed important for real investment, what can lower-income countries

[8]Comparable cross-country data on the price of capital goods are extremely scarce. The key source is the ICP, which collects detailed price data through cross-country surveys every 5–10 years. Using data from the 1985 and 1996 ICP rounds, Eaton and Kortum (2001) and Hsieh and Klenow (2007) find a strong negative correlation between relative investment prices and the level of development, similar to findings in this chapter. At the same time, they find little correlation between absolute prices of capital goods and per capita GDP. As argued by Alfaro and Ahmed (2009), the absence of a correlation may be attributed to data quality issues, which were largely addressed by methodological improvements in the 2011 ICP round (Feenstra, Inklaar, and Timmer 2015; Deaton and Aten 2017). Mutreja and others (2014) demonstrate that the smaller dispersion in absolute prices does not necessarily imply the absence of large trade costs.

do to bring down the price of capital goods relative to the price of consumption in their economies?

The Relative Price of Capital Goods: A Simple Framework

Theoretically, the importance of the relative price of investment in investment decisions is not hard to establish. As economic agents decide how to allocate their limited resources between consuming today and investing in machinery and equipment that will increase their future output, the price at which they can trade consumption goods for capital goods will be among the key influences of that choice (see, for example, Sarel 1995 and Restuccia and Urrutia 2001 for a simple theoretical framework). All else equal, a decline in the price of capital goods relative to other prices in an economy would make it more attractive for agents to invest than to consume and hence lead to higher real investment rates (in other words, a higher ratio of real investment to real output).[9] Of course, investment decisions, which hinge on a comparison between the user cost of capital and its marginal product, are influenced by many other factors, such as expectations of economic prospects, the availability and cost of finance, the quantity of capital already in use relative to the desired capital stock, the rate of depreciation of capital goods, agents' impatience, and the like.

The relative price of capital goods, in turn, is shaped by several factors. Of prime importance is the efficiency with which an economy can produce machinery and equipment (or other tradable goods that it can exchange for investment goods) compared with the efficiency in other sectors.[10] In countries that import a significant fraction of investment goods (as in many emerging market and developing economies), the relative price of machinery and equipment also reflects prices that international suppliers charge for these goods and other factors that drive a wedge between international and domestic prices. These factors include transportation costs, the efficiency of the domestic distribution sector, import tariffs, customs regulations, and the time and cost associated with the logistics of importing goods. Tax policies, such as accelerated depreciation, investment tax credits, and subsidies, as well as the extent of corruption (see Chapter 2 of the April 2019 *Fiscal Monitor*), also influence the relative investment price.[11]

Guided by this simple framework, the chapter proceeds to examine empirically the key sources of differences in the relative prices of tradable capital goods across countries and the factors underpinning the dramatic declines in the relative price of machinery and equipment over time. In the subsequent section, the importance of changes in the relative prices of capital goods for real investment rates and output is quantified using model simulations and empirical analysis of country and sectoral data.

Drivers of Relative Investment Prices

Across Countries

Determining which factors explain the observed differences in the absolute and relative prices of tradable capital goods in the 2011 ICP data is a daunting task. Because price levels of capital goods that bear comparison across countries are available only at one point in time, it is difficult to disentangle the causal contribution of various potential drivers. The chapter examines each potential source of differences in capital goods prices across countries—namely, the prices charged by key exporters, trade costs, and relative efficiency in the production of tradable goods—and relates these to the relative price of capital goods from the 2011 ICP data.

To assess whether differences in prices charged by key capital goods exporters can explain the higher relative prices of capital goods observed in emerging market and developing economies (compared with advanced economies), the chapter examines highly disaggregated data on trade in capital goods. Given that a small number of countries account for the bulk of global exports of machinery and equipment (Figure 3.4, panels 1–2), and given that most emerging market and developing econo-

[9]In a closed economy, where investment goods are produced only domestically, the relationship between the relative price of capital goods and investment is less clear cut, as discussed in Foley and Sidrauski (1970).

[10]Hsieh and Klenow (2007) presents a simple two-sector model that delivers these patterns for relative prices, under the assumption that markups, factor intensities, and factor prices are equal across sectors. The relative productivity in the production of capital goods across countries is conceptually tightly linked to countries' relative efficiency in the production of all tradable goods, including tradable consumer goods (the well-known Balassa-Samuelson effect).

[11]See Estevadeordal and Taylor (2013) for the role of tariffs; Sarel (1995) for the role of taxes; and Justiniano, Primiceri, and Tambalotti (2011) for investment-specific technology shocks that would affect relative sectoral productivity. Cross-country differences in the relative prices of capital have been emphasized as an important factor explaining the lack of capital flows from rich to poor economies, as discussed in Caselli and Feyrer (2007).

Figure 3.4. Unit Values of Tradable Capital Goods across Countries

A relatively small number of advanced economies and China account for a large share of global production and exports of capital goods. Unit values of capital goods exports by five major exporters are not systematically correlated with the per capita income of the importing country.

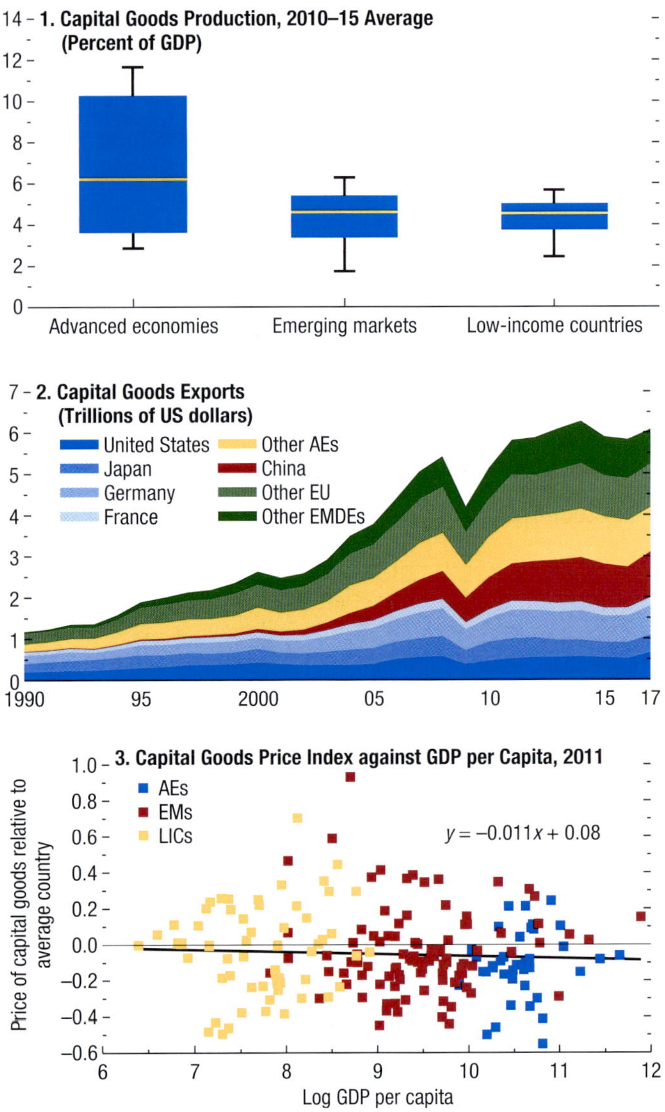

Sources: Eora Multi-Region Input-Output database; Eurostat; Ministry of Finance of Japan; UN Comtrade database; US Census Bureau; and IMF staff calculations.
Note: Panel 1 shows the cross-country distribution of the average 2010–15 production of capital goods as percent of GDP, using Eora sectors 9 and 10 to identify capital goods. The horizontal line inside each box represents the median; the upper and lower edges of each box show the top and bottom quartiles; and the black markers denote the top and bottom deciles. Panel 2 uses Comtrade SITC Revision 2, sector 7, to plot overall capital goods exports of the identified countries. Panel 3 uses export data for major capital goods exporters. For more details on data sources and methodology, see Online Annex 3.3. AEs = advanced economies; EMs = emerging market economies; EMDEs = emerging market and developing economies; EU = European Union; LICs = low-income countries.

mies import a significant proportion of these goods, unit values of various types of machinery and equipment from five of the largest capital goods exporters—the United States, China, Germany, France, and Japan—are compared across importing countries.[12] This approach, which builds on Alfaro and Ahmed (2009), ensures the cross-country comparability of capital goods, given that quality differences within such narrowly defined products sourced from the same exporter are likely minimal.[13] It also permits isolating the differences in the price charged by exporters from other sources of cross-country price variation that are reflected in the ICP data, such as trade, transportation, delivery, and installation costs paid by buyers and discounts that may be available to them.

The analysis uncovers little systematic correlation between the price of capital goods and the per capita income of the importing country when trade data from the five large capital goods exporters are pooled (Figure 3.4, panel 3). Trade costs, on the other hand, exhibit a clear pattern: they tend to be much lower for advanced economies.[14] Despite significant progress in liberalizing the international exchange of goods and services and reducing trade costs, emerging markets, and especially low-income developing countries, still have significantly higher policy-related barriers to trade than advanced economies, in addition to their larger natural trade barriers (Figure 3.5). They tend to be located farther from capital goods exporters and are less connected to global shipping networks. They impose significantly higher tariffs on imports of capital goods, and the time and cost associated with the logistics of importing goods—such as documentary and border compliance and domestic transportation—are substantially higher. Countries with higher trade costs in any of these measures tend to have higher absolute prices of machinery and equipment in the 2011 ICP data (Figure 3.6, panel 1).

[12]While exports of capital goods continue to be concentrated in a few countries, emerging market and developing economies have gained significant market share, accounting for about one-third of global exports in 2016, up from 5 percent in 1990. China has played a particularly prominent role, with its share in global exports rising from 1–2 percent in the 1990s to 18 percent in 2017.

[13]In particular, the analysis relates the unit value of each product to the importing country's per capita GDP, controlling for exporter-product-year fixed effects, similar to Schott (2004), Alfaro and Ahmed (2009), and Manova and Zhang (2012). See Online Annex 3.3 for details on the specification and findings.

[14]Data limitations prevent examination of the potential contribution of tax policies, such as accelerated depreciation or investment tax credits.

Figure 3.5. Trade Costs in 2011
(Median and interquartile range)

Trade costs are higher in emerging market and developing economies.

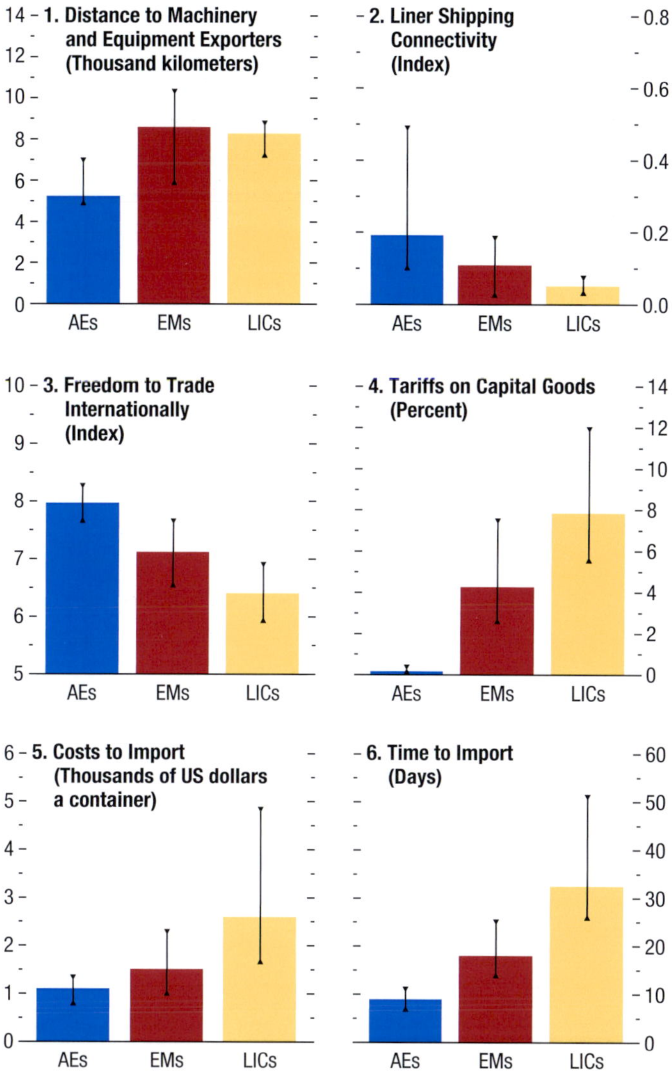

Sources: CEPII, GeoDist database; Eora Multi-Region Input-Output database; Feenstra and Romalis (2014); Fraser Institute; United Nations Conference on Trade and Development (UNCTAD); World Bank, Doing Business Indicators; and IMF staff calculations.
Note: Distance to exporters of machinery and equipment is calculated as the weighted average of a country's distance to all other countries, where the weights are equal to the partner countries' exports of capital goods as a share of global capital goods exports. The UNCTAD liner shipping connectivity index captures how well countries are connected to global shipping networks based on five components of the maritime transport sector: number of ships, their container-carrying capacity, maximum vessel size, number of services, and number of companies that deploy container ships in a country's port. The Fraser Institute's Freedom to Trade Internationally index is based on four different types of trade restrictions: tariffs, quotas, hidden administrative restraints, and controls on exchange rate and the movement of capital. The cost and time indicators measure the cost (excluding tariffs) and time associated with three sets of procedures—documentary compliance, border compliance, and domestic transport—within the overall process of importing a shipment of goods.
AEs = advanced economies; EMs = emerging market economies;
LICs = low-income countries.

Figure 3.6. Trade Costs, Relative Productivity, and the Price of Capital Goods in 2011

The absolute price of machinery and equipment in 2011 was higher in countries with larger trade costs. Trade costs and labor productivity in the tradable versus the nontradable sector can together explain a significant share of the cross-country variation in the relative price of machinery and equipment.

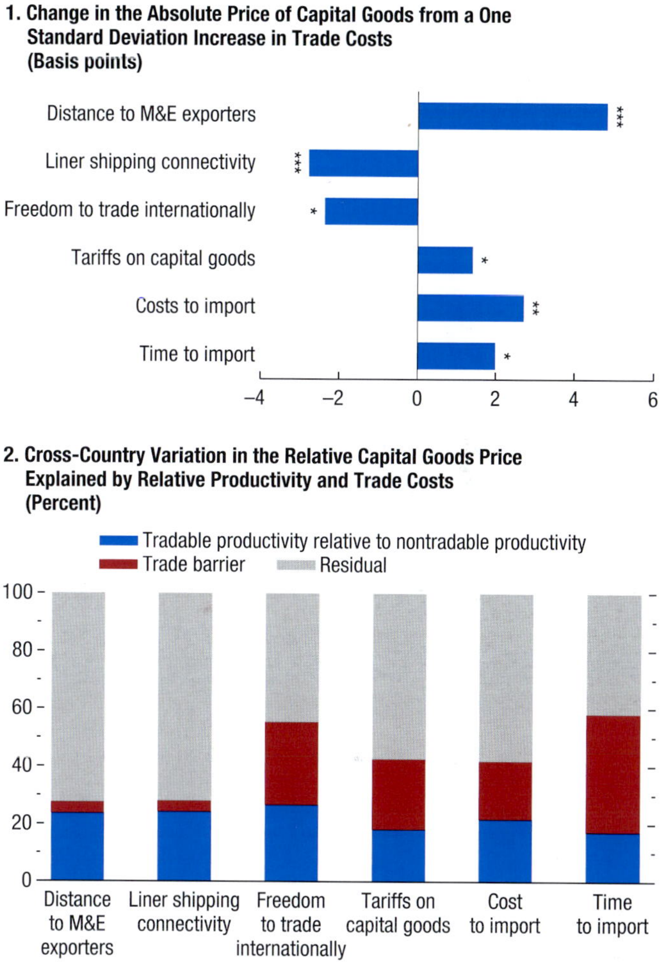

Source: IMF staff calculations.
Note: Panel 1 depicts the percent change in the 2011 International Comparison Program (ICP) absolute price of machinery and equipment associated with a one standard deviation increase in alternative measures of trade costs, based on estimates in Online Annex Table 3.4.1. In panel 2, the cross-country variation in the 2011 ICP price of machinery and equipment relative to consumption is decomposed into the share explained by differences in the labor productivity in the tradable goods sectors relative to the nontradable goods sectors, and alternative measures of trade costs, based on estimates in Online Annex Table 3.4.2. See notes to Figure 3.5 for definitions and sources of trade costs. M&E = machinery and equipment.
***$p < 0.01$; **$p < 0.05$; *$p < 0.1$.

Putting all the pieces together as outlined in the conceptual framework, the chapter next examines the contribution of efficiency in the production of tradable goods relative to efficiency in the nontradable sector, as well as alternative measures of trade costs' contribution to the cross-country variation in the relative prices of capital goods.[15] As shown in panel 2 of Figure 3.6, relative productivity differences in the production of tradable goods and trade costs can together explain up to 60 percent of the cross-country variation in the relative price of machinery and equipment, depending on which measure of trade cost is used.[16] Interestingly, policy-related trade barriers, such as tariffs and cost and time of importing, are a more powerful predictor of relative prices than are natural barriers to trade, such as distance and connectivity. While causal interpretation is difficult in the cross-country setting and, in light of the likely relationship between relative productivity and trade barriers, these findings are consistent with the idea that the relative prices of capital goods are higher in emerging market and developing economies due both to higher trade barriers and lower productivity in the production of capital goods and tradable goods more broadly.[17]

[15]The chapter estimates a simple ordinary least squares regression of the log of the relative price of machinery and equipment (using ICP 2011 data) on the log of the relative labor productivity in the tradable-goods-producing sectors and alternative measures of trade costs, which are included one at a time. In a second step, the regression estimates are used to decompose the variation in the log of relative prices into the variance that can be explained by the relative productivity measure versus trade costs. Given the cross-sectional nature of the data, this analysis is purely illustrative. As elaborated in the next section, relative productivity and trade costs are not independent of one another, complicating the interpretation of their estimated contribution to the variation in relative prices. The relative productivity in the tradable goods sector may be affected by trade barriers, as production of tradable goods likely relies on imported inputs. Furthermore, policy-related trade barriers may be erected with the goal of protecting low-productivity tradable goods sectors. See Online Annex 3.4 for further details on the specification and findings.

[16]Given the high correlation among different components of trade costs, including all of the measures considered in the same regression does not significantly increase the share of variation in relative prices that can be explained by trade costs.

[17]Sposi (2015) similarly argues that trade barriers play an important role in explaining the relative price of tradable goods and services across countries, noting that removing trade barriers would eliminate more than one-half of the observed gap in relative prices between rich and poor countries.

Over Time

While cross-country variation in relative capital goods prices has been the focus so far, this section aims to shed light on the drivers of the big declines in the relative prices of tradable capital goods seen in most countries over the past 30 years. The analysis attempts to disentangle the roles of technological progress—which may have boosted productivity of the capital goods sectors—and deepening trade integration. To do so, it follows a two-step approach. First, sectoral producer price data across 40 advanced and emerging market economies during 1995–2011 from the World Input-Output Database are analyzed to estimate the elasticity of producer prices to changes in sectoral labor productivity and exposure to international trade (as measured by import penetration—the ratio of imports to domestic value added). The analysis controls for all factors that affect prices equally across sectors within a country in a particular year (such as exchange rate fluctuations and policies, commodity price changes, aggregate demand and productivity shocks, and the like) and all time-invariant differences in prices across countries and sectors.[18] Given the endogenous nature of trade exposure, the analysis isolates changes in import penetration that were triggered by policy choice, by using import tariffs as an instrument.[19] Second, the estimated elasticities are combined with the change in relative labor productivity and trade exposure of the capital goods sector to estimate how much each factor can account for the decline in the relative prices of machinery and equipment during 2000–11. Recognizing that exposure to foreign competition affects relative domestic prices indirectly through its impact on sectoral productivity, the decomposition attempts to separate out the contributions made by trade-related changes in labor productivity and changes in productivity due to other factors (such as sectoral technological advances) in the decline in the sectoral price of machinery and equipment.[20]

[18]See Online Annex 3.5 for further details. The analysis relies on producer prices due to their availability for a wide range of sectors and countries. All sectoral variables are measured relative to their economy-wide equivalent.

[19]While widely used in the literature, the choice of tariffs as an instrument for trade integration does not fully address endogeneity concerns as policymakers may set tariff rates in response to various political economy considerations.

[20]For evidence on the productivity-enhancing effects of trade reforms, see, among others, Amiti and Konings (2007); Topalova and Khandelwal (2011); and Ahn and others (2019).

Table 3.1. Sectoral Producer Prices

	Relative Producer Prices			Relative Productivity
	OLS	OLS	IV	IV
Dependent Variables:	(1)	(2)	(3)	(4)
Relative Import Penetration$_{t-1}$	−0.135***	−0.107***	−0.574***	1.363***
	(0.033)	(0.037)	(0.163)	(0.363)
Difference for Capital Goods Sectors		−0.191**	0.033	1.407**
		(0.081)	(0.322)	(0.671)
Relative Productivity$_{t-1}$	−0.316***	−0.314***	−0.328***	
	(0.035)	(0.035)	(0.032)	
Number of Observations	16,077	16,077	16,077	16,077
R^2	0.62	0.62	0.56	0.91
Relative Import Penetration for Capital Goods Sectors		−0.298***	−0.541*	2.770***
		(0.071)	(0.287)	(0.564)

Source: IMF staff calculations.
Note: All regressions include country-year and country-sector fixed effects. Standard errors clustered at the country and sector level are in parentheses. Difference for capital goods sectors refers to the interaction term between import penetration and a dummy indicating whether a sector produces capital goods. IV = instrumental variable; OLS = ordinary least squares. See Online Annex 3.5 for details.
***$p < 0.01$; **$p < 0.05$; *$p < 0.1$.

The econometric analysis (details of which can be found in Online Annex 3.5 and Table 3.1) confirms that both greater exposure to trade and faster productivity growth lead to lower domestic producer prices. A 1 percent increase in the import ratio, which can be achieved by a 0.7 percentage point cut in tariffs, reduces the sectoral producer price by about 0.5 percent. Changes in labor productivity also have a significant impact on producer prices, with a 1 percent increase in sectoral labor productivity reducing producer prices by about 0.3 percent. Confirming findings of other studies, the analysis also uncovers a strong positive effect of policy-induced changes in import penetration on labor productivity at the sector level (Table 3.1, column 4). Labor productivity of the capital-goods-producing sector is particularly sensitive to deepening trade integration—a finding consistent with the larger reliance on global value chains for the production of these goods (Figure 3.1, panel 7).[21]

Figure 3.7 decomposes the decline in the relative price of the machinery and equipment producing sectors relative to the price of consumption between 2000 and 2011 into four parts: (1) the direct effect of deepening trade integration; (2) the effect of trade integration through higher labor productivity; (3) the effect of higher labor productivity, which is not due to

[21]These results suggest that, if low-income countries were to bring capital goods tariffs to the level of those in advanced economies (in other words, they reduce tariffs by roughly 8 percentage points), the price of investment goods would decline by about 16 percent (with roughly 40 percent of the decline coming from the direct trade integration effect and the rest coming from higher productivity in the capital goods sector due to greater import competition).

Figure 3.7. Contributions to Changes in Relative Producer Prices of Capital Goods: 2000–11
(Percent)

The decline in the price of capital goods relative to the price of consumption has been supported by faster labor productivity growth and deepening trade integration.

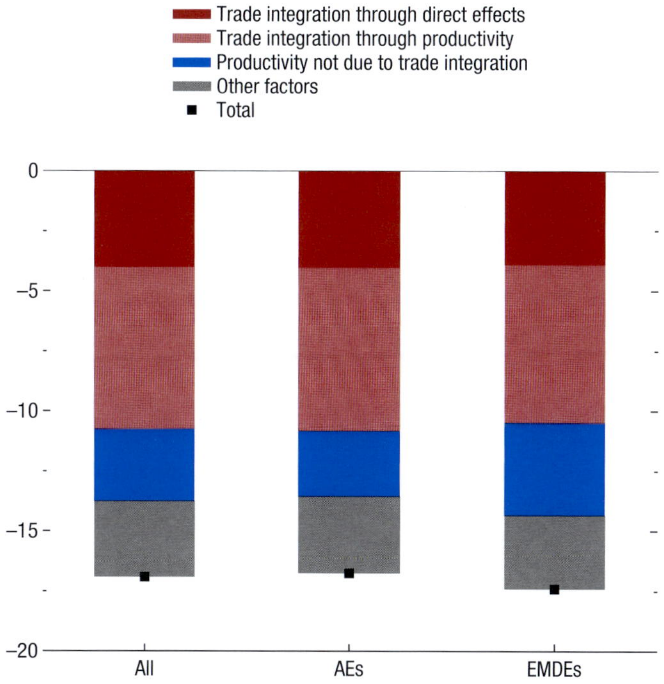

Source: IMF staff calculations.
Note: The figure combines the estimated elasticities of producer prices to trade integration and relative labor productivity from Table 3.1 and changes in these factors for the capital goods sector between 2000 and 2011 to compute their contribution to the observed change in the producer price of capital goods relative to the price of consumption. See Online Annex 3.5 for a detailed description of country coverage, data sources, and methodology. AEs = advanced economies; EMDEs = emerging market and developing economies.

deepening trade integration; and (4) a residual. Deepening trade integration accounts for the bulk of the decline in relative prices of machinery and equipment, both through its direct effect on producer prices and, indirectly, through higher labor productivity of domestic capital goods producers. Productivity gains in the capital-goods-producing sectors, which cannot be directly linked to trade integration, are also a significant factor.

The empirical exercise also suggests that a nontrivial portion of the decline in the price of investment goods, especially in emerging market and developing economies, can be attributed to other factors. These could include the downward trend in world interest rates, financial liberalization, and the emergence of China as a key supplier of tradable investment goods over this period (see Figure 3.4, panel 2 and Online Annex 3.3).[22]

Macroeconomic Implications of Shocks to the Price of Capital Goods

The last section of this chapter aims to quantify the relevance of relative investment prices for macroeconomic outcomes. How much does the relative price of capital goods matter for a country's real investment rate? What share of the dramatic increase in machinery and equipment investment over the past 30 years can be attributed to the decline in the relative price of these goods? To answer these questions, the analysis relies both on model-based explorations and on empirical evidence.[23]

As discussed in Box 3.3, analysis of the macroeconomic effects of the relative price of investment within a structural model is insightful as it captures the aggregate effect of exogenous changes in relative investment prices in a general equilibrium environment, which accounts for all feedback mechanisms in the economy. Moreover, given that relative prices within an economy are endogenously determined, model simulations make it possible to isolate changes in these prices that are driven by specific exogenous shocks. As a result, their effects on investment rates and other macroeconomic outcomes can be credibly traced. Using the IMF's Global Integrated Monetary and Fiscal model, the analysis reveals that both shocks to the relative productivity of the investment-goods-producing sector and tariff cuts that permanently lower the price of capital goods imports lead to sizable and long-lasting increases in the real investment rate in a representative emerging market economy. Shocks that result in a 1 percent decline in the price of investment relative to consumption lead to a roughly 0.8 percent increase in the ratio of real investment to real GDP in the medium term.[24] Guided by these findings, the empirical analysis sets out to examine whether the model predictions are reflected in the historical relationship between the relative prices of machinery and equipment and real investment rates, at both the country and sectoral levels.

Cross-Country Empirical Evidence

The cross-country analysis relies on over 60 years of data across 180 advanced and emerging market and developing economies from the latest release of the Penn World Table database. Using a reduced-form framework, the analysis relates real investment in machinery and equipment as a share of a country's real output and the price of machinery and equipment relative to the price of consumption. The analysis controls for all global shocks (for example, global financial conditions, commodity price changes, uncertainty, and world economic prospects), all time-invariant country characteristics, and a host of other country-specific and time-varying factors shown by economic theory and previous studies to shape investment rates. These include proxies for the availability and cost of finance within each country, the strength of economic prospects, exposure to global markets and commodity price fluctuations, and the quality of institutions and infrastructure. The estimation is based on five-year averages to smooth out cyclical fluctuations and approximate more closely the medium-term relationship between the relative price and investment rate uncovered in the structural model simulations.

Estimation results, detailed in Online Annex 3.6, confirm that real investment rates are shaped by

[22]Capital-goods-producing sectors tend to be more capital intensive than other sectors in developing economies. Hence, easier access to financing may benefit capital goods production more than other sectors, contributing to a decline in the relative price of investment.

[23]As discussed in the conceptual framework, investment decisions are shaped by numerous factors. A comprehensive analysis of the relative importance of all potential factors is beyond the scope of this chapter. The goal of the analysis is to zoom in on the relative price as a potential driver of real investment rates and attempt to provide suggestive evidence of its quantitative importance.

[24]For an average emerging market and developing economy with a ratio of real investment to real output of about 22 percent, this finding would imply that a 1 percent decline in the relative price of investment would lead to an increase in the investment rate to 22.2 percent.

Table 3.2 Real Investment Rate and the Relative Price of Machinery and Equipment

Dependent Variable: Log Real Investment-to-GDP Ratio	Cross-Country Regressions: All (1)	Post-1990 (2)	EMDEs (3)	Sectoral Regressions (4)	(5)
Log Relative Price	−0.377***	−0.292*	−0.491***	−0.326***	−0.528***
	(0.116)	(0.171)	(0.161)	(0.078)	(0.068)
Number of Observations	658	553	457	971	971
Number of Countries	127	127	93	18	18
R^2	0.41	0.36	0.38	0.94	0.93
First Stage F-Statistic	118.80	81.81	64.04	644.60	728.80

Source: IMF staff calculations.
Note: The dependent variable is log real machinery and equipment investment-to-GDP ratio. Regressions are estimated with data averaged over nonoverlapping five-year windows using instrumental variable regressions, where the main independent variable—log price of machinery and equipment relative to consumption—is instrumented with its lagged value. All cross-country panel regressions in columns (1)–(3) control for country and period fixed effects, and a set of other determinants of investment-to-GDP ratios. Sectoral regression in column (4) is estimated with country-period and country-sector fixed effects, and in column (5) with period and country-sector fixed effects, where period refers to the nonoverlapping five-year windows. Standard errors clustered at the country level are in parentheses. See Online Annexes 3.6 and 3.7 for details. EMDEs = emerging market and developing economies.
***$p < 0.01$; **$p < 0.05$; *$p < 0.1$.

a variety of factors. Although estimates are often imprecise, a stronger regulatory environment, higher trade and financial integration, lower-cost finance, and greater financial development—as well as better infrastructure—are all associated with a higher ratio of real investment in machinery and equipment to real output. Importantly, the analysis reveals a strong and statistically significant negative relationship between real investment in machinery and equipment and its relative price (Table 3.2). The findings are robust to alternative specifications, focusing on the post-1990 period, examining the sample of emerging market and developing economies only, and using alternative instrumental variable strategies to correct for the negative bias that may arise from potentially correlated measurement errors in the real investment rate and its price. A 1 percent decline in the relative prices of tradable capital goods is associated with a 0.3–0.5 percent increase in the real investment rate over a five-year period. It is important to note that these empirical estimates likely represent an upper bound of the true effect of changes in relative price on real investment rates. As discussed above, relative investment prices are endogenous and reflect many factors, including changes in policies that could have a direct impact on investment rates.

Sectoral Empirical Evidence

A sectoral perspective can complement the cross-country analysis in an important way. The relative price of capital goods is but one of the considerations that shape investment decisions. While the cross-country analysis attempts to control for many factors, the estimated relationship between real investment rates and prices could be biased due to the omission of factors that may correlate with relative prices but are not properly captured in the estimation. Sectoral analysis makes it possible to isolate the relationship between real investment rates and the price of investment across different sectors while properly accounting for the role of all factors that affect overall investment within a country in a particular year. These include financial conditions, economy-wide growth prospects, quality of regulations that affect investment returns, exchange rate fluctuations and policies, international capital flows, availability of complementary public infrastructure, and the like.

The analysis relies on EU and World KLEMS data covering 18 (mostly advanced) economies over 1971–2015 to construct measures of real investment in machinery and equipment and the relative prices of these capital goods specific to 15 broad economic sectors.[25] As in the cross-country analysis, the baseline estimation relates machinery and equipment investment as a share of sectoral real value added to relative prices, using five-year averages. The estimated elasticity, according to which a 1 percent decline in the relative price of machinery and equipment is associated with a 0.2–0.5 percent increase in the real investment rate in these capital goods, is comparable to those uncovered in the cross-country analysis. Further, as in the model simulations presented in Box 3.3, declining investment

[25]See Online Annex 3.7 for details.

Figure 3.8. Elasticity of Real Investment-to-GDP Ratio to Relative Price of Capital Goods: Model Simulations versus Empirical Evidence
(Percent)

Model simulations and empirical evidence deliver broadly consistent estimates of the elasticity of the real investment-to-real GDP ratio to the relative price of capital goods.

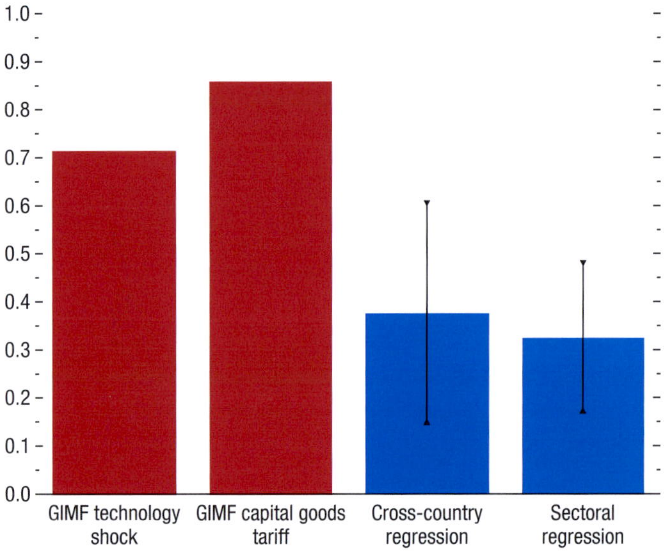

Source: IMF staff calculations.
Note: The bars depict the simulated/estimated elasticity of the real investment-to-GDP ratio to the price of capital goods relative to the price of consumption. See Box 3.3 for details on the model, and Online Annexes 3.6–7 for details on the empirical analyses. GIMF = Global Integrated Monetary and Fiscal model.

Figure 3.9. Contributions of Relative Prices to Increases in Real Investment in Machinery and Equipment, 1990–94 to 2010–14
(Percent)

Between 1990–94 and 2010–14, real investment-to-real GDP ratios in machinery and equipment grew by approximately 60 percent. A significant portion of this increase can be explained by the precipitous fall in the relative price of machinery and equipment.

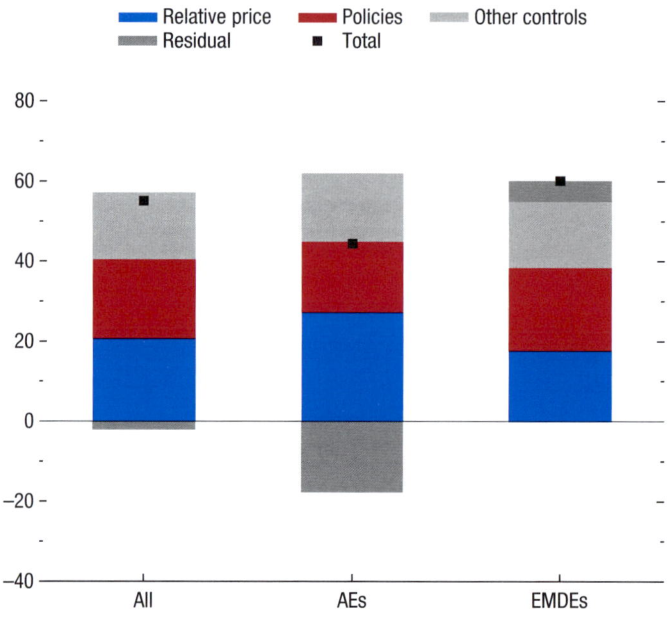

Source: IMF staff calculations.
Note: The figure presents the contribution to the observed increase in real machinery and transport equipment investment-to-GDP ratios between 1990–94 and 2010–14 from the relative price of machinery and transport equipment, various policies, and other controls. See Online Annex 3.6 for a detailed description of the estimated model. Black square indicates the total change in real machinery equipment investment-to-real GDP ratios. AEs = advanced economies; EMDEs = emerging market and developing economies.

prices are linked to higher output in the sector and marginally higher labor productivity. Analysis of firm-level data from Colombia further confirms that lower capital goods prices resulting from a sizable tariff cut following trade reform in 2011 prompted firms to boost investment (see Box 3.4).

Figure 3.8 compares the findings across the structural model, cross-country, and sectoral analyses, revealing a consistent pattern. Across all three approaches, the evidence that the relative price of capital goods matters for investment decisions is strong. It is challenging to obtain an unbiased estimate of the elasticity of real investment with regard to prices, given the endogenous nature of relative price changes and problems with measurement. With those difficulties in mind, Figure 3.9—as a purely illustrative exercise—uses the estimated elasticity from the cross-country analysis (Table 3.2) and the post-1990 change in the relative price of capital goods in each country to decompose the change in the real investment rate. These changes comprise the parts attributable to (1) the decline in real investment prices; (2) the change in relevant policies; (3) other factors, such as global trends in investment, convergence, and growth expectations; and (4) the residual. Improvements in policies and policy frameworks have contributed significantly to the rise of real investment in machinery and equipment in both advanced as well as emerging market and developing economies. The dramatic decline in the relative prices of tradable capital goods that occurred alongside can also explain a sizable share of the increase in investment in tradable capital goods in advanced and emerging market and developing economies. The anecdotal evidence presented in Box 3.1 on the rapid rise in investment in low-carbon technologies with steeper declines in production costs—and firm-level evidence from Colombia on the investment effects of arguably exogenous changes in the price of capital goods, discussed in Box 3.4—also point to relatively high price-elasticity of investment.

Summary and Policy Implications

The strengthening of investment in emerging market and developing economies over the past three decades was supported by their improved macroeconomic policy and institutional frameworks, the synchronized pickup in economic activity until the global financial crisis of 2008–09, and falling global real interest rates. But it also coincided with dramatic declines in the relative price of tradable capital goods, likely reflecting efficiency gains from international trade and advances in information and communications technology that led to more efficient production of capital goods. Could rising trade tensions, slower trade integration, and sluggish productivity growth threaten this potential driver of investment going forward?

This chapter sets out to answer this question by (1) examining whether declines in the relative prices of machinery and equipment have historically provided a quantitatively important boost to investment rates, and (2) shedding light on the drivers of the precipitous fall in the price of tradable investment goods relative to other prices in the economy.

Using both structural model simulations and empirical evidence, the chapter finds that the relative price of investment goods is an important driver of real investment rates in both advanced as well as emerging market and developing economies. The global financial crisis left lasting scars on investment worldwide. However, from a long-term perspective, real investment rates in machinery and equipment have increased significantly in both groups of economies. While exact quantification is challenging, empirical evidence suggests that a nontrivial share of the rise in the real investment rates in machinery and equipment in both groups of economies can be attributed to the dramatic fall in the relative price of these goods over the past three decades. The chapter's sectoral analysis of relative producer prices reveals that the significant decline in the price of machinery and equipment, in turn, was driven by faster productivity growth in the capital-goods-producing sector and deepening trade integration, which has bolstered price competition in domestic markets and improved the efficiency of production processes in the investment goods sector.

Taken together, the chapter's analyses suggest that the slowing pace of trade liberalization since the mid-2000s, and especially the possibility of its reversal in some advanced economies, could interfere with the tailwind to machinery and equipment investment generated by the falling price of capital goods. This finding provides an additional, often overlooked, argument in support of policies aimed at reducing trade costs and reinvigorating international trade.

Many emerging market and developing economies still maintain tariff and other trade barriers that significantly raise the relative price of investment paid by domestic investors.[26] Effective import tariffs on capital goods in 2011 were about 4 percent in emerging market and 8 percent in low-income developing countries, compared with close to zero in advanced economies (Figure 3.5, panel 4). Fully implementing commitments under the World Trade Organization's Trade Facilitation Agreement could reduce non-tariff barriers by an equivalent of a 15-percentage point tariff cut in less-developed economies (WTO 2015).

In advanced economies, which have similarly benefited from declining capital goods prices over the past three decades, avoiding protectionist measures and resolving disagreements without raising trade costs, will be crucial to prevent further weakening of the lackluster investment growth since the global financial crisis of a decade ago.[27] For all economies, reviving trade liberalization, reducing trade costs from both tariff and other barriers, and addressing areas most relevant for continued integration in the contemporary global economy—such as regulatory cooperation, e-commerce, and leveraging complementarities between investment and trade—would help maintain the pace of decline in relative capital goods prices and further spur investment. These benefits would complement the better-known welfare and productivity gains

[26]While the vast majority of emerging market and developing economies still have large investment needs, other countries (such as China) face the complex task of rebalancing growth models toward consumption and services, after decades of investment-led stimulus and policy interventions aimed at strengthening capital goods production and exports. Policy challenges are also different in some low-income developing countries where import tariffs represent a significant source of government revenue, and tariff reform would need to be accompanied by measures to compensate for revenue losses.

[27]Cavallo and Landry (2018) find that the rise in capital imports in the United States has added 5 percent to its output per hour since the 1970s, and that the imposition of tariffs on capital goods could lead to sizable productivity losses over the next decade.

from international trade (for a discussion, see Chapter 2 of the October 2016 WEO).

The analyses in this chapter also highlight the importance of continued technological advances and innovation in the capital-goods-producing sector in both advanced as well as emerging market and developing economies. By lowering the relative price of investment goods, these generate dividends beyond the effect of such advances on aggregate productivity growth. As discussed in Adler and others (2017) and Chapter 2 of the April 2016 *Fiscal Monitor,* policies that encourage research and development, entrepreneurship, and technology transfer more broadly, could also help the capital-goods-producing sector, as would continued investment in education and public infrastructure.

The economic benefits of declining capital goods prices notwithstanding, policymakers need to be mindful of their distributional consequences and potential for job disruptions. As discussed in Chapter 3 of the April 2017 WEO, the decline in the relative price of investment has eroded the share of economic output that goes to labor in economies where many jobs can be easily automated and performed by machines. Policies should be designed to help workers better cope with disruptions caused by technological progress and global integration, including through long-term investment in education, programs for skill upgrading throughout workers' careers, and policies facilitating the reallocation of displaced workers to new jobs (see IMF/WB/WTO 2017).

Box 3.1. The Price of Manufactured Low-Carbon Energy Technologies

Increasing use of renewable energy sources could help curb carbon emissions substantially—a necessary step to slow the pace of climate change, which threatens the economic future of countries across the globe (Chapter 3 of the October 2017 *World Economic Outlook*). Once considered uneconomical, in recent years, the cost of installing low-carbon electric generation capacity has declined dramatically for some renewable energy sources.[1] Between 2009 and 2017, prices of solar photovoltaics and onshore wind turbines fell most rapidly, dropping by 76 percent and 34 percent, respectively—making these energy sources competitive alternatives to fossil fuels and more traditional low-carbon sources (Figure 3.1.1).

The authors of this box are Christian Bogmans and Lama Kiyasseh.

[1]This cost is typically measured by the so-called levelized cost of electricity, which measures the lifetime costs of building and operating a power plant divided by its lifetime energy production, based on recently financed projects in countries where deployment took place.

Cost reductions, coupled with favorable policies, have indeed led to a substantial increase in global renewable energy capacity, which grew by about 6.5 percent a year between 2000 and 2017 and captured more than two-thirds of global investment in new generation capacity in recent years. It is only in the past decade, however, with solar and wind emerging as cost-effective power sources, that total investment in renewable energy capacity accelerated, suggesting a strong link between investment and its relative price. While hydropower dominated renewable energy investment up to 2008, investment in wind technologies took the lead in 2009. With their relative price falling precipitously, solar photovoltaics became the most popular investment choice in 2016 (Figure 3.1.2). In 2017, more was invested in solar photovoltaics than in all other low-carbon sources combined.

However, not all low-carbon energy technologies declined in cost. Nuclear energy and hydropower costs rose by 21 percent and 9 percent, respectively, over this period. What explains these divergent price

Figure 3.1.1. Levelized Cost of Electricity of Low-Carbon Energy Sources
(US dollars a megawatt hour)

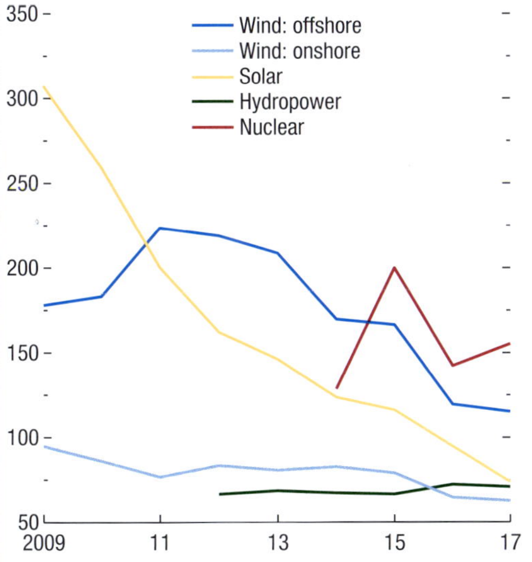

Sources: Bloomberg New Energy Finance; Federal Reserve Economic Data; and IMF staff calculations.
Note: Levelized cost of electricity data has been deflated using GDP deflator and does not include subsidies and taxes.

Figure 3.1.2. Annual Additions to Global Electricity Capacity
(Thousand megawatts)

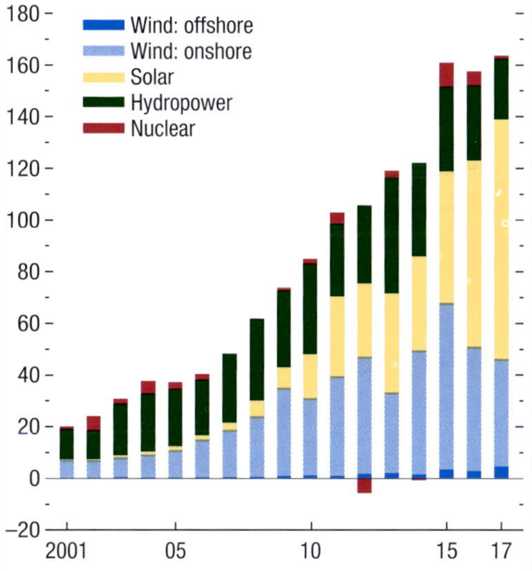

Sources: International Atomic Energy Agency; International Renewable Energy Agency; and IMF staff calculations.
Note: Solar includes solar photovoltaics and concentrated solar power. Hydropower refers to renewable hydropower and excludes pumped storage.

Box 3.1 *(continued)*

paths for energy technologies? The different trajectories of prices of machinery and equipment and those of residential and nonresidential structures (see Figure 3.2) certainly played a role. Nuclear energy and hydropower share similarities with large-scale civil engineering projects, such as the construction of bridges and railroads. Potential cost reduction for these kinds of projects is limited by the lumpiness of investment, relatively little component standardization (Sovacool, Nugent, and Gilbert 2014), construction delays (Berthélemy and Rangel 2015), and increasingly stringent—though necessary—local environmental and safety concerns.

In contrast, research and development in solar and wind technologies, their standardization, and economies of scale (through larger manufacturing plants) have resulted in increasingly efficient solar photovoltaics modules and larger wind turbines, with millions of quasi-identical experiences leading to continuous cost reductions achieved through learning by doing (Kavlak, McNerney, and Trancik 2018). Significant cost reductions in those sectors bode well for prices of electric batteries, whose production could become significantly more efficient with standardization and economies of scale and whose increased use could lastingly reduce carbon emissions, particularly those from the transportation sector.

Box 3.2. Evidence from Big Data: Capital Goods Prices across Countries

The International Comparison Project (ICP) has traditionally been the only data source for prices of comparable baskets of capital goods across countries. However, despite significant improvements, concerns about comparability across countries and methods of price collection remain. These potentially confound cross-country price comparisons (see, for example, Alfaro and Ahmed 2009; Deaton and Heston 2010; Inklaar and Rao 2017). A promising alternative is the use of big data, which allows the comparison of online prices of identical (capital) goods sold across the world. The newly available Billion Prices Project database (Cavallo, Neiman, and Rigobon 2014), used in this box, allows precisely that kind of comparison.

The analysis takes online price information for 674 distinct Apple products across 27 economies, with a monthly frequency from 2009 to 2012.[1] Normalized by US prices, the prices charged for each product sold within the same month across the 27 economies in the sample are compared.

Online retail prices of identical goods across countries differ because they include markups, local taxes and subsidies, transportation costs, and tariffs and other nontariff barriers. Across the 27, mostly advanced, economies for which data are available, significant differences are observed in absolute prices of Apple products, although no clear correlation with the countries' per capita income is seen (Figure 3.2.1, panels 1 and 3). Relative to the overall GDP price level, however, the Billion Prices Project data confirm the regularity established with ICP data and reported in previous studies: the relative prices of capital goods tend to be significantly lower in richer countries (Figure 3.2.1, panels 2 and 4).

Figure 3.2.1. Price of Apple Products and Income
(Percent)

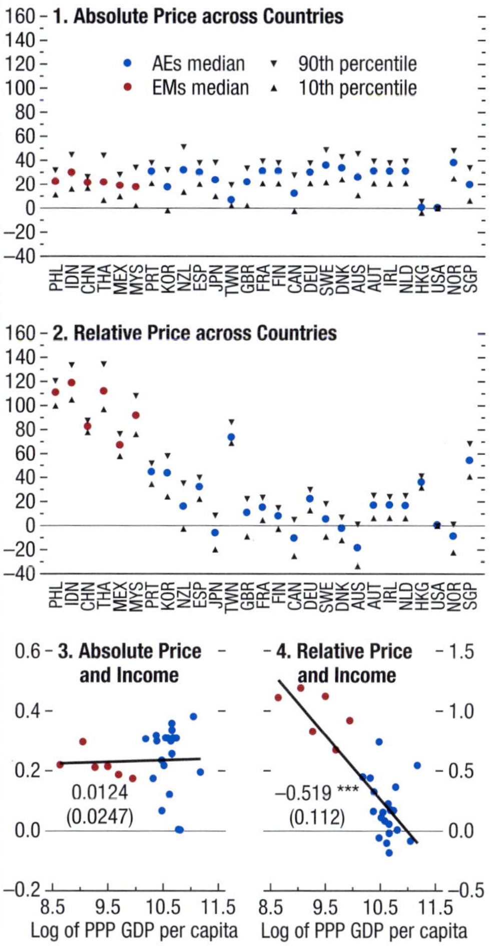

Sources: Billion Prices Project; International Comparison Program; and IMF staff calculations.
Note: Countries on the *x*-axis in panels 1 and 2 are sorted by real GDP per capita in purchasing-power-parity international dollars. Dots denote medians of log prices for each country. Solid lines in panels 3 and 4 denote product-level regression results at monthly frequency, with product-time fixed effects, and standard errors clustered at the country level. Products sold on the website of Apple Inc. but not produced by Apple Inc. are excluded from the sample. Country labels in panels 1 and 2 use International Organization for Standardization (ISO) country codes. AEs = advanced economies; EMs = emerging markets; PPP = purchasing power parity. ***$p < 0.01$; **$p < 0.05$; *$p < 0.1$.

The author of this box is Jilun Xing.

[1]Product categories are, for example, MacBooks, iPhones, iPods, and cables and accessories. Product identifiers specify model, memory, storage, display size, and so on. The online price information from the Billion Price Project database is identical to the offline price of Apple products, except for shipping cost, local taxes, and store promotions (Cavallo, Neiman, and Rigobon 2014). Although Apple products could be considered consumer goods, they are increasingly used as capital goods—for example, roughly half of all iPads are bought by corporate and government users (Goel 2016).

Box 3.3. On the Underlying Source of Changes in Capital Goods Prices: A Model-Based Analysis

The price of investment goods relative to other goods plays a significant role in capital accumulation. The price of investment goods in any country reflects multiple factors, such as the relative (1) price of investment goods in other, capital-goods-exporting, countries; (2) productivity of domestic investment-goods-producing sectors; (3) markups across sectors; and (4) incidence of tariffs and other trade costs. Although changes in any of these factors can affect the price of investment goods, and therefore trigger changes in capital accumulation, the macroeconomic effects may vary, depending on the underlying source of variation.

A structural model helps to formalize and quantify these possible differences. In this box, we use the IMF's Global Integrated Monetary and Fiscal model to study the medium-term macroeconomic effects—in a small emerging market economy—of two scenarios where the relative domestic price of investment goods (relative to the consumer price index) decreases. In the first scenario, the emerging market economy becomes permanently more efficient at producing new capital, in the spirit of Greenwood, Hercowitz, and Krussell (1997); in the second scenario, tariffs charged on imports of capital goods are permanently lowered.

The investment-specific technological change in the first scenario can be interpreted in several ways: greater international diffusion of technological know-how (possibly via global value chains) that disproportionately affects the production of capital (or durables more generally); lower domestic costs incurred by firms in capital goods sectors (for example, thanks to improvements in the regulatory environment); improved organizational efficiency; and so on.[1] In response, and assuming markups do not increase, firms in these sectors would lower their prices relative to the rest of the economy. The second scenario illustrates the effects of a decline in tariffs—or trade costs more broadly—on all imported capital. In this case, the decline in the overall investment price index reflects lower domestic prices of imported capital goods. Both simulations are normalized to obtain a 1 percent decline in the relative price of capital in the long term. Given the model's assumed share of capital goods imports in overall investment spending (about 33 percent), this requires a 4 percentage point permanent decline in investment goods tariffs in the second scenario, with a recurrent fiscal cost of about 0.25 percent of annual GDP.[2]

Figure 3.3.1. Model Simulations
(Deviation from the original steady state, percent)

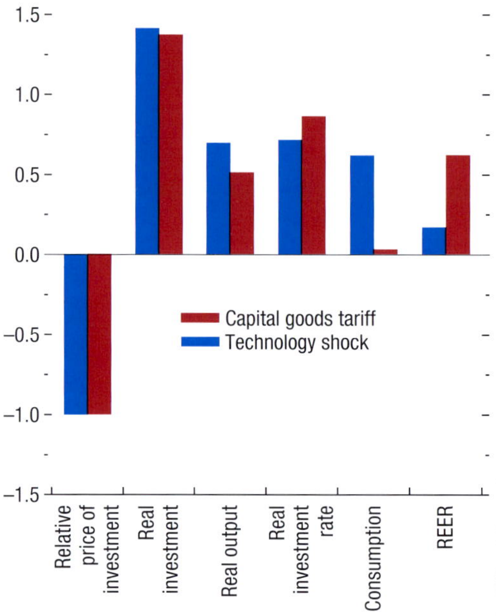

Source: IMF staff calculations.
Note: REER = real effective exchange rate.

The medium-term impact (10 years after the shock) is presented in Figure 3.3.1. In both scenarios, the same decline in capital goods prices increases the returns to capital by similar amounts, thus triggering a similar increase in investment. The effect on output is different, however (0.7 percent of GDP and 0.5 percent of GDP, respectively). This difference is the result of a permanent increase in the efficiency of newly produced capital goods that expands the production possibility frontier of the local economy. As the economy becomes more productive, household income and consumption increase permanently.[3]

The authors of this box are Michal Andrle and Rafael Portillo.

[1]It can be argued that there is greater scope for efficiency gains in capital goods sectors in emerging markets given the greater complexity of production.

[2]The required decrease in tariffs also reflects the real exchange rate depreciation observed in this scenario.

[3]A 1 percent decrease in investment goods prices caused by a decrease in markups in the investment goods sector produces very similar effects to an increase in investment-specific productivity.

Box 3.3 *(continued)*

In the case of the decline in the tariff, there is no such initial expansion in the production possibility frontier (in the capital-goods-producing sector). The incentives to capital accumulation that come from lower capital goods prices can instead be thought of as reflecting a subsidy. Although it becomes cheaper to invest in capital projects, the tariff revenue forgone leads to a government revenue shortfall, which is resolved by lowering public transfers to households. Lower public transfers generate a headwind to private consumption. From a balance of payments perspective, higher relative demand for imports puts pressure on the real effective exchange rate to depreciate, which means an additional headwind to consumption because the domestic consumer basket becomes more expensive. As a result, there is little increase in consumption.

It is worth stressing that the supply-side effects in both scenarios are largely a result of lower investment costs. To illustrate this point, we also simulate a decrease in general tariffs equivalent in fiscal revenue terms to the investment-specific tariff decrease. In this case, there is no visible effect on the domestic relative price of investment. As a result, the increase in investment is much smaller (0.23 percent versus 1.34 percent in the investment-specific tariff scenario), as is the effect on output (0.18 percent versus 0.5 percent).

As these results emphasize, lowering barriers that hamper trade in capital goods and promoting research and development that improve efficiency in the capital goods sectors are good for output, investment, and consumption in the long term, even if they entail some fiscal costs.

Box 3.4. Capital Goods Tariffs and Investment: Firm-Level Evidence from Colombia

This box uses data from Colombia to shed light on the effect of a reduction in the price of capital goods—induced by cuts in capital goods tariffs—on firm-level investment. Given that capital goods prices within an economy are endogenously determined, it is difficult to pin down their causal effect on investment. Firm-level analysis helps overcome this issue by making use of differential, and arguably exogenous, changes in the prices of capital and other goods triggered by a substantial tariff reform in Colombia in 2011. The Colombian tariff reform aimed to simplify the tariff structure and boost economic growth (Torres and Romero 2013). Consequently, between 2010 and 2011, the average tariff rate on imported goods declined by close to 4 percentage points, from 12.5 percent in 2010 to 8.7 percent in 2011 (Figure 3.4.1).

Using an event study analysis, this box examines two different channels through which trade liberalization could affect firms' investment decisions: (1) increased competition, and (2) enhanced access to cheaper and potentially higher-quality inputs, including capital goods. While several studies have examined the productivity effect of tariff cuts through these channels (see, for example, Amiti and Konings 2007), evidence about their effect on investment is scant. The empirical approach relates the change in the firm-level investment rate before and after the tariff reform, which led to reductions in capital goods input tariffs, other input tariffs, and output tariffs. In particular, the following equation is estimated:

$$\Delta Investment_i = \alpha + \beta_1 \Delta Capital\ Input\ Tariff_{s(i)} + \beta_2 \Delta Other\ Input\ Tariff_{s(i)} + \beta_3 \Delta Output\ Tariff_{s(i)} + \epsilon_i,$$

in which $Investment_i$ is defined as investment over total fixed assets for a given firm i.[1] $Output\ Tariff_{s(i)}$

The authors of this box are Sergii Meleshchuk and Yannick Timmer.

[1]The data for investment are taken from Encuesta Anual Manufacturera, an annual survey of manufacturing firms in Colombia. The data on tariffs come from Felbermayr, Teti, and

Figure 3.4.1. Distribution of Tariff Changes between 2010 and 2011
(Percent)

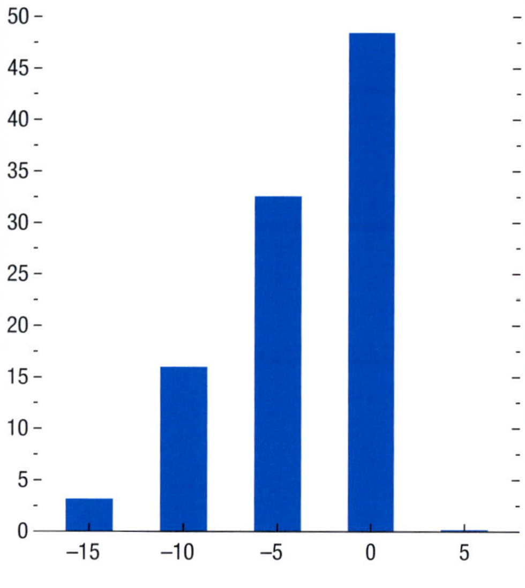

Sources: Meleshchuk and Timmer (2019); and IMF staff calculations.
Note: The histogram shows the change in tariffs on the *x*-axis and the percent of imported goods affected by this tariff change on the *y*-axis.

Figure 3.4.2. Effect on Investment from Cuts in Tariffs on Capital Goods Inputs, Other Inputs, and Output
(Percent)

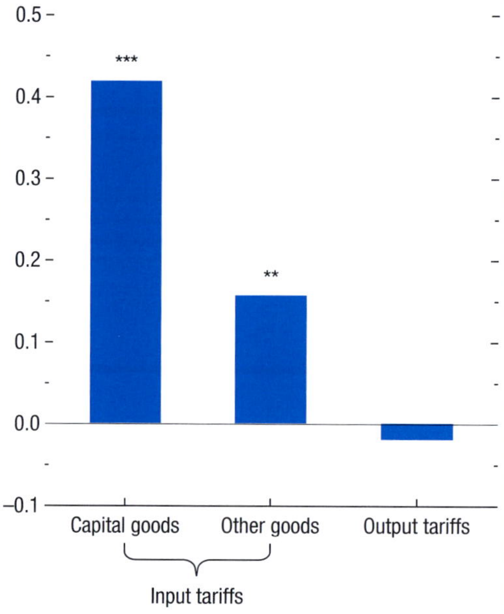

Sources: Meleshchuk and Timmer (2019); and IMF staff calculations.
Note: ***$p < 0.01$; **$p < 0.05$; *$p < 0.1$.

Box 3.4 *(continued)*

is the simple average of most-favored-nation tariffs across Harmonized System six-digit products within the 33 sectors, $s(i)$, and is meant to capture the effect of higher competition on investment rates. *Capital Input Tariff*$_{s(i)}$ and *Other Input Tariff*$_{s(i)}$ are constructed following Amiti and Konings (2007) as weighted averages of output tariffs in all capital goods and other sectors, with weights reflecting the share of inputs from each of the sectors used in the production of the sector ***s*** output, based on the 2007 input-output table. The input tariff variables capture the effect of access to cheaper inputs. Unlike earlier studies, the analysis allows for a differential investment response to cuts in the tariffs on capital goods versus other inputs.

Figure 3.4.2 shows the estimated coefficients on the three types of tariffs. A 1 percentage point reduction in capital goods input tariffs is associated with a 0.4 percentage point increase in investment, a point estimate that is statistically significant at the 1 percent level.[2] A reduction in noncapital input tariffs leads to a smaller (0.15 percentage point) yet still statistically significant increase in investment. This finding echoes the results of model simulations discussed in Box 3.3, which similarly uncover a much smaller investment response to a general tariff cut, compared with a cut in capital goods tariffs. The effect of a reduction in output tariffs is not associated with significant changes in firms' investment decisions, at least in the short term.[3]

These findings present further evidence—from a recent trade reform in a large emerging market economy—that firms' investment choices are sensitive to the price of capital goods.

Yalcin (2018). Use of fixed input-output matrices at the sector level alleviates endogeneity concerns that arise when firm-level input-output matrices are employed.

[2]The coefficients on changes in input tariffs can be interpreted as the effects of changes in prices on investment rates under the assumption that tariffs are fully passed into the prices importers pay. If there is only partial pass-through, the estimated coefficients are attenuated toward zero relative to the true effect of prices.

[3]The results are robust to including standard controls, such as firm size or sales growth. The results are presented using a one-year window, but are also robust to using a wider time window around the tariff cuts.

References

Adler, Gustavo, Romain Duval, Davide Furceri, Sinem Kilic Celik, Ksenia Koloskova, and Marcos Polawski-Ribeiro. 2017. "Gone with the Headwinds: Global Productivity." IMF Staff Discussion Note 17/04, International Monetary Fund, Washington, DC.

Ahn, JaeBin, Era Dabla-Norris, Romain Duval, Bingjie Hu, and Lamin Njie. 2019. "Reassessing the Productivity Gains from Trade Liberalization." *Review of International Economics*, 27(1): 130–54.

Alfaro, Laura, and Faisal Z. Ahmed. 2009. "The Price of Capital: Evidence from Trade Data." Harvard Business School Working Paper 07–073, Harvard Business School, Boston.

Amiti, Mary, and Jozef Konings. 2007. "Trade Liberalization, Intermediate Inputs, and Productivity: Evidence from Indonesia." *American Economic Review* 97 (5): 1611–638.

Armenter, Roc, and Amartya Lahiri. 2012. "Accounting for Development through Investment Prices." *Journal of Monetary Economics* 59: 550–64.

Berthélemy, Michel, and Lina Escobar Rangel. 2015. "Nuclear Reactors' Construction Costs: The Role of Lead-Time, Standardization and Technological Progress." *Energy Policy* 82: 118–30.

Calderón, César, Enrique Moral-Benito, and Luis Servén. 2015. "Is Infrastructure Capital Productive? A Dynamic Heterogeneous Approach." *Journal of Applied Econometrics* 30 (2): 177–98.

Caceres, Carlos, Yan Carriere-Swallow, Ishak Demir, and Bertrand Gruss. 2016. "US Monetary Policy Normalization and Global Interest Rates." IMF Working Paper 16/195, International Monetary Fund, Washington, DC.

Caselli, Francesco, and James Feyrer. 2007. "The Marginal Product of Capital." *The Quarterly Journal of Economics* 122 (2): 535–68.

Cavallo, Alberto, Brent Neiman, and Roberto Rigobon. 2014. "Currency Unions, Product Introductions, and the Real Exchange Rate." *The Quarterly Journal of Economics* 129 (2): 529–95.

Cavallo, Michele, and Anthony Landry. 2018. "Capital-Goods Imports and US Growth." Bank of Canada Staff Working Paper, Bank of Canada, Ottawa.

Chinn, Menzie D., and Hiro Ito. 2006. "What Matters for Financial Development? Capital Controls, Institutions, and Interactions." *Journal of Development Economics* 81 (1): 163–92.

Collins, William J., and Jeffrey G. Williamson. 2001. "Capital Goods Prices and Investment 1879–1950." *Journal of Economic History* 61 (1): 59–94.

DeLong, J. Bradford, and Lawrence H. Summers. 1991. "Equipment Investment and Economic Growth." *Quarterly Journal of Economics* 106: 445–502.

———. 1992. "Equipment Spending and Economic Growth: How Strong is the Nexus?" *Brookings Papers on Economic Activity* (2): 157–99.

———. 1993. "How Strongly Do Developing Economies Benefit from Equipment Investment?" *Journal of Monetary Economics* 32: 395–415.

Deaton, Angus, and Bettina Aten. 2017. "Trying to Understand the PPPs in ICP 2011: Why Are the Results So Different?" *American Economic Journal: Macroeconomics* 9 (1): 243–64.

Deaton, Angus, and Alan Heston. 2010 "Understanding PPPs and PPP-Based National Accounts." *American Economic Journal: Macroeconomics* 2 (4): 1–35.

Eaton, Jonathan, and Samuel Kortum. 2001. "Trade in Capital Goods." *European Economic Review* 45: 1195–235.

Estevadeordal, Antoni, and Alan M. Taylor. 2013. "Is the Washington Consensus Dead? Growth, Openness, and the Great Liberalization, 1970s–2000s." *Review of Economics and Statistics* 95 (5): 1669–690.

Feenstra, Robert, Robert Inklaar, and Marcel Timmer. 2015. "The Next Generation of the Penn World Tables." *American Economic Review* 105 (10): 3150–182.

Feenstra, Robert, and John Romalis. 2014. "International Prices and Endogenous Quality." *Quarterly Journal of Economics* 129 (2): 477–527.

Felbermayr, Gabriel, Feodora Teti, and Erdal Yalcin. 2018. "On the Profitability of Trade Deflection and the Need for Rules of Origin." CESifo Working Paper Series 6929, CESifo Group, Munich.

Foley, Duncan K., and Miguel Sidrauski. 1970. "Portfolio Choice, Investment, and Growth." *American Economic Review* 60 (1): 44–63.

Gaspar, Victor, David Amaglobelo, Mercedes Garcia-Escribano, Delphine Prady, and Mauricio Soto. 2019. "Fiscal Policy and Development: Human, Social and Physical Investment for the SDGs." IMF Staff Discussion Note 19/03, International Monetary Fund, Washington, DC.

Goel, Vindu. 2016. "Once Taunted by Steve Jobs, Companies Are Now Big Customers of Apple." *The New York Times*, August 7.

Greenwood, Jeremy, Zvi Hercowitz, and Per Krussell. 1997. "Long-Run Implication of Investment-Specific Technological Change." *American Economic Review* 87 (3): 342–62.

Gruss, Bertrand, and Suhaib Kebhajz. 2019. "Commodity Terms of Trade: A New Database." IMF Working Paper 19/21, International Monetary Fund, Washington, DC.

Hsieh, Chang-Tai, and Peter J. Klenow. 2007. "Relative Prices and Relative Prosperity." *American Economic Review* 97: 562–85.

Inklaar, Robert, and D.S. Prasada Rao. 2017 "Cross-Country Income Levels over Time: Did the Developing World Suddenly Become Much Richer?" *American Economic Journal: Macroeconomics* 9 (1): 265–90.

International Monetary Fund, World Bank, and World Trade Organization (IMF/WB/WTO). 2017. "Making Trade and Engine of Growth for All: The Case for Trade and for Policies to Facilitate Adjustment." Policy Papers for Discussion at the Meeting of G20 Sherpas, Frankfurt, March 23–24.

Johri, Alok, and Md Mahbubur Rahman. 2017. "The Rise and Fall of India's Relative Investment Price: A Tale of Policy Error and Reform." Unpublished, McMaster University.

Jones, Chad. 1994. "Economic Growth and the Relative Price of Capital." *Journal of Monetary Economics* 34: 359–82.

Justiniano, Alejandro, Giorgio E. Primiceri, and Andrea Tambalotti. 2011. "Investment Shocks and the Relative Price of Investment." *Review of Economic Dynamics* 14 (1): 102–21.

Karabarbounis, Loukas, and Brent Neiman. 2013. "The Global Decline of the Labor Share." *Quarterly Journal of Economics* 129 (1): 61–103.

Kavlak, Goksin, James McNerney, and Jessika E. Trancik. 2018. "Evaluating the Causes of Cost Reduction in Photovoltaic Modules." *Energy Policy* 123: 700–10.

Lim, Jamus Jerome. 2013. "Institutional and Structural Determinants of Investment Worldwide." World Bank Policy Research Working Paper 6591, World Bank, Washington, DC.

Manova, Kalina, and Zhiwei Zhang. 2012. "Export Prices across Firms and Destinations." *Quarterly Journal of Economics* 127: 379–436.

Magud, Nicolás, and Sebastián Sosa. 2017. "Corporate Investment in Emerging Markets: The Role of Commodity Prices." *Economía* 18 (1): 157–95.

Meleshchuk, Sergii, and Yannick Timmer. 2019. "Trade Liberalization and Firm Investment: Evidence from Colombia." Unpublished.

Mutreja, Piyusha, B. Ravikumar, Raymond Riezman, and Michael Sposi. 2014. "Price Equalization, Trade Flows, and Barriers to Trade." *European Economic Review* 70: 383–98.

Mutreja, Piyusha, B. Ravikumar, and Michael Sposi. 2018. "Capital Goods Trade, Relative Prices, and Economic Development." *Review of Economic Dynamics* 27: 101–22.

REN21. 2018. *Renewables 2018 Global Status Report*. Paris: REN21 Secretariat.

Restuccia, Diego, and Carlos Urrutia. 2001. "Relative Prices and Investment Rates." *Journal of Monetary Economics* 47 (1): 93–121.

Salahuddin, Mohammad, and Rabiul Islam. 2008. "Factors Affecting Investment in Developing Countries: A Panel Data Study." *The Journal of Developing Areas* 42 (1): 21–37.

Sarel, Michael. 1995. "Relative Prices, Economic Growth and Tax Policy." IMF Working Paper 95/113, International Monetary Fund, Washington, DC.

Schott, Peter. 2004. "Across-Product versus Within-Product Specialization in International Trade." *Quarterly Journal of Economics* 119 (2): 647–78.

Schreyer, Paul. 2002. "Computer Price Indices and International Growth and Productivity Comparisons." *Review of Income and Wealth* 48 (1): 15–31.

Sen, Kunal. 2002. "Trade Policy, Equipment Investment and Growth in India." *Oxford Development Studies* 30 (3): 317–31.

Shorrocks, A.F. 1982. "Inequality Decomposition by Factor Components." *Econometrica* 50 (1): 193–211.

Sposi, Michael. 2015. "Trade Barriers and the Relative Price of Tradables." *Journal of International Economics* 96 (2): 398–411.

Sovacool, Benjamin. K., Daniel Nugent, and Alex Gilbert. 2014. "Construction Cost Overruns and Electricity Infrastructure: An Unavoidable Risk?" *The Electricity Journal* 27 (4): 112–20.

Taylor, Alan M. 1998a. "On the Costs of Inward-Looking Development: Price Distortions, Growth, and Divergence in Latin America." *Journal of Economic History* 58: 1–28.

———. 1998b. "Argentina and the World Capital Market: Saving, Investment, and International Capital Mobility in the Twentieth Century." *Journal of Development Economics* 57: 147–84.

Topalova, Petia, and Amit Khandelwal. 2011. "Trade Liberalization and Firm Productivity: The Case of India." *The Review of Economics and Statistics* 93 (3): 995–1009.

Torres, Mauricio, and Germán Romero. 2013. "Efectos de la Reforma Estructural Arancelaria en la Protección Efectiva Arancelaria de la Economía Colombiana." *Cuadernos de Economía* 32 (59): 265–303.

World Trade Organization (WTO). 2015. *World Trade Report 2015: Speeding Up Trade: Benefits and Challenges of Implementing the WTO Trade Facilitation Agreement*. Geneva.

CHAPTER 4

THE DRIVERS OF BILATERAL TRADE AND THE SPILLOVERS FROM TARIFFS

The presence of large and rising bilateral trade balances has raised concerns that asymmetric obstacles to trade may distort the international trade system. This chapter examines the drivers of bilateral trade balances, distinguishing between the roles of macroeconomic factors, the international division of labor, and bilateral tariffs. It also examines how, through their impact on the ways production is organized within and across countries, tariffs affect productivity, output, and employment. Three main findings emerge. First, the evolution of bilateral trade balances since the mid-1990s reflects mostly macroeconomic forces known to determine aggregate trade balances at the country level. Second, changes in bilateral tariffs played a smaller role than macroeconomic conditions in explaining the evolution of bilateral trade balances over the past two decades, reflecting tariffs' already-low levels in many countries and the fact that reciprocal tariff reductions had offsetting effects on bilateral trade balances. But other policy distortions—such as supply policies—may have played a role. Third, declining tariffs have lifted productivity by allowing greater international division of labor and further specialization by countries, including through participation in global value chains. The integrated nature of the current trade system suggests that a sharp increase in tariffs would create significant spillovers, leaving the global economy worse off. These findings support two main policy conclusions. First, the discussion of external imbalances (of which trade balances are the largest part for most countries) is rightly focused on the macroeconomic factors—for example, fiscal policy—which tend to determine trade and current account balances at the aggregate level. Targeting particular bilateral trade balances will likely only lead to trade diversion and offsetting changes in trade balances with other partners. Second, multilateral reductions in tariffs and other nontariff barriers will benefit trade and, over the longer term, improve macroeconomic outcomes.

The authors of this chapter are Johannes Eugster, Florence Jaumotte (team leader), Margaux MacDonald, and Roberto Piazza, with contributions from Carlos Caceres, Diego Cerdeiro, Kyun Suk Chang, Swarnali Ahmed Hannan, Rui Mano, Sergii Meleshchuk, Rafael Portillo, and Marika Santoro, and support from Pankhuri Dutt, Chanpheng Fizzarotti, Menexenia Tsaroucha, and Ilse Peirtsegaele.

Introduction

In both advanced and emerging market economies, more than 80 percent of the public views trade in a positive light—yet, fewer than half of these people are convinced that trade benefits jobs, wages, or prices. This skepticism is particularly pronounced in advanced economies.[1] These mixed views reflect the fact that the benefits of trade can come at a cost. On one hand, trade allows countries to specialize according to comparative advantage, enhances competition, and enables knowledge and technology to flow across borders, boosting the productivity and income of all countries (see, for example, Chapter 4 of the April 2018 *World Economic Outlook* (WEO)). Lower trade barriers and efficiency gains from the globalization of production have also contributed to strong declines in the relative price of capital goods, thereby contributing to drive strong real investment and narrowing income gaps for emerging market and developing economies (Chapter 3 of the April 2019 WEO). And trade benefits consumers by widening the choice and lowering the price of goods and services, especially those that account for a large share of lower-income households' consumption. On the other hand, there are serious concerns that trade can be associated with dislocations and involve costly adjustment for some groups of workers and communities. However, the overwhelming consensus of the large and still-growing empirical literature is that, on balance, open and fair trade, with lower or no tariffs or other obstacles to trade, can bring lasting net benefits to all involved if the right policies are in place to ensure that the gains are widely shared and those bearing the brunt of adjustment receive the help they deserve.[2]

In this context, the presence of large and rising bilateral trade balances has come under scrutiny, raising the question of whether they may be a sign of asymmetric obstacles to trade and pose concerns for policymakers. If, however, bilateral trade balances reflect mostly the macroeconomic forces known to determine countries'

[1]Pew Research Center spring 2018 *Global Attitudes Survey*. In emerging market economies, slightly more than half of respondents agree with the statement "trade creates jobs."

[2]See IMF (2017a) and IMF/WB/WTO (2017, 2018).

aggregate trade balances—such as fiscal policy strengthening or a weakening of demand relative to what is produced domestically—the behavior of trade at the bilateral level would be of little relevance, and the focus should be on addressing possible macroeconomic policy distortions. At the same time, the analysis of bilateral trade patterns promises insights into the economic costs that obstacles to trade, such as tariffs, could have—beyond their impact on bilateral trade balances—through their longer-term effect on the international division of labor, productivity, output, and employment.

With this in mind, the chapter aims to answer the following questions:

- What drives bilateral trade balances—specifically, what is the role of macroeconomic factors compared with tariffs and other determinants that are more micro-structural in nature and impact comparative advantage and the international division of labor?[3]
- What is the link between aggregate trade balances (and their drivers) and bilateral balances?
- What are the consequences for countries involved when bilateral tariffs are raised? And what spillovers arise for others when accounting for the presence of global value chains?

The chapter starts by examining what drives changes in bilateral trade balances, using the gravity model for bilateral trade flows. Model estimates are used to explain changes observed in bilateral trade balances, disentangling the impact of trade costs (including tariffs), the international division of labor, and macroeconomic factors. While the gravity model remains the workhorse model of the trade literature, it is worthwhile keeping certain limitations to this exercise in mind. First, the variables included in the gravity model do not capture completely all the time-invariant factors that determine the level of the trade balance between two countries. Hence, the chapter focuses on explaining changes in bilateral balances over time. Second, macroeconomic factors include all factors that determine aggregate supply and demand of a country. This includes macroeconomic policies and fundamental drivers, such as demographics, but also longer-term effects of large and persistent tariff changes and supply-side policies (for example, widespread subsidies) that are more difficult to measure systematically across countries. To give a more complete account of the role of policies, the chapter then takes a closer look at macroeconomic factors and how they are shaped by macroeconomic policies and other measurable determinants.

The second part of the chapter examines the impact of tariff changes beyond bilateral trade balances, on measures of economic activity more closely related to welfare, such as output, employment, and productivity. It highlights the role of greater supply chain connections and estimates the impact of tariffs through several channels: protection for domestic producers, effects on producers up and down the supply chain, and trade diversion. Simulations of a hypothetical tariff war scenario between the United States and China conclude the chapter, with different modeling approaches used to examine potential effects on the two economies and the spillovers on bystanders.

The findings of the chapter are as follows.

- Overall trade balances matter more than bilateral trade balances. Changes in overall (that is, aggregate) trade balances tend to affect most bilateral trade balances while—absent changes in macroeconomic conditions—a change in a bilateral trade balance tends to be offset by changes in bilateral balances with other trading partners, with little or no impact on the overall trade balance.
- The evolution of bilateral trade balances over the past two decades was, to a significant extent, driven by macroeconomic factors—specifically, the relative movement of aggregate demand and supply in both trading partners and their underlying drivers. These drivers included fundamental factors, such as demographics and the level of economic and institutional development; macroeconomic policies, in particular fiscal policy and credit cycles; and—in some cases—exchange rate policies and domestic supply-side policies (for example, subsidies to production costs).
- In contrast, changes in bilateral tariffs played a smaller role in the evolution of bilateral trade balances, reflecting their already-low starting levels in many countries and the fact that most countries reduced tariffs at the same time, creating offsetting effects on net trade. At the same time, however, the level of tariffs is an important part of bilateral trade costs, which help shape the international division of labor and, thereby, the way changing macroeconomic factors impact bilateral trade and trade balances.
- For the same reason, tariffs have important effects on productivity, output, and employment over the longer term. The decline of tariffs to lower

[3]More specifically, trade can arise from the fact that trading partners have a different sectoral composition of supply and demand, which in part reflects the international division of labor according to comparative advantage.

levels enabled a greater international division of labor—including through global value chains—and enhanced competition and access to foreign inputs, resulting in strong productivity improvements. This suggests scope for significant positive spillovers from shifts to lower tariffs, but also negative spillovers from tariff wars. Increases in bilateral tariffs will hurt output, employment, and productivity, not only in the affected economies, but also in bystanders up and down value chains. While some countries may benefit from trade diversion, higher tariffs would leave the global economy worse off.

These findings suggest two main policy conclusions. First, discussion of external balances is rightly focused on macroeconomic determinants of trade and current account balances. Changes in macroeconomic policies (for example, fiscal policy) will affect all bilateral balances. An important implication is that, unless macroeconomic conditions are addressed, targeting a particular subset of bilateral trade balances will likely result only in trade diversion and offsetting changes in trade balances with other partners. Second, broad-based, multilateral reductions in tariffs and other nontariff barriers will benefit trade and, over the longer term, improve macroeconomic outcomes. Reductions in tariffs lead to efficiency and dynamic gains by allowing countries to further specialize according to their comparative advantage, to integrate into supply chains, and improve access to foreign inputs. In contrast, higher tariffs on bilateral trade can come at significant economic cost, not only for the countries involved, but also for others. These effects are greatly amplified by global supply chains, which transmit spillovers from bilateral tariffs, affecting countries up and down the value chain. While some countries may benefit from trade diversion, negative confidence effects and tighter global financial conditions triggered by trade tensions would affect all countries negatively (Chapter 1 of the October 2018 WEO).

While these findings suggest that reducing barriers to trade would benefit the global economy, there are valid concerns about the distributional effects of trade. It is important to put in place specific policies to ensure that the gains from trade are widely shared and that those left behind are adequately protected (IMF 2017a; IMF/WB/WTO 2017, 2018). Policies to help those harmed by structural adjustment or dislocations include enhancing social safety nets in affected economies—for example, with modern income support programs and unemployment assistance programs—policies to retrain and reintegrate the dislocated groups into the labor market, and changes in tax and benefit policies to redistribute the gains from trade more evenly.

Stylized Facts

From the perspective of a single country, the overall trade balance is the sum of its bilateral trade balances, which in turn account for the difference between the values of exports and imports with each trading partner. This suggests aggregate and bilateral balances are highly related—and, indeed, for countries with large overall trade imbalances, bilateral trade balances appear to be more one-sided, either on the positive side (for example, Germany) or on the negative side (for example, the United States) (Figure 4.1). At the same time, a striking degree of variation of bilateral trade balances is apparent across trading partners: most countries have positive and negative bilateral trade balances, and even countries with small overall trade balances can have large (and offsetting) bilateral trade balances. Similar observations hold more broadly beyond the countries shown in the figure.

These stylized facts suggest that bilateral trade balances are shaped by two broad forces: (1) macroeconomic factors, more specifically countries' imbalances between aggregate domestic supply and domestic spending, as captured by their overall trade balances; and (2) tariffs and more micro-structural factors that determine varying bilateral trade intensities between two countries.

The relationship between overall and bilateral trade balances is also evident at a global level (Figure 4.2). Measured in absolute value to highlight their sizes, global bilateral and overall trade balances have evolved broadly in parallel over the past two decades, increasing strongly up to the 2008–09 global financial crisis and dipping during the crisis.[4] However, some differences can be seen, too—for example, bilateral balances increased more than aggregate trade balances and did not decline as much as aggregate trade balances after the crisis. A few countries with large overall balances, such as China, the United States, Germany, Korea, and Japan, are also big contributors to global bilat-

[4]Specifically, global bilateral balances are measured by taking the sum of the absolute values of all countries' bilateral balances. Similarly, for global overall balances, the sum of the absolute value of all countries' overall trade balances is calculated.

Figure 4.1. Bilateral Trade Balances, by Major Partners[1]
(Percent of global GDP)

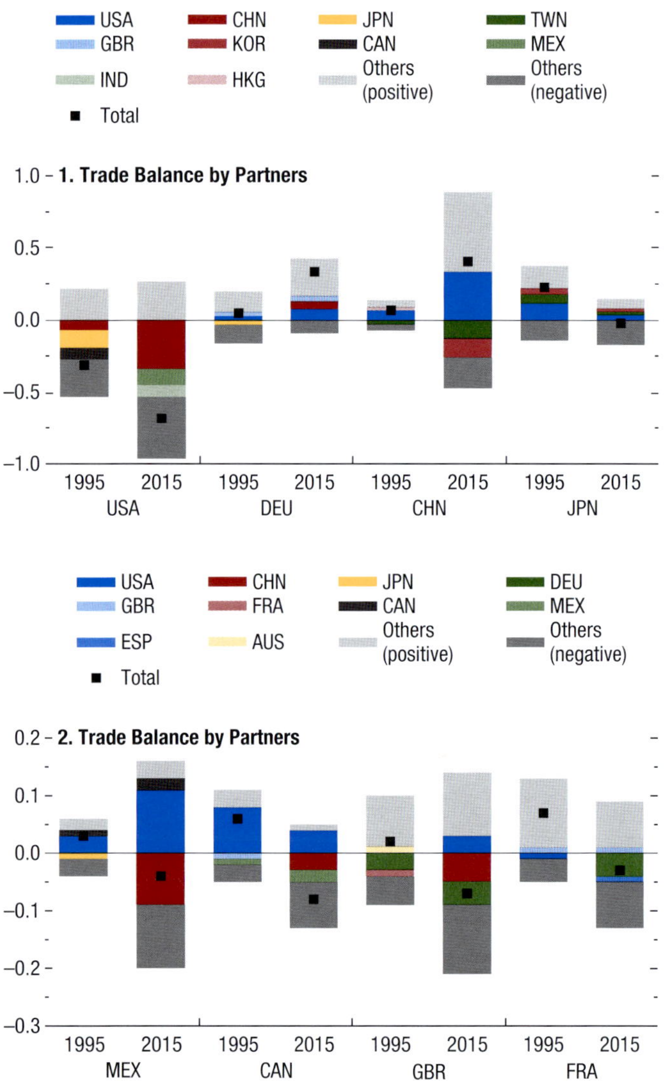

Sources: Organisation for Economic Co-operation and Development, Trade in Value Added database; and IMF staff calculations.
Note: Data labels use International Organization of Standardization (ISO) country codes.
[1]Top three partners shown per year.

Figure 4.2. Global Trade Imbalances

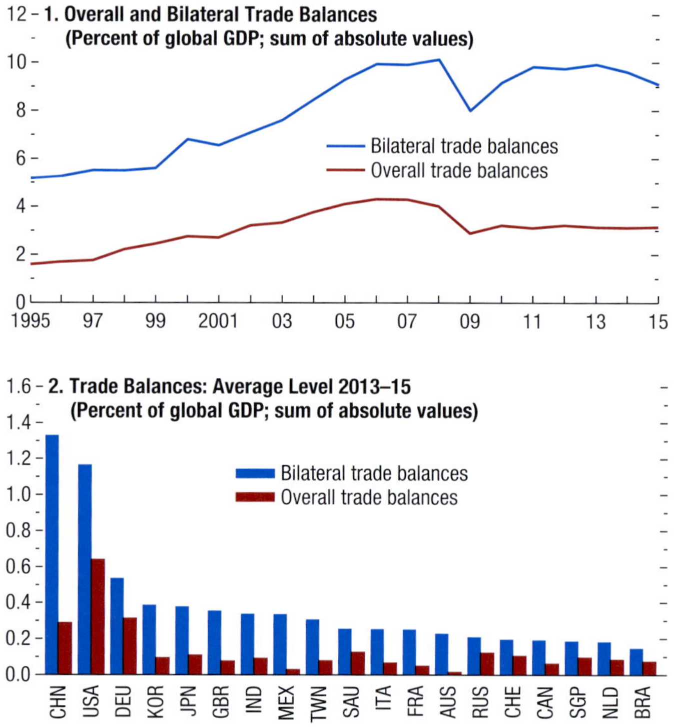

Sources: Organisation for Economic Co-operation and Development, Trade in Value Added database; and IMF staff calculations.
Note: Data labels use International Organization for Standardization (ISO) country codes.

eral balances. However, in all these cases, bilateral trade balances are significantly wider than the overall trade balances.

Global trade integration has been crucial to all these developments and was fostered by a persistent fall in trade costs. The average bilateral *trade intensity* across country pairs, discussed later in the chapter, captures the relative size of impediments to trade attributable, at a first approximation, to the presence of trading costs (Figure 4.3). Higher trade intensity for a given pair suggests that trade between those countries is easier. Looking at the evolution between 1995–99 and 2010–15, it is clear that, for most country pairs, trade has become relatively easier. This finding is not surprising, in light of the observation that barriers that hinder trade flows have fallen over time. Improvements in transportation technologies have reduced shipping costs over long distances. Policy changes have also been crucial, with the expansion of World Trade Organization membership leading to a generalized decline in import tariffs. Reductions were particularly marked where tariffs were initially high, as in China and in other emerging market economies. At the same time, large variability of bilateral trade intensity is seen across country pairs. This reflects bilateral trade costs, such as tariffs and more micro-structural factors, and suggests some variation in the way macroeconomic factors affect the various bilateral trade balances of a country.

Another determinant of the bilateral intensity of trade between two countries is their international spe-

Figure 4.3. Trade Intensity and Barriers to Trade

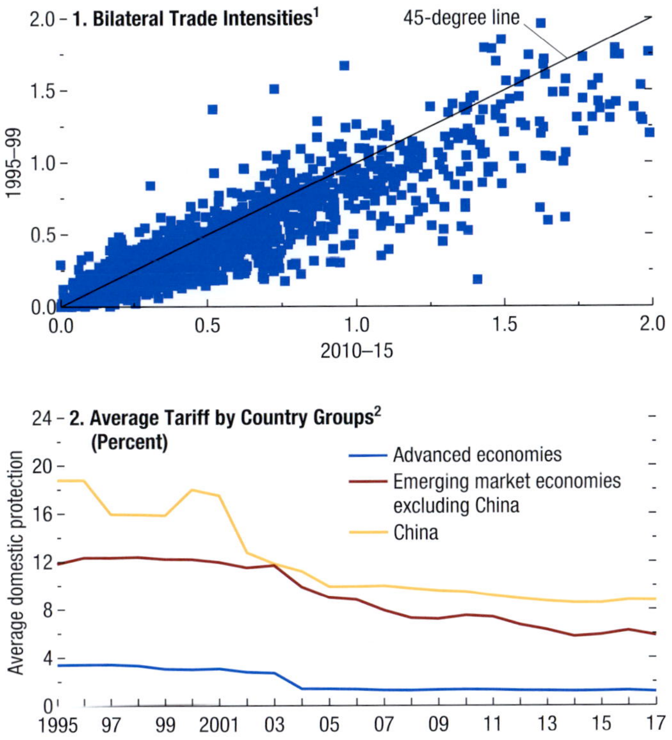

Sources: Organisation for Economic Co-operation and Development, Trade in Value Added database; World Bank, World Integrated Trade Solution database; and IMF staff calculations.

[1]Each dot represents a country pair. For a given pair of countries, the estimated trade intensity provides the impact on exports of the pair-specific bilateral and multilateral trading costs. To improve readability, pairs with intensity greater than two have been excluded.

[2]Averages are aggregated from the country-sector level using constant (2000) value-added shares as weights.

Figure 4.4. Revealed Comparative Advantage[1]

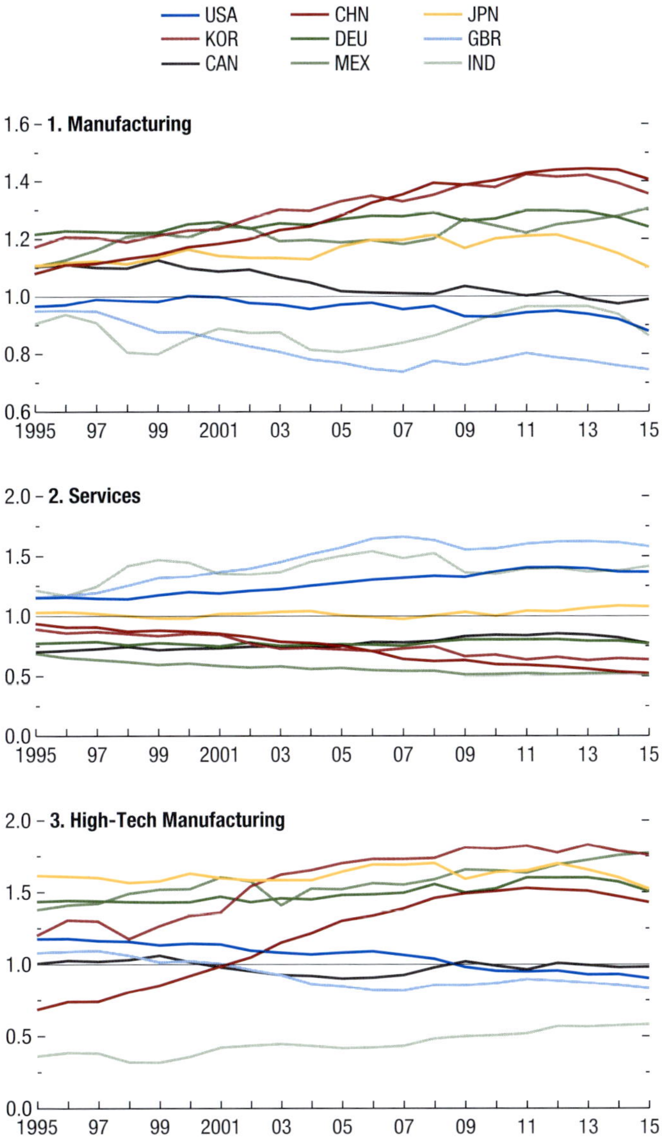

Sources: Organisation for Economic Co-operation and Development, Trade in Value Added database; and IMF staff calculations.

Note: Data labels use International Organization for Standardization (ISO) country codes.

[1]Values greater than 1 indicate a revealed comparative advantage in the sector.

cialization. As the cost of trading declined, countries tended to further specialize in what they were best at producing (their comparative advantage)—at least at a broad sectoral level—while importing other products from other countries—deepening the international division of labor and realizing further gains from trade. The country-specific demand and supply structures can generate complex multicountry trade patterns, whereby trade flows across countries occur because countries consume and produce specific goods with different intensities. Countries that had a revealed comparative advantage in manufacturing in 1995 reinforced their specialization in manufacturing—notably, China, Korea, Germany, Japan, and Mexico (Figure 4.4).[5]

[5]Revealed comparative advantage is measured by the share of a sector in a country's exports relative to the sector's share in world exports.

Conversely, relative de-specialization in manufacturing exports took place in countries that had an initial comparative disadvantage in this sector, such as the United States and the United Kingdom. A similar pattern can be observed in services, where the United Kingdom, India, and the United States built on their initial comparative advantage. The evolution of these comparative advantages was also reflected in these countries' manu-

Figure 4.5. Largest Trade Flows, 1995 versus 2015
(Billions of US dollars)

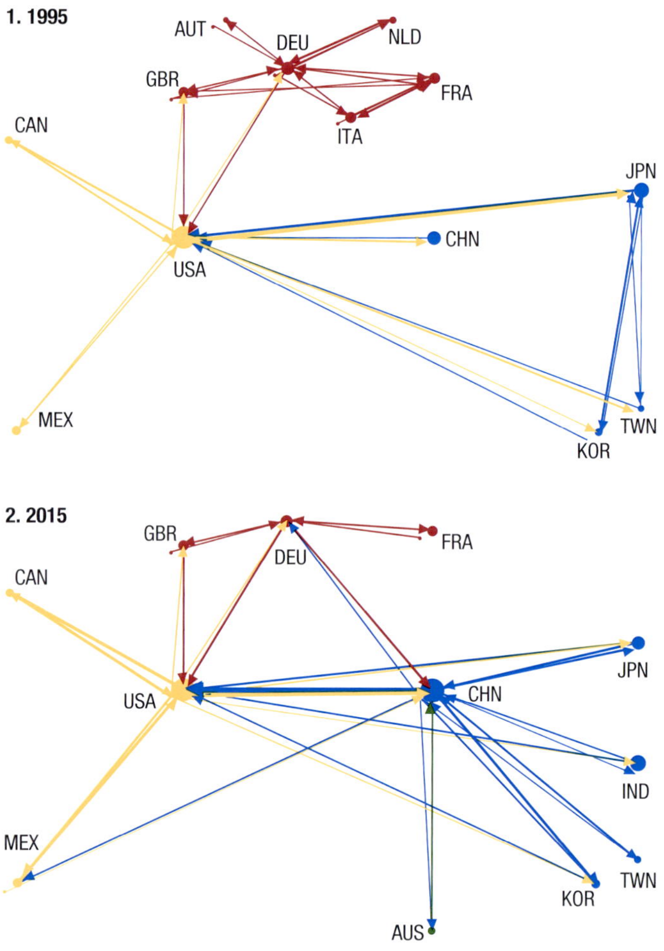

Sources: Organisation for Economic Co-operation and Development, Trade in Value Added database; and IMF staff calculations.
Note: Countries with largest export in year (>= 1 percent of world GDP in 1995 and 2015, respectively), deflated by the US GDP deflator. The size of the bubbles represents the world share of a country's GDP. Data labels use International Organization for Standardization (ISO) country codes.

facturing and services trade balances, with the United States, for example, increasing its surplus in services.

However, the evolution of comparative advantage is not determined by declining trade costs alone. Korea and China are examples of countries developing high-tech manufacturing sectors with a strong global trade impact despite a lack of (or in the case of Korea, modest) initial comparative advantage in this area. Other examples can be found at a more disaggregated level.[6] These developments could reflect, among other things, relatively higher productivity growth in certain sectors due to innovation. At the same time, there is much debate about the role of supply-side policies in helping build such comparative advantage.[7]

The development of global supply chains has also deepened the specialization of countries across and within sectors, amplifying multicountry trade patterns. A focus on the largest bilateral trade flows in 1995 and 2015 suggests that global production is broadly organized around three poles, though with changing intensity (Figure 4.5): the North America pole (or "factory") organized around the United States with Canada and Mexico; the European factory centered around Germany; and the Asian factory.[8] There are also important links between the three production poles, in particular between the United States and Asia. While poles remained broadly intact from a regional perspective between 1995 and 2015, they changed within and intensified over time—with Asia experiencing the most notable changes. In 1995, Japan was at the center of factory Asia, whereas China now plays a central role, and some goods that Japanese firms used to ship directly to the United States are now first shipped to China for further processing. Greater participation in such global value chains should be expected to generate larger bilateral balances (measured by the sum of their absolute values) but not necessarily a larger overall trade balance.[9] Indeed, data suggest a strong positive relationship between a country's participation in global value chains and the size of its bilateral balances, while the relationship is much weaker when it comes to the size of the overall trade balance (Figure 4.6).

Another implication of these trends is that the difference between traditional gross trade measures and value-added measures (which capture the actual value added exchanged between two countries) has increased because the good sold incorporates value added from

[6]See Daruich, Easterly, and Reshef (2019) for a more detailed analysis of changes in specialization of countries at a more disaggregated level.

[7]Such policies could include, among other measures, sectoral subsidies, incentivization of innovation (for example, China's patent promotion policy; see Chapter 4 of the April 2018 WEO), and technology transfer policies and practices. Supply-side policies are discussed later in the chapter.

[8]See Baldwin and Lopez-Gonzalez (2013) for a more detailed analysis of global patterns of supply-chain trade.

[9]For instance, consider a global value chain located in three countries and characterized by a flow of intermediate goods from the first country to the second, and from the second to the third. In this case, an intensification of the global value chain link would imply an increase in the trade deficit of the second country with respect to the first, and an increase in its surplus with respect to the third. See Ahn and others (forthcoming) for a discussion of the correlation between bilateral trade balances and participation in global value chains.

various countries along the value chain (Box 4.1).[10] This is particularly relevant and accounted for in the analysis of the impact of tariffs on value added and employment in the section titled "A Closer Look at Tariffs and Their Spillovers."

Determinants of Bilateral Trade Balances

To understand and quantify the drivers of bilateral trade, this chapter uses the workhorse model of the trade literature, the so-called gravity model. A wide body of theoretical and empirical literature shows that this model does a good job of explaining bilateral exports as a function of trade costs, aggregate supply and demand of trade partners, and the sectoral composition of demand and supply. The estimated determinants of bilateral exports can then be mapped to estimated bilateral imports and to bilateral net trade patterns. This method allows bilateral trade balances to be broken down into the components that drive them—namely, specific trade policy actions and broad macroeconomic policies and conditions.[11]

The Gravity Model in a Nutshell

The gravity model explains *bilateral exports* as a function of three sets of determinants (see, among others, Anderson and van Wincoop 2003).

- *Macroeconomic factors:* Specifically, bilateral exports increase with the aggregate supply (gross output) of the exporting country and the aggregate demand (gross spending) of the importing country, scaled by world output. The analysis uses *gross* output and spending (instead of value added and final spending) to account for growth in global-value-chain-related intermediates' trade, which is included in export measures.
- *Trade costs:* These include natural trade costs and man-made—or policy-related—trade costs. Two countries are more likely to trade with each other if they are in close geographic proximity, have historical ties, or have lower overt trade costs (lower tariffs, trade agreements).[12] In addition to bilateral trade costs between the two countries, it is important to control for the average trade costs faced by the exporter across all trading partners and the average trade costs imposed by the importer to capture that the effect of bilateral tariffs is relative to trade costs with other partners. These factors capture the general equilibrium effects of trade costs.[13]

Figure 4.6. The Role of Global Value Chains[1]

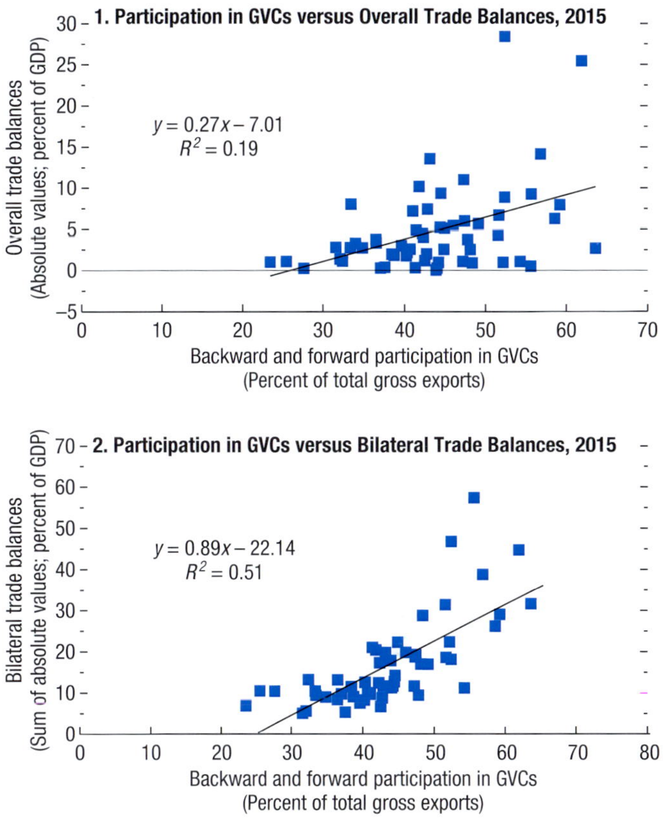

Source: Organisation for Economic Co-operation and Development, Trade in Value Added database.
Note: GVCs = global value chains.
[1]Each dot represents a country.

[10]See Johnson and Noguera (2012a, 2012b, 2017); and Koopman, Wang, and Wei (2014).

[11]See, for instance, Feenstra (2004); Silva and Tenreyro (2006); Baldwin and Taglioni (2011); Bacchetta and others (2012); and Yotov and others (2016) for a discussion of the estimation of the gravity model for bilateral exports. There is very little empirical literature that attempts to identify determinants of bilateral trade balances (for example, Davis and Weinstein 2002).

[12]The model used here includes geographic distance between trading partners; bilateral tariffs; and dummy variables for a common border, a common language, common colonial history, and a common free trade agreement. The traditional gravity literature does not explicitly consider the role of exchange rate arrangements. For instance, common currency areas, such as the euro area, can help reduce real trade costs among participants by eliminating the need for currency hedging. In standard gravity regressions, such effects would be in part picked up, through collinearity, by the geographic proximity variables or the free trade agreement dummies.

[13]General equilibrium effects, include, for example, effects of trade costs of a third country on trade between the bilateral pair. The literature also speaks about multilateral trade costs as "multilateral

- *Sectoral composition of supply and demand:* The sectoral composition of supply and demand—which reflects the international division of labor—will affect how much two countries trade in various sectors and, hence, how much they trade in the aggregate. For instance, if a country specializes in producing manufacturing goods, and its trading partner spends more on manufacturing goods than it produces, it will generate a larger trade flow between the two countries. Estimating the gravity model at the sectoral level and aggregating to the country level allows identification of the role of differences in the sectoral structure of exporters' supply and importers' demand on bilateral trade flows.

It is important to recognize up front the limitations of this approach. First, while the gravity model clearly distinguishes between the principal drivers of bilateral trade, these can be more difficult to disentangle in practice. For example, as discussed, changes in tariffs do not only affect bilateral trade. Over the longer term, large and persistent changes in tariffs can also influence the international division of labor and, thereby, macroeconomic factors—an issue further investigated in the section titled "A Closer Look at Tariffs and Their Spillovers." The results presented are thus best interpreted as partial-equilibrium effects and not necessarily as a reflection of the complete dynamic interaction of trade, macroeconomic factors, and tariffs over time. Second, macroeconomic factors capture all factors and policies that impact aggregate supply and demand, including fundamental factors (such as demographics or institutional development), macroeconomic policies, and supply-side policies. However, the latter are difficult to identify separately given the lack of consistent measures across countries—this is particularly true for measures of macroeconomic policy distortions, such as widespread export or production subsidies that distort trade similarly across all trading partners.[14] The section titled "The Role of Macroeconomic Factors" explores in more detail these underlying drivers.

With these caveats in mind, the model of bilateral exports is estimated at the country and the sector levels, using the Organization for Economic Co-operation and Development's Trade in Value Added database. The database reports bilateral export data for 63 countries at the International Standard Industrial Classification of All Economic Activities 3 level for 34 sectors from 1995 to 2015. All variables are expressed in nominal US dollars. In line with the literature, the estimation is carried out over five-year periods to remove the short-term effect of nominal variables, such as nominal exchange rate movements.[15] Online Annex 4.1 provides more details about the estimation and results.[16]

The estimated effects are consistent with other studies (see, for example, Bacchetta and others 2012; and Yotov and others 2016). They confirm that domestic aggregate supply of the exporter and aggregate demand of the importer are key determinants of bilateral export flows. Trade costs are estimated to be important barriers to trade, with the estimated elasticity implying that a 1 percent increase in gross ad valorem tariffs reduces gross bilateral exports by about 3–6 percent.[17] These country-level results are highly robust to the sector-level specification, which allows for introduction of the role of specialization in determining trade. As expected, important differences exist between services and non-services sectors, which can be observed only in sector-level data. For instance, although distance is a significant hindrance to both types of trade, it is more important for trade in services. Overall, the model explains bilateral exports (and imports) very well across all specifications.

resistance" or, equivalently, as indices of market potential or access (see, for example, Head and Mayer 2014). In the empirical application, a common proxy for multilateral trade costs is the GDP-weighted trade costs against all trading partners.

[14]One example of concern over such distortionary policies is the Group of Twenty policymakers' agreement to avoid market-distorting subsidies and other support measures that contribute to excess capacity in steel production—see, for example, G20 (2018).

[15]The traditional gravity model is therefore better interpreted as capturing the determinants of bilateral exports over the medium term. For instance, a sudden depreciation of the exporter's currency would have neutral medium-term effects on the US dollar price of its exports. In fact, as time goes by, firms would compensate for the initial depreciation of the domestic currency by increasing their domestically denominated export prices. The gravity model also does not control for other relative price changes between the importer and exporter (such as those driven by commodity prices). However, adding measures of exporter and importer price indices does not have a notable effect on the other coefficients and adds little explanatory power to the model.

[16]All annexes are available at www.imf.org/en/Publications/WEO.

[17]This approach focuses on the partial equilibrium effect of these variables, and the range of effects reflects the different sector- and country-level estimates reported in Online Annex 4.1. The section titled "A Closer Look at Tariffs and Their Spillovers" discusses some of the general equilibrium implications.

Decomposing Bilateral Trade Balances through the Gravity Lens

The model of bilateral exports (or imports) also provides information about the determinants of bilateral trade balances—defined as the difference between bilateral exports and imports. The gravity model loses explanatory power when applied to the level of bilateral trade balances, reflecting the difficulty in accounting for structural factors—beyond tariffs and broad sectoral specialization—that are time invariant and that determine the balance of trade between two countries (see Online Annex 4.1).[18] This chapter therefore focuses on explaining changes in bilateral trade balances.

An intuitive way to understand and quantify how trade costs, macroeconomic factors, and changes in sectoral composition explain an observed change in a bilateral trade balance over the sample period 1995–2015 is to look at the estimated contribution of each explanatory variable in the model to that change (see Online Annex 4.1 for the derivation). The contributions to changes in the bilateral trade balances are presented for the major trading partners of three of the largest trading countries and manufacturing centers globally—the United States, China, and Germany (Figure 4.7).[19] The figure highlights the prominent role that macroeconomic factors play in explaining changes in bilateral trade balances. Trade costs contribute, too, although to a lesser degree. Another observation is that the precise impact of macroeconomic factors on bilateral trade balances depends on the initial state of this relationship—in particular, whether the bilateral balance was large and positive or negative. Since trade

Figure 4.7. Contributions to Changes in Bilateral Trade Balances, 1995–2015[1]

(Billions of US dollars)

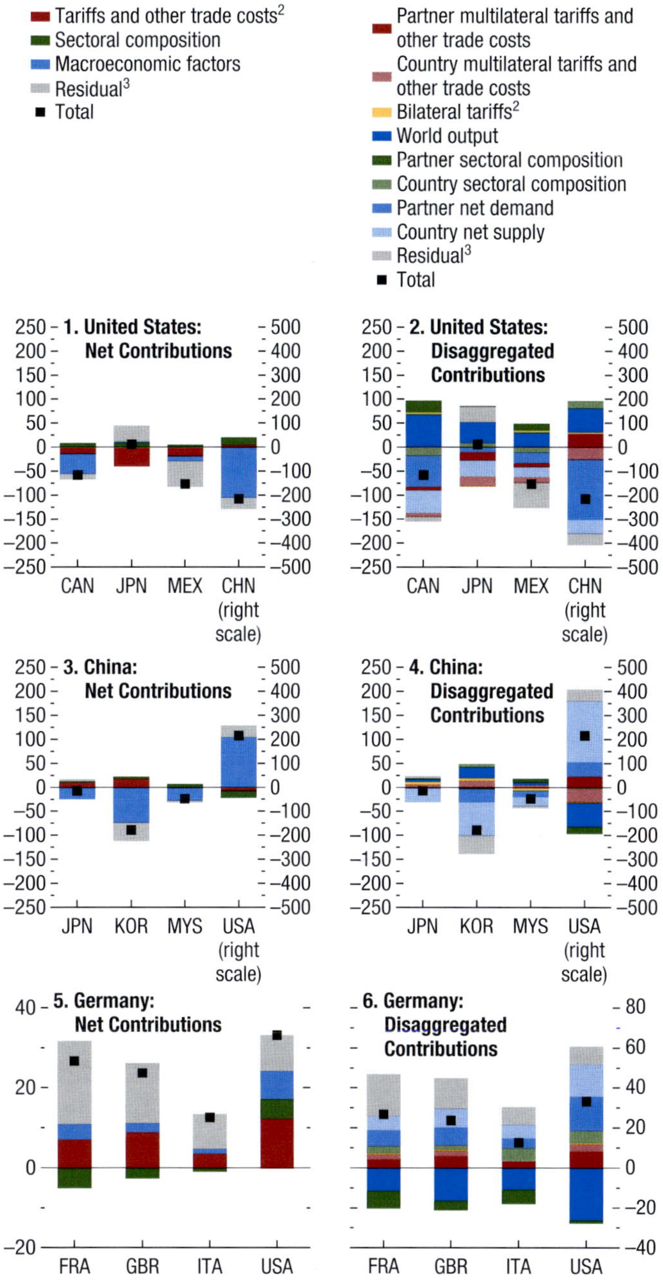

Sources: Organisation for Economic Co-operation and Development, Trade in Value Added database; and IMF staff calculations.
Note: Panels 1, 3, and 5 present the macroeconomic, sectoral, and trade cost terms on a net basis. Panels 2, 4, and 6 separate these net terms into their components as follows: macroeconomic factor into country net supply, partner net demand, and world output; sectoral composition into country sectoral composition and partner sectoral composition; and tariffs and other trade costs into bilateral tariffs, country multilateral trade costs, and partner multilateral trade costs. Data labels use International Organization for Standardization (ISO) country codes.
[1]Average value 2010–15 minus average value 1995–99.
[2]This includes tariffs and free or preferential trade agreements.
[3]The residual is the sum of the model residuals plus the approximation error.

[18]One possible candidate is the increasing international division of labor and integration of countries made possible by global value chains, which is only imperfectly captured by the standard gravity model. For example, Ahn and others (forthcoming) shows that, in a gravity equation estimated with country-time fixed effects, estimation residuals increase over time and can be accounted for by the increasing participation of countries into global value chains. This is in line with the section titled "A Closer Look at Tariffs and Their Spillovers" and Box 4.4, which stress the importance of considering the key current role of global value chains when thinking about the role of tariffs. In addition, as indicated by Figure 4.6, panel 1, macro factors and global value chain participation are not significantly correlated and thus provide potentially independent information regarding the evolution of trade patterns.

[19]Panel 1 presents the macroeconomic, sectoral, and trade cost contributions on a net basis. Panel 2 separates these net contributions into their components as follows: macroeconomic factors into country net supply, partner net demand, and world output; sectoral composition into country sectoral composition and partner sectoral composition; and tariffs and other trade costs into bilateral tariffs, country multilateral trade costs, and partner multilateral trade costs.

costs, along with other more micro-structural factors, determine countries' comparative advantage and the international division of labor over the longer term, this suggest another way that tariffs can leave a mark on the path of bilateral trade balances over time.[20]

Role of macroeconomic factors. Macroeconomic factors—both domestic and foreign—appear to be, by far, the largest contributors to changes in bilateral trade balances over the period of analysis. That both domestic and foreign macroeconomic conditions matter suggests that the relative evolution of the *aggregate* trade balances of the two trading partners has a role to play—a notion that is explored in the section titled "The Role of Macroeconomic Factors."

- *Domestic macroeconomic conditions* reflect the evolution of gross output and gross spending in a particular country. The magnitude of impact depends on the initial bilateral trade balance between the two countries, as determined by trade costs, the international division of labor, initial macroeconomic conditions, and other structural factors.[21] For instance, over 1995–2015, US domestic macroeconomic factors had a negative effect on its bilateral trade balances across trading partners because US gross output was growing more slowly than spending. Put simply, the United States was, in the aggregate, spending more than it was producing, so it had to import more goods from its trading partners.[22] In contrast, Germany's domestic macroeconomic factors had a positive effect on its bilateral trade balances, reflecting faster growth of output than spending. Finally, output was also growing faster than spending in China over this period—in part reflecting domestic supply-side policies, such as subsidies to the cost of production of manufactured (traded) goods (see, for example, IMF 2011, 2017b; and the 2017 *External Sector Report*). Where China initially had a bilateral surplus (for example, with the United States), reflecting its strong comparative advantage in manufacturing goods, its faster growth of output than spending amplified the bilateral surplus. In contrast, for trading partners with which it maintained an initial trade deficit, such as Korea and Malaysia, the growth of spending, applied to much larger initial imports, had a larger impact than the growth of supply, amplifying the bilateral deficit.
- *Foreign macroeconomic factors* are the contributions of the evolution of spending and output in partner countries. As with the contribution of domestic macroeconomic factors, the initial structure of trade matters in the determination of the change in the bilateral trade balances. For instance, in the case of Germany, foreign macroeconomic factors contributed to its bilateral surpluses, reflecting the faster growth of spending relative to output in partner countries and the initial surplus position that Germany held with its partners.

Role of sectoral specialization: Changes in the sectoral composition of aggregate demand and supply play a nontrivial role for many bilateral imbalances.[23] Overall, a positive effect on the bilateral trade balance indicates that the output share of sectors where a country had large initial exports rose (more than the spending share)—supporting the idea that countries build on existing production structures and comparative advantage—or that the spending share of sectors where the country had high initial demand fell (more than the output share). In the case of the United States, sectoral changes in its supply and demand seem to have contributed positively to its bilateral balances with China, Germany, and Japan. The same holds true for Germany's bilateral trade balances with Italy and the United States.

Role of trade costs: Although declines in bilateral tariffs contributed to growth in the level of gross trade (exports and imports), they had a more muted impact on trade balances (that is, "net" trade—the difference between exports and imports). This, in part, reflects the fact that tariffs were already low in the mid-1990s in many countries and that tariff reductions were reciprocal, with offsetting effects on bilateral trade balances. For example, changes in bilateral tariffs contributed slightly positively to changes in US bilateral trade balances with Canada, China, and Mexico because these countries' tariffs on US goods were falling faster than tariffs imposed by the United States on their goods (albeit from a higher level). All else equal, this mechanically promoted a greater rise in US exports to these countries than in their exports to the United States. For example, if Chinese tariffs on US goods had remained at their 1995 level, the estimation suggests that the US–China trade deficit would have been, on average, $30 billion (about 12 percent) larger

[20]Note, however, in the case of the US–China trade balance, that trade was relatively small in 1995 (see Figure 4.1).

[21]On a technical level, this is because of the multiplicative form in which the different determinants of bilateral trade interact with each other.

[22]The section titled "The Role of Macroeconomic Factors" takes a closer look at the drivers of these macroeconomic factors.

[23]For a discussion of the relationship between sectoral specialization, asymmetric trade costs across sectors, and external balances, see Barattieri (2014); Joy and others (2018); and Boz, Li, and Zhang (2019).

over 2010–15. Of course, this would not have translated into an equal deterioration in the US overall trade balance, given that trade diversion effects would have led to larger US exports to other countries.

In many cases, changes in the average trade costs faced by countries across all their trading partners played a larger role during the sample period than changes in particular bilateral tariffs. As noted above, world output shares of emerging market economies, especially China, rose over time. For most countries, this resulted in additional trade with these emerging market economies, while reducing trade with some others. However, at the same time, trade patterns also adjusted to the fact that those rapidly growing countries happened to display higher tariffs than the typical advanced economy, which drove up average trade costs. All else equal, this increase in average trading costs made trade between lower-cost country pairs more attractive, contributing positively to trade intensity between many countries and amplifying bilateral trade balances—for example, widening US bilateral deficits and increasing Germany's bilateral surpluses.

Compared with macroeconomic factors, changes in bilateral tariffs played a smaller role in the evolution of bilateral balances, but their role should not be underestimated. As discussed further in the section titled "A Closer Look at Tariffs and Their Spillovers," over the longer term, large and persistent changes in tariffs can have a significant impact on the international division of labor, productivity, and macroeconomic factors. Indeed, an increase in bilateral tariffs to prohibitive levels would cripple trade, whether at the bilateral or global level, with severe consequences for the economies involved.

The Role of Macroeconomic Factors

The previous section shows that changes in a country's bilateral trade balances are, to a significant extent, driven by changes in the imbalance between gross production and the spending of each trading partner. This imbalance (in its unweighted form) is simply the country's *aggregate* trade balance. Starting from this observation, this section provides a more detailed view of the role of macroeconomic factors by decomposing the aggregate trade balance into a set of specific macroeconomic drivers, including the effect of macroeconomic policies.

It is possible to manipulate the usual gravity equation to show more clearly that, under mild assumptions, any bilateral trade balance depends on the *relative* size of the two countries' aggregate trade balance-to-GDP ratios, the two countries' sizes relative to the world economy, and bilateral trade intensities. Box 4.2 discusses this relationship and illustrates how changes in the aggregate trade balances of the United States and China can account for most of the evolution in their bilateral trade balance. In particular, once aggregate and bilateral trade balances are scaled in a theory-consistent way (that is, by taking into account the changing sizes of the trading partners), it becomes clear that the shrinking of the aggregate trade balances of the United States and China after the global financial crisis was matched by a corresponding contraction in their bilateral trade balance.

The precise way a given change in a country's aggregate trade balance is reflected in its bilateral balances depends on a set of partner-specific *trade intensities*. A simple example illustrates this point: consider a ½ percentage point exogenous decrease in Germany's overall trade balance—holding everything else constant, Germany's bilateral trade balances with, among others, China, the Netherlands, and the United States would decline by about 0.1 percent of Germany's GDP, while bilateral trade balances with the United Kingdom and France would decline by 0.05 percent of Germany's GDP (Figure 4.8).[24] A greater effect on bilateral balances reflects either a higher trade intensity with Germany (for example, in the case of the Netherlands) or a higher share in world output (for example, in the case of the United States).

From a policy perspective, it is important to understand the factors behind the movement of aggregate trade balances over time. This question can be answered through the IMF's External Balance Assessment (EBA) framework, which relates the current account of a country to macroeconomic policies and other drivers. Given that the current account of a country consists of the aggregate trade balance and net foreign incomes and transfers, the EBA model can also be applied to the trade balance directly (see Online Annex 4.2).[25] The main EBA determinants fall into four broad groups:[26]

[24]This example considers only partial effects and does not include important general equilibrium responses.

[25]In the exercise presented here, countries' aggregate trade balance-to-GDP ratios are regressed on the standard EBA drivers. As noted, given that the trade balance is just a subcomponent of the current account, the EBA drivers remain valid explanatory variables, but their quantitative role can change. The current account and the trade balance EBA regressions turn out to be quite consistent with each other (see Online Annex 4.2).

[26]The IMF's EBA methodology, which has been in place since 2013, estimates the level of the current account and exchange rate consistent with fundamentals and desired macroeconomic policies. The scope of the trade balance exercise presented here, instead, does not discuss desired policies. For this reason, and for ease of

Figure 4.8. Effect of a Deterioration of Germany's Aggregate Trade Balance on Selected Bilateral Balances

(Percent of Germany's GDP)

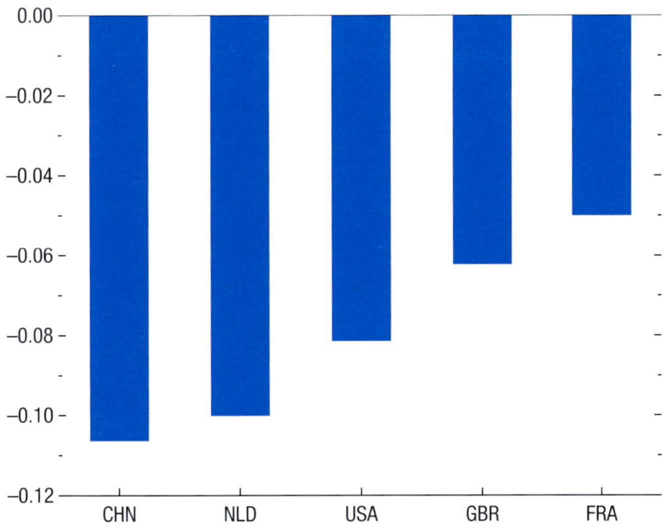

Sources: Organisation for Economic Co-operation and Development, Trade in Value Added database; and IMF staff calculations.
Note: Data labels use International Organization for Standardization (ISO) country codes. The figure shows the effect on selected bilateral balances of a 0.5 percentage point deterioration in Germany's aggregate trade balance to GDP.

Figure 4.9. Contributions of Macroeconomic Drivers to Aggregate Trade Balances, Average 2010–17[1]

(Percent of GDP)

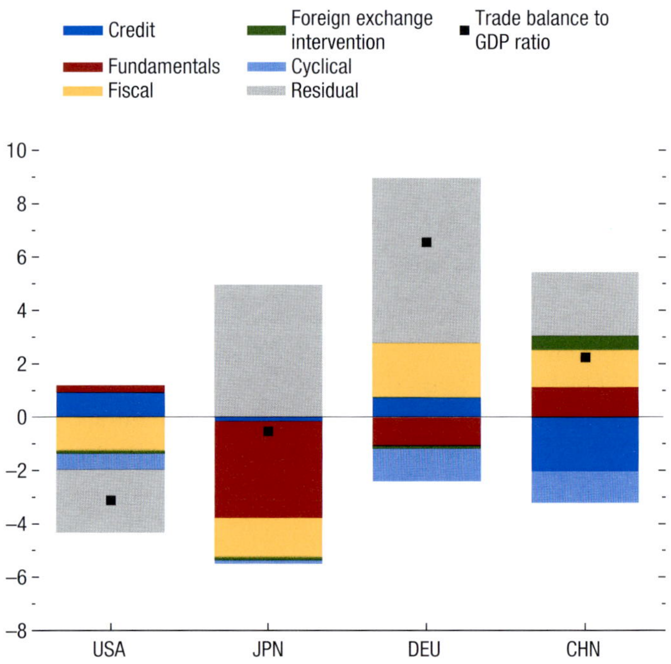

Source: IMF staff calculations.
Note: Data labels use International Organization for Standardization (ISO) country codes.
[1]Contributions were obtained by regressing the countries' trade balance-to-GDP ratio on the standard IMF External Balance Assessment variables.

- *Macroeconomic policies*: Those included are fiscal policy (cyclically adjusted fiscal balance) and exchange rate policy (foreign exchange interventions). Macroeconomic policy distortions (for example, widespread export or production subsidies that distort trade similarly across all trading partners) could also affect macroeconomic imbalances, however, these policies are difficult to measure systematically across countries and are not explicitly captured here.
- *Credit*: This dimension is captured by detrended private credit to GDP.
- *Cyclical*: This represents temporary factors of a cyclical nature, such as the output gap and the commodity terms of trade, capturing fluctuations in commodity prices.
- *Fundamentals*: This includes such factors as demographics, the level of economic and institutional development, social safety nets, reliance on commodity exports, the country's net foreign asset position, and the country's role as a provider of safe and reserve assets.

Applying the EBA analysis to the United States, Japan, Germany, and China (as examples) highlights the role of macroeconomic policies and of financial variables in the evolution of external trade imbalances during 2010–17 (Figure 4.9). In recent years, financial conditions (captured by credit) have contributed to the reduction in external imbalances. This is the case in the United States, where the contribution of credit conditions to the trade balance is now positive after the correction of the credit boom before the global financial crisis, and in China, where the credit expansion after the crisis led to an increase in domestic demand and to a reduction in the external surplus. Fiscal policies also matter. For example, a tight fiscal policy in Germany contributed to a large trade surplus while, in Japan, a relatively loose fiscal stance contributed to balancing the external trade position. In the United States, the relatively expansionary fiscal stance after the global financial crisis offset other improvements in the trade balance and, going forward, the recent fiscal stimulus is projected to further widen the trade deficit.[27] Among

presentation, the EBA explanatory variables have been grouped in a somewhat different way than in the original EBA framework.

[27]The fiscal contribution for China here is calculated under the official, legal-based, definition of the government sector. However,

the other drivers, foreign exchange interventions have had only a limited impact on aggregate trade balances and, for China, have largely disappeared in recent years, while cyclical factors have provided, on average, a significant negative component in all countries, except Japan. Among the group of fundamental drivers, the level of development—a proxy for growth prospects and investment opportunities—is estimated to have made a positive contribution to the aggregate trade balance of advanced economies, and a negative contribution for China, consistent with the idea that goods and services should flow "downhill" from advanced to emerging market economies. Moreover, demographic variables make a negative contribution to the trade balance of countries in the late stage of the aging process.[28] Finally, the unexplained residual is quantitively significant, but in line with the original EBA regression. The residual is likely to reflect, among other things, the role of macroeconomic distortions not directly accounted for by the EBA drivers. These include supply-side policies, such as production subsidies and regulatory policies that affect aggregate supply. Such policies have been pointed to in the case of China (see, for example, IMF 2011, 2017b; and the 2017 *External Sector Report*).[29]

As a further cross-check of the role of aggregate macroeconomic factors in driving external imbalances, Box 4.3 discusses the relationship between bilateral and overall trade balances during episodes of large trade deficit adjustments. It finds that empirically large changes in overall trade balances tend to go along with similar changes in a country's bilateral trade relationships, while the opposite does not hold. That is, large adjustments in specific bilateral deficits do not necessarily lead to large adjustments in the overall trade balances (Figure 4.10), suggesting that, absent changes in macroeconomic conditions, large changes in one of the bilateral trade balances of a country tend to result in compensating adjustments in other bilateral balances.

Figure 4.10. Bilateral Trade Deficit Reversal Episodes
(Number of episodes)

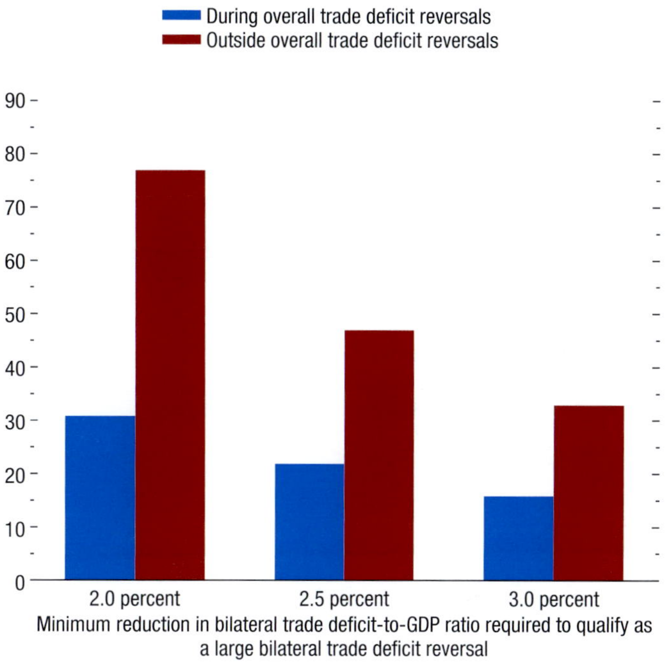

Source: IMF, Direction of Trade Statistics database.
Note: See Box 4.3 for definition of large overall and bilateral trade deficit reversals. There are 92 overall trade deficit reversals.

A Closer Look at Tariffs and Their Spillovers

The analysis so far finds that the direct impact of tariffs on trade balances is small relative to macroeconomic factors. However, as discussed, in the longer term, large, sustained changes in tariffs can shape the international division of labor, as firms adjust domestic and international investment and production structures, including by organizing themselves into global value chains. Indeed, the reduction in tariffs and transportation and communications costs since the mid-1990s has gone hand in hand with a significant increase in complex global value chain participation, which—loosely speaking—is the share of exports that crosses at least two borders (Figure 4.11). Changes in tariffs can thus have important ramifications for

under the IMF staff's economic-based ("augmented") definition of the general government sector, it would likely be negative.

[28]Goods and services are expected to flow "downhill" from advanced economies to raise investment by emerging market economies, which explains the sign of the contribution to the trade balance of the level of development driver. This result is in line with what is obtained in the original, current account-based EBA regression. Instead, while the original EBA finds that demographic variables make a *positive* contribution to the current account of countries in the late stage of the aging process, the contribution in the trade balance regression is *negative*. This is intuitive, given that aging is expected to boost the net income account of a country, stemming from the return on the net foreign assets previously accumulated abroad. At the same time, given that part of this income is later repatriated and consumed by an aging population, the trade balance deteriorates.

[29]More generally, the list of EBA drivers does not include tariffs. This choice is not particularly problematic as long as tariffs are relatively low. It is also important to recognize that macroeconomic policies directly captured in the EBA drivers may be devised as a response to other distortions that operate at the aggregate level.

Figure 4.11. Tariffs and Global Value Chain Participation[1]
(Value added-weighted average over countries and sectors; percent)

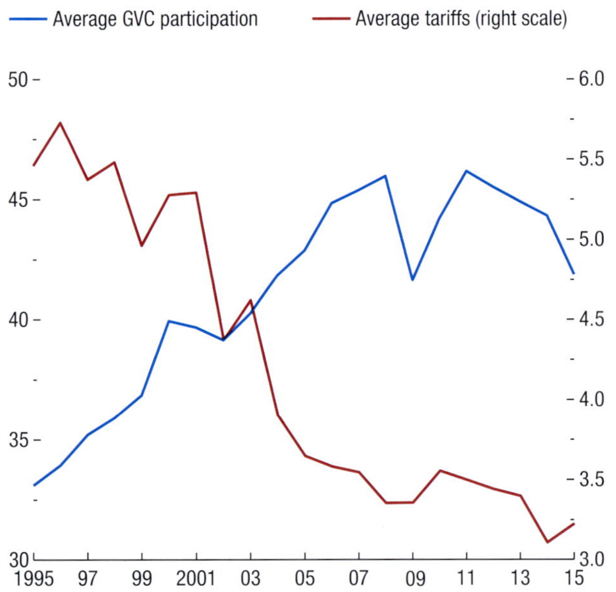

Sources: Organisation for Economic Co-operation and Development, Trade in Value Added database; World Bank, World Integrated Trade Solution database; and IMF staff calculations.
Note: GVC participation is the backward and forward participation in GVCs as a percent of total exports. Tariffs are for agriculture, mining, and manufacturing sectors. GVC = global value chain.
[1]2012–15 extrapolated based on Trade in Value Added database (2018).

productivity, output, and employment.[30] For instance, Amiti and others (2017) finds that China's tariff reductions—associated with its accession to the World Trade Organization—lowered the cost of inputs, boosted Chinese firms' productivity, and, in conjunction with reduced US tariff uncertainty, expanded export participation to the United States.

Increased global integration of production through global value chains creates scope for specialization and productivity improvement—but, at the same time, it increases the risk of international spillovers, including from increases in tariffs and trade wars.[31] As firms use intermediate inputs from other sectors and countries, tariffs imposed in those sectors and countries can affect their cost of production. The effect of tariffs up the value chain (that is, tariffs on direct or indirect suppliers of inputs) is most direct if intermediate inputs are imported. However, effects can also arise indirectly through other sectors and countries. What holds for tariffs upstream also applies to tariffs down the value chain (that is, tariffs imposed by direct or indirect users of the country's output). The firm selling intermediate goods to a sector or country that imposes a new tariff can be affected through reduced demand from customers. Finally, it is possible that tariffs have effects even on countries not directly related to the two parties involved. Relative prices impact trade at all levels, and so do relative tariffs. A change in the tariffs imposed on competitors can therefore affect a firm's international competitiveness and demand for its output; this is similar to the idea of trade diversion, when imposing tariffs on a trading partner's goods leads to a switch of demand to another trading partner's goods on which there are no tariffs.

Measuring Spillovers from Tariffs

What is the impact of tariffs on production, employment, and productivity, accounting for how firms operating in a global value chain context are affected, both domestically and internationally? To capture the various effects of tariffs, four measures are constructed:[32]

- The *upstream tariff* is the average cumulative tariff applied to the intermediate inputs as a share of the sector's output. It captures the average effect tariffs have on the cost of production. It is calculated using the global input-output matrix, in which individual elements are scaled by the relevant sectoral output.
- The *domestic protection tariff* captures the average tariff (import-weighted) imposed on imports that compete with the output of the domestic sector. Its level will most directly affect domestic demand for the sector's output.
- The *downstream tariff* is the average cumulative tariff the sector's output faces when exported either directly or indirectly through other (intermediate-output-using) sectors and countries. Just as for the upstream tariff, it is calculated using a global input-output matrix, scaled by the sector's output. Its level affects the international demand for the sector's output.

[30]The question of the empirical effects of tariffs on economic outcome variables relates to a vast literature (for example, Amiti and Konings 2007; Topalova and Khandelwal 2011; Ahn and others 2016; and Furceri and others 2018); see Online Annex 4.3 for a discussion. Criscuolo and Timmis (2017) provides a discussion of the relationship between global value chains and productivity.

[31]It takes time for firms to change their production structure to minimize the consequences of tariff increases. These short-term costs can be magnified by policy uncertainty, which delays firms' investment decisions.

[32]The construction of upstream and downstream tariffs relies on Vandenbussche, Connell, and Simons (2017) for a theoretical justification and follows Rouzet and Miroudot (2013) in terms of practical implementation. See Online Annex 4.3 for further details.

Table 4.1. Sign and Significance of Tariff Effects on Economic Variables

	(1) Real Value Added	(2) Number Employees	(3) Labor Productivity	(4) Total Factor Productivity
Upstream Tariff	–	–	–	–
Domestic Protection	+	–	–	+
Downstream Tariff	–	–	–	–
Diversion Tariff	+	+	+	–

Source: IMF staff calculations.
Note: Dependent variables are expressed in natural logarithm. Errors are clustered at the country-sector level. Pattern coding: white is not significant at the 10 percent level; light color is significant at the 10 percent level; medium color is signifcant at the 5 percent level; full color is significant at the 1 percent level; green for positive coefficients; red for negative ones.

- The *diversion tariff* captures the weighted average tariff that partner countries impose on all other suppliers except the country-sector in question. The relative weights are a function of the importance of the exporter and importer countries.

The empirical analysis—from a large panel data set of 35 countries and 13 manufacturing sectors, controlling for country-specific macroeconomic changes and country-industry characteristics—suggests that tariffs have significant and economically sizable effects both along the value chain and horizontally on real value added, employment, and productivity (Table 4.1; Online Annex 4.3).

Two main conclusions emerge. First, tariffs up and down the value chain matter for output and productivity generally much more than domestic protection of the given sector. Upstream and downstream tariffs have statistically significant negative effects on value added, consistent with the idea that either they increase input costs (upstream tariff) or reduce international demand for the sector's output (downstream tariff). Both labor productivity and total factor productivity are also significantly reduced by higher upstream or downstream tariffs because they either make foreign inputs more expensive or reduce the ability to benefit from returns to scale by participating in international markets. In contrast, tariffs aimed at increasing protection for domestic producers do not appear to have significant effects, except for a small negative effect on employment. This may reflect a rough offset of negative effects of reduced competition by a larger market share of domestic suppliers. Second, there is evidence of trade diversion. The diversion tariff is positive and statistically significant for value added and employment, consistent with the idea that firms, and therefore sectors, can benefit from a tariff imposed on competitors. The effect, however, does not extend to labor productivity and total factor productivity, for which the diversion tariff is insignificant.

Illustrative Simulations of Tariff Changes

Simulations can illustrate the economic significance of the estimated effects and how a given tariff change affects different countries through different channels. In line with the empirical model discussed above, the simulations illustrate partial equilibrium effects and do not include channels other than the direct trade effects (for example, policy uncertainty, confidence effect, and financial conditions).[33] A different approach using general equilibrium models is discussed later in this chapter.

Impact of Greater Integration on Tariff Spillovers

Closer integration into global value chains has increased the sensitivity of the upstream and downstream tariffs to nominal tariff changes, amplifying their effect. A 1 percentage point tariff increase by all countries would have a larger negative effect today than in 1995 (Figure 4.12).[34] The effect of a nominal tariff hike on real value added has become more negative for all countries, but to varying degrees. For countries such as Germany and Korea and, to a slightly lesser extent, China and Japan, whose manufacturing sectors are both rather big and particularly integrated

[33]The inclusion of the different fixed effects in the estimated model helps make a precise identification of the tariff effect by controlling for country-specific macroeconomic changes or constant characteristics of a given country-industry. The related caveat is that, by absorbing those, the estimated coefficients show partial equilibrium effects. For example, general equilibrium effects of widespread tariff increases on the exchange rate would not be captured by the model. Historically, changes in relative tariffs were predominantly due to tariff declines. In principle, a tariff increase could have a different effect from a tariff decline, even over the medium to long term, but this potential asymmetry is not explored here.

[34]Given data requirements and infrequent data releases, 2011 was the most recent year for which the simulation could be carried out. This is, however, a good approximation of today's links as most of the increase in global value chain integration took place before 2011 (see Figure 4.11). The simulations use the coefficients estimated over the entire sample. Changes in the effects thus reflect changes in weights, notably closer integration of production, as captured by the global input-output matrix.

Figure 4.12. Illustration of the Effect of Tariff Changes on Real Value Added
(Percent of GDP)

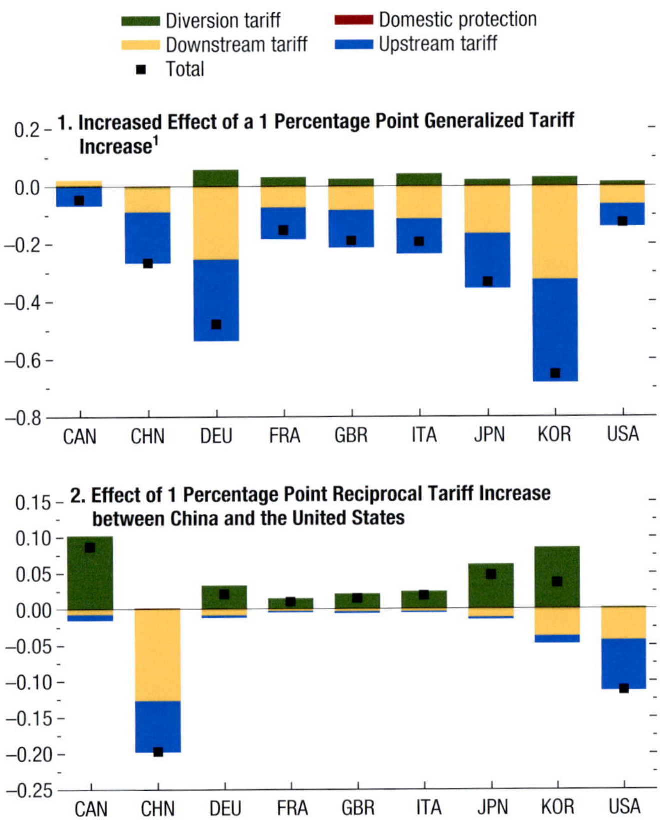

Source: IMF staff calculations.
Note: Data labels use International Organization for Standardization (ISO) country codes.
[1]The figure shows the change in the simulated tariff spillovers between 1995 and 2011, the last year for which such an exercise is possible given data constraints. 2011 is a good approximation of current global value chain links because most of the growth in global value chain integration took place before 2011.

into global value chains, the effects in terms of overall GDP are larger. For Canada and the United States, whose manufacturing sectors are smaller and have evolved less in terms of global integration, the effects tend to be smaller.

Spillovers from Bilateral Tariffs

When tariff changes are more discriminatory and less generalized across countries, the relative importance of the different tariff measures changes, and trade diversion becomes a relevant force for third countries. This becomes apparent when the 1 percentage point tariff increase is limited to trade between China and the United States (see Figure 4.12). China and the United States are the countries most affected and are both hurt by the move.[35] For China, the effects of the downstream and—to a slightly lesser extent—upstream tariffs dominate. For the United States, upstream tariffs are more important because intermediate imports from China play a relatively bigger role. This underlines how tariffs can be harmful to the countries imposing them when they target those with which they are closely integrated through supply chains. For third countries, trade diversion offsets negative spillovers from value chain links with China and the United States. Japan and Korea, which supply inputs to China, are affected by downstream tariffs, but also benefit from trade diversion. For Canada, the relative importance of trade diversion is most pronounced, and the overall effect is most likely to be positive.

The analysis so far has focused on small, first-round sectoral effects of tariffs, abstracting from, among other things, the additional domestic and international effects that stem from resulting aggregate changes in productivity, employment, or output. For a better understanding of the global general equilibrium effects, a hypothetical, large US–China trade dispute is simulated using three different modeling approaches that each emphasize different transmission channels (Box 4.4). China and the United States are found to suffer the largest losses from their reciprocal tariff increases, due to the collapse in bilateral trade—with only partial substitution from other sources—and lower returns to capital, reflecting tariff distortions. Trade diversion leads to substitution of China's exports to the United States: Mexico and Canada benefit most, reflecting their close proximity to, and strong trade relations with, the United States; east Asia also benefits to some extent. At the same time, these countries increase imports of intermediates from China and from other countries. While the level of bilateral trade between China and the United States is much reduced, there is no economically significant change in either country's aggregate trade balance. Overall, macroeconomic spillover effects in third countries are modest in size, but sectoral spillovers are larger as global value chains are repositioned. In particular, over the long term, sizable shifts in manufacturing capacity away from China (and the United States) toward Mexico, Canada, and east Asia would occur (Figure 4.13). These sectoral shifts would imply sizable job losses in specific sectors, especially in China and the United States.

The trade diversion effects—found both in the sectoral empirical analysis and in the general equilibrium simulations—suggest that attempts to target one

[35]The smaller cost on the United States in percent of GDP reflects the relatively smaller weight of the US manufacturing sector in US GDP; the change in manufacturing value added itself is actually somewhat larger for the United States than for China.

bilateral trade balance through tariffs or other distortions will likely be met with offsetting changes in the trade balances with other partners. Under given macroeconomic conditions, changes in bilateral trade balances are unlikely to translate into sustained changes in the overall trade balance. Finally, while some third countries may benefit from trade diversion, a trade war between China and the United States would also trigger increased uncertainty, negative confidence effects, and a tightening of global financial conditions, with negative effects on most countries (Chapter 1 of the October 2018 WEO). Therefore, most countries are likely to be worse off, even those that benefit from trade diversion.

Conclusion

The findings in this chapter strongly suggest that aggregate imbalances tend to be reflected at the bilateral level, while bilateral imbalances are of little consequence for the aggregate—indeed, unless macroeconomic conditions change, attempts to influence a particular bilateral trade balance are likely to lead to compensating adjustments elsewhere, leaving the overall trade balance unchanged.

Over the past two decades, macroeconomic factors played a key role in explaining changes in bilateral balances. The path of bilateral imbalances was, to a significant extent, determined by the relative movement of the two partners' domestic imbalance between supply and demand—as mirrored in their respective overall trade balance. Macroeconomic factors reflected a variety of drivers, including fundamental factors, macroeconomic policies—such as fiscal policies and credit cycles—and, in some cases, exchange rate policies and supply-side policies.

At the same time, bilateral balances are also a reflection of the international division of labor and economic benefits accruing through trade. Declines in tariffs and other trade costs have allowed global value chains to grow and countries to further specialize according to their comparative advantage while production arrangements spread across borders and became more efficient.

Looking beyond the effects on bilateral trade balances, higher tariffs would have significant negative impacts on value added, employment, and productivity for the countries involved and for third countries through value chain links. Greater international division of labor, in particular through global value chains, has increased the scope for negative spillovers of tariffs on other countries and spillback effects on countries imposing the tariffs. While some countries may benefit from trade diversion, all will be affected by adverse confidence effects and tighter financial conditions as trade tensions escalate.

Figure 4.13. Sectoral Effects from a 25 Percent Increase in Tariffs Affecting All US–China Trade: World Real Value Added
(Contributions to total percent change from baseline)

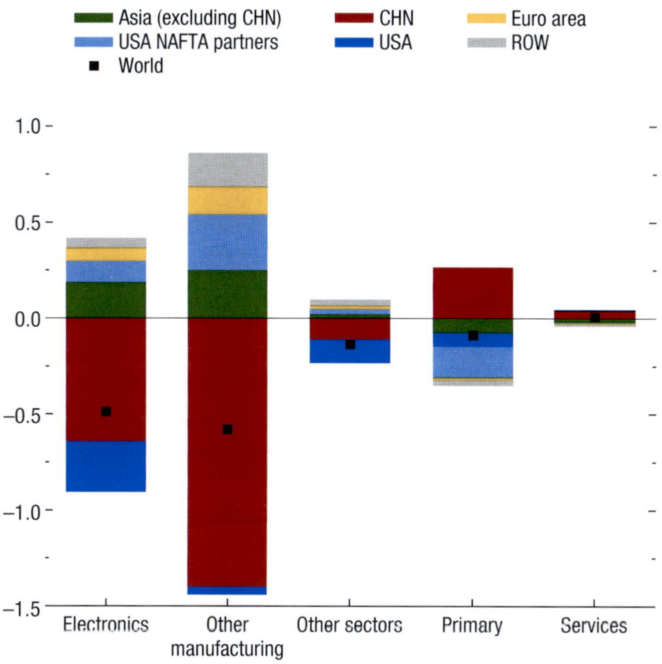

Source: IMF calculations using the model in Caliendo and others (2017).
Note: NAFTA = North American Free Trade Agreement; ROW = rest of the world. Data labels use International Organization for Standardization (ISO) country codes.

Two main policy conclusions emerge from the analysis. First, given the important role of macroeconomic imbalances in bilateral trade and trade balances, the discussion of external balances is rightly focused on aggregate trade balances and current accounts—as well as the macroeconomic policies and distortions driving them. Aggregate external imbalances are not bad in and of themselves, given that they allow countries to borrow to finance investment and future growth, or to smooth consumption at times when income is temporarily lost. But policymakers should avoid distortive macroeconomic policies that create excessive—and possibly unsustainable—imbalances.

Second, there is a strong case for lowering tariffs. The evidence provided here implies that lower tariffs will not only boost trade, they will also allow adjustment in the international division of labor to more fully reflect comparative advantage—which in turn leads to output, employment, and productivity gains for countries themselves and for others up and down the value chain. But as highlighted elsewhere, it is important to have policies in place to ensure that the benefits from trade are widely shared and the burden of adjustment does not fall on only a few (IMF 2017a; IMF/WB/WTO 2017, 2018).

Box 4.1. Gross versus Value-Added Trade

Popular debate about bilateral trade balances usually focuses on the standard measure of *gross balances*—that is, exports to a country minus imports from the same country. However, over the past few years, the literature has emphasized that a more complete picture of bilateral trade relations needs to include the evolution of *value-added balances* (Johnson and Noguera 2012a, 2012b, 2017; Koopman, Wang, and Wei 2014). The importance of differentiating between gross and value-added bilateral balances has become more relevant as global value chains continue to develop.

The point can be explained using, as an example, trade among China, Korea, and the United States in electrical goods, such as smart phones or televisions (WB and others 2017). If only final goods were traded internationally, then any good that the United States exports to Korea would stay in Korea. In this case, gross exports of the United States to Korea would give a correct representation of how much value produced in the first country actually reaches the other. However, this is not how production of electrical goods is carried out in today's global value chains, where trade occurs largely in intermediate goods. The United States exports some inputs (such as design) to Korea, which adds new inputs (semiconductors and processors) to the production stage and exports the resulting new intermediates to China, which in turn completes production by assembling the inputs and ships the final goods back to the United States. In the example of these goods, the United States accumulates a *gross* bilateral surplus with Korea and a deficit with China. These values, however, do not reflect the true origin and destination of the value of production generated—and consumed—in each country. Imports of the United States from China, in fact, reflect only partially the value generated in China, given that they incorporate not only the extra value generated in Korea, but also the value initially generated in the United States. Therefore, the trade deficit of the United States with regard to China is smaller if calculated in *value-added* terms.

Panel 1 of Figure 4.1.1 shows the 10 largest bilateral imbalances in 2015, in both gross and value-added terms. It is clear that, while large gross bilateral imbalances are, in general, also accompanied by large value-added imbalances, the imbalances in value-added

Figure 4.1.1. Gross versus Value-Added Trade Balance
(Billions of US dollars)

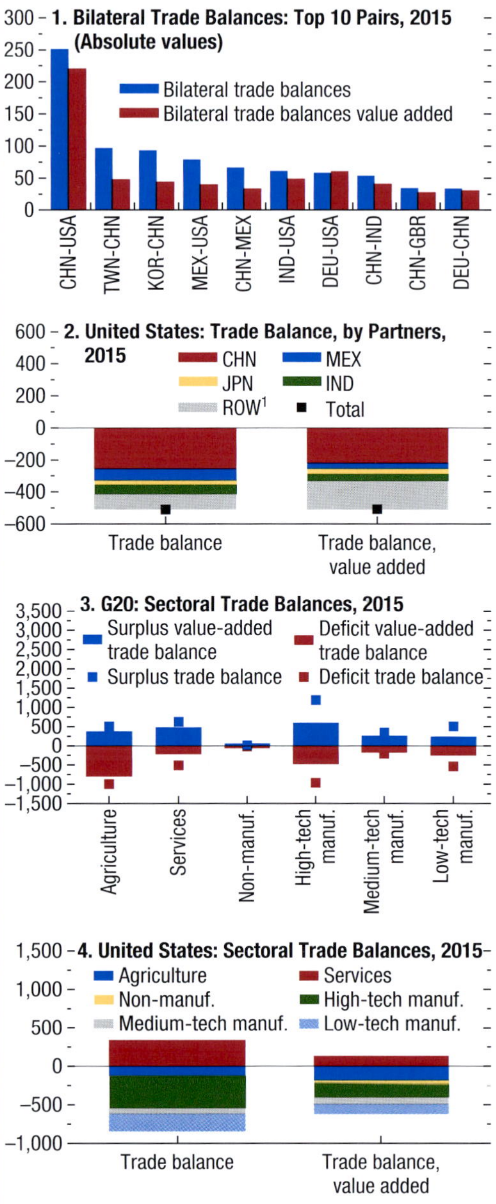

Sources: Organisation for Economic Co-operation and Development, Trade in Value Added database; and IMF staff calculations.
Note: G20 = Group of Twenty; manuf. = manufacturing; ROW = rest of the world. Data labels use International Organization for Standardization (ISO) country codes.
[1]Includes statistical discrepancy.

The author of this box is Roberto Piazza.

Box 4.1 *(continued)*

terms are smaller. For example, Korea's surplus with China is smaller in value-added terms because Korea's figure for gross exports incorporates value added from other countries. Panel 2 looks specifically at the largest bilateral imbalances for the United States and shows that the trade deficits with Mexico and China shrink when measured in value-added terms. Clearly, when measured against the totality of the rest of the world, a country's overall trade balance is the same, regardless of whether it is measured in gross or in value-added terms.

Similar considerations hold when looking at the sectoral composition of trade imbalances. Panel 3 presents, for each of six sectors, the sum of surplus and of deficits across Group of Twenty countries. Sectoral trade surpluses and deficits are typically smaller on a value added than on a gross basis, reflecting the round-trip of production through different sectors. Panel 4 looks at imbalances for the United States. When measured in value added, the US surplus in services is reduced, and its manufacturing deficit shrinks. This happens, for example, when US services (such as intellectual property) are used as inputs in the manufacturing sector of other countries, and these manufactured goods are then imported back to the United States.

Box 4.2. Bilateral and Aggregate Trade Balances

This box derives an explicit relationship between bilateral and aggregate trade balances and illustrates, as an example, the role of macroeconomic factors for the US–China bilateral trade balance.

Under the relatively mild assumption that trade costs are symmetric—that is, the cost of shipping goods from country *i* to country *j* is the same as the cost of shipping from *j* to *i*—the standard gravity relationship that underpins the analysis in the previous section can be rearranged to obtain

$$\frac{TB_{ij}}{Y_i Y_j^W} = m_{ij} \cdot \left(\frac{TB_i}{Y_i} - \frac{TB_j}{Y_j}\right),$$

in which *TB* denotes trade balance and *Y* output, with one of the two outputs (Y_j^W in the equation) expressed as a share of world output (see Online Annex 4.2 for the derivation). The equation makes clear that the bilateral trade balance between two countries (appropriately scaled) depends on the relative evolution of the aggregate trade balance-to-GDP ratio of each of the two countries.

The appropriate scaling of the bilateral trade balance between countries *i* and *j* jointly accounts for the output level of both. This captures the intuition that, as the two countries grow, all else equal, their bilateral trade balance would tend to increase in absolute value. Figure 4.2.1, panel 1, shows that, when scaled by US GDP, the bilateral trade imbalance between the United States and China did not shrink after the 2008–09 global financial crisis. However, when the double scaling is applied—and therefore the growing share of China in the world economy is factored in—a notable reduction emerges. This is consistent with the decline in global imbalances seen after the global financial crisis.

Finally, the equation also makes clear that changes in a country's aggregate trade imbalance (driven by fundamentals, such as fiscal policy and credit cycles) are amplified or dampened at the bilateral level by the corresponding bilateral trade intensity m_{ij}, which summarizes how a specific trade relationship is affected by the pair-specific bilateral and multilateral trading costs (and other more micro-structural determinants) identified by the gravity framework.

Applying this relationship to the US–China bilateral trade balance confirms that macroeconomic imbalances played a key role in its evolution. Figure 4.2.1 (panel 2) plots again the scaled bilateral trade balance ("actual"), but now against a "predicted" value constructed as the product of a constant estimate for m_{ij} times the difference in the aggregate trade-balance-to-GDP ratios of the two countries. The fact that the two lines track quite closely shows that variations in aggregate trade balances explain the evolution of the (scaled) US–China bilateral balance very well. The imperfection of the relationship indicates that variations in trade intensity—for example, because of the changing constellation of world trade costs, also play a role.

The author of this box is Roberto Piazza.

Figure 4.2.1. US–China Bilateral and Aggregate Trade Balances
(Percent)

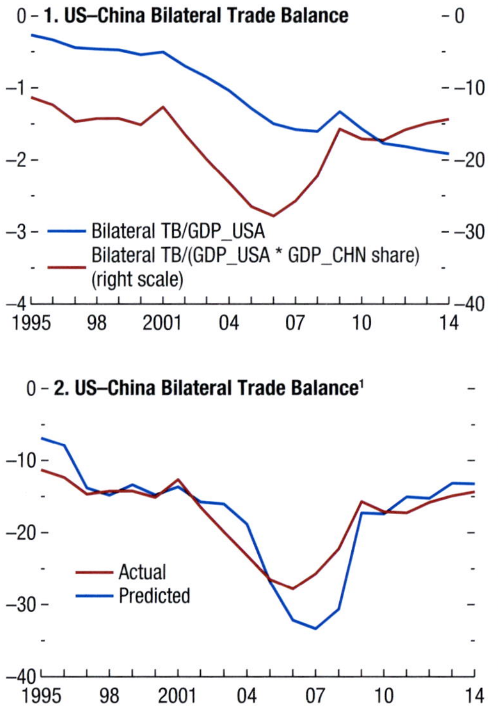

Sources: Organisation for Economic Co-operation and Development, Trade in Value Added database; and IMF staff calculations.
Note: TB = Trade Balance. Data labels use International Organization for Standardization (ISO) country codes.
[1]As a percentage of US GDP times the world share of China's GDP.

Box 4.3. Understanding Trade Deficit Adjustments: Does Bilateral Trade Play a Special Role?

Will a policy of targeting bilateral trade deficits reduce a country's overall current account deficit? This box tackles this question by documenting the role of bilateral trade balances in past episodes of large trade deficit adjustments. The results suggest that (1) overall trade deficit adjustments are not necessarily driven by disproportionate or large trade adjustments of trading partners with the biggest deficits; and (2) large adjustments of these high-deficit trading partners are no guarantee that large adjustments in overall trade balances will take place.

Large Trade Deficit Reversal Episodes

Following the literature on current account deficit reversals (see Milesi-Ferretti and Razin 1998), episodes of large trade deficit adjustments are identified using three criteria: (1) the average reduction in the overall trade deficit is at least 3 percentage points of GDP over three years relative to the three-year average before the event, (2) the maximum trade deficit in the three years after the reversal is lower than the minimum deficit in the three years preceding the reversal, and (3) there is no other episode in the following six years. Episodes of large bilateral trade deficit adjustments relative to the trading partners with the five biggest deficits are then computed using the same concept.[1]

Using IMF Direction of Trade Statistics data from 1980–2017 for countries with nominal GDP above the world median in 2017 (excluding fuel exporters), 92 large deficit-adjustment episodes were identified. Of these, only 17 percent (16 out of 92) were associated with large bilateral trade adjustment by at least one of the five biggest deficit partners. Results are generally robust to the adjustment threshold for bilateral trade adjustments (for example, a lower threshold of 2½ percentage points would increase the number of episodes with large bilateral trade adjustments from 16 to 22). The findings suggest that the overall trade adjustments are not generally driven by large adjustments in a country's top trading partners (Figure 4.10 in Chapter 4, blue bar). Interestingly, in many cases, large adjustments in at least one of the five biggest deficit partners took place without a large reversal in the overall trade deficit (Figure 4.10 in Chapter 4, orange bar), suggesting that large adjustments of key bilateral deficit partners do not guarantee large adjustments in the overall trade balance.

Figure 4.3.1. Improvement in Bilateral Trade Deficits during Overall Trade Deficit Reversal Episodes
(Percent)

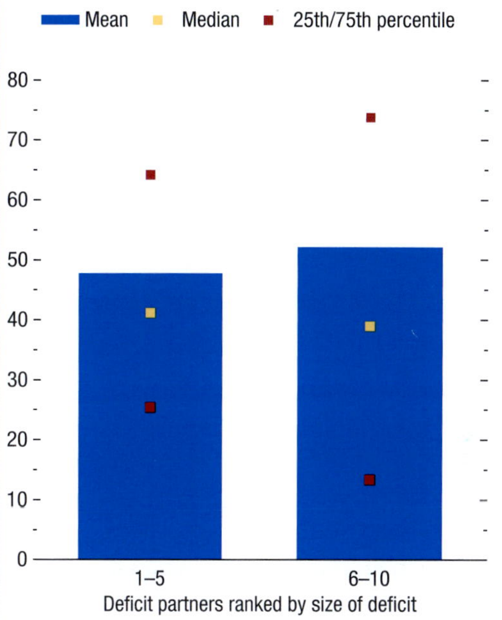

Source: IMF, Direction of Trade Statistics database.
Note: Improvement in bilateral trade balance deficit to GDP relative to initial level is calculated using the following formula: change in bilateral trade balance to GDP (between three-year average of trade balance to GDP prior to reversal and three-year average after the reversal) relative to the absolute value of initial bilateral trade balance to GDP level (three-year average of trade balance to GDP prior to reversal year). Positive value represents improvement in trade balance deficit against deficit trading partners.

How Broad Based Are Trade Deficit Adjustments?

As expected, absolute adjustments are concentrated at the top. The five biggest deficit partners are, on average, responsible for 54 percent of deficit correction, the next five are responsible for 12 percent of the correction, and the following five explain 8 percent of the correction. These results are not surprising, given that trade is fairly concentrated across trading partners, especially in advanced economies, where about half of trade is conducted with fewer than six partners.

Relative adjustments, however, are more evenly distributed. Adjustments are generally broad based or proportional across trading partners, such that the

The authors of this box are Kyun Suk Chang, Swarnali Ahmed Hannan, and Sergii Meleshchuk.

[1]To be conservative, the episodes of large bilateral trade deficit adjustments are initially computed using the first two requirements and then matched with the overall episodes. For bilateral episodes matched with overall episodes, any further bilateral episode within plus or minus six years is removed from the sample. Bilateral episodes happening outside overall reversal episodes are based on the remaining sample.

Box 4.3 *(continued)*

improvement in bilateral trade balances—adjusted for their initial trade balance—is similar across the top five and the sixth to tenth deficit partners (Figure 4.3.1). Specifically, the mean adjustment for the top five deficit partners is about 48 percent of their initial level, slightly lower than 52 percent of adjustment by the deficit partners ranked six to ten. Regression analysis confirms that all trading partners (top or bottom) contribute to trade deficit adjustments and that disproportionate reductions in the trade balances with top trading partners are by no means a necessary condition for the overall trade balance reduction.

In sum, the findings in this box suggest that targeting bilateral trade balances would likely not help to reduce a country's overall current account deficit. This is consistent with the conventional economic wisdom that changes in current account balances—the difference between national saving and investment—is best achieved through adjustments to macroeconomic policies, not trade policies.

Box 4.4. The Global Macro and Micro Effects of a US–China Trade Dispute: Insights from Three Models

Recent trade measures between the United States and China have revived interest in the macroeconomic effects of tariffs. Because most of the tariffs (implemented or envisaged) target trade between two large economies, an important question is the extent to which other countries not directly involved in the dispute (third countries) could be affected. The possible spillovers are both macro—affecting GDP and overall trade—and micro—including value-chain and sectoral disruptions.

This box provides a range of estimates for China, the United States, and third countries, in a hypothetical and illustrative scenario in which tariffs on all US–China goods trade increase by 25 percentage points. It covers a range of models used by macroeconomists, trade policy experts, and academic trade theorists: a dynamic stochastic general equilibrium model of the global economy (the IMF's Global Integrated Monetary and Fiscal model, or GIMF); a multisector perfect-competition computable general equilibrium model often used for trade policy analysis (the Global Trade Analysis Project, or GTAP); and a multisector heterogenous-firm model with entry and exit à la Melitz (Caliendo and others 2017, henceforth CFRT). Each model emphasizes different transmission channels.[1] GIMF focuses on the aggregate effects over time, with a distinction between the short term, during which nominal and real rigidities tend to amplify the expenditure-switching effects of tariffs, and the medium to long term, during which the effect stems mainly from the (distortionary) permanent impact of tariffs on the levels of key factors of production, capital, and labor. Given their rich sectoral and regional disaggregation, the two trade models (GTAP and CFRT) emphasize, instead, the disruption that tariffs cause by reallocating factors of production—inefficiently and unevenly—across sectors within countries over the medium to the long term. In CFRT, the extent of reallocation is amplified by the presence of increasing returns to scale associated with firm-level fixed costs of entering domestic and export markets.

Two preliminary remarks are in order. First, the emphasis of this box is on trade-related channels. The negative spillovers from trade policy uncertainty were previously analyzed with GIMF in the October 2018 *World Economic Outlook* and are not included here. Second—and as is typical in trade policy simulations—the results depend crucially on the ease with which producers can substitute inputs from different countries (trade elasticities). In line with estimates found in the literature, results are based on a calibration in which substitution between any two foreign suppliers is easier than substitution between a foreign supplier and a domestic firm.[2] This tends to amplify the (positive) effects on third countries, given that production tends to be diverted toward them rather than re-shored to the countries imposing the tariffs.

Effects on the United States and China

Figures 4.4.1 and 4.4.2 show that the United States and China suffer the largest losses. This result is broadly robust across models. The starting point is a collapse in

The authors of this box are Carlos Caceres, Diego Cerdeiro, Rui Mano, Rafael Portillo, and Marika Santoro.

[1]All models feature trade in intermediate goods, though to a varying degree, depending on the extent of the sectoral and regional disaggregation in the model.

[2]This is the case in both trade models and in the short term in GIMF. The elasticities between domestic and foreign production in CFRT are calibrated using the estimates in Feenstra and others (2018); they broadly match the elasticities in GTAP.

Box 4.4 *(continued)*

Figure 4.4.1. Macro Effects from a 25 Percent Increase in Tariffs Affecting All US–China Trade: Real GDP
(Percentage point change from baseline)

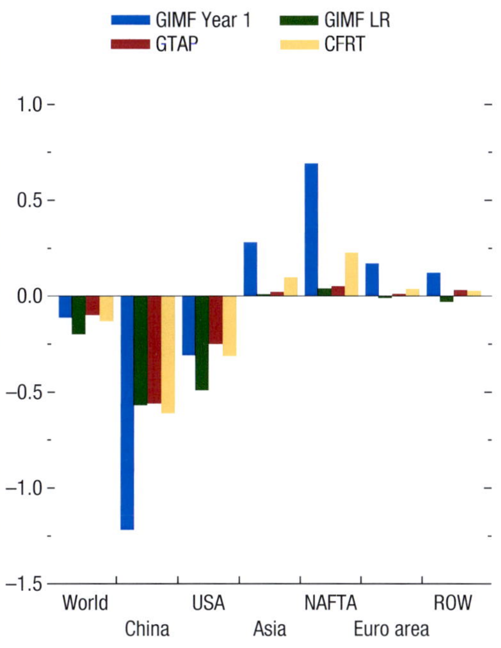

Source: IMF calculation using the model in Caliendo and others (2017).
Note: CFRT = Caliendo and others (2017) model; EA = euro area; GIMF = Global Integrated Monetary and Fiscal model; GTAP = Global Trade Analysis Project; LR = long run; NAFTA = North American Free Trade Agreement; ROW = rest of the world.

Figure 4.4.2. Macro Effects from a 25 Percent Increase in Tariffs Affecting All US–China Trade: Real Exports
(Percentage point change from baseline)

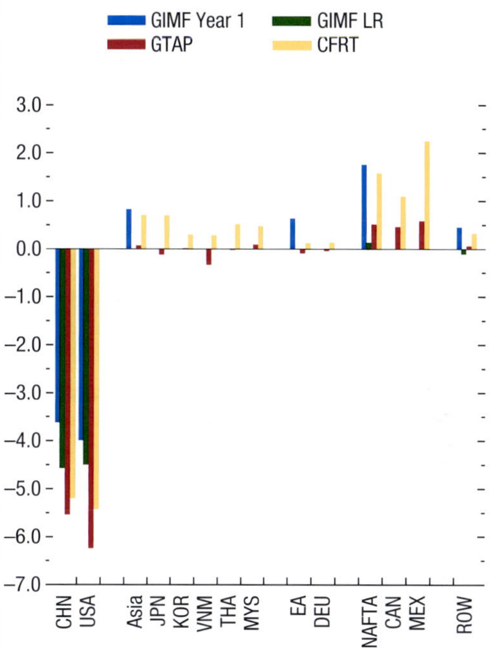

Source: IMF calculation using the model in Caliendo and others (2017).
Note: CFRT = Caliendo and others (2017) model; EA = euro area; GIMF = Global Integrated Monetary and Fiscal model; GTAP = Global Trade Analysis Project; LR = long run; NAFTA = North American Free Trade Agreement; ROW = rest of the world. Data labels use International Organization for Standardization (ISO) country codes.

US–China trade, which falls by 25–30 percent in the short term (GIMF) and somewhere between 30 percent and 70 percent over the long term, depending on the model and the direction of trade (Table 4.4.1). The decrease in external demand leads to a decline in total exports and in GDP in both countries. Annual real GDP losses range from –0.3 percent to –0.6 percent for the United States and from –0.5 percent to –1.5 percent for China. The effect on China is typically larger across all models, as exports to the United States represent a larger share of the Chinese economy (than vice versa). In GIMF, the effects on China are more pronounced in the short term, given that wages and prices do not adjust sufficiently to help offset the decrease in external demand; the negative effects on the United States become larger over the long term, as higher tariffs and a more appreciated exchange rate (not shown) lower the returns to capital. In CFRT, instead, the effects on China are amplified by the loss of economies of scale. The asymmetry in the effects of the tariff dispute is also reflected in each country's terms of trade: these improve in the United States and worsen in China. Finally, although the US–China bilateral trade deficit is reduced, there is no economically significant change in each country's multilateral trade balance.[3]

Macro Spillovers

Figure 4.4.2 and Table 4.4.1 show the effects on total exports and bilateral exports to China and the United States by regions of the world and selected

[3]The latter result (shown in Table 4.4.1) is based on GIMF simulations only, as the two trade models are solved under the explicit assumption that each country's multilateral trade balance does not change.

Box 4.4 *(continued)*

Table 4.4.1. Macro Effects from a 25 Percent Increase in Tariffs Affecting All US–China Trade: Bilateral Trade Flows with Third Countries

	GIMF		GTAP	CFRT
Macro Variables	Year 1	Long Run		
Trade Balance (percent of GDP)				
China	–0.2	–0.3	. . .	. . .
United States	–0.2	–0.3	. . .	. . .
Exports to the United States				
China	–20.9	–25.1	–71.3	–56.0
Asia	3.7	1.8	10.6	7.7
Japan	. . .	. . .	9.2	5.8
Korea	. . .	. . .	10.3	7.7
Vietnam	. . .	. . .	13.9	9.7
Thailand	. . .	. . .	10.8	9.3
Malaysia	. . .	. . .	10.9	7.7
Euro Area	3.8	1.7	8.4	5.7
Germany	. . .	. . .	8.6	4.9
NAFTA	2.6	0.7	3.2	3.2
Canada	. . .	. . .	7.5	2.5
Mexico	. . .	. . .	2.8	4.3
Rest of the World	3.1	1.7	6.1	5.8
Exports to China				
United States	–27.5	–36.4	–77.6	–63.7
Asia	0.5	–1.5	–4.9	–1.1
Japan	. . .	. . .	–5.3	–0.8
Korea	. . .	. . .	–5.3	–1.3
Vietnam	. . .	. . .	–3.4	–3.4
Thailand	. . .	. . .	–4.4	–2.1
Malaysia	. . .	. . .	–4.9	–0.6
Euro Area	1.3	–1.6	–4.3	–1.4
Germany	. . .	. . .	–4.4	–1.4
NAFTA	–0.4	–2.6	–4.4	–2.9
Canada	. . .	. . .	–0.1	–2.8
Mexico	. . .	. . .	–6.3	–3.5
Rest of the World	–0.1	–1.6	–1.0	–2.8

Source: IMF staff calculations.
Note: CFRT = Caliendo and others (2017); GIMF = Global Integrated Monetary and Fiscal model; GTAP = Global Trade Analysis Project.

countries.[4] A very robust result across models is that, while third countries experience an increase in exports to the United States, they also experience a decrease in exports to China. Much of the trade diversion at the global level is therefore about third countries increasing their exports to the United States at the expense of China (as well as importing more intermediate goods from China; more on this follows). The effect on third countries' overall exports is, in general, positive, with Mexico and Canada benefitting the most, thanks to their proximity to, and strong trade relations with, the United States. Across models, the increase in third-country exports is most notable in GIMF in the short term and in CFRT, with GTAP showing weaker, and in some cases negative, responses.

There is more variation across models in terms of the effects on output in third countries, though these are typically modest in size. GIMF shows positive effects in the short term, including relatively large ones in other North America (excluding the United States), which reflect the strength of trade diversion in the presence of nominal rigidities.[5] The effects are small but negative over the long term, however, in every region except other North America (excluding the United States), as some of the capital-reducing distor-

[4]This version of GIMF includes four other regions (Asia excluding China, North America excluding the United States, the euro area, and remaining countries) besides the United States and China.

[5]As already mentioned, this study does not focus on possible trade-policy-related uncertainty, which can create short-term negative spillovers for third countries that can more than offset the positive effects from the trade diversion.

Box 4.4 *(continued)*

Figure 4.4.3. US Imports of Electronics and Machinery before and after Tariffs

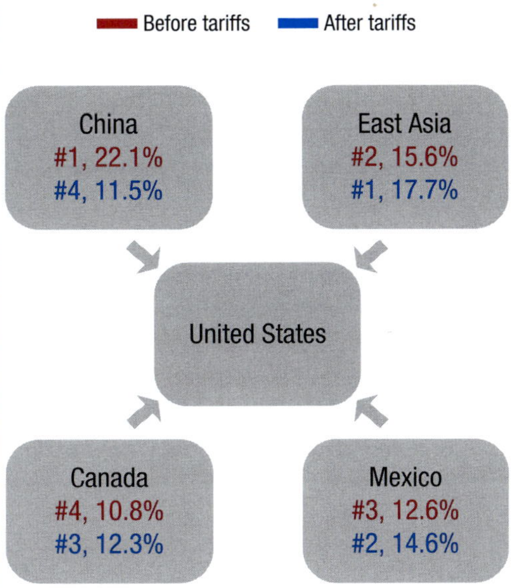

Sources: Caliendo and others (2017) model; and IMF staff calculations.
Note: #x means rank, xx% means share in total US imports of electronics.

Figure 4.4.4. Mexico's Imports of Intermediate Inputs for the Electronics and Manufacturing Sectors
(Percent of GDP)

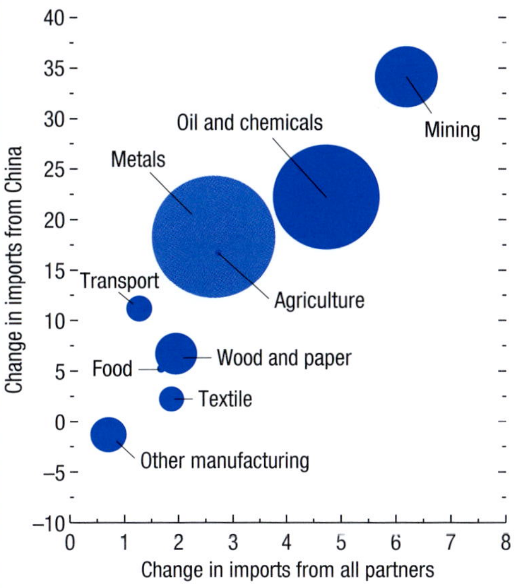

Source: IMF staff calculations.
Note: Excluding machinery and electronics. Dot size is proportional to input intensity in Mexico's machinery and electronics sector.

tions from higher tariffs mentioned earlier spill over to third countries. GTAP shows positive but small effects, while CFRT shows a number of countries (such as Mexico, Canada, Malaysia, Thailand, and Korea) experiencing a relatively large expansion in output and benefiting from economies of scale.

Sectoral Reallocations across Countries

Results from the two trade models illustrate that, while, in the aggregate, the spillovers tend to be moderate, this is not true at the sectoral level. The manufacturing sector shows a large worldwide contraction, with major fallout in the electronics and other manufacturing sectors in China (see Figure 4.13 in the main text). In contrast, manufacturing sectors expand in Mexico, Canada, and in Asian countries. Services expand in China and contract in the other countries mentioned previously, while the US agricultural sector experiences a sizable contraction. The magnitude of the reallocation varies across models; it is larger in CFRT due to economies of scale.

These sectoral reallocations imply sizable job losses in specific sectors, which compound the macroeconomic adjustment for those experiencing an overall contraction (mainly the United States and China). For example, in CFRT, large sectors in both countries shed a significant number of jobs—about 1 percent of the workforce in the US agricultural and transportation equipment sectors, and 5 percent in China's other manufacturing sector.

Repositioning of Global Value Chains

Finally, the sectoral reallocations also have implications for global value chains and the structure of international trade. The electronics and machinery sector provides a good illustration, given its importance in global trade (about 20 percent of world imports). In CFRT—the model in which the reallocation effects are most pronounced—China would eventually stop being the number one exporter of electronics and machinery to the United States, with other countries in Asia, Canada, and Mexico replacing China (Figure 4.4.3). In, for example, Mexico, the sizable entry of new firms into the electronics sector would then lead to large increases in imports of intermediates from everywhere else and especially from China (Figure 4.4.4).

References

Ahn, JaeBin, Emine Boz, Mauric Obstfeld, and Petia Topalova. Forthcoming. "Bilateral Trade Balances and Global Value Chains." International Monetary Fund, Washington, DC.

Ahn, JaeBin, Era Dabla-Norris, Romain Duval, Bingjie Hu, and Lamin Njie. 2016. "Reassessing the Productivity Gains from Trade Liberalization." IMF Working Paper 16/77, International Monetary Fund, Washington, DC.

Amiti, Mary, Mi Dai, Robert C. Feenstra, and John Romalis. 2017. "How Did China's WTO Entry Affect US Prices?" NBER Working Paper 23487, National Bureau of Economic Research, Cambridge, MA.

Amiti, Mary, and Jozef Konings. 2007. "Trade Liberalization, Intermediate Inputs, and Productivity: Evidence from Indonesia." *American Economic Review* 97 (5): 1611–638.

Anderson, James E., and Eric van Wincoop. 2003. "Gravity with Gravitas: A Solution to the Border Puzzle." *American Economic Review* 93 (1): 170–92.

Bacchetta, Marc, Cosimo Beverelli, Olivier Cadot, Marco Fugazza, Jean-Marie Grether, Matthias Helble, Alessandro Nicita, and Roberta Piermartini. 2012. "A Practical Guide to Trade Policy Analysis." World Trade Organization, Geneva.

Baldwin, Richard, and Javier Lopez-Gonzalez. 2013. "Supply-Chain Trade: A Portrait of Global Patterns and Several Testable Hypotheses." NBER Working Papers 18957, National Bureau of Economic Research, Cambridge, MA.

Baldwin, Richard, and Daria Taglioni. 2011. "Gravity Chains: Estimating Bilateral Trade Flows When Parts and Components Trade is Important." *Journal of Banking and Financial Economics* 2 (2): 61–82.

Barattieri, Alessandro. 2014. "Comparative Advantage, Service Trade, and Global Imbalances." *Journal of International Economics* 92 (1): 1–13.

Boz, Emine, Nan Li, and Hongrui Zhang. 2019. "Effective Trade Costs and the Current Account: An Empirical Analysis." IMF Working Paper 19/8, International Monetary Fund, Washington, DC.

Caliendo, Lorenzo, Robert C. Feenstra, John Romalis, and Alan Taylor. 2017. "Tariff Reductions, Entry, and Welfare: Theory and Evidence for the Last Two Decades." NBER Working Paper 21768, National Bureau of Economic Research, Cambridge, MA.

Caliendo, Lorenzo, and Fernando Parro. 2015. "Estimates of the Trade and Welfare Effects of NAFTA." *The Review of Economic Studies* 82 (1): 1–44.

Criscuolo, Chiara, and Jonathan Timmis. 2017. "The Relationship between Global Value Chains and Productivity." Centre for the Study of Living Standards, *International Productivity Monitor* 32 (Spring): 61–83.

Daruich, Diego, William Easterly, and Ariell Reshef. 2019. "The Surprising Instability of Export Specializations." *Journal of Development Economics* 137: 36–65.

Davis, Donald, and David Weinstein. 2002. "The Mystery of the Excess Trade (Balances)." *American Economic Review* 92 (2): 170–74.

Feenstra, Robert C. 2004. *Advanced International Trade: Theory and Evidence*. Princeton, NJ, and Oxford: Princeton University Press.

Feenstra, Robert C., Philip Luck, Maurice Obstfeld, and Katheryn Russ. 2018. "In Search of the Armington Elasticity." *Review of Economics and Statistics* 100 (1): 135–50.

Furceri, Davide, Swarnali A. Hannan, Jonathan D. Ostry, and Andrew K. Rose. 2018. "Macroeconomic Consequences of Tariffs." CEPR Discussion Papers 13389, Center for Economic and Policy Research, Washington, DC.

Group of Twenty (G20). 2018. "G20 Global Forum on Steel Excess Capacity Ministerial Meeting, Ministerial Report." September 20, Paris.

Head, Keith, and Thierry Mayer. 2014. "Gravity Equations: Workhorse, Toolkit, and Cookbook." In *Handbook of International Economics*, Volume 4, edited by Gita Gopinath, Elhanan Helpman, and Kenneth Rogoff. Oxford: Elsevier.

International Monetary Fund (IMF). 2011. "People's Republic of China: Spillover Report for the 2011 Article IV Consultation and Selected Issues." IMF Country Report 11/193, Washington, DC.

———. 2017a. "Fostering Inclusive Growth." Prepared for discussion at the July 2017 Group of Twenty Leaders' Summit.

———. 2017b. "People's Republic of China 2017 Article IV Consultation—Press Release; Staff Report; and Statement by the Executive Director for the People's Republic of China." IMF Country Report 17/247, Washington, DC.

International Monetary Fund, World Bank, and World Trade Organization (IMF/WB/WTO). 2017. "Making Trade an Engine of Growth for All: The Case for Trade and for Policies to Facilitate Adjustment." Prepared for discussion at the March 2017 meeting of Group of Twenty 20 Sherpas by staffs of the International Monetary Fund, World Bank, and World Trade Organization.

———. 2018. "Reinvigorating Trade and Inclusive Growth." Prepared for discussion at the March 2017 meeting of the Group of Twenty Sherpas by staffs of the International Monetary Fund, World Bank, and World Trade Organization.

Joy, Mark, Noëmie Lisack, Simon Lloyd, Dennis Reinhardt, Rana Sajedi, and Simon Whitaker. 2018. "Mind the (Current Account) Gap." Bank of England Financial Stability Paper 43, London.

Johnson, Robert C., and Guillermo Noguera. 2012a. "Accounting for Intermediates: Production Sharing and Trade in Value Added." *Journal of International Economics* 86 (2): 224–36.

———. 2012b. "Proximity and Production Fragmentation." *American Economic Review Papers and Proceedings* 102 (3): 407–11.

———. 2017. "A Portrait of Trade in Value Added over Four Decades." *Review of Economics and Statistics* 99 (5): 896–911.

Koopman, Robert, Zhi Wang, and Shang-Jin Wei. (2014). Tracing Value Added and Double Counting in Gross Exports. *American Economic Review* 104 (2): 459–94.

Milesi-Ferretti, Gian Maria, and Assaf Razin. 1998. “Sharp Reductions in Current Account Deficits: An Empirical Analysis.” *European Economic Review* 42 (3–5): 897–908.

Rouzet, Dorothée, and Sébastien Miroudot. 2013. “The Cumulative Impact of Trade Barriers along the Value Chain: An Empirical Assessment Using the OECD Inter-Country Input-Output Model.” Organisation for Economic Co-operation and Development, Paris.

Silva, JMC Santos, and Silvana Tenreyro. 2006. “The Log of Gravity.” *The Review of Economics and Statistics* 88 (4): 641–58.

Topalova, Petia, and Amit Khandelwal. 2011. “Trade Liberalization and Firm Productivity: The Case of India.” *The Review of Economics and Statistics* 93 (3): 995–1009.

Vandenbussche, Hylke, William Connell, and Woutel Simons. 2017. “Global Value Chains, Trade Shocks, and Jobs: An Application to Brexit.” CEPR Discussion Paper 12303, Centre for Economic Policy Research, London.

World Bank (WB), World Trade Organization, Organisation for Economic Co-operation and Development, and University of International Business and Economics. 2017. *Global Value Chain Development Report 2017: Measuring and Analyzing the Impact of GVCs on Economic Development.* Washington, DC: World Bank.

Yotov, Yoto V., Roberta Piermartini, José-Antonio Monteiro, and Mario Larch. 2016. “An Advanced Guide to Trade Policy Analysis: The Structural Gravity Model.” World Trade Organization, Geneva.

STATISTICAL APPENDIX

The Statistical Appendix presents historical data as well as projections. It comprises seven sections: Assumptions, What's New, Data and Conventions, Country Notes, Classification of Countries, Key Data Documentation, and Statistical Tables.

The assumptions underlying the estimates and projections for 2019–20 and the medium-term scenario for 2021–24 are summarized in the first section. The second section presents a brief description of the changes to the database and statistical tables since the October 2018 *World Economic Outlook* (WEO). The third section provides a general description of the data and the conventions used for calculating country group composites. The fourth section summarizes selected key information for each country. The fifth section summarizes the classification of countries in the various groups presented in the WEO. The sixth section provides information on methods and reporting standards for the member countries' national account and government finance indicators included in the report.

The last, and main, section comprises the statistical tables. (Statistical Appendix A is included here; Statistical Appendix B is available online at www.imf.org/en/Publications/WEO. Data in these tables have been compiled on the basis of information available through March 29, 2019. The figures for 2019 and beyond are shown with the same degree of precision as the historical figures solely for convenience; because they are projections, the same degree of accuracy is not to be inferred.

Assumptions

Real effective *exchange rates* for the advanced economies are assumed to remain constant at their average levels measured during the period January 14 to February 11, 2019. For 2019 and 2020, these assumptions imply average US dollar–special drawing right (SDR) conversion rates of 1.397 and 1.407, US dollar–euro conversion rates of 1.144 and 1.156, and yen–US dollar conversion rates of 107.8 and 103.2, respectively.

It is assumed that the *price of oil* will average $59.16 a barrel in 2019 and $59.02 a barrel in 2020.

Established *policies* of national authorities are assumed to be maintained. The more specific policy assumptions underlying the projections for selected economies are described in Box A1.

With regard to *interest rates*, it is assumed that the London interbank offered rate (LIBOR) on six-month US dollar deposits will average 3.2 percent in 2019 and 3.8 percent in 2020, that three-month euro deposits will average –0.3 percent in 2019 and –0.2 percent in 2020, and that six-month yen deposits will average 0.0 percent in 2019 and 2020, respectively.

As a reminder, in regard to the *introduction of the euro*, on December 31, 1998, the Council of the European Union decided that, effective January 1, 1999, the irrevocably fixed conversion rates between the euro and currencies of the member countries adopting the euro are as described in Box 5.4 of the October 1998 WEO.

1 euro	=	13.7603	Austrian schillings
	=	40.3399	Belgian francs
	=	0.585274	Cyprus pound[1]
	=	1.95583	Deutsche marks
	=	15.6466	Estonian krooni[2]
	=	5.94573	Finnish markkaa
	=	6.55957	French francs
	=	340.750	Greek drachmas[3]
	=	0.787564	Irish pound
	=	1,936.27	Italian lire
	=	0.702804	Latvian lat[4]
	=	3.45280	Lithuanian litas[5]
	=	40.3399	Luxembourg francs
	=	0.42930	Maltese lira[1]
	=	2.20371	Netherlands guilders
	=	200.482	Portuguese escudos
	=	30.1260	Slovak koruna[6]
	=	239.640	Slovenian tolars[7]
	=	166.386	Spanish pesetas

[1]Established on January 1, 2008.
[2]Established on January 1, 2011.
[3]Established on January 1, 2001.
[4]Established on January 1, 2014.
[5]Established on January 1, 2015.
[6]Established on January 1, 2009.
[7]Established on January 1, 2007.

What's New

- *FYR Macedonia* is now called *North Macedonia*.
- In February 2019, *Zimbabwe* adopted a new local currency unit, the RTGS dollar, which has become the official unit of account. Efforts are underway to revise and update all national accounts series to the new RTGS dollar. Current data are based on IMF staff estimates of price and exchange rate developments in US (and RTGS) dollars. Staff estimates of US dollar values may differ from authorities' estimates.

Data and Conventions

Data and projections for 194 economies form the statistical basis of the WEO database. The data are maintained jointly by the IMF's Research Department and regional departments, with the latter regularly updating country projections based on consistent global assumptions.

Although national statistical agencies are the ultimate providers of historical data and definitions, international organizations are also involved in statistical issues, with the objective of harmonizing methodologies for the compilation of national statistics, including analytical frameworks, concepts, definitions, classifications, and valuation procedures used in the production of economic statistics. The WEO database reflects information from both national source agencies and international organizations.

Most countries' macroeconomic data presented in the WEO conform broadly to the 2008 version of the *System of National Accounts* (SNA). The IMF's sector statistical standards—the sixth edition of the *Balance of Payments and International Investment Position Manual* (BPM6), the *Monetary and Financial Statistics Manual and Compilation Guide* (MFSMCG), and the *Government Finance Statistics Manual 2014* (GFSM 2014)—have been or are being aligned with the SNA 2008. These standards reflect the IMF's special interest in countries' external positions, financial sector stability, and public sector fiscal positions. The process of adapting country data to the new standards begins in earnest when the manuals are released. However, full concordance with the manuals is ultimately dependent on the provision by national statistical compilers of revised country data; hence, the WEO estimates are only partially adapted to these manuals. Nonetheless, for many countries, the impact on major balances and aggregates of conversion to the updated standards will be small. Many other countries have partially adopted the latest standards and will continue implementation over a period of years.[1]

The fiscal gross and net debt data reported in the WEO are drawn from official data sources and IMF staff estimates. While attempts are made to align gross and net debt data with the definitions in the GFSM, as a result of data limitations or specific country circumstances, these data can sometimes deviate from the formal definitions. Although every effort is made to ensure the WEO data are relevant and internationally comparable, differences in both sectoral and instrument coverage mean that the data are not universally comparable. As more information becomes available, changes in either data sources or instrument coverage can give rise to data revisions that can sometimes be substantial. For clarification on the deviations in sectoral or instrument coverage, please refer to the metadata for the online WEO database.

Composite data for country groups in the WEO are either sums or weighted averages of data for individual countries. Unless noted otherwise, multiyear averages of growth rates are expressed as compound annual rates of change.[2] Arithmetically weighted averages are used for all data for the emerging market and developing economies group—except data on inflation and money growth, for which geometric averages are used. The following conventions apply:

Country group composites for exchange rates, interest rates, and growth rates of monetary aggregates are weighted by GDP converted to US dollars at market exchange rates (averaged over the preceding three years) as a share of group GDP.

Composites for other data relating to the domestic economy, whether growth rates or ratios, are weighted by GDP valued at purchasing power parity as a share of total world or group GDP.[3] Annual inflation rates are simple percentage changes from the previous years, except in the case of emerging market and developing economies, for which the rates are based on logarithmic differences.

Composites for real GDP per capita in *purchasing power parity* terms are sums of individual country data after conversion to the international dollar in the years indicated.

Unless noted otherwise, composites for all sectors for the euro area are corrected for reporting discrepancies in intra-area transactions. Unadjusted annual GDP data are used for the euro area and for the majority of individual countries, except for Cyprus, Germany, Ireland, and Portugal, which report calendar-adjusted data. For data

[1] Many countries are implementing the SNA 2008 or European System of National and Regional Accounts (ESA) 2010, and a few countries use versions of the SNA older than that from 1993. A similar adoption pattern is expected for the BPM6 and GFSM 2014. Please refer to Table G, which lists the statistical standards adhered to by each country.

[2] Averages for real GDP and its components, employment, inflation, factor productivity, GDP per capita, trade, and commodity prices are calculated based on the compound annual rate of change, except in the case of the unemployment rate, which is based on the simple arithmetic average.

[3] See "Revised Purchasing Power Parity Weights" the July 2014 WEO *Update* for a summary of the revised purchasing-power-parity-based weights, as well as Box A2 of the April 2004 WEO and Annex IV of the May 1993 WEO. See also Anne-Marie Gulde and Marianne Schulze-Ghattas, "Purchasing Power Parity Based Weights for the *World Economic Outlook*," in *Staff Studies for the World Economic Outlook* (Washington, DC: International Monetary Fund, December 1993), 106–23..

prior to 1999, data aggregations apply 1995 European currency unit exchange rates.

Composites for fiscal data are sums of individual country data after conversion to US dollars at the average market exchange rates in the years indicated.

Composite unemployment rates and employment growth are weighted by labor force as a share of group labor force.

Composites relating to external sector statistics are sums of individual country data after conversion to US dollars at the average market exchange rates in the years indicated for balance of payments data and at end-of-year market exchange rates for debt denominated in currencies other than US dollars.

Composites of changes in foreign trade volumes and prices, however, are arithmetic averages of percent changes for individual countries weighted by the US dollar value of exports or imports as a share of total world or group exports or imports (in the preceding year).

Unless noted otherwise, group composites are computed if 90 percent or more of the share of group weights is represented.

Data refer to calendar years, except in the case of a few countries that use fiscal years; Table F lists the economies with exceptional reporting periods for national accounts and government finance data for each country.

For some countries, the figures for 2018 and earlier are based on estimates rather than actual outturns; Table G lists the latest actual outturns for the indicators in the national accounts, prices, government finance, and balance of payments indicators for each country.

Country Notes

The consumer price data for *Argentina* before December 2013 reflect the consumer price index (CPI) for the Greater Buenos Aires Area (CPI-GBA), while from December 2013 to October 2015 the data reflect the national CPI (IPCNu). The government that took office in December 2015 discontinued the IPCNu, stating that it was flawed, and released a new CPI for the Greater Buenos Aires Area on June 15, 2016 (a new national CPI has been disseminated starting in June 2017). At its November 9, 2016, meeting, the IMF Executive Board considered the new CPI series to be in line with international standards and lifted the declaration of censure issued in 2013. Given the differences in geographical coverage, weights, sampling, and methodology of these series, the average CPI inflation for 2014, 2015, and 2016 and end-of-period inflation for 2015 and 2016 are not reported in the April 2019 WEO.

Argentina's authorities discontinued the publication of labor market data in December 2015 and released new series starting in the second quarter of 2016.

India's real GDP growth rates are calculated as per national accounts: for 1998 to 2011 with base year 2004/05 and, thereafter, with base year 2011/12.

Against the backdrop of a civil war and weak capacity, the reliability of *Libya*'s data, especially medium-term projections, is low.

Data for *Syria* are excluded from 2011 onward because of the uncertain political situation.

Trinidad and Tobago's growth estimates for 2018 are based on full-year energy sector data from the Ministry of Energy and Ministry of Finance, preliminary national accounts data for the first three quarters of the year from the Central Statistical Office, and staff projections for the fourth quarter nonenergy output based on available information. Growth estimates are subject to revision once the finalized data for the full year become available.

Starting from October 2018, *Uruguay*'s public pension system has been receiving transfers in the context of a new law that compensates persons affected by the creation of the mixed pension system (amounting to 1.3 percent of GDP in 2018). These funds are recorded as revenue, consistent with IMF methodology. Therefore, data and projections for 2018–22 are affected by these transfers.

Projecting the economic outlook in *Venezuela*, including assessing past and current economic developments as the basis for the projections, is complicated by the lack of discussions with the authorities (the last Article IV consultation took place in 2004), incomplete understanding of the reported data, and difficulties in interpreting certain reported economic indicators given economic developments. The fiscal accounts include the budgetary central government; social security; FOGADE (insurance deposit institution); and a sample of public enterprises, including Petróleos de Venezuela, S.A. (PDVSA); and data for 2018–24 are IMF staff estimates. The effects of hyperinflation and the paucity of reported data mean that the IMF staff's projected macroeconomic indicators need to be interpreted with caution. For example, nominal GDP is estimated assuming the GDP deflator rises in line with the IMF staff's projection of average inflation. Public external debt in relation to GDP is projected using the IMF staff's estimate of the average exchange rate for the year. Wide uncertainty surrounds these projections. *Venezuela*'s consumer prices (CPI) are excluded from all WEO group composites.

Classification of Countries

Summary of the Country Classification

The country classification in the WEO divides the world into two major groups: advanced economies and emerging market and developing economies.[4] This classification is not based on strict criteria, economic or otherwise, and has evolved over time. The objective is to facilitate analysis by providing a reasonably meaningful method of organizing data. Table A provides an overview of the country classification, showing the number of countries in each group by region and summarizing some key indicators of their relative size (GDP valued at purchasing power parity, total exports of goods and services, and population).

Some countries remain outside the country classification and therefore are not included in the analysis. Cuba and the Democratic People's Republic of Korea are examples of countries that are not IMF members, and their economies therefore are not monitored by the IMF.

General Features and Composition of Groups in the *World Economic Outlook* Classification

Advanced Economies

The 39 advanced economies are listed in Table B. The seven largest in terms of GDP based on market exchange rates—the United States, Japan, Germany, France, Italy, the United Kingdom, and Canada—constitute the subgroup of major advanced economies, often referred to as the Group of Seven (G7). The members of the euro area are also distinguished as a subgroup. Composite data shown in the tables for the euro area cover the current members for all years, even though the membership has increased over time.

Table C lists the member countries of the European Union, not all of which are classified as advanced economies in the WEO.

Emerging Market and Developing Economies

The group of emerging market and developing economies (155) includes all those that are not classified as advanced economies.

The regional breakdowns of emerging market and developing economies are Commonwealth of Independent States (CIS); emerging and developing Asia; emerging and developing Europe (sometimes also referred to as "central and eastern Europe"); Latin America and the Caribbean (LAC); Middle East, North Africa, Afghanistan, and Pakistan (MENAP); and sub-Saharan Africa (SSA).

Emerging market and developing economies are also classified according to analytical criteria. The *analytical criteria* reflect the composition of export earnings and a distinction between net creditor and net debtor economies. The detailed composition of emerging market and developing economies in the regional and analytical groups is shown in Tables D and E.

The analytical criterion *source of export earnings* distinguishes between the categories fuel (Standard International Trade Classification (SITC) 3) and *nonfuel* and then focuses on *nonfuel primary products* (SITCs 0, 1, 2, 4, and 68). Economies are categorized into one of these groups if their main source of export earnings exceeded 50 percent of total exports on average between 2013 and 2017.

The financial criteria focus on *net creditor economies, net debtor economies, heavily indebted poor countries* (HIPCs), and *low-income developing countries* (LIDCs). Economies are categorized as net debtors when their latest net international investment position, where available, was less than zero or their current account balance accumulations from 1972 (or earliest available data) to 2017 were negative. Net debtor economies are further differentiated on the basis of *experience with debt servicing*.[5]

The HIPC group comprises the countries that are or have been considered by the IMF and the World Bank for participation in their debt initiative known as the HIPC Initiative, which aims to reduce the external debt burdens of all the eligible HIPCs to a "sustainable" level in a reasonably short period of time.[6] Many of these countries have already benefited from debt relief and have graduated from the initiative.

The LIDCs are countries that have per capita income levels below a certain threshold (set at $2,700 in 2016 as measured by the World Bank's Atlas method), structural features consistent with limited development and structural transformation, and external financial linkages insufficiently close for them to be widely seen as emerging market economies.

[4] As used here, the terms "country" and "economy" do not always refer to a territorial entity that is a state as understood by international law and practice. Some territorial entities included here are not states, although their statistical data are maintained on a separate and independent basis.

[5] During 2013–17, 27 economies incurred external payments arrears or entered into official or commercial bank debt-rescheduling agreements. This group is referred to as *economies with arrears and/or rescheduling during 2013–17*.

[6] See David Andrews, Anthony R. Boote, Syed S. Rizavi, and Sukwinder Singh, "Debt Relief for Low-Income Countries: The Enhanced HIPC Initiative," IMF Pamphlet Series 51 (Washington, DC: International Monetary Fund, November 1999).

Table A. Classification by *World Economic Outlook* Groups and Their Shares in Aggregate GDP, Exports of Goods and Services, and Population, 2018[1]
(Percent of total for group or world)

	Number of Economies	GDP		Exports of Goods and Services		Population	
		Advanced Economies	World	Advanced Economies	World	Advanced Economies	World
Advanced Economies	**39**	**100.0**	**40.8**	**100.0**	**63.0**	**100.0**	**14.3**
United States		37.2	15.2	16.1	10.1	30.6	4.4
Euro Area	19	28.0	11.4	41.8	26.3	31.7	4.5
Germany		7.9	3.2	12.0	7.6	7.8	1.1
France		5.4	2.2	5.7	3.6	6.1	0.9
Italy		4.4	1.8	4.2	2.6	5.7	0.8
Spain		3.4	1.4	3.1	2.0	4.3	0.6
Japan		10.2	4.1	5.9	3.7	11.8	1.7
United Kingdom		5.5	2.2	5.4	3.4	6.2	0.9
Canada		3.3	1.4	3.5	2.2	3.5	0.5
Other Advanced Economies	16	15.8	6.4	27.3	17.2	16.1	2.3
Memorandum							
Major Advanced Economies	7	73.8	30.1	52.8	33.2	71.6	10.3
		Emerging Market and Developing Economies	World	Emerging Market and Developing Economies	World	Emerging Market and Developing Economies	World
Emerging Market and Developing Economies	**155**	**100.0**	**59.2**	**100.0**	**37.0**	**100.0**	**85.7**
Regional Groups							
Commonwealth of Independent States[2]	12	7.5	4.4	8.1	3.0	4.5	3.9
Russia		5.3	3.1	5.5	2.0	2.3	1.9
Emerging and Developing Asia	30	56.2	33.3	48.9	18.1	56.4	48.3
China		31.6	18.7	28.8	10.7	21.8	18.7
India		13.1	7.8	6.2	2.3	20.9	17.9
Excluding China and India	28	11.5	6.8	13.9	5.2	13.7	11.7
Emerging and Developing Europe	12	6.1	3.6	9.8	3.6	2.8	2.4
Latin America and the Caribbean	33	12.6	7.5	13.7	5.1	9.8	8.4
Brazil		4.2	2.5	3.0	1.1	3.3	2.8
Mexico		3.2	1.9	5.2	1.9	2.0	1.7
Middle East, North Africa, Afghanistan, and Pakistan	23	12.5	7.4	15.0	5.6	11.0	9.4
Middle East and North Africa	21	10.9	6.5	14.7	5.4	7.3	6.2
Sub-Saharan Africa	45	5.1	3.0	4.5	1.7	15.6	13.4
Excluding Nigeria and South Africa	43	2.7	1.6	2.6	1.0	11.7	10.0
Analytical Groups[3]							
By Source of Export Earnings							
Fuel	28	17.3	10.2	22.0	8.2	11.8	10.1
Nonfuel	126	82.7	49.0	78.0	28.9	88.2	75.6
Of Which, Primary Products	35	5.0	3.0	5.1	1.9	8.9	7.6
By External Financing Source							
Net Debtor Economies	122	51.5	30.5	49.4	18.3	68.3	58.5
Net Debtor Economies by Debt-Servicing Experience							
Economies with Arrears and/or Rescheduling during 2013–17	27	3.5	2.1	2.5	0.9	6.5	5.5
Other Groups							
Heavily Indebted Poor Countries	39	2.5	1.5	1.9	0.7	11.7	10.0
Low-Income Developing Countries	59	7.3	4.3	6.9	2.5	23.0	19.7

[1]The GDP shares are based on the purchasing-power-parity valuation of economies' GDP. The number of economies comprising each group reflects those for which data are included in the group aggregates.
[2]Georgia, Turkmenistan, and Ukraine, which are not members of the Commonwealth of Independent States, are included in this group for reasons of geography and similarity in economic structure.
[3]Syria is omitted from the source of export earnings, and South Sudan and Syria are omitted from the net external position group composites because of insufficient data.

Table B. Advanced Economies by Subgroup

Major Currency Areas		
United States		
Euro Area		
Japan		
Euro Area		
Austria	Greece	Netherlands
Belgium	Ireland	Portugal
Cyprus	Italy	Slovak Republic
Estonia	Latvia	Slovenia
Finland	Lithuania	Spain
France	Luxembourg	
Germany	Malta	
Major Advanced Economies		
Canada	Italy	United States
France	Japan	
Germany	United Kingdom	
Other Advanced Economies		
Australia	Korea	Singapore
Czech Republic	Macao SAR[2]	Sweden
Denmark	New Zealand	Switzerland
Hong Kong SAR[1]	Norway	Taiwan Province of China
Iceland	Puerto Rico	
Israel	San Marino	

[1]On July 1, 1997, Hong Kong was returned to the People's Republic of China and became a Special Administrative Region of China.
[2]On December 20, 1999, Macao was returned to the People's Republic of China and became a Special Administrative Region of China.

Table C. European Union

Austria	Germany	Poland
Belgium	Greece	Portugal
Bulgaria	Hungary	Romania
Croatia	Ireland	Slovak Republic
Cyprus	Italy	Slovenia
Czech Republic	Latvia	Spain
Denmark	Lithuania	Sweden
Estonia	Luxembourg	United Kingdom
Finland	Malta	
France	Netherlands	

Table D. Emerging Market and Developing Economies by Region and Main Source of Export Earnings

	Fuel	Nonfuel Primary Products
Commonwealth of Independent States		
	Azerbaijan	Tajikistan
	Kazakhstan	Uzbekistan
	Russia	
	Turkmenistan[1]	
Emerging and Developing Asia		
	Brunei Darussalam	Kiribati
	Timor-Leste	Lao P.D.R.
		Marshall Islands
		Mongolia
		Papua New Guinea
		Solomon Islands
		Tuvalu
Latin America and the Caribbean		
	Bolivia	Argentina
	Ecuador	Chile
	Trinidad and Tobago	Guyana
	Venezuela	Paraguay
		Peru
		Suriname
		Uruguay
Middle East, North Africa, Afghanistan, and Pakistan		
	Algeria	Afghanistan
	Bahrain	Mauritania
	Iran	Somalia
	Iraq	Sudan
	Kuwait	
	Libya	
	Oman	
	Qatar	
	Saudi Arabia	
	United Arab Emirates	
	Yemen	
Sub-Saharan Africa		
	Angola	Burkina Faso
	Chad	Burundi
	Republic of Congo	Central African Republic
	Equatorial Guinea	Democratic Republic of the Congo
	Gabon	Côte d'Ivoire
	Nigeria	Eritrea
	South Sudan	Guinea
		Guinea-Bissau
		Liberia
		Malawi
		Mali
		Sierra Leone
		South Africa
		Zambia
		Zimbabwe

[1]Turkmenistan, which is not a member of the Commonwealth of Independent States, is included in this group for reasons of geography and similarity in economic structure.

Table E. Emerging Market and Developing Economies by Region, Net External Position, and Status as Heavily Indebted Poor Countries and Low-Income Developing Countries

	Net External Position[1]	Heavily Indebted Poor Countries[2]	Low-Income Developing Countries
Commonwealth of Independent States			
Armenia	*		
Azerbaijan	•		
Belarus	*		
Georgia[3]	*		
Kazakhstan	*		
Kyrgyz Republic	*		*
Moldova	*		*
Russia	•		
Tajikistan	*		*
Turkmenistan[3]	*		
Ukraine[3]	*		
Uzbekistan	•		*
Emerging and Developing Asia			
Bangladesh	*		*
Bhutan	*		*
Brunei Darussalam	•		
Cambodia	*		*
China	•		
Fiji	*		
India	*		
Indonesia	*		
Kiribati	•		*
Lao P.D.R.	*		*
Malaysia	*		
Maldives	*		
Marshall Islands	*		
Micronesia	•		
Mongolia	*		
Myanmar	*		*
Nauru	*		
Nepal	•		*
Palau	•		
Papua New Guinea	*		*
Philippines	*		
Samoa	*		
Solomon Islands	*		*
Sri Lanka	*		
Thailand	*		
Timor-Leste	•		*
Tonga	*		
Tuvalu	•		
Vanuatu	*		
Vietnam	*		*

	Net External Position[1]	Heavily Indebted Poor Countries[2]	Low-Income Developing Countries
Emerging and Developing Europe			
Albania	*		
Bosnia and Herzegovina	*		
Bulgaria	*		
Croatia	*		
Hungary	*		
Kosovo	*		
Montenegro	*		
North Macedonia	*		
Poland	*		
Romania	*		
Serbia	*		
Turkey	*		
Latin America and the Caribbean			
Antigua and Barbuda	*		
Argentina	•		
Aruba	*		
The Bahamas	*		
Barbados	*		
Belize	*		
Bolivia	*	•	
Brazil	*		
Chile	*		
Colombia	*		
Costa Rica	*		
Dominica	•		
Dominican Republic	*		
Ecuador	*		
El Salvador	*		
Grenada	*		
Guatemala	*		
Guyana	*	•	
Haiti	*	•	*
Honduras	*	•	*
Jamaica	*		
Mexico	*		
Nicaragua	*	•	*
Panama	*		
Paraguay	*		
Peru	*		
St. Kitts and Nevis	*		
St. Lucia	*		
St. Vincent and the Grenadines	*		
Suriname	*		
Trinidad and Tobago	•		
Uruguay	*		
Venezuela	•		

Table E. Emerging Market and Developing Economies by Region, Net External Position, and Status as Heavily Indebted Poor Countries and Low-Income Developing Countries *(continued)*

	Net External Position[1]	Heavily Indebted Poor Countries[2]	Low-Income Developing Countries
Middle East, North Africa, Afghanistan, and Pakistan			
Afghanistan	•	•	*
Algeria	•		
Bahrain	•		
Djibouti	*		*
Egypt	*		
Iran	•		
Iraq	•		
Jordan	*		
Kuwait	•		
Lebanon	*		
Libya	•		
Mauritania	*	•	*
Morocco	*		
Oman	•		
Pakistan	*		
Qatar	•		
Saudi Arabia	•		
Somalia	*	*	*
Sudan	*	*	*
Syria[4]	. . .		
Tunisia	*		
United Arab Emirates	•		
Yemen	*		*
Sub-Saharan Africa			
Angola	*		
Benin	*	•	*
Botswana	•		
Burkina Faso	*	•	*
Burundi	*	•	*
Cabo Verde	*		
Cameroon	*	•	*
Central African Republic	*	•	*
Chad	*	•	*
Comoros	*	•	*
Democratic Republic of the Congo	*	•	*
Republic of Congo	*	•	*
Côte d'Ivoire	*	•	*
Equatorial Guinea	*		
Eritrea	*	*	*
Eswatini	•		
Ethiopia	*	•	*
Gabon	•		
The Gambia	*	•	*
Ghana	*	•	*
Guinea	*	•	*
Guinea-Bissau	*	•	*
Kenya	*		*
Lesotho	*		*
Liberia	*	•	*
Madagascar	*	•	*
Malawi	*	•	*
Mali	*	•	*
Mauritius	•		
Mozambique	*	•	*
Namibia	*		
Niger	*	•	*
Nigeria	*		*
Rwanda	*	•	*
São Tomé and Príncipe	*	•	*
Senegal	*	•	*
Seychelles	*		
Sierra Leone	*	•	*
South Africa	•		
South Sudan[4]	. . .		*
Tanzania	*	•	*
Togo	*	•	*
Uganda	*	•	*
Zambia	*	•	*
Zimbabwe	*		*

[1]Dot (star) indicates that the country is a net creditor (net debtor).

[2]Dot instead of star indicates that the country has reached the completion point, which allows it to receive the full debt relief committed to at the decision point.

[3]Georgia, Turkmenistan, and Ukraine, which are not members of the Commonwealth of Independent States, are included in this group for reasons of geography and similarity in economic structure.

[4]South Sudan and Syria are omitted from the net external position group composite for lack of a fully developed database.

Table F. Economies with Exceptional Reporting Periods[1]

	National Accounts	Government Finance
The Bahamas		Jul/Jun
Barbados		Apr/Mar
Bhutan	Jul/Jun	Jul/Jun
Botswana		Apr/Mar
Dominica		Jul/Jun
Egypt	Jul/Jun	Jul/Jun
Eswatini		Apr/Mar
Ethiopia	Jul/Jun	Jul/Jun
Haiti	Oct/Sep	Oct/Sep
Hong Kong SAR		Apr/Mar
India	Apr/Mar	Apr/Mar
Iran	Apr/Mar	Apr/Mar
Jamaica		Apr/Mar
Lesotho	Apr/Mar	Apr/Mar
Malawi		Jul/Jun
Marshall Islands	Oct/Sep	Oct/Sep
Mauritius		Jul/Jun
Micronesia	Oct/Sep	Oct/Sep
Myanmar	Oct/Sep	Oct/Sep
Nauru	Jul/Jun	Jul/Jun
Nepal	Aug/Jul	Aug/Jul
Pakistan	Jul/Jun	Jul/Jun
Palau	Oct/Sep	Oct/Sep
Puerto Rico	Jul/Jun	Jul/Jun
St. Lucia		Apr/Mar
Samoa	Jul/Jun	Jul/Jun
Singapore		Apr/Mar
Thailand		Oct/Sep
Trinidad and Tobago		Oct/Sep

[1]Unless noted otherwise, all data refer to calendar years.

Table G. Key Data Documentation

		National Accounts					Prices (CPI)	
Country	Currency	Historical Data Source[1]	Latest Actual Annual Data	Base Year[2]	System of National Accounts	Use of Chain-Weighted Methodology[3]	Historical Data Source[1]	Latest Actual Annual Data
Afghanistan	Afghan afghani	NSO	2017	2002/03	SNA 1993		NSO	2017
Albania	Albanian lek	IMF staff	2017	1996	ESA 2010	From 1996	NSO	2018
Algeria	Algerian dinar	NSO	2017	2001	SNA 1993	From 2005	NSO	2017
Angola	Angolan kwanza	NSO and MEP	2017	2002	ESA 1995		NSO	2018
Antigua and Barbuda	Eastern Caribbean dollar	CB	2017	2006[6]	SNA 1993		NSO	2017
Argentina	Argentine peso	NSO	2018	2004	SNA 2008		NSO	2018
Armenia	Armenian dram	NSO	2017	2005	SNA 2008		NSO	2018
Aruba	Aruban Florin	NSO	2017	2000	SNA 1993	From 2000	NSO	2017
Australia	Australian dollar	NSO	2018	2015/16	SNA 2008	From 1980	NSO	2018
Austria	Euro	NSO	2017	2010	ESA 2010	From 1995	NSO	2018
Azerbaijan	Azerbaijan manat	NSO	2017	2005	SNA 1993	From 1994	NSO	2017
The Bahamas	Bahamian dollar	NSO	2017	2012	SNA 1993		NSO	2017
Bahrain	Bahrain dinar	NSO	2017	2010	SNA 2008		NSO	2017
Bangladesh	Bangladesh taka	NSO	2017	2005/06	SNA 1993		NSO	2017
Barbados	Barbados dollar	NSO and CB	2018	2010	SNA 1993		NSO	2017
Belarus	Belarusian ruble	NSO	2017	2014	SNA 2008	From 2005	NSO	2017
Belgium	Euro	CB	2017	2016	ESA 2010	From 1995	CB	2017
Belize	Belize dollar	NSO	2017	2000	SNA 1993		NSO	2017
Benin	CFA franc	NSO	2015	2007	SNA 1993		NSO	2017
Bhutan	Bhutanese ngultrum	NSO	2015/16	2000/01[6]	SNA 1993		CB	2016/17
Bolivia	Bolivian boliviano	NSO	2017	1990	SNA 2008		NSO	2018
Bosnia and Herzegovina	Bosnian convertible marka	NSO	2017	2010	ESA 2010	From 2000	NSO	2018
Botswana	Botswana pula	NSO	2017	2006	SNA 1993		NSO	2018
Brazil	Brazilian real	NSO	2018	1995	SNA 2008		NSO	2018
Brunei Darussalam	Brunei dollar	NSO and GAD	2017	2010	SNA 1993		NSO and GAD	2017
Bulgaria	Bulgarian lev	NSO	2018	2010	ESA 2010	From 1996	NSO	2018
Burkina Faso	CFA franc	NSO and MEP	2017	1999	SNA 1993		NSO	2017
Burundi	Burundi franc	NSO	2015	2005	SNA 1993		NSO	2017
Cabo Verde	Cabo Verdean escudo	NSO	2017	2007	SNA 2008	From 2011	NSO	2017
Cambodia	Cambodian riel	NSO	2017	2000	SNA 1993		NSO	2018
Cameroon	CFA franc	NSO	2017	2005	SNA 2008		NSO	2018
Canada	Canadian dollar	NSO	2018	2012	SNA 2008	From 1980	NSO	2018
Central African Republic	CFA franc	NSO	2012	2005	SNA 1993		NSO	2015
Chad	CFA franc	CB	2017	2005	SNA 1993		NSO	2017
Chile	Chilean peso	CB	2018	2013[6]	SNA 2008	From 2003	NSO	2018
China	Chinese yuan	NSO	2018	2015	SNA 2008		NSO	2018
Colombia	Colombian peso	NSO	2017	2015	SNA 1993	From 2000	NSO	2017
Comoros	Comorian franc	MEP	2017	2000	...		NSO	2017
Democratic Republic of the Congo	Congolese franc	NSO	2018	2005	SNA 1993		CB	2018
Republic of Congo	CFA franc	NSO	2017	1990	SNA 1993		NSO	2018
Costa Rica	Costa Rican colón	CB	2016	2012	SNA 2008		CB	2016

Table G. Key Data Documentation *(continued)*

	Government Finance					Balance of Payments		
Country	Historical Data Source[1]	Latest Actual Annual Data	Statistics Manual in Use at Source	Subsectors Coverage[4]	Accounting Practice[5]	Historical Data Source[1]	Latest Actual Annual Data	Statistics Manual in Use at Source
Afghanistan	MoF	2017	2001	CG	C	NSO, MoF, and CB	2017	BPM 5
Albania	IMF staff	2018	1986	CG,LG,SS,MPC, NFPC	. . .	CB	2017	BPM 6
Algeria	MoF	2017	1986	CG	C	CB	2017	BPM 6
Angola	MoF	2017	2001	CG,LG	. . .	CB	2017	BPM 6
Antigua and Barbuda	MoF	2017	2001	CG	C	CB	2016	BPM 6
Argentina	MEP	2018	1986	CG,SG,SS	C	NSO	2018	BPM 6
Armenia	MoF	2017	2001	CG	C	CB	2018	BPM 6
Aruba	MoF	2017	2001	CG	Mixed	CB	2017	BPM 5
Australia	MoF	2017	2014	CG,SG,LG,TG	A	NSO	2018	BPM 6
Austria	NSO	2017	2001	CG,SG,LG,SS	A	CB	2018	BPM 6
Azerbaijan	MoF	2017	. . .	CG	C	CB	2017	BPM 6
The Bahamas	MoF	2017/18	2001	CG	C	CB	2017	BPM 5
Bahrain	MoF	2017	2001	CG	C	CB	2017	BPM 6
Bangladesh	MoF	2017	. . .	CG	C	CB	2017	BPM 6
Barbados	MoF	2018/19	1986	BCG	C	CB	2017	BPM 5
Belarus	MoF	2017	2001	CG,LG,SS	C	CB	2017	BPM 6
Belgium	CB	2017	ESA 2010	CG,SG,LG,SS	A	CB	2017	BPM 6
Belize	MoF	2017	1986	CG,MPC	Mixed	CB	2017	BPM 6
Benin	MoF	2017	1986	CG	C	CB	2016	BPM 6
Bhutan	MoF	2016/17	1986	CG	C	CB	2015/16	BPM 6
Bolivia	MoF	2017	2001	CG,LG,SS,NMPC, NFPC	C	CB	2017	BPM 6
Bosnia and Herzegovina	MoF	2017	2001	CG,SG,LG,SS	Mixed	CB	2018	BPM 6
Botswana	MoF	2017/18	1986	CG	C	CB	2017	BPM 6
Brazil	MoF	2018	2001	CG,SG,LG,SS, MPC,NFPC	C	CB	2017	BPM 6
Brunei Darussalam	MoF	2017	. . .	CG, BCG	C	NSO, MEP, and GAD	2017	BPM 6
Bulgaria	MoF	2018	2001	CG,LG,SS	C	CB	2018	BPM 6
Burkina Faso	MoF	2017	2001	CG	CB	CB	2016	BPM 6
Burundi	MoF	2015	2001	CG	A	CB	2016	BPM 6
Cabo Verde	MoF	2017	2001	CG	A	NSO	2017	BPM 6
Cambodia	MoF	2017	1986	CG,LG	A	CB	2017	BPM 5
Cameroon	MoF	2017	2001	CG,NFPC	C	MoF	2017	BPM 6
Canada	MoF	2017	2001	CG,SG,LG,SS,other	A	NSO	2018	BPM 6
Central African Republic	MoF	2016	2001	CG	C	CB	2015	BPM 5
Chad	MoF	2017	1986	CG,NFPC	C	CB	2015	BPM 6
Chile	MoF	2018	2001	CG,LG	A	CB	2018	BPM 6
China	MoF	2018	. . .	CG,LG	C	GAD	2018	BPM 6
Colombia	MoF	2017	2001	CG,SG,LG,SS	. . .	CB and NSO	2017	BPM 6
Comoros	MoF	2017	1986	CG	Mixed	CB and IMF staff	2017	BPM 5
Democratic Republic of the Congo	MoF	2018	2001	CG,LG	A	CB	2016	BPM 5
Republic of Congo	MoF	2018	2001	CG	A	CB	2017	BPM 6
Costa Rica	MoF and CB	2016	1986	CG	C	CB	2016	BPM 6

Table G. Key Data Documentation *(continued)*

		National Accounts					Prices (CPI)	
Country	Currency	Historical Data Source[1]	Latest Actual Annual Data	Base Year[2]	System of National Accounts	Use of Chain-Weighted Methodology[3]	Historical Data Source[1]	Latest Actual Annual Data
Côte d'Ivoire	CFA franc	NSO	2016	2009	SNA 1993		NSO	2017
Croatia	Croatian kuna	NSO	2017	2010	ESA 2010		NSO	2018
Cyprus	Euro	NSO	2018	2010	ESA 2010	From 1995	NSO	2018
Czech Republic	Czech koruna	NSO	2017	2010	ESA 2010	From 1995	NSO	2018
Denmark	Danish krone	NSO	2018	2010	ESA 2010	From 1980	NSO	2018
Djibouti	Djibouti franc	NSO	2018	1990	SNA 1993		NSO	2018
Dominica	Eastern Caribbean dollar	NSO	2016	2006	SNA 1993		NSO	2016
Dominican Republic	Dominican peso	CB	2017	2007	SNA 2008	From 2007	CB	2017
Ecuador	US dollar	CB	2018	2007	SNA 1993		NSO and CB	2018
Egypt	Egyptian pound	MEP	2017/18	2011/12	SNA 2008		NSO	2017/18
El Salvador	US dollar	CB	2018	2014	SNA 2008		NSO	2018
Equatorial Guinea	CFA franc	MEP and CB	2017	2006	SNA 1993		MEP	2018
Eritrea	Eritrean nakfa	IMF staff	2006	2005	SNA 1993		NSO	2009
Estonia	Euro	NSO	2018	2010	ESA 2010	From 2010	NSO	2018
Eswatini	Swazi lilangeni	NSO	2017	2011	SNA 1993		NSO	2018
Ethiopia	Ethiopian birr	NSO	2016/17	2015/16	SNA 1993		NSO	2017
Fiji	Fijian dollar	NSO	2017	2011[6]	SNA 1993		NSO	2017
Finland	Euro	NSO	2018	2010	ESA 2010	From 1980	NSO	2017
France	Euro	NSO	2017	2014	ESA 2010	From 1980	NSO	2018
Gabon	CFA franc	MoF	2017	2001	SNA 1993		NSO	2018
The Gambia	Gambian dalasi	NSO	2018	2013	SNA 1993		NSO	2018
Georgia	Georgian lari	NSO	2016	2010	SNA 1993	From 1996	NSO	2017
Germany	Euro	NSO	2018	2010	ESA 2010	From 1991	NSO	2018
Ghana	Ghanaian cedi	NSO	2017	2013	SNA 1993		NSO	2017
Greece	Euro	NSO	2017	2010	ESA 2010	From 1995	NSO	2018
Grenada	Eastern Caribbean dollar	NSO	2017	2006	SNA 1993		NSO	2018
Guatemala	Guatemalan quetzal	CB	2017	2001	SNA 1993	From 2001	NSO	2018
Guinea	Guinean franc	NSO	2016	2010	SNA 1993		NSO	2017
Guinea-Bissau	CFA franc	NSO	2017	2005	SNA 1993		NSO	2017
Guyana	Guyanese dollar	NSO	2017	2006[6]	SNA 1993		NSO	2017
Haiti	Haitian gourde	NSO	2017/18	1986/87	SNA 1993		NSO	2017/18
Honduras	Honduran lempira	CB	2017	2000	SNA 1993		CB	2018
Hong Kong SAR	Hong Kong dollar	NSO	2018	2016	SNA 2008	From 1980	NSO	2018
Hungary	Hungarian forint	NSO	2018	2005	ESA 2010	From 2005	IEO	2018
Iceland	Icelandic króna	NSO	2018	2005	ESA 2010	From 1990	NSO	2018
India	Indian rupee	NSO	2017/18	2011/12	SNA 2008		NSO	2017/18
Indonesia	Indonesian rupiah	NSO	2018	2010	SNA 2008		NSO	2018
Iran	Iranian rial	CB	2017/18	2011/12	SNA 1993		CB	2017/18
Iraq	Iraqi dinar	NSO	2017	2007	SNA 1968/93		NSO	2017
Ireland	Euro	NSO	2017	2016	ESA 2010	From 1995	NSO	2018
Israel	New Israeli shekel	NSO	2017	2015	SNA 2008	From 1995	NSO	2017
Italy	Euro	NSO	2017	2010	ESA 2010	From 1980	NSO	2018
Jamaica	Jamaican dollar	NSO	2017	2007	SNA 1993		NSO	2018

Table G. Key Data Documentation *(continued)*

	Government Finance					Balance of Payments		
Country	Historical Data Source[1]	Latest Actual Annual Data	Statistics Manual in Use at Source	Subsectors Coverage[4]	Accounting Practice[5]	Historical Data Source[1]	Latest Actual Annual Data	Statistics Manual in Use at Source
Côte d'Ivoire	MoF	2017	1986	CG	A	CB	2016	BPM 6
Croatia	MoF	2017	2001	CG,LG	A	CB	2017	BPM 6
Cyprus	NSO	2018	ESA 2010	CG,LG,SS	A	CB	2017	BPM 6
Czech Republic	MoF	2017	2001	CG,LG,SS	A	NSO	2017	BPM 6
Denmark	NSO	2017	2001	CG,LG,SS	A	NSO	2018	BPM 6
Djibouti	MoF	2018	2001	CG	A	CB	2018	BPM 5
Dominica	MoF	2016/17	1986	CG	C	CB	2016	BPM 6
Dominican Republic	MoF	2017	2001	CG,SG,LG,SS, NMPC	Mixed	CB	2017	BPM 6
Ecuador	CB and MoF	2018	1986	CG,SG,LG,SS, NFPC	C	CB	2018	BPM 6
Egypt	MoF	2017/18	2001	CG,LG,SS,MPC	C	CB	2017/18	BPM 5
El Salvador	MoF and CB	2018	1986	CG,LG,SS	C	CB	2018	BPM 6
Equatorial Guinea	MoF and MEP	2017	1986	CG	C	CB	2017	BPM 5
Eritrea	MoF	2008	2001	CG	C	CB	2008	BPM 5
Estonia	MoF	2017	1986/2001	CG,LG,SS	C	CB	2018	BPM 6
Eswatini	MoF	2017/18	2001	CG	A	CB	2017	BPM 6
Ethiopia	MoF	2015/16	1986	CG,SG,LG,NFPC	C	CB	2016/17	BPM 5
Fiji	MoF	2017	1986	CG	C	CB	2017	BPM 6
Finland	MoF	2016	2001	CG,LG,SS	A	NSO	2017	BPM 6
France	NSO	2017	2001	CG,LG,SS	A	CB	2018	BPM 6
Gabon	IMF staff	2018	2001	CG	A	CB	2017	BPM 5
The Gambia	MoF	2018	1986	CG	C	CB and IMF staff	2018	BPM 5
Georgia	MoF	2017	2001	CG,LG	C	NSO and CB	2016	BPM 6
Germany	NSO	2018	2001	CG,SG,LG,SS	A	CB	2018	BPM 6
Ghana	MoF	2018	2001	CG	C	CB	2018	BPM 5
Greece	NSO	2017	2014	CG,LG,SS	A	CB	2017	BPM 6
Grenada	MoF	2017	2014	CG	CB	CB	2017	BPM 6
Guatemala	MoF	2017	2001	CG	C	CB	2017	BPM 6
Guinea	MoF	2017	2001	CG	C	CB and MEP	2017	BPM 6
Guinea-Bissau	MoF	2017	2001	CG	A	CB	2017	BPM 6
Guyana	MoF	2017	1986	CG,SS,NFPC	C	CB	2017	BPM 6
Haiti	MoF	2017/18	2001	CG	C	CB	2017/18	BPM 5
Honduras	MoF	2018	2014	CG,LG,SS,other	Mixed	CB	2018	BPM 6
Hong Kong SAR	NSO	2018/19	2001	CG	C	NSO	2017	BPM 6
Hungary	MEP and NSO	2017	ESA 2010	CG,LG,SS,NMPC	A	CB	2018	BPM 6
Iceland	NSO	2017	2001	CG,LG,SS	A	CB	2018	BPM 6
India	MoF and IMF staff	2017/18	1986	CG,SG	C	CB	2017/18	BPM 6
Indonesia	MoF	2018	2001	CG,LG	C	CB	2018	BPM 6
Iran	MoF	2016/17	2001	CG	C	CB	2016/17	BPM 5
Iraq	MoF	2017	2001	CG	C	CB	2017	BPM 6
Ireland	MoF and NSO	2017	2001	CG,LG,SS	A	NSO	2017	BPM 6
Israel	MoF and NSO	2017	2001	CG,LG,SS	. . .	NSO	2017	BPM 6
Italy	NSO	2017	2001	CG,LG,SS	A	NSO	2017	BPM 6
Jamaica	MoF	2017/18	1986	CG	C	CB	2017	BPM 5

Table G. Key Data Documentation *(continued)*

		National Accounts					Prices (CPI)	
Country	Currency	Historical Data Source[1]	Latest Actual Annual Data	Base Year[2]	System of National Accounts	Use of Chain-Weighted Methodology[3]	Historical Data Source[1]	Latest Actual Annual Data
Japan	Japanese yen	GAD	2018	2011	SNA 2008	From 1980	GAD	2018
Jordan	Jordanian dinar	NSO	2017	2016	SNA 2008		NSO	2018
Kazakhstan	Kazakhstani tenge	NSO	2017	2007	SNA 1993	From 1994	CB	2017
Kenya	Kenyan shilling	NSO	2017	2009	SNA 2008		NSO	2018
Kiribati	Australian dollar	NSO	2017	2006	SNA 2008		NSO	2017
Korea	South Korean won	CB	2017	2010	SNA 2008	From 1980	NSO	2017
Kosovo	Euro	NSO	2018	2016	ESA 2010		NSO	2018
Kuwait	Kuwaiti dinar	MEP and NSO	2017	2010	SNA 1993		NSO and MEP	2018
Kyrgyz Republic	Kyrgyz som	NSO	2016	2005	SNA 1993		NSO	2017
Lao P.D.R.	Lao kip	NSO	2017	2012	SNA 1993		NSO	2018
Latvia	Euro	NSO	2018	2010	ESA 2010	From 1995	NSO	2018
Lebanon	Lebanese pound	NSO	2017	2010	SNA 2008	From 2010	NSO	2017/18
Lesotho	Lesotho loti	NSO	2015/16	2012/13	SNA 2008		NSO	2017
Liberia	US dollar	CB	2017	1992	SNA 1993		CB	2017
Libya	Libyan dinar	MEP	2016	2003	SNA 1993		NSO	2017
Lithuania	Euro	NSO	2018	2010	ESA 2010	From 2005	NSO	2018
Luxembourg	Euro	NSO	2017	2010	ESA 2010	From 1995	NSO	2018
Macao SAR	Macanese pataca	NSO	2017	2016	SNA 2008	From 2001	NSO	2017
Madagascar	Malagasy ariary	NSO	2016	2000	SNA 1968		NSO	2017
Malawi	Malawian kwacha	NSO	2011	2010	SNA 2008		NSO	2018
Malaysia	Malaysian ringgit	NSO	2018	2010	SNA 2008		NSO	2018
Maldives	Maldivian rufiyaa	MoF and NSO	2017	2014	SNA 1993		CB	2017
Mali	CFA franc	NSO	2016	1999	SNA 1993		NSO	2017
Malta	Euro	NSO	2017	2010	ESA 2010	From 2000	NSO	2018
Marshall Islands	US dollar	NSO	2016/17	2003/04	SNA 1993		NSO	2016/17
Mauritania	Mauritanian ouguiya	NSO	2014	2004	SNA 1993		NSO	2017
Mauritius	Mauritian rupee	NSO	2018	2006	SNA 1993	From 1999	NSO	2018
Mexico	Mexican peso	NSO	2017	2013	SNA 2008		NSO	2018
Micronesia	US dollar	NSO	2016/17	2004	SNA 1993		NSO	2015/16
Moldova	Moldovan leu	NSO	2017	2010	SNA 2008		NSO	2017
Mongolia	Mongolian tögrög	NSO	2016	2010	SNA 1993		NSO	2016/17
Montenegro	Euro	NSO	2017	2006	ESA 2010		NSO	2018
Morocco	Moroccan dirham	NSO	2016	2007	SNA 1993	From 1998	NSO	2017
Mozambique	Mozambican metical	NSO	2017	2009	SNA 1993/2008		NSO	2017
Myanmar	Myanmar kyat	MEP	2017/18	2010/11	. . .		NSO	2017/18
Namibia	Namibian dollar	NSO	2017	2000	SNA 1993		NSO	2017
Nauru	Australian dollar	. . .	2015/16	2006/07	SNA 1993		NSO	2016/17
Nepal	Nepalese rupee	NSO	2017/18	2000/01	SNA 1993		CB	2017/18
Netherlands	Euro	NSO	2018	2015	ESA 2010	From 1980	NSO	2018
New Zealand	New Zealand dollar	NSO	2017	2009/10	SNA 2008	From 1987	NSO	2017
Nicaragua	Nicaraguan córdoba	CB	2017	2006	SNA 1993	From 1994	CB	2018
Niger	CFA franc	NSO	2016	2000	SNA 1993		NSO	2018
Nigeria	Nigerian naira	NSO	2018	2010	SNA 2008		NSO	2018
North Macedonia	Macedonian denar	NSO	2018	2005	ESA 2010		NSO	2018
Norway	Norwegian krone	NSO	2017	2016	ESA 2010	From 1980	NSO	2018

Table G. Key Data Documentation *(continued)*

	Government Finance					Balance of Payments		
Country	Historical Data Source[1]	Latest Actual Annual Data	Statistics Manual in Use at Source	Subsectors Coverage[4]	Accounting Practice[5]	Historical Data Source[1]	Latest Actual Annual Data	Statistics Manual in Use at Source
Japan	GAD	2017	2014	CG,LG,SS	A	MoF	2018	BPM 6
Jordan	MoF	2017	2001	CG,NFPC	C	CB	2017	BPM 6
Kazakhstan	NSO	2017	2001	CG,LG	A	CB	2017	BPM 6
Kenya	MoF	2017	2001	CG	A	CB	2017	BPM 6
Kiribati	MoF	2017	1986	CG,LG	C	NSO	2016	BPM 6
Korea	MoF	2017	2001	CG,SS	C	CB	2017	BPM 6
Kosovo	MoF	2018	. . .	CG,LG	C	CB	2018	BPM 6
Kuwait	MoF	2017	1986	CG	Mixed	CB	2017	BPM 6
Kyrgyz Republic	MoF	2017	. . .	CG,LG,SS	C	CB	2017	BPM 5
Lao P.D.R.	MoF	2016	2001	CG	C	CB	2016	BPM 5
Latvia	MoF	2017	ESA 2010	CG,LG,SS	C	CB	2018	BPM 6
Lebanon	MoF	2017	2001	CG	Mixed	CB and IMF staff	2017	BPM 5
Lesotho	MoF	2017/18	2001	CG,LG	C	CB	2017/18	BPM 5
Liberia	MoF	2017	2001	CG	A	CB	2017	BPM 5
Libya	MoF	2018	1986	CG,SG,LG	C	CB	2017	BPM 5
Lithuania	MoF	2017	2014	CG,LG,SS	A	CB	2017	BPM 6
Luxembourg	MoF	2017	2001	CG,LG,SS	A	NSO	2017	BPM 6
Macao SAR	MoF	2017	2014	CG,SS	C	NSO	2017	BPM 6
Madagascar	MoF	2017	1986	CG,LG	C	CB	2017	BPM 5
Malawi	MoF	2017/18	1986	CG	C	NSO and GAD	2017	BPM 6
Malaysia	MoF	2017	2001	CG,SG,LG	C	NSO	2018	BPM 6
Maldives	MoF	2017	1986	CG	C	CB	2017	BPM 5
Mali	MoF	2016	2001	CG	Mixed	CB	2016	BPM 6
Malta	NSO	2017	2001	CG,SS	A	NSO	2017	BPM 6
Marshall Islands	MoF	2016/17	2001	CG,LG,SS	A	NSO	2016/17	BPM 6
Mauritania	MoF	2017	1986	CG	C	CB	2016	BPM 5
Mauritius	MoF	2017/18	2001	CG,LG,NFPC	C	CB	2017	BPM 6
Mexico	MoF	2018	2014	CG,SS,NMPC,NFPC	C	CB	2018	BPM 6
Micronesia	MoF	2016/17	2001	CG,SG,LG,SS	. . .	NSO	2016/17	BPM 5
Moldova	MoF	2017	1986	CG	C	CB	2017	BPM 5
Mongolia	MoF	2016	2001	CG,SG,LG,SS	C	CB	2016	BPM 6
Montenegro	MoF	2018	1986/2001	CG,LG,SS	C	CB	2017	BPM 6
Morocco	MEP	2017	2001	CG	A	GAD	2017	BPM 6
Mozambique	MoF	2017	2001	CG,SG	Mixed	CB	2017	BPM 6
Myanmar	MoF	2017/18	2014	CG,NFPC	C	IMF staff	2017/18	BPM 6
Namibia	MoF	2017	2001	CG	C	CB	2017	BPM 6
Nauru	MoF	2016/17	2001	CG	Mixed	IMF staff	2014/15	BPM 6
Nepal	MoF	2017/18	2001	CG	C	CB	2017/18	BPM 5
Netherlands	MoF	2017	2001	CG,LG,SS	A	CB	2017	BPM 6
New Zealand	MoF	2017/18	2001	CG, LG	A	NSO	2017	BPM 6
Nicaragua	MoF	2017	1986	CG,LG,SS	C	IMF staff	2017	BPM 6
Niger	MoF	2017	1986	CG	A	CB	2018	BPM 6
Nigeria	MoF	2018	2001	CG,SG,LG	C	CB	2018	BPM 6
North Macedonia	MoF	2018	1986	CG,SG,SS	C	CB	2018	BPM 6
Norway	NSO and MoF	2016	2014	CG,LG,SS	A	NSO	2017	BPM 6

Table G. Key Data Documentation *(continued)*

		National Accounts					Prices (CPI)	
Country	Currency	Historical Data Source[1]	Latest Actual Annual Data	Base Year[2]	System of National Accounts	Use of Chain-Weighted Methodology[3]	Historical Data Source[1]	Latest Actual Annual Data
Oman	Omani rial	NSO	2017	2010	SNA 1993		NSO	2018
Pakistan	Pakistan rupee	NSO	2017/18	2005/06[6]	. . .		NSO	2017/18
Palau	US dollar	MoF	2016/17	2014/15	SNA 1993		MoF	2016/17
Panama	US dollar	NSO	2017	2007	SNA 1993	From 2007	NSO	2017
Papua New Guinea	Papua New Guinea kina	NSO and MoF	2015	2013	SNA 1993		NSO	2015
Paraguay	Paraguayan guaraní	CB	2017	2014	SNA 2008		CB	2017
Peru	Peruvian nuevo sol	CB	2018	2007	SNA 1993		CB	2018
Philippines	Philippine peso	NSO	2018	2000	SNA 2008		NSO	2018
Poland	Polish zloty	NSO	2018	2010	ESA 2010	From 1995	NSO	2018
Portugal	Euro	NSO	2017	2011	ESA 2010	From 1980	NSO	2018
Puerto Rico	US dollar	NSO	2016/17	1954	SNA1968		NSO	2016/17
Qatar	Qatari riyal	NSO and MEP	2018	2013	SNA 1993		NSO and MEP	2018
Romania	Romanian leu	NSO	2018	2010	ESA 2010	From 2000	NSO	2018
Russia	Russian ruble	NSO	2017	2016	SNA 2008	From 1995	NSO	2018
Rwanda	Rwandan franc	NSO	2017	2014	SNA 2008		NSO	2017
Samoa	Samoan tala	NSO	2016/17	2009/10	SNA 1993		NSO	2016/17
San Marino	Euro	NSO	2017	2007	. . .		NSO	2017
São Tomé and Príncipe	São Tomé and Príncipe dobra	NSO	2017	2008	SNA 1993		NSO	2018
Saudi Arabia	Saudi riyal	NSO and MEP	2018	2010	SNA 1993		NSO and MEP	2018
Senegal	CFA franc	NSO	2018	2014	SNA 1993		NSO	2018
Serbia	Serbian dinar	NSO	2017	2010	ESA 2010	From 2010	NSO	2018
Seychelles	Seychelles rupee	NSO	2016	2006	SNA 1993		NSO	2016
Sierra Leone	Sierra Leonean leone	NSO	2017	2006	SNA 1993	From 2010	NSO	2017
Singapore	Singapore dollar	NSO	2017	2010	SNA 2008		NSO	2017
Slovak Republic	Euro	NSO	2017	2010	ESA 2010	From 1997	NSO	2018
Slovenia	Euro	NSO	2017	2010	ESA 2010	From 2000	NSO	2018
Solomon Islands	Solomon Islands dollar	CB	2016	2004	SNA 1993		NSO	2017
Somalia	US dollar	CB	2016	2012	SNA 1993		CB	2014
South Africa	South African rand	NSO	2017	2010	SNA 2008		NSO	2017
South Sudan	South Sudanese pound	NSO	2017	2010	SNA 1993		NSO	2017
Spain	Euro	NSO	2018	2010	ESA 2010	From 1995	NSO	2018
Sri Lanka	Sri Lankan rupee	NSO	2017	2010	SNA 1993		NSO	2018
St. Kitts and Nevis	Eastern Caribbean dollar	NSO	2017	2006	SNA 1993		NSO	2017
St. Lucia	Eastern Caribbean dollar	NSO	2017	2006	SNA 1993		NSO	2017
St. Vincent and the Grenadines	Eastern Caribbean dollar	NSO	2017	2006[6]	SNA 1993		NSO	2017
Sudan	Sudanese pound	NSO	2014	1982	SNA 1968		NSO	2018
Suriname	Surinamese dollar	NSO	2017	2007	SNA 1993		NSO	2018

Table G. Key Data Documentation *(continued)*

	Government Finance					Balance of Payments		
Country	Historical Data Source[1]	Latest Actual Annual Data	Statistics Manual in Use at Source	Subsectors Coverage[4]	Accounting Practice[5]	Historical Data Source[1]	Latest Actual Annual Data	Statistics Manual in Use at Source
Oman	MoF	2017	2001	CG	C	CB	2017	BPM 5
Pakistan	MoF	2017/18	1986	CG,SG,LG	C	CB	2017/18	BPM 6
Palau	MoF	2016/17	2001	CG	. . .	MoF	2016/17	BPM 6
Panama	MoF	2017	1986	CG,SG,LG,SS, NFPC	C	NSO	2017	BPM 6
Papua New Guinea	MoF	2015	1986	CG	C	CB	2015	BPM 5
Paraguay	MoF	2017	2001	CG,SG,LG,SS,MPC, NFPC	C	CB	2017	BPM 6
Peru	CB and MoF	2018	2001	CG,SG,LG,SS	Mixed	CB	2018	BPM 5
Philippines	MoF	2017	2001	CG,LG,SS	C	CB	2017	BPM 6
Poland	MoF and NSO	2017	ESA 2010	CG,LG,SS	A	CB	2017	BPM 6
Portugal	NSO	2017	2001	CG,LG,SS	A	CB	2018	BPM 6
Puerto Rico	MEP	2015/16	2001	. . .	A	. . .	. . .	. . .
Qatar	MoF	2018	1986	CG	C	CB and IMF staff	2018	BPM 5
Romania	MoF	2018	2001	CG,LG,SS	C	CB	2018	BPM 6
Russia	MoF	2017	2001	CG,SG,SS	Mixed	CB	2018	BPM 6
Rwanda	MoF	2016	1986	CG,LG	Mixed	CB	2017	BPM 6
Samoa	MoF	2016/17	2001	CG	A	CB	2016/17	BPM 6
San Marino	MoF	2017	. . .	CG	. . .	Other	2017	. . .
São Tomé and Príncipe	MoF and Customs	2017	2001	CG	C	CB	2017	BPM 6
Saudi Arabia	MoF	2018	2014	CG	C	CB	2018	BPM 6
Senegal	MoF	2018	2001	CG	C	CB and IMF staff	2018	BPM 6
Serbia	MoF	2017	1986/2001	CG,SG,LG,SS,other	C	CB	2017	BPM 6
Seychelles	MoF	2017	1986	CG,SS	C	CB	2016	BPM 6
Sierra Leone	MoF	2017	1986	CG	C	CB	2017	BPM 5
Singapore	MoF	2018/19	2001	CG	C	NSO	2017	BPM 6
Slovak Republic	NSO	2017	2001	CG,LG,SS	A	CB	2017	BPM 6
Slovenia	MoF	2017	1986	CG,SG,LG,SS	C	NSO	2017	BPM 6
Solomon Islands	MoF	2017	1986	CG	C	CB	2016	BPM 6
Somalia	MoF	2016	2001	CG	C	CB	2016	BPM 5
South Africa	MoF	2017	2001	CG,SG,SS	C	CB	2017	BPM 6
South Sudan	MoF and MEP	2017	. . .	CG	C	MoF, NSO, and MEP	2017	BPM 6
Spain	MoF and NSO	2017	ESA 2010	CG,SG,LG,SS	A	CB	2017	BPM 6
Sri Lanka	MoF	2017	2001	CG	C	CB	2017	BPM 6
St. Kitts and Nevis	MoF	2017	1986	CG, SG	C	CB	2017	BPM 6
St. Lucia	MoF	2017/18	1986	CG	C	CB	2017	BPM 6
St. Vincent and the Grenadines	MoF	2017	1986	CG	C	CB	2017	BPM 6
Sudan	MoF	2018	2001	CG	Mixed	CB	2018	BPM 6
Suriname	MoF	2017	1986	CG	Mixed	CB	2017	BPM 5

Table G. Key Data Documentation *(continued)*

		National Accounts					Prices (CPI)	
Country	Currency	Historical Data Source[1]	Latest Actual Annual Data	Base Year[2]	System of National Accounts	Use of Chain-Weighted Methodology[3]	Historical Data Source[1]	Latest Actual Annual Data
Sweden	Swedish krona	NSO	2018	2017	ESA 2010	From 1993	NSO	2018
Switzerland	Swiss franc	NSO	2017	2010	ESA 2010	From 1980	NSO	2017
Syria	Syrian pound	NSO	2010	2000	SNA 1993		NSO	2011
Taiwan Province of China	New Taiwan dollar	NSO	2018	2011	SNA 2008		NSO	2018
Tajikistan	Tajik somoni	NSO	2017	1995	SNA 1993		NSO	2017
Tanzania	Tanzanian shilling	NSO	2017	2015	SNA 2008		NSO	2017
Thailand	Thai baht	MEP	2017	2002	SNA 1993	From 1993	MEP	2018
Timor-Leste	US dollar	MoF	2016	2015[6]	SNA 2008		NSO	2018
Togo	CFA franc	NSO	2016	2007	SNA 1993		NSO	2018
Tonga	Tongan pa'anga	CB	2017	2010	SNA 1993		CB	2017
Trinidad and Tobago	Trinidad and Tobago dollar	NSO	2017	2012	SNA 1993		NSO	2018
Tunisia	Tunisian dinar	NSO	2017	2010	SNA 1993	From 2009	NSO	2016
Turkey	Turkish lira	NSO	2018	2009	ESA 2010	From 2009	NSO	2018
Turkmenistan	New Turkmen manat	NSO	2017	2008	SNA 1993	From 2000	NSO	2017
Tuvalu	Australian dollar	PFTAC advisors	2015	2005	SNA 1993		NSO	2017
Uganda	Ugandan shilling	NSO	2017	2010	SNA 1993		CB	2017/18
Ukraine	Ukrainian hryvnia	NSO	2017	2010	SNA 2008	From 2005	NSO	2017
United Arab Emirates	U.A.E. dirham	NSO	2017	2010	SNA 2008		NSO	2018
United Kingdom	British pound	NSO	2018	2016	ESA 2010	From 1980	NSO	2018
United States	US dollar	NSO	2018	2012	SNA 2008	From 1980	NSO	2018
Uruguay	Uruguayan peso	CB	2017	2005	SNA 1993		NSO	2018
Uzbekistan	Uzbek sum	NSO	2017	2015	SNA 1993		NSO, and IMF staff	2018
Vanuatu	Vanuatu vatu	NSO	2017	2006	SNA 1993		NSO	2017
Venezuela	Venezuelan bolívar soberano	CB	2017	1997	SNA 2008		CB	2017
Vietnam	Vietnamese dong	NSO	2018	2010	SNA 1993		NSO	2018
Yemen	Yemeni rial	IMF staff	2017	1990	SNA 1993		NSO,CB, and IMF staff	2017
Zambia	Zambian kwacha	NSO	2017	2010	SNA 2008		NSO	2018
Zimbabwe	RTGS dollar	NSO	2015	2012	. . .		NSO	2018

Table G. Key Data Documentation *(continued)*

	Government Finance					Balance of Payments		
Country	Historical Data Source[1]	Latest Actual Annual Data	Statistics Manual in Use at Source	Subsectors Coverage[4]	Accounting Practice[5]	Historical Data Source[1]	Latest Actual Annual Data	Statistics Manual in Use at Source
Sweden	MoF	2017	2001	CG,LG,SS	A	NSO	2018	BPM 6
Switzerland	MoF	2016	2001	CG,SG,LG,SS	A	CB	2017	BPM 6
Syria	MoF	2009	1986	CG	C	CB	2009	BPM 5
Taiwan Province of China	MoF	2018	2001	CG,LG,SS	C	CB	2018	BPM 6
Tajikistan	MoF	2017	1986	CG,LG,SS	C	CB	2016	BPM 6
Tanzania	MoF	2016	1986	CG,LG	C	CB	2016	BPM 5
Thailand	MoF	2017/18	2001	CG,BCG,LG,SS	A	CB	2017	BPM 6
Timor-Leste	MoF	2017	2001	CG	C	CB	2017	BPM 6
Togo	MoF	2017	2001	CG	C	CB	2017	BPM 6
Tonga	MoF	2017	2014	CG	C	CB and NSO	2018	BPM 6
Trinidad and Tobago	MoF	2017/18	1986	CG	C	CB	2017	BPM 6
Tunisia	MoF	2016	1986	CG	C	CB	2018	BPM 5
Turkey	MoF	2017	2001	CG,LG,SS,other	A	CB	2018	BPM 6
Turkmenistan	MoF	2017	1986	CG,LG	C	NSO and IMF staff	2015	BPM 6
Tuvalu	MoF	2017	. . .	CG	Mixed	IMF staff	2012	BPM 6
Uganda	MoF	2017	2001	CG	C	CB	2017	BPM 6
Ukraine	MoF	2017	2001	CG,SG,LG,SS	C	CB	2017	BPM 6
United Arab Emirates	MoF	2017	2001	CG,BCG,SG,SS	C	CB	2017	BPM 5
United Kingdom	NSO	2018	2001	CG,LG	A	NSO	2018	BPM 6
United States	MEP	2017	2014	CG,SG,LG	A	NSO	2017	BPM 6
Uruguay	MoF	2018	1986	CG,LG,SS,MPC, NFPC	C	CB	2017	BPM 6
Uzbekistan	MoF	2018	2014	CG,SG,LG,SS	C	MEP	2017	BPM 6
Vanuatu	MoF	2017	2001	CG	C	CB	2017	BPM 6
Venezuela	MoF	2017	2001	BCG,NFPC	C	CB	2017	BPM 5
Vietnam	MoF	2016	2001	CG,SG,LG	C	CB	2017	BPM 5
Yemen	MoF	2017	2001	CG,LG	C	IMF staff	2017	BPM 5
Zambia	MoF	2017	1986	CG	C	CB	2017	BPM 6
Zimbabwe	MoF	2017	1986	CG	C	CB and MoF	2017	BPM 6

Note: BPM = *Balance of Payments Manual*; CPI = consumer price index; ESA = European System of National Accounts; SNA = System of National Accounts.

[1]CB = central bank; Customs = Customs Authority; GAD = General Administration Department; IEO = international economic organization; MEP = Ministry of Economy, Planning, Commerce, and/or Development; MoF = Ministry of Finance and/or Treasury; NSO = National Statistics Office; PFTAC = Pacific Financial Technical Assistance Centre.

[2]National accounts base year is the period with which other periods are compared and the period for which prices appear in the denominators of the price relationships used to calculate the index.

[3]Use of chain-weighted methodology allows countries to measure GDP growth more accurately by reducing or eliminating the downward biases in volume series built on index numbers that average volume components using weights from a year in the moderately distant past.

[4]BCG = budgetary central government; CG = central government; EUA = extrabudgetary units/accounts; LG = local government; MPC = monetary public corporation, including central bank; NFPC = nonfinancial public corporation; NMPC = nonmonetary financial public corporation; SG = state government; SS = social security fund; TG = territorial governments.

[5]Accounting standard: A = accrual accounting; C = cash accounting; CB = commitments basis accounting; Mixed = combination of accrual and cash accounting.

[6]Base year is not equal to 100 because the nominal GDP is not measured in the same way as real GDP or the data are seasonally adjusted.

Box A1. Economic Policy Assumptions Underlying the Projections for Selected Economies

Fiscal Policy Assumptions

The short-term fiscal policy assumptions used in the *World Economic Outlook* (WEO) are normally based on officially announced budgets, adjusted for differences between the national authorities and the IMF staff regarding macroeconomic assumptions and projected fiscal outturns. When no official budget has been announced, projections incorporate policy measures that are judged likely to be implemented. The medium-term fiscal projections are similarly based on a judgment about the most likely path of policies. For cases in which the IMF staff has insufficient information to assess the authorities' budget intentions and prospects for policy implementation, an unchanged structural primary balance is assumed unless indicated otherwise. Specific assumptions used in regard to some of the advanced economies follow. (See also Tables B5 to B9 in the online section of the Statistical Appendix for data on fiscal net lending/borrowing and structural balances.)[1]

Argentina: Fiscal projections are based on the available information regarding budget outturn and budget plans for the federal and provincial governments, fiscal measures announced by the authorities, and the IMF staff's macroeconomic projections.

Australia: Fiscal projections are based on Australian Bureau of Statistics data, the fiscal year 2018/19 budgets of the Commonwealth and states and territories, 2018/19 midyear fiscal and economic reviews by states and territories, and the IMF staff's estimates and projections.

Austria: Fiscal projections are based on data from Statistics Austria, the authorities' projections, and the IMF staff's estimates and projections.

Belgium: Projections are based on the 2018–21 Stability Programme and other available information on the authorities' fiscal plans, with adjustments for the IMF staff's assumptions.

Brazil: Fiscal projections for 2019 take into account the deficit target approved in the budget law.

Canada: Projections use the baseline forecasts in the 2018 federal budget and the latest provincial budget updates as available. The IMF staff makes some adjustments to these forecasts, including for differences in macroeconomic projections. The IMF staff's forecast also incorporates the most recent data releases from Statistics Canada's Canadian System of National Economic Accounts, including federal, provincial, and territorial budgetary outturns through the third quarter of 2018.

Chile: Projections are based on the authorities' budget projections, adjusted to reflect the IMF staff's projections for GDP and copper prices.

China: Fiscal expansion is expected for 2019 as a result of personal income tax reform and other measures to respond to economic slowdown.

Denmark: Estimates for 2018 are aligned with the latest official budget numbers, adjusted where appropriate for the IMF staff's macroeconomic assumptions. For 2019, the projections incorporate key features of the medium-term fiscal plan as embodied in the authorities' Convergence Programme 2018 submitted to the European Union.

France: Projections for 2018 and beyond are based on the measures of the 2018 budget law, the multiyear law for 2018–22, and the 2019 budget law adjusted for differences in assumptions on macroeconomic and financial variables, and revenue projections. Historical fiscal data reflect the September 2018 revisions and update of the historical fiscal accounts, debt data, and national accounts.

Germany: The IMF staff's projections for 2019 and beyond are based on the 2019 Draft Budgetary Plan and data updates from the national statistical agency, adjusted for the differences in the IMF staff's macroeconomic framework and assumptions concerning revenue elasticities. The estimate of gross debt includes portfolios of impaired assets and noncore business transferred to institutions that are winding up, as well as other financial sector and EU support operations.

Greece: Greece's general government primary balance estimate for 2018 is based on preliminary data up to November 2018, provided by the Ministry of Finance as of February 1, 2019. Historical data since 2010 reflect adjustments in line with the primary balance definition under the enhanced surveillance framework for Greece.

[1] The output gap is actual minus potential output, as a percentage of potential output. Structural balances are expressed as a percentage of potential output. The structural balance is the actual net lending/borrowing minus the effects of cyclical output from potential output, corrected for one-time and other factors, such as asset and commodity prices and output composition effects. Changes in the structural balance consequently include effects of temporary fiscal measures, the impact of fluctuations in interest rates and debt-service costs, and other noncyclical fluctuations in net lending/borrowing. The computations of structural balances are based on the IMF staff's estimates of potential GDP and revenue and expenditure elasticities. (See Annex I of the October 1993 WEO.) Net debt is calculated as gross debt minus financial assets corresponding to debt instruments. Estimates of the output gap and of the structural balance are subject to significant margins of uncertainty.

Box A1 *(continued)*

Hong Kong Special Administrative Region: Projections are based on the authorities' medium-term fiscal projections on expenditures.

Hungary: Fiscal projections include the IMF staff's projections of the macroeconomic framework and of the impact of recent legislative measures, as well as fiscal policy plans announced in the 2018 budget.

India: Historical data are based on budgetary execution data. Projections are based on available information on the authorities' fiscal plans, with adjustments for the IMF staff's assumptions. Subnational data are incorporated with a lag of up to one year; general government data are thus finalized well after central government data. IMF and Indian presentations differ, particularly regarding divestment and license auction proceeds, net versus gross recording of revenues in certain minor categories, and some public sector lending.

Indonesia: IMF projections are based on moderate tax policy and administration reforms and a gradual increase in social and capital spending over the medium term in line with fiscal space.

Ireland: Fiscal projections are based on the country's Budget 2019.

Israel: Historical data are based on Government Finance Statistics data prepared by the Central Bureau of Statistics. The central government deficit is assumed to increase to 3.5 percent of GDP in 2019. It is assumed to decline afterward, but not in line with medium-term fiscal targets, consistent with long experience of revisions to those targets.

Italy: The IMF staff's estimates and projections are informed by the fiscal plans included in the government's 2019 draft budget. The IMF staff assumes that the automatic value-added tax hikes for next year will be canceled.

Japan: The projections reflect fiscal measures already announced by the government, including the consumption tax hike in October 2019 and the mitigating measures included in the FY2019 budget and tax reform.

Korea: The medium-term forecast incorporates the medium-term path for public spending announced by the government.

Mexico: Fiscal projections for 2018 are broadly in line with the approved budget; projections for 2019 and beyond assume compliance with rules established in the Fiscal Responsibility Law.

Netherlands: Fiscal projections for 2018–24 are based on the authorities' Bureau for Economic Policy Analysis budget projections, after adjustment for differences in macroeconomic assumptions. Historical data were revised following the June 2014 Central Bureau of Statistics release of revised macroeconomic data because of the adoption of ESA 2010 and the revisions of data sources.

New Zealand: Fiscal projections are based on the fiscal year 2018/19 budget and 2018 Half-Year Economic and Fiscal Update and the IMF staff's estimates.

Portugal: The projections for the current year are based on the authorities' approved budget, adjusted to reflect the IMF staff's macroeconomic forecast. Projections thereafter are based on the assumption of unchanged policies.

Puerto Rico: Fiscal projections are based on the Puerto Rico Fiscal and Economic Growth Plans (FEGPs), which were prepared in October 2018, and are certified by the Oversight Board. In line with this plan's assumptions, IMF projections assume federal aid for rebuilding after Hurricane Maria, which devastated the island in September 2017. The projections also assume revenue losses from the following: elimination of federal funding for the Affordable Care Act starting in 2020 for Puerto Rico; elimination of federal tax incentives starting in 2018 that had neutralized the effects of Puerto Rico's Act 154 on foreign firms; and the effects of the Tax Cuts and Jobs Act, which reduce the tax advantage of US firms producing in Puerto Rico. Given sizable policy uncertainty, some FEGP and IMF assumptions may differ, in particular those relating to the effects of the corporate tax reform, tax compliance, and tax adjustments (fees and rates); reduction of subsidies and expenses, freezing of payroll operational costs, and improvement of mobility; reduction of expenses; and increased health care efficiency. On the expenditure side, measures include extension of Act 66, which freezes much government spending, through 2020; reduction of operating costs; decreases in government subsidies; and spending cuts in education. Although IMF policy assumptions are similar to those in the FEGP scenario with full measures, the IMF's projections of fiscal revenues, expenditures, and balance are different from the FEGPs'. This stems from two main differences in methodologies: first, while IMF projections are on an accrual basis, the FEGPs' are on a cash basis. Second, the IMF and FEGPs make very different macroeconomic assumptions.

Russia: Projections for 2018–21 are the IMF staff's estimates, based on the authorities' budget. Projections for 2022–24 are based on the new oil price rule, with adjustments by the IMF staff.

Box A1 *(continued)*

Saudi Arabia: The IMF staff baseline projections of total government revenues, except exported oil revenues, are based on IMF staff understanding of government policies as announced in the 2019 Budget and Fiscal Balance Program 2019 Update. Exported oil revenues are based on WEO baseline oil prices and the assumption that Saudi Arabia will continue to meet its commitments under the OPEC+ agreement. Expenditure projections take the 2019 budget and the Fiscal Balance Program 2019 Update as a starting point and reflect IMF staff estimates of the latest changes in policies and economic developments.

Singapore: For fiscal year 2019/20, projections are based on budget numbers. For the rest of the projection period, the IMF staff assumes unchanged policies.

South Africa: Fiscal assumptions are based on the 2019 Budget Review. Nontax revenue excludes transactions in financial assets and liabilities, as they involve primarily revenues associated with realized exchange rate valuation gains from the holding of foreign currency deposits, sale of assets, and conceptually similar items.

Spain: For 2019, projections assume expenditures under the 2018 budget extension scenario and already legislated measures, including pension and public wage increases, and the IMF staff's projection of revenues. For 2020 and beyond, fiscal projections are IMF staff projections, which assume an unchanged structural primary balance.

Sweden: Fiscal projections take into account the authorities' projections based on the 2018 December Budget. The impact of cyclical developments on the fiscal accounts is calculated using the 2014 Organisation for Economic Co-operation and Development's elasticity (Price, Dang and Guillemette (2014)) to take into account output and employment gaps.

Switzerland: The projections assume that fiscal policy is adjusted as necessary to keep fiscal balances in line with the requirements of Switzerland's fiscal rules.

Turkey: The fiscal projections assume a more negative primary and overall balance than envisaged in the authorities' New Economic Program 2019–21, based partly on the IMF staff's lower growth forecast and partly on definitional differences: the basis for the projections in the WEO and *Fiscal Monitor* is the IMF-defined fiscal balance, which excludes some revenue and expenditure items that are included in the authorities' headline balance.

United Kingdom: Fiscal projections are based on the country's Spring 2019 Budget, with expenditure projections based on the budgeted nominal values and with revenue projections adjusted for differences between the IMF staff's forecasts of macroeconomic variables (such as GDP growth and inflation) and the forecasts of these variables assumed in the authorities' fiscal projections. The IMF staff's data exclude public sector banks and the effect of transferring assets from the Royal Mail Pension Plan to the public sector in April 2012. Real government consumption and investment are part of the real GDP path, which, according to the IMF staff, may or may not be the same as projected by the UK Office for Budget Responsibility.

United States: Fiscal projections are based on the January 2019 Congressional Budget Office baseline, adjusted for the IMF staff's policy and macroeconomic assumptions. Projections incorporate the effects of tax reform (the Tax Cuts and Jobs Act, signed into law at the end of 2017) as well as the Bipartisan Budget Act of 2018, passed in February 2018. Finally, fiscal projections are adjusted to reflect the IMF staff's forecasts for key macroeconomic and financial variables—and different accounting treatment of financial sector support and defined-benefit pension plans—and are converted to a general government basis. Data are compiled using SNA 2008 and, when translated into government finance statistics, this is in accordance with the *Government Finance Statistics Manual 2014*. Because of data limitations, most series begin in 2001.

Monetary Policy Assumptions

Monetary policy assumptions are based on the established policy framework in each country. In most cases, this implies a nonaccommodative stance over the business cycle: official interest rates will increase when economic indicators suggest that inflation will rise above its acceptable rate or range; they will decrease when indicators suggest inflation will not exceed the acceptable rate or range, that output growth is below its potential rate, and that the margin of slack in the economy is significant. On this basis, the London interbank offered rate on six-month US dollar deposits is assumed to average 3.2 percent in 2019 and 3.8 percent in 2020 (see Table 1.1). The rate on three-month euro deposits is assumed to average –0.3 percent in 2019 and –0.2 percent in 2020. The interest rate on six-month Japanese yen deposits is assumed to average 0.0 percent in 2019 and 2020.

Box A1 *(continued)*

Argentina: Monetary policy assumptions are consistent with the current monetary policy framework, which targets zero base money growth in seasonally adjusted terms.

Australia: Monetary policy assumptions are in line with market expectations.

Brazil: Monetary policy assumptions are consistent with gradual convergence of inflation toward the middle of the target range.

Canada: Monetary policy assumptions are in line with market expectations.

China: Monetary policy is expected to remain on hold.

Denmark: The monetary policy is to maintain the peg to the euro.

Euro area: Monetary policy assumptions for euro area member countries are in line with market expectations.

Hong Kong Special Administrative Region: The IMF staff assumes that the currency board system will remain intact.

India: Monetary policy projections are consistent with achieving the Reserve Bank of India's inflation target over the medium term.

Indonesia: Monetary policy assumptions are in line with the maintenance of inflation within the central bank's targeted band.

Japan: Monetary policy assumptions are in line with market expectations.

Korea: Monetary policy assumptions are in line with market expectations.

Mexico: Monetary policy assumptions are consistent with attaining the inflation target.

Russia: Monetary projections assume that the Central Bank of Russia is pausing the transition to a neutral stance.

Saudi Arabia: Monetary policy projections are based on the continuation of the exchange rate peg to the US dollar.

Singapore: Broad money is projected to grow in line with the projected growth in nominal GDP.

South Africa: Monetary policy will remain neutral.

Sweden: Monetary projections are in line with Riksbank projections.

Switzerland: The projections assume no change in the policy rate in 2018–19.

Turkey: The outlook for monetary and financial conditions assumes no changes to the current policy stance.

United Kingdom: The short-term interest rate path is based on market interest rate expectations.

United States: The IMF staff expects continued gradual normalization of the federal funds target rate, in line with the broader macroeconomic outlook.

List of Tables

Table A1. Summary of World Output[1]

(Annual percent change)

	Average									Projections		
	2001–10	2011	2012	2013	2014	2015	2016	2017	2018	2019	2020	2024
World	**3.9**	**4.3**	**3.5**	**3.5**	**3.6**	**3.4**	**3.4**	**3.8**	**3.6**	**3.3**	**3.6**	**3.7**
Advanced Economies	**1.7**	**1.7**	**1.2**	**1.4**	**2.1**	**2.3**	**1.7**	**2.4**	**2.2**	**1.8**	**1.7**	**1.6**
United States	1.7	1.6	2.2	1.8	2.5	2.9	1.6	2.2	2.9	2.3	1.9	1.6
Euro Area	1.2	1.6	–0.9	–0.2	1.4	2.1	2.0	2.4	1.8	1.3	1.5	1.4
Japan	0.6	–0.1	1.5	2.0	0.4	1.2	0.6	1.9	0.8	1.0	0.5	0.5
Other Advanced Economies[2]	2.8	3.0	2.0	2.3	3.0	2.0	2.1	2.7	2.2	1.9	2.2	2.2
Emerging Market and Developing Economies	**6.2**	**6.4**	**5.4**	**5.1**	**4.7**	**4.3**	**4.6**	**4.8**	**4.5**	**4.4**	**4.8**	**4.9**
Regional Groups												
Commonwealth of Independent States[3]	5.5	5.3	3.6	2.5	1.0	–1.9	0.8	2.4	2.8	2.2	2.3	2.4
Emerging and Developing Asia	8.4	7.9	7.0	6.9	6.8	6.8	6.7	6.6	6.4	6.3	6.3	6.1
Emerging and Developing Europe	3.9	6.7	2.6	4.9	3.9	4.8	3.3	6.0	3.6	0.8	2.8	3.1
Latin America and the Caribbean	3.2	4.6	2.9	2.9	1.3	0.3	–0.6	1.2	1.0	1.4	2.4	2.8
Middle East, North Africa, Afghanistan, and Pakistan	5.1	4.4	4.8	2.6	2.9	2.6	5.2	2.2	1.8	1.5	3.2	2.8
Middle East and North Africa	5.1	4.4	4.9	2.4	2.7	2.4	5.3	1.8	1.4	1.3	3.2	2.8
Sub-Saharan Africa	5.9	5.3	4.7	5.2	5.1	3.2	1.4	2.9	3.0	3.5	3.7	4.0
Memorandum												
European Union	1.6	1.8	–0.3	0.3	1.9	2.4	2.1	2.7	2.1	1.6	1.7	1.6
Low-Income Developing Countries	6.5	5.3	4.7	6.0	6.0	4.6	3.6	4.9	4.6	5.0	5.1	5.3
Analytical Groups												
By Source of Export Earnings												
Fuel	5.5	5.2	5.0	2.6	2.2	0.3	2.1	1.0	1.0	0.7	2.3	2.1
Nonfuel	6.4	6.7	5.4	5.7	5.3	5.2	5.1	5.6	5.3	5.1	5.3	5.3
Of Which, Primary Products	4.2	5.0	2.5	4.1	2.1	2.8	1.8	3.0	1.7	2.1	3.1	3.7
By External Financing Source												
Net Debtor Economies	5.1	5.3	4.4	4.7	4.5	4.1	4.1	4.8	4.6	4.4	4.8	5.2
Net Debtor Economies by Debt-Servicing Experience												
Economies with Arrears and/or Rescheduling during 2013–17	4.7	2.6	1.6	3.0	1.9	1.0	2.8	3.3	3.8	3.8	4.5	5.0
Memorandum												
Median Growth Rate												
Advanced Economies	2.2	1.9	1.0	1.5	2.5	2.3	2.4	2.8	2.7	2.1	2.2	2.0
Emerging Market and Developing Economies	4.5	4.7	4.4	4.2	3.7	3.3	3.3	3.5	3.2	3.5	3.5	3.6
Low-Income Developing Countries	5.2	6.0	5.1	5.2	5.0	3.9	4.2	4.7	3.9	5.0	5.0	5.0
Output per Capita[4]												
Advanced Economies	1.1	1.2	0.7	0.9	1.6	1.7	1.2	1.9	1.8	1.3	1.3	1.2
Emerging Market and Developing Economies	4.6	4.9	3.6	3.6	3.2	2.8	3.1	3.3	3.2	3.0	3.5	3.6
Low-Income Developing Countries	3.8	3.6	1.7	3.7	3.7	2.2	1.2	2.6	2.4	2.7	2.9	3.1
World Growth Rate Based on Market Exchange Rates	**2.5**	**3.1**	**2.5**	**2.6**	**2.8**	**2.8**	**2.5**	**3.2**	**3.1**	**2.7**	**2.9**	**2.9**
Value of World Output (billions of US dollars)												
At Market Exchange Rates	49,851	73,245	74,639	76,770	78,852	74,689	75,735	80,145	84,740	87,265	92,310	114,577
At Purchasing Power Parities	70,655	95,045	99,926	105,120	110,836	115,750	120,828	127,693	135,178	142,046	150,169	187,689

[1]Real GDP.

[2]Excludes the United States, euro area countries, and Japan.

[3]Georgia, Turkmenistan, and Ukraine, which are not members of the Commonwealth of Independent States, are included in this group for reasons of geography and similarity in economic structure.

[4]Output per capita is in international currency at purchasing power parity.

Table A2. Advanced Economies: Real GDP and Total Domestic Demand[1]

(Annual percent change)

	Average									Projections			Fourth Quarter[2]	Projections	
	2001–10	2011	2012	2013	2014	2015	2016	2017	2018	2019	2020	2024	2018:Q4	2019:Q4	2020:Q4
Real GDP															
Advanced Economies	**1.7**	**1.7**	**1.2**	**1.4**	**2.1**	**2.3**	**1.7**	**2.4**	**2.2**	**1.8**	**1.7**	**1.6**	**2.0**	**1.8**	**1.8**
United States	1.7	1.6	2.2	1.8	2.5	2.9	1.6	2.2	2.9	2.3	1.9	1.6	3.0	2.2	1.7
Euro Area	1.2	1.6	–0.9	–0.2	1.4	2.1	2.0	2.4	1.8	1.3	1.5	1.4	1.1	1.6	1.4
Germany	0.9	3.7	0.7	0.6	2.2	1.5	2.2	2.5	1.5	0.8	1.4	1.2	0.6	1.4	1.3
France	1.3	2.2	0.3	0.6	1.0	1.1	1.2	2.2	1.5	1.3	1.4	1.5	0.9	1.6	1.3
Italy	0.3	0.6	–2.8	–1.7	0.1	0.9	1.1	1.6	0.9	0.1	0.9	0.6	0.0	0.6	0.8
Spain	2.2	–1.0	–2.9	–1.7	1.4	3.6	3.2	3.0	2.5	2.1	1.9	1.6	2.4	1.9	1.7
Netherlands	1.4	1.5	–1.0	–0.1	1.4	2.0	2.2	2.9	2.5	1.8	1.7	1.5	1.7	1.8	1.7
Belgium	1.6	1.8	0.2	0.2	1.3	1.7	1.5	1.7	1.4	1.3	1.4	1.5	1.2	1.3	1.4
Austria	1.5	2.9	0.7	0.0	0.7	1.1	2.0	2.6	2.7	2.0	1.7	1.5	1.7	2.5	1.6
Greece	1.8	–9.1	–7.3	–3.2	0.7	–0.4	–0.2	1.5	2.1	2.4	2.2	1.2	2.3	2.7	1.8
Portugal	0.7	–1.8	–4.0	–1.1	0.9	1.8	1.9	2.8	2.1	1.7	1.5	1.4	1.7	1.6	1.6
Ireland	2.9	3.7	0.2	1.3	8.7	25.0	4.9	7.2	6.8	4.1	3.4	2.7	4.0	4.0	3.5
Finland	1.7	2.6	–1.4	–0.8	–0.6	0.1	2.5	2.8	2.4	1.9	1.7	1.3	2.5	1.6	2.4
Slovak Republic	4.9	2.8	1.7	1.5	2.8	4.2	3.1	3.2	4.1	3.7	3.5	2.5	4.0	3.7	3.5
Lithuania	4.3	6.0	3.8	3.5	3.5	2.0	2.4	4.1	3.4	2.9	2.6	2.0	3.6	2.5	2.4
Slovenia	2.7	0.6	–2.7	–1.1	3.0	2.3	3.1	4.9	4.5	3.4	2.8	2.1	3.4	4.1	2.0
Luxembourg	2.7	2.5	–0.4	3.7	4.3	3.9	2.4	1.5	3.0	2.7	2.8	2.6	2.0	3.3	2.4
Latvia	3.8	6.4	4.0	2.4	1.9	3.0	2.1	4.6	4.8	3.2	3.1	3.0	5.6	1.7	3.7
Estonia	3.3	7.6	4.3	1.9	2.9	1.9	3.5	4.9	3.9	3.0	2.9	2.8	4.3	1.3	3.9
Cyprus	3.3	0.4	–2.9	–5.8	–1.3	2.0	4.8	4.5	3.9	3.5	3.3	2.4	3.8	3.2	3.7
Malta	2.0	1.4	2.7	4.6	8.6	10.6	5.7	6.6	6.4	5.2	4.4	3.2	7.0	5.2	3.3
Japan	0.6	–0.1	1.5	2.0	0.4	1.2	0.6	1.9	0.8	1.0	0.5	0.5	0.3	0.3	1.4
United Kingdom	1.6	1.6	1.4	2.0	2.9	2.3	1.8	1.8	1.4	1.2	1.4	1.6	1.4	1.0	1.5
Korea	4.4	3.7	2.3	2.9	3.3	2.8	2.9	3.1	2.7	2.6	2.8	2.9	3.2	2.3	3.2
Canada	1.9	3.1	1.8	2.3	2.9	0.7	1.1	3.0	1.8	1.5	1.9	1.6	1.6	1.8	1.8
Australia	3.1	2.8	3.9	2.1	2.6	2.5	2.8	2.4	2.8	2.1	2.8	2.6	2.3	2.6	2.8
Taiwan Province of China	4.2	3.8	2.1	2.2	4.0	0.8	1.5	3.1	2.6	2.5	2.5	2.1	1.8	2.6	2.7
Switzerland	1.8	1.8	1.0	1.9	2.5	1.3	1.6	1.7	2.5	1.1	1.5	1.6	1.6	1.4	1.6
Sweden	2.1	2.7	–0.3	1.2	2.6	4.5	2.7	2.1	2.3	1.2	1.8	2.0	2.4	0.8	2.2
Singapore	5.8	6.5	4.3	5.0	4.1	2.5	2.8	3.9	3.2	2.3	2.4	2.6	1.9	3.4	1.3
Hong Kong SAR	4.1	4.8	1.7	3.1	2.8	2.4	2.2	3.8	3.0	2.7	3.0	3.0	1.3	4.1	2.9
Norway	1.6	1.0	2.7	1.0	2.0	2.0	1.2	2.0	1.4	2.0	1.9	1.7	1.8	0.7	2.6
Czech Republic	3.2	1.8	–0.8	–0.5	2.7	5.3	2.5	4.4	2.9	2.9	2.7	2.5	2.8	2.7	2.9
Israel	3.2	5.1	2.2	4.3	3.9	2.6	4.0	3.5	3.3	3.3	3.3	3.0	2.6	3.6	3.2
Denmark	0.8	1.3	0.2	0.9	1.6	2.3	2.4	2.3	1.2	1.7	1.8	1.6	2.2	1.6	1.7
New Zealand	2.7	1.9	2.5	2.2	3.1	4.0	4.2	2.6	3.0	2.5	2.9	2.5	3.3	2.2	3.1
Puerto Rico	0.7	–0.4	0.0	–0.3	–1.2	–1.0	–1.3	–2.4	–2.3	–1.1	–0.7	–0.8	. . .	. . .	. . .
Macao SAR	. . .	21.7	9.2	11.2	–1.2	–21.6	–0.9	9.7	4.7	4.3	4.2	4.1	. . .	. . .	. . .
Iceland	2.6	1.9	1.3	4.1	2.1	4.7	6.6	4.6	4.6	1.7	2.9	2.5	3.8	3.0	2.3
San Marino	. . .	–8.3	–7.0	–0.8	–0.7	2.5	2.5	0.6	1.1	0.8	0.7	0.5	. . .	. . .	. . .
Memorandum															
Major Advanced Economies	1.3	1.6	1.4	1.5	1.9	2.1	1.4	2.2	2.1	1.6	1.5	1.3	1.8	1.6	1.5
Real Total Domestic Demand															
Advanced Economies	**1.6**	**1.4**	**0.8**	**1.1**	**2.1**	**2.6**	**1.9**	**2.3**	**2.2**	**1.9**	**1.7**	**1.6**	**2.2**	**1.7**	**1.8**
United States	1.7	1.5	2.2	1.6	2.6	3.6	1.8	2.5	3.0	2.5	1.7	1.4	3.1	2.2	1.7
Euro Area	1.1	0.7	–2.4	–0.6	1.3	2.4	2.4	1.7	1.7	1.3	1.6	1.6	1.5	1.4	1.5
Germany	0.3	3.0	–0.8	1.0	1.6	1.4	2.9	2.2	1.9	1.1	1.7	1.3	1.9	1.0	1.9
France	1.5	2.1	–0.4	0.7	1.5	1.5	1.7	2.1	1.0	1.0	1.1	2.0	0.5	1.4	0.9
Italy	0.5	–0.6	–5.6	–2.6	0.2	1.5	1.5	1.4	1.0	–0.2	1.0	0.7	0.0	0.5	0.9
Spain	2.3	–3.1	–5.1	–3.2	2.0	4.0	2.4	3.0	3.0	2.2	1.7	1.4	2.8	2.1	1.5
Japan	0.2	0.7	2.3	2.4	0.4	0.8	0.0	1.4	0.6	1.3	0.3	0.4	0.8	–0.4	1.7
United Kingdom	1.7	–0.2	1.8	2.1	3.2	2.3	2.4	1.4	1.6	1.4	1.2	1.6	2.0	0.9	1.5
Canada	2.9	3.4	2.0	2.2	1.7	–0.1	0.7	3.9	1.7	0.6	1.8	1.6	0.0	1.7	1.6
Other Advanced Economies[3]	2.9	3.2	2.0	1.5	2.8	2.4	2.3	3.4	2.5	2.3	2.6	2.6	2.3	2.8	2.5
Memorandum															
Major Advanced Economies	1.3	1.4	1.2	1.4	2.0	2.4	1.6	2.2	2.1	1.7	1.4	1.3	2.1	1.4	1.6

[1]In this and other tables, when countries are not listed alphabetically, they are ordered on the basis of economic size.
[2]From the fourth quarter of the preceding year.
[3]Excludes the Group of Seven (Canada, France, Germany, Italy, Japan, United Kingdom, United States) and euro area countries.

Table A3. Advanced Economies: Components of Real GDP

(Annual percent change)

	Averages										Projections	
	2001–10	2011–20	2011	2012	2013	2014	2015	2016	2017	2018	2019	2020
Private Consumer Expenditure												
Advanced Economies	**1.8**	**1.7**	**1.1**	**0.9**	**1.2**	**1.8**	**2.5**	**2.2**	**2.2**	**2.0**	**1.6**	**1.5**
United States	2.1	2.3	1.9	1.5	1.5	2.9	3.7	2.7	2.5	2.6	2.2	1.8
Euro Area	1.1	0.8	0.0	–1.2	–0.6	0.9	1.8	2.0	1.6	1.3	1.1	1.3
Germany	0.5	1.3	1.3	1.4	0.8	1.1	1.6	1.9	2.0	0.9	0.8	1.3
France	1.8	0.9	0.6	–0.4	0.5	0.8	1.5	2.1	1.0	0.9	0.8	1.0
Italy	0.5	0.0	0.0	–4.0	–2.4	0.2	1.9	1.3	1.5	0.6	0.3	1.0
Spain	2.0	0.7	–2.4	–3.5	–3.1	1.5	3.0	2.9	2.5	2.4	2.0	1.7
Japan	0.9	0.4	–0.4	2.0	2.4	–0.9	–0.2	–0.1	1.1	0.4	0.4	–0.5
United Kingdom	1.8	1.6	–0.7	1.5	1.8	2.0	2.6	3.1	2.1	1.7	1.1	1.2
Canada	3.1	2.2	2.3	1.9	2.6	2.6	2.3	2.2	3.5	2.1	0.8	1.4
Other Advanced Economies[1]	3.0	2.6	3.1	2.2	2.3	2.4	2.8	2.5	2.7	2.5	2.4	2.7
Memorandum												
Major Advanced Economies	1.6	1.6	1.1	1.1	1.3	1.8	2.5	2.1	2.1	1.8	1.4	1.3
Public Consumption												
Advanced Economies	**2.1**	**0.8**	**–0.6**	**–0.1**	**–0.1**	**0.5**	**1.7**	**1.9**	**0.7**	**1.6**	**1.6**	**1.4**
United States	2.1	–0.1	–3.0	–1.5	–1.9	–0.8	1.7	1.5	–0.1	1.2	1.0	0.7
Euro Area	1.9	0.8	–0.1	–0.3	0.4	0.7	1.3	1.8	1.1	1.0	1.3	1.1
Germany	1.2	1.8	0.9	1.1	1.3	1.6	2.9	4.0	1.6	1.0	2.1	1.4
France	1.6	1.1	1.1	1.6	1.5	1.3	1.0	1.4	1.3	1.0	0.8	0.5
Italy	1.0	–0.4	–1.8	–1.4	–0.3	–0.7	–0.6	0.1	–0.2	0.2	–0.4	0.8
Spain	4.7	0.2	–0.3	–4.7	–2.1	–0.3	2.0	1.0	1.9	2.3	1.7	0.8
Japan	1.5	1.3	1.9	1.7	1.5	0.5	1.5	1.4	0.3	0.8	1.3	1.8
United Kingdom	2.6	1.0	0.1	1.2	–0.2	2.2	1.4	0.8	–0.2	0.4	2.2	1.7
Canada	2.5	1.0	1.3	0.7	–0.8	0.6	1.4	1.8	2.1	2.5	0.3	0.6
Other Advanced Economies[1]	2.9	2.7	1.6	1.9	2.3	2.4	2.6	3.5	2.3	3.9	3.7	3.0
Memorandum												
Major Advanced Economies	1.9	0.5	–1.1	–0.2	–0.5	0.1	1.6	1.6	0.3	1.1	1.1	1.0
Gross Fixed Capital Formation												
Advanced Economies	**0.5**	**2.8**	**3.2**	**2.6**	**1.7**	**3.5**	**3.2**	**2.0**	**3.8**	**3.1**	**2.5**	**2.4**
United States	0.0	3.9	4.6	6.9	3.6	4.9	3.3	1.7	4.0	4.8	3.6	2.2
Euro Area	0.4	1.7	1.5	–3.4	–2.3	1.7	4.9	4.0	2.6	3.0	2.4	2.6
Germany	–0.2	2.7	7.4	–0.1	–1.2	3.9	1.1	3.3	3.6	2.7	3.0	3.1
France	1.2	1.6	2.0	0.2	–0.8	0.0	1.0	2.8	4.5	2.9	1.8	1.8
Italy	0.1	–0.8	–1.9	–9.3	–6.6	–2.3	2.1	3.5	4.4	3.4	–1.0	0.8
Spain	1.2	1.0	–6.9	–8.6	–3.4	4.7	6.7	2.9	4.8	5.2	2.9	2.7
Japan	–2.2	2.1	1.7	3.5	4.9	3.1	1.6	–0.3	3.0	1.3	1.9	0.9
United Kingdom	0.3	2.7	2.6	2.1	3.4	7.2	3.4	2.3	3.5	0.2	0.6	2.3
Canada	3.8	1.1	4.6	4.9	1.4	2.3	–5.2	–4.3	3.0	0.8	0.5	3.9
Other Advanced Economies[1]	2.7	2.7	4.1	3.0	2.5	2.6	2.0	2.7	4.3	1.0	1.4	3.0
Memorandum												
Major Advanced Economies	0.0	2.9	3.7	3.7	2.2	3.8	2.2	1.5	3.8	3.4	2.5	2.1

Table A3. Advanced Economies: Components of Real GDP *(continued)*

(Annual percent change)

	Averages										Projections	
	2001–10	2011–20	2011	2012	2013	2014	2015	2016	2017	2018	2019	2020
Final Domestic Demand												
Advanced Economies	**1.6**	**1.8**	**1.3**	**1.1**	**1.1**	**2.0**	**2.5**	**2.1**	**2.3**	**2.1**	**1.9**	**1.7**
United States	1.7	2.3	1.6	2.0	1.3	2.8	3.3	2.3	2.5	2.9	2.3	1.7
Euro Area	1.1	1.0	0.3	–1.5	–0.8	1.0	2.3	2.4	1.7	1.6	1.4	1.6
Germany	0.5	1.7	2.5	1.0	0.5	1.8	1.8	2.6	2.3	1.3	1.5	1.7
France	1.6	1.1	1.0	0.2	0.5	0.8	1.3	2.1	1.8	1.4	1.0	1.1
Italy	0.5	–0.2	–0.8	–4.5	–2.8	–0.4	1.4	1.4	1.7	1.0	–0.1	0.9
Spain	2.3	0.6	–3.0	–4.8	–3.0	1.8	3.6	2.5	2.9	3.0	2.1	1.7
Japan	0.2	1.0	0.5	2.3	2.8	0.2	0.6	0.1	1.4	0.6	1.2	0.3
United Kingdom	1.7	1.7	0.0	1.6	1.7	2.9	2.5	2.5	1.9	1.2	1.2	1.5
Canada	3.1	1.7	2.6	2.4	1.6	2.1	0.3	0.6	3.1	1.9	0.7	1.8
Other Advanced Economies[1]	2.9	2.6	3.0	2.4	2.4	2.5	2.6	2.7	3.1	2.2	2.3	2.8
Memorandum												
Major Advanced Economies	1.3	1.7	1.3	1.4	1.2	1.9	2.3	1.9	2.2	2.0	1.7	1.4
Stock Building[2]												
Advanced Economies	**0.0**	**0.0**	**0.2**	**–0.2**	**0.0**	**0.1**	**0.1**	**–0.3**	**0.0**	**0.1**	**0.1**	**0.1**
United States	0.0	0.1	–0.1	0.2	0.2	–0.1	0.3	–0.5	0.0	0.1	0.2	0.2
Euro Area	–0.1	0.0	0.5	–0.9	0.2	0.3	0.0	0.1	0.0	0.1	–0.1	0.0
Germany	–0.1	–0.1	0.5	–1.7	0.5	–0.2	–0.3	0.3	–0.1	0.5	–0.4	0.0
France	–0.1	0.1	1.1	–0.6	0.2	0.7	0.3	–0.4	0.2	–0.4	0.0	0.0
Italy	0.0	0.0	0.2	–1.1	0.2	0.6	0.1	0.1	–0.3	–0.1	0.0	0.1
Spain	0.0	0.0	–0.1	–0.2	–0.3	0.2	0.5	–0.1	0.1	0.1	0.1	0.0
Japan	0.0	0.0	0.2	0.0	–0.4	0.1	0.3	–0.1	0.0	0.2	0.0	0.0
United Kingdom	0.0	0.0	–0.2	0.2	0.2	0.7	–0.2	–0.1	–0.6	0.4	0.2	–0.2
Canada	–0.1	0.1	0.7	–0.3	0.5	–0.4	–0.4	0.0	0.8	–0.2	0.0	0.0
Other Advanced Economies[1]	0.0	–0.1	0.2	–0.3	–0.8	0.2	0.0	–0.4	0.2	0.3	0.0	–0.1
Memorandum												
Major Advanced Economies	0.0	0.0	0.2	–0.2	0.2	0.1	0.1	–0.3	0.0	0.1	0.1	0.1
Foreign Balance[2]												
Advanced Economies	**0.1**	**0.0**	**0.3**	**0.4**	**0.3**	**0.0**	**–0.3**	**–0.2**	**0.1**	**0.0**	**–0.1**	**0.0**
United States	0.0	–0.2	0.0	0.0	0.2	–0.3	–0.8	–0.3	–0.3	–0.2	–0.3	–0.1
Euro Area	0.1	0.3	0.9	1.5	0.3	0.1	–0.2	–0.4	0.8	0.2	0.1	0.1
Germany	0.5	0.2	0.9	1.4	–0.3	0.7	0.2	–0.6	0.3	–0.4	–0.2	–0.2
France	–0.2	0.0	0.1	0.7	–0.1	–0.5	–0.4	–0.5	0.1	0.6	0.3	0.3
Italy	–0.2	0.4	1.2	2.8	0.8	–0.1	–0.5	–0.4	0.2	–0.1	0.2	0.0
Spain	–0.2	0.6	2.1	2.2	1.5	–0.5	–0.3	0.8	0.1	–0.4	0.0	0.2
Japan	0.3	–0.1	–0.9	–0.8	–0.4	0.0	0.3	0.6	0.5	0.0	0.0	0.1
United Kingdom	–0.1	–0.1	1.5	–0.4	–0.5	–0.4	–0.3	–0.7	0.5	–0.2	–0.2	0.1
Canada	–1.1	0.2	–0.3	–0.4	0.1	1.2	0.9	0.4	–1.1	0.1	0.8	0.1
Other Advanced Economies[1]	0.6	0.2	0.5	0.5	0.9	0.4	–0.1	0.0	–0.5	0.3	0.0	0.0
Memorandum												
Major Advanced Economies	0.0	–0.1	0.1	0.2	0.0	–0.1	–0.4	–0.2	0.0	–0.1	–0.1	0.0

[1]Excludes the Group of Seven (Canada, France, Germany, Italy, Japan, United Kingdom, United States) and euro area countries.
[2]Changes expressed as percent of GDP in the preceding period.

Table A4. Emerging Market and Developing Economies: Real GDP

(Annual percent change)

	Average									Projections		
	2001–10	2011	2012	2013	2014	2015	2016	2017	2018	2019	2020	2024
Commonwealth of Independent States[1,2]	**5.5**	**5.3**	**3.6**	**2.5**	**1.0**	**–1.9**	**0.8**	**2.4**	**2.8**	**2.2**	**2.3**	**2.4**
Russia	4.8	5.1	3.7	1.8	0.7	–2.5	0.3	1.6	2.3	1.6	1.7	1.6
Excluding Russia	7.3	6.0	3.5	4.2	1.9	–0.5	2.1	4.1	3.9	3.5	3.7	4.0
Armenia	8.1	4.7	7.1	3.3	3.6	3.3	0.3	7.5	5.0	4.6	4.5	4.5
Azerbaijan	14.4	–1.6	2.2	5.8	2.8	1.0	–3.1	0.1	1.4	3.4	3.1	1.7
Belarus	7.4	5.5	1.7	1.0	1.7	–3.8	–2.5	2.5	3.0	1.8	2.2	2.0
Georgia	6.3	7.2	6.4	3.4	4.6	2.9	2.8	4.8	4.7	4.6	5.0	5.2
Kazakhstan	8.3	7.4	4.8	6.0	4.2	1.2	1.1	4.1	4.1	3.2	3.2	4.5
Kyrgyz Republic	4.0	6.0	–0.1	10.9	4.0	3.9	4.3	4.7	3.5	3.8	3.4	3.4
Moldova	5.1	5.8	–0.6	9.0	5.0	–0.3	4.4	4.7	4.0	3.5	3.8	3.8
Tajikistan	8.0	7.4	7.5	7.4	6.7	6.0	6.9	7.1	7.0	5.0	4.5	4.0
Turkmenistan	13.2	14.7	11.1	10.2	10.3	6.5	6.2	6.5	6.2	6.3	6.0	5.7
Ukraine[3]	3.9	5.5	0.2	0.0	–6.6	–9.8	2.4	2.5	3.3	2.7	3.0	3.3
Uzbekistan	6.9	8.3	8.2	8.0	8.0	7.9	9.0	8.9	5.0	5.0	5.5	6.0
Emerging and Developing Asia	**8.4**	**7.9**	**7.0**	**6.9**	**6.8**	**6.8**	**6.7**	**6.6**	**6.4**	**6.3**	**6.3**	**6.1**
Bangladesh	5.8	6.5	6.3	6.0	6.3	6.8	7.2	7.6	7.7	7.3	7.0	7.0
Bhutan	8.4	9.7	6.4	3.6	4.0	6.2	7.3	7.4	5.8	4.8	6.3	6.5
Brunei Darussalam	1.4	3.7	0.9	–2.1	–2.5	–0.4	–2.5	1.3	–0.2	4.8	6.6	2.2
Cambodia	8.0	7.1	7.3	7.4	7.1	7.0	6.9	7.0	7.3	6.8	6.7	6.0
China	10.5	9.5	7.9	7.8	7.3	6.9	6.7	6.8	6.6	6.3	6.1	5.5
Fiji	1.3	2.7	1.4	4.7	5.6	3.8	0.7	3.0	3.2	3.4	3.3	3.2
India[4]	7.5	6.6	5.5	6.4	7.4	8.0	8.2	7.2	7.1	7.3	7.5	7.7
Indonesia	5.4	6.2	6.0	5.6	5.0	4.9	5.0	5.1	5.2	5.2	5.2	5.3
Kiribati	0.7	1.6	4.7	4.2	–0.7	10.4	5.1	0.3	2.3	2.3	2.3	1.8
Lao P.D.R.	7.2	8.0	7.8	8.0	7.6	7.3	7.0	6.8	6.5	6.7	6.8	6.8
Malaysia	4.6	5.3	5.5	4.7	6.0	5.1	4.2	5.9	4.7	4.7	4.8	4.8
Maldives	6.5	8.4	2.4	7.3	7.3	2.9	7.3	6.9	7.0	6.3	5.5	5.5
Marshall Islands	1.6	3.2	2.8	–0.7	–0.6	1.8	4.5	2.6	2.4	2.3	2.0	1.3
Micronesia	0.2	3.3	–2.0	–3.9	–2.2	5.0	0.7	2.4	2.1	1.2	0.7	0.6
Mongolia	6.3	17.3	12.3	11.6	7.9	2.4	1.2	5.3	6.9	6.3	4.9	5.5
Myanmar	10.3	5.6	7.3	8.4	8.0	7.0	5.9	6.8	2.1	6.4	6.6	7.0
Nauru	. . .	11.7	10.1	34.2	36.5	2.8	10.4	4.0	–2.4	–1.0	0.1	2.0
Nepal	4.0	3.4	4.8	4.1	6.0	3.3	0.6	7.9	6.3	6.5	6.3	5.0
Palau	0.5	5.5	4.8	–1.7	3.0	10.4	0.5	–3.7	0.4	2.0	2.5	2.0
Papua New Guinea	4.0	1.1	4.6	3.8	15.4	5.3	1.7	2.4	0.0	3.8	3.1	3.9
Philippines	4.8	3.7	6.7	7.1	6.1	6.1	6.9	6.7	6.2	6.5	6.6	6.8
Samoa	2.5	5.6	0.4	–1.9	1.2	1.7	7.2	2.7	0.7	3.3	4.6	2.2
Solomon Islands	3.4	13.2	4.6	3.0	2.3	2.5	3.5	3.5	3.4	2.9	2.8	2.9
Sri Lanka	5.1	8.4	9.1	3.4	5.0	5.0	4.5	3.3	3.0	3.5	4.0	4.8
Thailand	4.6	0.8	7.2	2.7	1.0	3.1	3.4	4.0	4.1	3.5	3.5	3.6
Timor-Leste[5]	4.3	7.7	5.5	2.5	4.1	4.0	5.3	–4.6	0.8	5.0	4.8	4.8
Tonga	1.4	1.8	–1.1	–0.6	2.9	3.5	4.2	2.5	1.8	4.6	4.9	1.1
Tuvalu	0.9	7.9	–3.8	4.6	1.3	9.1	3.0	3.2	4.3	4.1	4.4	2.7
Vanuatu	2.9	1.2	1.8	2.0	2.3	0.2	3.5	4.4	3.2	3.0	2.8	2.8
Vietnam	6.8	6.2	5.2	5.4	6.0	6.7	6.2	6.8	7.1	6.5	6.5	6.5
Emerging and Developing Europe	**3.9**	**6.7**	**2.6**	**4.9**	**3.9**	**4.8**	**3.3**	**6.0**	**3.6**	**0.8**	**2.8**	**3.1**
Albania	5.6	2.5	1.4	1.0	1.8	2.2	3.3	3.8	4.2	3.7	3.9	4.0
Bosnia and Herzegovina	3.9	0.9	–0.7	2.4	1.1	3.1	3.2	3.0	3.1	3.1	3.2	3.5
Bulgaria	4.6	1.9	0.0	0.5	1.8	3.5	3.9	3.8	3.2	3.3	3.0	2.8
Croatia	2.5	–0.3	–2.3	–0.5	–0.1	2.4	3.5	2.9	2.7	2.6	2.5	2.0
Hungary	2.0	1.7	–1.6	2.1	4.2	3.5	2.3	4.1	4.9	3.6	2.7	2.2
Kosovo	4.6	4.4	2.8	3.4	1.2	4.1	4.1	4.2	4.0	4.2	4.0	4.0
Montenegro	3.3	3.2	–2.7	3.5	1.8	3.4	2.9	4.7	4.5	2.8	2.5	2.9
North Macedonia	3.0	2.3	–0.5	2.9	3.6	3.9	2.8	0.2	2.7	3.0	3.1	3.5
Poland	3.9	5.0	1.6	1.4	3.3	3.8	3.1	4.8	5.1	3.8	3.1	2.8
Romania	4.2	2.0	2.1	3.5	3.4	3.9	4.8	7.0	4.1	3.1	3.0	3.0
Serbia	5.0	2.0	–0.7	2.9	–1.6	1.8	3.3	2.0	4.4	3.5	4.0	4.0
Turkey	4.0	11.1	4.8	8.5	5.2	6.1	3.2	7.4	2.6	–2.5	2.5	3.5

Table A4. Emerging Market and Developing Economies: Real GDP *(continued)*

(Annual percent change)

	Average 2001–10	2011	2012	2013	2014	2015	2016	2017	2018	Projections 2019	2020	2024
Latin America and the Caribbean	**3.2**	**4.6**	**2.9**	**2.9**	**1.3**	**0.3**	**–0.6**	**1.2**	**1.0**	**1.4**	**2.4**	**2.8**
Antigua and Barbuda	1.4	–2.1	3.5	–0.1	4.7	4.0	4.8	3.6	5.3	4.0	3.3	2.0
Argentina	3.4	6.0	–1.0	2.4	–2.5	2.7	–2.1	2.7	–2.5	–1.2	2.2	3.6
Aruba	–0.8	3.5	–1.4	4.2	0.9	–0.4	0.5	2.3	1.2	0.7	0.9	1.1
The Bahamas	0.7	0.6	3.1	–0.4	–0.1	1.0	–1.7	1.4	2.3	2.1	1.6	1.5
Barbados	0.7	–0.8	–0.1	–1.4	–0.2	2.2	2.3	–0.2	–0.5	–0.1	0.6	1.8
Belize	3.9	2.2	2.9	0.9	3.7	3.4	–0.6	1.4	3.0	2.5	2.1	1.7
Bolivia	3.8	5.2	5.1	6.8	5.5	4.9	4.3	4.2	4.3	4.0	3.9	3.7
Brazil	3.7	4.0	1.9	3.0	0.5	–3.5	–3.3	1.1	1.1	2.1	2.5	2.2
Chile	4.2	6.1	5.3	4.0	1.8	2.3	1.7	1.3	4.0	3.4	3.2	3.0
Colombia	4.0	7.4	3.9	4.6	4.7	3.0	2.1	1.4	2.7	3.5	3.6	3.6
Costa Rica	4.3	4.3	4.8	2.3	3.5	3.6	4.2	3.4	2.7	2.9	2.8	3.5
Dominica	2.4	–0.2	–1.1	0.8	4.2	–3.7	2.6	–5.4	–12.0	8.0	7.0	1.5
Dominican Republic	4.6	3.1	2.7	4.9	7.6	7.0	6.6	4.6	7.0	5.1	5.0	5.0
Ecuador	4.1	7.9	5.6	4.9	3.8	0.1	–1.2	2.4	1.1	–0.5	0.2	2.1
El Salvador	1.6	3.8	2.8	2.2	1.7	2.4	2.5	2.3	2.5	2.5	2.3	2.2
Grenada	1.8	0.8	–1.2	2.4	7.3	6.4	3.7	5.1	4.8	4.2	2.4	2.7
Guatemala	3.3	4.2	3.0	3.7	4.2	4.1	3.1	2.8	3.1	3.5	3.6	3.5
Guyana	2.4	5.4	5.0	5.0	3.9	3.1	3.4	2.1	3.4	3.8	29.6	17.9
Haiti	0.1	5.5	2.9	4.2	2.8	1.2	1.5	1.2	1.5	1.5	1.5	1.6
Honduras	4.1	3.8	4.1	2.8	3.1	3.8	3.8	4.9	3.7	3.4	3.4	3.7
Jamaica	0.6	1.4	–0.5	0.2	0.6	0.9	1.5	0.7	1.4	1.7	1.9	2.4
Mexico	1.5	3.7	3.6	1.4	2.8	3.3	2.9	2.1	2.0	1.6	1.9	2.7
Nicaragua	2.9	6.3	6.5	4.9	4.8	4.8	4.7	4.9	–4.0	–5.0	–0.2	3.0
Panama	5.9	11.3	9.8	6.9	5.1	5.7	5.0	5.3	3.9	6.0	5.5	5.5
Paraguay	3.7	4.2	–0.5	8.4	4.9	3.1	4.3	5.0	3.7	3.5	4.0	4.0
Peru	5.6	6.5	6.0	5.8	2.4	3.3	4.0	2.5	4.0	3.9	4.0	3.8
St. Kitts and Nevis	2.2	1.8	–0.7	5.5	6.1	2.1	2.3	1.2	3.0	3.5	3.5	2.7
St. Lucia	2.0	4.1	–0.3	–2.0	0.0	0.3	3.9	3.7	1.0	3.3	2.7	1.5
St. Vincent and the Grenadines	2.6	0.2	1.3	2.5	0.2	0.8	0.8	0.7	2.0	2.3	2.4	2.3
Suriname	5.0	5.8	2.7	2.9	0.3	–3.4	–5.6	1.7	2.0	2.2	2.5	3.0
Trinidad and Tobago[4]	5.7	–0.2	–0.7	2.3	–1.3	1.9	–6.5	–2.0	0.3	0.0	1.5	1.7
Uruguay	3.2	5.2	3.5	4.6	3.2	0.4	1.7	2.7	2.1	1.9	3.0	3.0
Venezuela	3.1	4.2	5.6	1.3	–3.9	–6.2	–17.0	–15.7	–18.0	–25.0	–10.0	–1.5
Middle East, North Africa, Afghanistan, and Pakistan	**5.1**	**4.4**	**4.8**	**2.6**	**2.9**	**2.6**	**5.2**	**2.2**	**1.8**	**1.5**	**3.2**	**2.8**
Afghanistan	. . .	6.5	14.0	5.7	2.7	1.0	2.2	2.7	2.3	3.0	3.5	5.5
Algeria	3.9	2.8	3.4	2.8	3.8	3.7	3.2	1.4	2.1	2.3	1.8	0.4
Bahrain	5.4	2.0	3.7	5.4	4.4	2.9	3.5	3.8	1.8	1.8	2.1	3.0
Djibouti	3.5	7.3	4.8	5.0	6.0	6.5	6.5	6.7	6.7	6.7	6.0	6.0
Egypt	4.9	1.8	2.2	3.3	2.9	4.4	4.3	4.2	5.3	5.5	5.9	6.0
Iran	4.7	3.1	–7.7	–0.3	3.2	–1.6	12.5	3.7	–3.9	–6.0	0.2	1.1
Iraq	12.1	7.5	13.9	7.6	0.7	2.5	13.6	–1.7	0.6	2.8	8.1	1.9
Jordan	6.0	2.6	2.7	2.8	3.1	2.4	2.0	2.1	2.0	2.2	2.4	3.0
Kuwait	4.6	9.6	6.6	1.2	0.5	0.6	2.9	–3.5	1.7	2.5	2.9	2.9
Lebanon	5.7	0.9	2.7	2.6	1.9	0.4	1.6	0.6	0.2	1.3	2.0	3.3
Libya[4]	4.1	–66.7	124.7	–36.8	–53.0	–13.0	–7.4	64.0	17.9	4.3	1.4	1.5
Mauritania	4.9	4.7	5.8	6.1	5.6	0.4	1.8	3.0	3.0	6.4	4.7	8.1
Morocco	4.9	5.2	3.0	4.5	2.7	4.5	1.1	4.1	3.1	3.2	3.8	4.5
Oman	3.0	2.6	9.1	5.1	1.4	4.7	5.0	–0.9	2.1	1.1	6.2	1.7
Pakistan	4.5	3.6	3.8	3.7	4.1	4.1	4.6	5.4	5.2	2.9	2.8	2.5
Qatar	13.1	13.4	4.7	4.4	4.0	3.7	2.1	1.6	2.2	2.6	3.2	3.0
Saudi Arabia	3.4	10.0	5.4	2.7	3.7	4.1	1.7	–0.7	2.2	1.8	2.1	2.3
Somalia	. . .	. . .	1.2	–0.8	0.4	3.8	4.9	2.3	3.1	3.5	3.5	3.5
Sudan[6]	5.1	–2.8	–17.0	2.0	4.7	1.9	2.9	1.7	–2.1	–2.3	–1.3	1.5
Syria[7]	4.5	. . .	. . .	. . .	. . .	. . .	. . .	. . .	. . .	. . .	. . .	. . .
Tunisia	4.2	–1.9	4.0	2.9	3.0	1.2	1.1	2.0	2.5	2.7	3.2	4.1
United Arab Emirates	3.9	6.9	4.5	5.1	4.4	5.1	3.0	0.8	1.7	2.8	3.3	2.7
Yemen	4.3	–12.7	2.4	4.8	–0.2	–16.7	–13.6	–5.9	–2.7	2.1	10.0	3.7

Table A4. Emerging Market and Developing Economies: Real GDP *(continued)*
(Annual percent change)

	Average 2001–10	2011	2012	2013	2014	2015	2016	2017	2018	Projections 2019	2020	2024
Sub-Saharan Africa	**5.9**	**5.3**	**4.7**	**5.2**	**5.1**	**3.2**	**1.4**	**2.9**	**3.0**	**3.5**	**3.7**	**4.0**
Angola	8.8	3.5	8.5	5.0	4.8	0.9	–2.6	–0.2	–1.7	0.4	2.9	3.9
Benin	3.9	3.0	4.8	7.2	6.4	2.1	4.0	5.8	6.5	6.5	6.5	6.5
Botswana	4.1	6.0	4.5	11.3	4.1	–1.7	4.3	2.9	4.6	3.9	4.1	3.9
Burkina Faso	5.9	6.6	6.5	5.8	4.3	3.9	5.9	6.3	6.0	6.0	6.0	6.0
Burundi	3.7	4.0	4.4	5.9	4.5	–4.0	–1.0	0.0	0.1	0.4	0.5	0.5
Cabo Verde	5.4	4.0	1.1	0.8	0.6	1.0	4.7	4.0	4.7	5.0	5.0	5.0
Cameroon	3.9	4.1	4.5	5.4	5.9	5.7	4.6	3.5	4.0	4.3	4.7	5.5
Central African Republic	1.5	3.3	4.1	–36.7	1.0	4.8	4.5	4.3	4.3	5.0	5.0	5.0
Chad	9.8	0.1	8.8	5.8	6.9	1.8	–6.4	–3.1	3.1	4.5	6.0	3.8
Comoros	2.0	2.2	3.0	3.5	2.0	1.0	2.2	2.7	2.8	2.8	2.9	3.3
Democratic Republic of the Congo	4.7	6.9	7.1	8.5	9.5	6.9	2.4	3.4	3.9	4.3	4.4	4.9
Republic of Congo	4.7	3.4	3.8	3.3	6.8	2.6	–2.8	–3.1	0.8	5.4	1.5	2.2
Côte d'Ivoire	1.1	–4.9	10.9	9.3	8.8	8.8	8.0	7.7	7.4	7.5	7.2	6.5
Equatorial Guinea	15.2	6.5	8.3	–4.1	0.4	–9.1	–8.8	–4.7	–5.7	–4.0	–4.7	1.5
Eritrea	0.9	8.7	7.0	4.6	2.9	2.6	1.9	5.0	4.2	3.8	4.1	4.4
Eswatini	3.5	2.2	4.7	6.4	1.9	0.4	3.2	1.9	0.2	–0.4	0.2	2.2
Ethiopia	8.5	11.4	8.7	9.9	10.3	10.4	8.0	10.1	7.7	7.7	7.5	7.0
Gabon	1.4	7.1	5.3	5.5	4.4	3.9	2.1	0.5	1.2	3.1	3.9	4.4
The Gambia	3.8	–4.3	5.6	4.8	–0.9	5.9	0.4	4.6	6.6	5.4	5.2	4.8
Ghana	5.8	17.4	9.0	7.9	2.9	2.2	3.4	8.1	5.6	8.8	5.8	3.8
Guinea	3.1	5.6	5.9	3.9	3.7	3.8	10.5	9.9	5.8	5.9	6.0	5.0
Guinea-Bissau	2.5	8.1	–1.7	3.3	1.0	6.1	6.3	5.9	3.8	5.0	5.0	5.0
Kenya	4.2	6.1	4.6	5.9	5.4	5.7	5.9	4.9	6.0	5.8	5.9	6.0
Lesotho	3.9	6.7	4.9	2.2	3.0	2.5	3.1	–1.6	1.5	3.9	0.3	1.7
Liberia	2.0	7.7	8.4	8.8	0.7	0.0	–1.6	2.5	1.2	0.4	1.6	3.7
Madagascar	2.6	1.4	3.0	2.2	3.3	3.1	4.2	4.3	5.2	5.2	5.3	4.8
Malawi	4.9	4.9	1.9	5.2	5.7	2.9	2.3	4.0	3.2	4.0	5.0	6.5
Mali	5.8	3.2	–0.8	2.3	7.1	6.2	5.8	5.4	4.9	5.0	4.9	4.8
Mauritius	4.0	4.1	3.5	3.4	3.7	3.6	3.8	3.8	3.8	3.9	3.9	4.0
Mozambique	8.2	7.1	7.2	7.1	7.4	6.6	3.8	3.7	3.3	4.0	4.0	11.7
Namibia	4.0	5.1	5.1	5.6	6.4	6.1	0.6	–0.9	–0.1	1.4	2.0	3.3
Niger	5.4	2.2	11.8	5.3	7.5	4.3	4.9	4.9	5.2	6.5	6.0	5.5
Nigeria	8.9	4.9	4.3	5.4	6.3	2.7	–1.6	0.8	1.9	2.1	2.5	2.6
Rwanda	8.2	7.8	8.8	4.7	7.6	8.9	6.0	6.2	8.6	7.8	8.1	7.5
São Tomé and Príncipe	5.2	4.4	3.1	4.8	6.5	3.8	4.2	3.9	3.0	4.0	4.5	5.0
Senegal	4.0	1.5	5.1	2.8	6.6	6.4	6.2	7.2	6.2	6.9	7.5	6.0
Seychelles	2.0	5.4	3.7	6.0	4.5	4.9	4.5	5.3	3.6	3.4	3.3	3.6
Sierra Leone	8.9	6.3	15.2	20.7	4.6	–20.5	6.4	3.8	3.7	5.4	5.4	5.1
South Africa	3.5	3.3	2.2	2.5	1.8	1.2	0.4	1.4	0.8	1.2	1.5	1.8
South Sudan	. . .	. . .	–52.4	29.3	2.9	–0.2	–16.7	–5.5	–1.2	8.8	5.2	5.0
Tanzania	6.3	7.9	5.1	6.8	6.7	6.2	6.9	6.8	6.6	4.0	4.2	4.9
Togo	2.2	6.4	6.5	6.1	5.9	5.7	5.6	4.4	4.7	5.0	5.3	5.4
Uganda	7.9	6.8	2.2	4.7	4.6	5.7	2.3	5.0	6.2	6.3	6.2	6.7
Zambia	7.4	5.6	7.6	5.1	4.7	2.9	3.8	3.4	3.5	3.1	2.9	2.5
Zimbabwe[8]	–3.9	14.2	16.7	2.0	2.4	1.8	0.7	4.7	3.4	–5.2	3.3	4.0

[1]Data for some countries refer to real net material product (NMP) or are estimates based on NMP. The figures should be interpreted only as indicative of broad orders of magnitude because reliable, comparable data are not generally available. In particular, the growth of output of new private enterprises of the informal economy is not fully reflected in the recent figures.
[2]Georgia, Turkmenistan, and Ukraine, which are not members of the Commonwealth of Independent States, are included in this group for reasons of geography and similarity in economic structure.
[3]Data are based on the 2008 System of National Accounts. The revised national accounts data are available beginning in 2000 and exclude Crimea and Sevastopol from 2010 onward.
[4]See country-specific notes for India, Libya, and Trinidad and Tobago in the "Country Notes" section of the Statistical Appendix.
[5]In this table only, the data for Timor-Leste are based on non-oil GDP.
[6]Data for 2011 exclude South Sudan after July 9. Data for 2012 and onward pertain to the current Sudan.
[7]Data for Syria are excluded for 2011 onward owing to the uncertain political situation.
[8]The Zimbabwe dollar ceased circulating in early 2009. Data are based on IMF staff estimates of price and exchange rate developments in US dollars. IMF staff estimates of US dollar values may differ from authorities' estimates. Real GDP is in constant 2009 prices.

Table A5. Summary of Inflation
(Percent)

	Average 2001–10	2011	2012	2013	2014	2015	2016	2017	2018	Projections 2019	2020	2024
GDP Deflators												
Advanced Economies	**1.7**	**1.3**	**1.3**	**1.3**	**1.5**	**1.3**	**1.0**	**1.5**	**1.6**	**1.5**	**1.8**	**1.9**
United States	2.1	2.1	1.9	1.8	1.9	1.1	1.1	1.9	2.3	1.8	2.1	2.1
Euro Area	1.9	1.0	1.3	1.2	0.9	1.4	0.8	1.1	1.4	1.5	1.8	2.0
Japan	–1.1	–1.7	–0.8	–0.3	1.7	2.1	0.3	–0.2	–0.1	0.6	1.2	0.7
Other Advanced Economies[1]	2.1	2.0	1.2	1.5	1.3	1.0	1.3	2.0	1.4	1.6	1.7	1.9
Consumer Prices												
Advanced Economies	**2.0**	**2.7**	**2.0**	**1.4**	**1.4**	**0.3**	**0.8**	**1.7**	**2.0**	**1.6**	**2.1**	**2.0**
United States	2.4	3.1	2.1	1.5	1.6	0.1	1.3	2.1	2.4	2.0	2.7	2.2
Euro Area[2]	2.1	2.7	2.5	1.3	0.4	0.2	0.2	1.5	1.8	1.3	1.6	2.0
Japan	–0.3	–0.3	–0.1	0.3	2.8	0.8	–0.1	0.5	1.0	1.1	1.5	1.4
Other Advanced Economies[1]	2.1	3.3	2.1	1.7	1.5	0.5	0.9	1.8	1.9	1.6	1.8	2.0
Emerging Market and Developing Economies[3]	**6.6**	**7.1**	**5.8**	**5.5**	**4.7**	**4.7**	**4.2**	**4.3**	**4.8**	**4.9**	**4.7**	**4.2**
Regional Groups												
Commonwealth of Independent States[4]	12.1	9.8	6.2	6.5	8.1	15.5	8.3	5.5	4.5	5.7	5.0	4.3
Emerging and Developing Asia	4.3	6.5	4.6	4.6	3.4	2.7	2.8	2.4	2.6	2.8	3.1	3.3
Emerging and Developing Europe	10.2	5.5	6.1	4.5	4.1	3.2	3.2	6.2	8.7	9.0	7.5	6.9
Latin America and the Caribbean	5.8	5.2	4.6	4.6	4.9	5.5	5.6	6.0	6.2	6.5	5.1	3.6
Middle East, North Africa, Afghanistan, and Pakistan	7.1	9.3	9.8	9.2	6.7	5.4	4.7	6.4	10.4	9.7	9.3	7.8
Middle East and North Africa	6.9	8.8	9.7	9.4	6.5	5.5	4.9	6.7	11.4	10.0	9.6	8.2
Sub-Saharan Africa	9.9	9.3	9.2	6.6	6.4	7.0	11.2	11.0	8.5	8.1	7.4	6.6
Memorandum												
European Union	2.4	3.1	2.6	1.5	0.5	0.1	0.2	1.7	1.9	1.6	1.7	2.0
Low-Income Developing Countries	9.7	11.7	9.8	8.0	7.2	6.9	8.6	9.6	9.1	8.2	7.9	7.3
Analytical Groups												
By Source of Export Earnings												
Fuel	9.7	8.6	8.0	8.1	6.4	8.6	6.9	5.4	7.2	7.6	7.2	6.5
Nonfuel	5.7	6.7	5.3	4.9	4.2	3.8	3.7	4.0	4.3	4.4	4.2	3.9
Of Which, Primary Products[5]	6.5	6.8	7.0	6.5	7.1	5.2	6.4	11.2	13.6	15.0	10.7	6.7
By External Financing Source												
Net Debtor Economies	7.4	7.6	6.9	6.2	5.6	5.4	5.1	5.5	5.4	5.2	5.0	4.5
Net Debtor Economies by Debt-Servicing Experience												
Economies with Arrears and/or Rescheduling during 2013–17	8.5	10.3	7.9	6.6	10.1	13.8	8.4	16.7	16.7	12.9	10.9	8.1
Memorandum												
Median Inflation Rate												
Advanced Economies	2.2	3.2	2.6	1.4	0.7	0.1	0.6	1.6	1.9	1.6	1.7	2.0
Emerging Market and Developing Economies[3]	5.1	5.4	4.5	3.8	3.1	2.7	2.7	3.3	3.1	3.1	3.2	3.0

[1]Excludes the United States, euro area countries, and Japan.
[2]Based on Eurostat's harmonized index of consumer prices.
[3]Excludes Venezuela but includes Argentina starting from 2017 onward. See country-specific notes for Venezuela and Argentina in the "Country Notes" section of the Statistical Appendix.
[4]Georgia, Turkmenistan, and Ukraine, which are not members of the Commonwealth of Independent States, are included in this group for reasons of geography and similarity in economic structure.
[5]Includes Argentina starting from 2017 onward. See country-specific note for Argentina in the "Country Notes" section of the Statistical Appendix.

Table A6. Advanced Economies: Consumer Prices[1]

(Annual percent change)

													End of Period[2]		
	Average									Projections				Projections	
	2001–10	2011	2012	2013	2014	2015	2016	2017	2018	2019	2020	2024	2018	2019	2020
Advanced Economies	**2.0**	**2.7**	**2.0**	**1.4**	**1.4**	**0.3**	**0.8**	**1.7**	**2.0**	**1.6**	**2.1**	**2.0**	**1.7**	**2.0**	**1.9**
United States	2.4	3.1	2.1	1.5	1.6	0.1	1.3	2.1	2.4	2.0	2.7	2.2	2.0	2.7	2.4
Euro Area[3]	2.1	2.7	2.5	1.3	0.4	0.2	0.2	1.5	1.8	1.3	1.6	2.0	1.5	1.4	1.6
Germany	1.6	2.5	2.2	1.6	0.8	0.7	0.4	1.7	1.9	1.3	1.7	2.2	1.8	1.6	1.8
France	1.9	2.3	2.2	1.0	0.6	0.1	0.3	1.2	2.1	1.3	1.5	1.9	2.0	1.2	1.6
Italy	2.2	2.9	3.3	1.2	0.2	0.1	–0.1	1.3	1.2	0.8	1.2	1.6	1.2	0.8	1.2
Spain	2.8	3.2	2.4	1.4	–0.2	–0.5	–0.2	2.0	1.7	1.2	1.6	1.9	1.2	1.3	1.7
Netherlands	2.1	2.5	2.8	2.6	0.3	0.2	0.1	1.3	1.6	2.3	1.6	2.0	1.9	2.0	1.7
Belgium	2.1	3.4	2.6	1.2	0.5	0.6	1.8	2.2	2.3	1.9	1.6	2.0	2.2	1.3	2.1
Austria	1.9	3.5	2.6	2.1	1.5	0.8	1.0	2.2	2.1	1.8	2.0	2.0	1.7	1.9	2.0
Greece	3.4	3.1	1.0	–0.9	–1.4	–1.1	0.0	1.1	0.8	1.1	1.4	1.8	0.6	0.8	1.6
Portugal	2.5	3.6	2.8	0.4	–0.2	0.5	0.6	1.6	1.2	1.0	1.7	2.0	0.6	4.0	–1.7
Ireland	2.2	1.2	1.9	0.6	0.3	0.0	–0.2	0.3	0.7	1.2	1.5	2.0	0.8	0.4	1.5
Finland	1.7	3.3	3.2	2.2	1.2	–0.2	0.4	0.8	1.2	1.3	1.5	2.0	1.3	1.4	1.5
Slovak Republic	4.1	4.1	3.7	1.5	–0.1	–0.3	–0.5	1.4	2.5	2.4	2.2	2.1	1.9	2.2	2.1
Lithuania	3.0	4.1	3.2	1.2	0.2	–0.7	0.7	3.7	2.5	2.3	2.3	2.5	1.8	2.3	2.3
Slovenia	4.2	1.8	2.6	1.8	0.2	–0.5	–0.1	1.4	1.7	1.4	1.6	2.0	1.4	1.3	1.9
Luxembourg	2.6	3.7	2.9	1.7	0.7	0.1	0.0	2.1	2.0	1.6	1.9	1.9	1.9	1.9	1.6
Latvia	5.4	4.2	2.3	0.0	0.7	0.2	0.1	2.9	2.6	2.4	2.4	2.1	2.5	2.4	2.4
Estonia	4.2	5.1	4.2	3.2	0.5	0.1	0.8	3.7	3.4	3.0	2.8	2.5	3.3	3.0	2.8
Cyprus	2.4	3.5	3.1	0.4	–0.3	–1.5	–1.2	0.7	0.8	0.5	1.6	2.0	1.1	1.2	1.3
Malta	2.4	2.5	3.2	1.0	0.8	1.2	0.9	1.3	1.7	1.8	1.9	2.0	1.2	1.9	1.9
Japan	–0.3	–0.3	–0.1	0.3	2.8	0.8	–0.1	0.5	1.0	1.1	1.5	1.4	0.8	1.7	1.0
United Kingdom	2.1	4.5	2.8	2.6	1.5	0.0	0.7	2.7	2.5	1.8	2.0	2.0	2.3	1.8	2.0
Korea	3.2	4.0	2.2	1.3	1.3	0.7	1.0	1.9	1.5	1.4	1.6	2.0	1.3	1.4	1.6
Canada	2.0	2.9	1.5	0.9	1.9	1.1	1.4	1.6	2.2	1.7	1.9	2.0	2.1	1.8	1.9
Australia	3.0	3.4	1.7	2.5	2.5	1.5	1.3	2.0	2.0	2.0	2.3	2.5	1.8	2.3	2.3
Taiwan Province of China	0.9	1.4	1.6	1.0	1.3	–0.6	1.0	1.1	1.5	1.1	1.2	1.4	–0.1	1.1	1.2
Switzerland	0.9	0.2	–0.7	–0.2	0.0	–1.1	–0.4	0.5	0.9	0.8	0.9	1.0	1.4	0.2	1.2
Sweden	1.9	1.4	0.9	0.4	0.2	0.7	1.1	1.9	2.0	1.9	1.7	2.0	2.2	1.8	1.7
Singapore	1.6	5.2	4.6	2.4	1.0	–0.5	–0.5	0.6	0.4	1.3	1.4	1.4	0.5	1.4	1.4
Hong Kong SAR	0.4	5.3	4.1	4.3	4.4	3.0	2.4	1.5	2.4	2.4	2.5	2.5	2.4	2.4	2.5
Norway	2.0	1.3	0.7	2.1	2.0	2.2	3.6	1.9	2.8	1.9	1.7	2.0	3.5	1.6	1.8
Czech Republic	2.5	1.9	3.3	1.4	0.4	0.3	0.7	2.5	2.2	2.3	2.0	2.0	2.1	2.1	2.0
Israel	2.1	3.4	1.7	1.5	0.5	–0.6	–0.5	0.2	0.8	0.9	1.7	2.0	0.8	1.3	2.0
Denmark	2.0	2.7	2.4	0.5	0.4	0.2	0.0	1.1	0.7	1.1	1.3	2.0	0.7	1.2	1.4
New Zealand	2.6	4.1	1.0	1.1	1.2	0.3	0.6	1.9	1.6	2.0	1.9	2.0	2.1	1.9	2.0
Puerto Rico	2.7	2.9	1.3	1.1	0.6	–0.8	–0.3	1.8	2.5	0.3	1.3	1.4	2.5	0.3	1.3
Macao SAR	. . .	5.8	6.1	5.5	6.0	4.6	2.4	1.2	3.0	2.5	2.7	3.0	2.9	2.5	2.7
Iceland	6.2	4.0	5.2	3.9	2.0	1.6	1.7	1.8	2.7	2.8	2.5	2.5	3.7	2.6	2.6
San Marino	. . .	2.0	2.8	1.6	1.1	0.1	0.6	1.0	1.6	1.6	1.7	1.8	1.6	1.6	1.7
Memorandum															
Major Advanced Economies	1.8	2.6	1.9	1.3	1.5	0.3	0.8	1.8	2.1	1.7	2.2	2.0	1.8	2.1	2.0

[1]Movements in consumer prices are shown as annual averages.
[2]Monthly year-over-year changes and, for several countries, on a quarterly basis.
[3]Based on Eurostat's harmonized index of consumer prices.

Table A7. Emerging Market and Developing Economies: Consumer Prices[1]
(Annual percent change)

	Average									Projections			End of Period[2]	Projections	
	2001–10	2011	2012	2013	2014	2015	2016	2017	2018	2019	2020	2024	2018	2019	2020
Commonwealth of Independent States[3,4]	**12.1**	**9.8**	**6.2**	**6.5**	**8.1**	**15.5**	**8.3**	**5.5**	**4.5**	**5.7**	**5.0**	**4.3**	**5.1**	**5.6**	**4.6**
Russia	12.5	8.4	5.1	6.8	7.8	15.5	7.1	3.7	2.9	5.0	4.5	4.0	4.3	4.8	4.2
Excluding Russia	11.0	13.3	9.2	5.7	8.7	15.5	11.3	9.9	8.3	7.5	6.1	4.8	7.2	7.2	5.7
Armenia	4.4	7.7	2.5	5.8	3.0	3.7	–1.4	0.9	2.5	2.1	3.0	3.4	1.9	2.6	3.2
Azerbaijan	7.4	7.8	1.0	2.4	1.4	4.0	12.4	12.8	2.3	2.5	2.5	3.0	2.3	2.5	2.5
Belarus	20.1	53.2	59.2	18.3	18.1	13.5	11.8	6.0	4.9	5.0	5.0	4.0	5.6	5.0	5.0
Georgia	6.6	8.5	–0.9	–0.5	3.1	4.0	2.1	6.0	2.6	2.5	3.0	3.0	1.5	3.0	3.0
Kazakhstan	8.6	8.3	5.1	5.8	6.7	6.7	14.6	7.4	6.0	5.5	5.0	4.0	5.3	5.5	4.5
Kyrgyz Republic	7.4	16.6	2.8	6.6	7.5	6.5	0.4	3.2	1.5	2.2	4.9	5.0	0.5	4.7	5.1
Moldova	9.5	7.6	4.6	4.6	5.1	9.6	6.4	6.6	3.1	3.3	5.1	5.0	0.9	5.1	5.0
Tajikistan	13.5	12.4	5.8	5.0	6.1	5.8	5.9	7.3	3.8	6.7	6.2	6.5	5.4	6.2	6.2
Turkmenistan	7.2	5.3	5.3	6.8	6.0	7.4	3.6	8.0	13.6	13.0	9.0	6.0	8.9	13.0	9.0
Ukraine[5]	11.1	8.0	0.6	–0.3	12.1	48.7	13.9	14.4	10.9	8.0	5.9	5.0	9.8	7.0	5.6
Uzbekistan	14.5	12.4	11.9	11.7	9.1	8.5	8.0	12.5	17.9	16.5	11.9	7.5	14.4	15.7	10.5
Emerging and Developing Asia	**4.3**	**6.5**	**4.6**	**4.6**	**3.4**	**2.7**	**2.8**	**2.4**	**2.6**	**2.8**	**3.1**	**3.3**	**2.3**	**2.9**	**3.1**
Bangladesh	6.3	11.5	6.2	7.5	7.0	6.2	5.7	5.6	5.6	5.4	5.4	5.5	5.4	5.4	5.5
Bhutan	4.6	7.3	9.3	11.3	9.5	7.6	7.6	5.5	3.6	4.0	4.5	4.5	3.2	3.4	4.2
Brunei Darussalam	0.5	0.1	0.1	0.4	–0.2	–0.4	–0.7	–0.2	0.1	0.3	0.5	0.5	0.0	0.5	0.5
Cambodia	5.1	5.5	2.9	3.0	3.9	1.2	3.0	2.9	2.4	2.5	2.8	3.0	1.6	2.6	2.8
China	2.1	5.4	2.6	2.6	2.0	1.4	2.0	1.6	2.1	2.3	2.5	3.0	1.9	2.2	2.5
Fiji	3.7	7.3	3.4	2.9	0.5	1.4	3.9	3.4	4.1	3.5	3.0	3.0	4.9	3.5	3.0
India	6.5	9.5	10.0	9.4	5.8	4.9	4.5	3.6	3.5	3.9	4.2	4.0	2.7	4.1	4.3
Indonesia	8.6	5.3	4.0	6.4	6.4	6.4	3.5	3.8	3.2	3.3	3.6	3.0	3.1	3.6	3.5
Kiribati	3.1	1.5	–3.0	–1.5	2.1	0.6	1.9	0.4	1.9	2.1	2.5	2.6	1.9	2.1	2.5
Lao P.D.R.	7.6	7.6	4.3	6.4	4.1	1.3	1.8	0.7	2.0	3.1	3.3	3.1	1.5	2.9	3.1
Malaysia	2.2	3.2	1.7	2.1	3.1	2.1	2.1	3.8	1.0	2.0	2.6	2.2	0.2	2.4	2.6
Maldives	4.0	11.3	10.9	3.8	2.1	1.9	0.8	2.3	1.5	2.2	2.3	2.0	1.3	2.1	2.4
Marshall Islands	. . .	5.4	4.3	1.9	1.1	–2.2	–1.5	0.0	0.8	0.2	2.1	2.1	0.8	0.2	2.1
Micronesia	3.2	4.1	6.3	2.2	0.7	–0.2	0.5	0.5	2.0	2.0	2.0	2.0	2.0	2.0	2.0
Mongolia	8.8	7.7	15.0	8.6	12.9	5.9	0.5	4.6	7.6	8.4	7.6	7.1	9.7	7.2	8.0
Myanmar	20.1	2.8	2.8	5.7	5.1	10.0	6.8	4.0	3.5	3.9	6.7	6.1	4.9	2.1	7.1
Nauru	. . .	–3.4	0.3	–1.1	0.3	9.8	8.2	5.1	3.8	2.5	2.0	2.0	3.0	2.8	2.3
Nepal	6.1	9.6	8.3	9.9	9.0	7.2	9.9	4.5	4.2	4.9	6.5	5.3	4.6	5.1	6.5
Palau	2.7	4.7	3.6	3.4	4.1	0.9	–1.0	0.9	2.8	2.3	2.0	2.0	2.8	2.4	2.0
Papua New Guinea	6.5	4.4	4.5	5.0	5.2	6.0	6.7	5.4	4.7	4.3	4.7	3.7	4.8	4.7	4.7
Philippines	5.2	4.8	3.0	2.6	3.6	0.7	1.3	2.9	5.2	3.8	3.3	3.0	5.1	3.5	3.1
Samoa	5.7	2.9	6.2	–0.2	–1.2	1.9	0.1	1.3	3.7	5.1	4.3	2.8	5.8	4.5	4.0
Solomon Islands	8.5	7.4	5.9	5.4	5.2	–0.6	0.5	0.5	1.0	1.7	2.6	4.4	3.2	3.3	3.6
Sri Lanka	9.7	6.7	7.5	6.9	2.8	2.2	4.0	6.6	4.3	4.5	4.6	5.0	2.8	4.5	4.7
Thailand	2.6	3.8	3.0	2.2	1.9	–0.9	0.2	0.7	1.1	1.0	1.3	2.0	0.4	1.9	0.6
Timor-Leste	4.5	13.2	10.9	9.5	0.8	0.6	–1.5	0.5	2.3	2.5	3.1	4.0	2.1	2.8	3.5
Tonga	7.7	6.3	1.1	2.1	1.2	–1.1	2.6	7.4	3.9	5.8	5.0	2.5	6.7	5.0	4.9
Tuvalu	2.9	0.5	1.4	2.0	1.1	3.1	3.5	4.1	4.2	3.7	3.5	2.4	4.0	3.4	3.5
Vanuatu	2.9	0.9	1.3	1.5	0.8	2.5	0.8	3.1	2.8	2.0	2.2	2.2	2.6	2.6	2.2
Vietnam	7.7	18.7	9.1	6.6	4.1	0.6	2.7	3.5	3.5	3.1	3.3	3.9	3.0	3.2	3.4
Emerging and Developing Europe	**10.2**	**5.5**	**6.1**	**4.5**	**4.1**	**3.2**	**3.2**	**6.2**	**8.7**	**9.0**	**7.5**	**6.9**	**10.2**	**8.3**	**7.4**
Albania	3.0	3.4	2.0	1.9	1.6	1.9	1.3	2.0	2.0	2.0	2.4	3.0	1.8	2.2	2.6
Bosnia and Herzegovina	2.1	3.7	2.1	–0.1	–0.9	–1.0	–1.1	1.2	1.4	1.5	1.6	2.0	1.6	1.6	1.6
Bulgaria[6]	6.0	3.4	2.4	0.4	–1.6	–1.1	–1.3	1.2	2.6	2.4	2.3	2.3	2.3	2.2	2.3
Croatia	2.8	2.3	3.4	2.2	–0.2	–0.5	–1.1	1.1	1.5	1.5	1.6	1.9	0.9	1.2	1.5
Hungary	5.6	3.9	5.7	1.7	–0.2	–0.1	0.4	2.4	2.8	3.2	3.1	3.0	2.7	3.5	3.0
Kosovo	2.8	7.3	2.5	1.8	0.4	–0.5	0.3	1.5	1.1	2.2	1.3	2.0	2.9	0.6	2.4
Montenegro	7.3	3.5	4.1	2.2	–0.7	1.5	–0.3	2.4	2.6	0.9	1.7	2.0	1.7	1.9	1.8
North Macedonia	2.1	3.9	3.3	2.8	–0.3	–0.3	–0.2	1.4	1.5	1.8	2.0	2.2	0.8	2.0	2.0
Poland	2.8	4.3	3.7	0.9	0.0	–0.9	–0.6	2.0	1.6	2.0	1.9	2.3	1.1	2.3	1.9
Romania	12.1	5.8	3.3	4.0	1.1	–0.6	–1.6	1.3	4.6	3.3	3.0	2.5	3.3	3.5	3.0
Serbia	14.7	11.1	7.3	7.7	2.1	1.4	1.1	3.1	2.0	2.0	2.5	3.0	2.0	2.5	2.5
Turkey	17.5	6.5	8.9	7.5	8.9	7.7	7.8	11.1	16.3	17.5	14.1	12.4	20.3	15.5	14.0

Table A7. Emerging Market and Developing Economies: Consumer Prices[1] *(continued)*

(Annual percent change)

	Average									Projections			End of Period[2]	Projections	
	2001–10	2011	2012	2013	2014	2015	2016	2017	2018	2019	2020	2024	2018	2019	2020
Latin America and the Caribbean[7]	**5.8**	**5.2**	**4.6**	**4.6**	**4.9**	**5.5**	**5.6**	**6.0**	**6.2**	**6.5**	**5.1**	**3.6**	**7.1**	**5.6**	**4.9**
Antigua and Barbuda	2.2	3.5	3.4	1.1	1.1	1.0	–0.5	2.4	1.3	2.0	2.0	2.0	2.2	2.0	2.0
Argentina[8]	9.5	9.8	10.0	10.6	. . .	. . .	. . .	25.7	34.3	43.7	23.2	5.8	47.6	30.5	21.2
Aruba	3.3	4.4	0.6	–2.4	0.4	0.5	–0.9	–0.5	3.5	1.4	1.9	2.2	3.7	1.0	2.7
The Bahamas	2.3	3.1	1.9	0.4	1.2	1.9	–0.3	1.4	2.2	2.6	2.4	2.2	2.8	2.4	2.3
Barbados	4.1	9.4	4.5	1.8	1.8	–1.1	1.5	4.4	3.6	1.3	1.9	2.3	0.0	1.4	2.3
Belize	2.5	1.7	1.2	0.5	1.2	–0.9	0.7	1.1	0.3	1.2	1.6	2.0	–0.1	2.4	0.8
Bolivia	4.6	9.9	4.5	5.7	5.8	4.1	3.6	2.8	2.3	2.3	3.6	5.0	1.9	3.0	4.0
Brazil	6.6	6.6	5.4	6.2	6.3	9.0	8.7	3.4	3.7	3.6	4.1	4.0	3.7	3.9	4.0
Chile	3.2	3.3	3.0	1.8	4.7	4.3	3.8	2.2	2.3	2.3	3.0	3.0	2.1	2.7	3.0
Colombia	5.6	3.4	3.2	2.0	2.9	5.0	7.5	4.3	3.2	3.4	3.2	3.0	3.2	3.2	3.0
Costa Rica	10.3	4.9	4.5	5.2	4.5	0.8	0.0	1.6	2.3	2.6	3.1	3.0	2.0	3.2	3.0
Dominica	2.2	1.1	1.4	0.0	0.8	–0.9	0.0	0.6	1.4	1.6	1.8	2.0	1.4	1.8	1.8
Dominican Republic	12.1	8.5	3.7	4.8	3.0	0.8	1.6	3.3	3.6	1.4	4.2	4.0	1.2	3.7	4.0
Ecuador	8.1	4.5	5.1	2.7	3.6	4.0	1.7	0.4	–0.2	0.6	1.2	1.0	0.3	0.5	1.6
El Salvador	3.4	5.1	1.7	0.8	1.1	–0.7	0.6	1.0	1.1	0.6	1.3	1.0	0.4	1.4	1.2
Grenada	3.0	3.0	2.4	0.0	–1.0	–0.6	1.7	0.9	1.1	1.7	1.9	1.9	1.7	1.5	1.9
Guatemala	6.8	6.2	3.8	4.3	3.4	2.4	4.4	4.4	3.8	3.4	3.7	4.2	2.3	3.8	4.1
Guyana	5.9	4.4	2.4	1.9	0.7	–0.9	0.8	2.0	1.3	2.9	3.1	2.8	2.2	3.0	3.2
Haiti	14.0	7.4	6.8	6.8	3.9	7.5	13.4	14.7	13.5	14.9	13.0	10.2	14.6	13.5	12.5
Honduras	7.6	6.8	5.2	5.2	6.1	3.2	2.7	3.9	4.3	4.7	4.5	4.0	4.2	4.7	4.5
Jamaica	11.8	7.5	6.9	9.4	8.3	3.7	2.3	4.4	3.7	3.6	4.9	5.0	2.4	4.9	5.0
Mexico	4.7	3.4	4.1	3.8	4.0	2.7	2.8	6.0	4.9	3.8	3.1	3.0	4.8	3.1	3.0
Nicaragua	8.3	8.1	7.2	7.1	6.0	4.0	3.5	3.9	5.0	5.1	3.9	5.0	3.9	5.5	3.9
Panama	2.6	5.9	5.7	4.0	2.6	0.1	0.7	0.9	0.8	1.5	2.0	2.0	0.2	1.5	2.0
Paraguay	7.8	8.2	3.7	2.7	5.0	3.1	4.1	3.6	4.0	3.6	4.0	4.0	3.2	4.0	4.0
Peru	2.4	3.4	3.7	2.8	3.2	3.5	3.6	2.8	1.3	2.4	2.0	2.0	2.2	2.2	2.0
St. Kitts and Nevis	3.3	5.8	0.8	1.1	0.2	–2.3	–0.3	0.0	–0.6	0.0	2.0	2.0	–2.0	2.0	2.0
St. Lucia	2.6	2.8	4.2	1.5	3.5	–1.0	–3.1	0.1	1.9	1.9	2.2	2.0	2.0	2.0	2.1
St. Vincent and the Grenadines	2.9	3.2	2.6	0.8	0.2	–1.7	–0.2	2.2	2.4	2.0	2.0	2.0	2.0	2.0	2.0
Suriname	13.1	17.7	5.0	1.9	3.4	6.9	55.5	22.0	6.9	5.4	5.3	3.5	5.4	5.3	5.4
Trinidad and Tobago	7.0	5.1	9.3	5.2	5.7	4.7	3.1	1.9	1.1	1.1	2.2	3.0	1.0	1.1	2.2
Uruguay	8.7	8.1	8.1	8.6	8.9	8.7	9.6	6.2	7.6	7.6	7.2	7.0	8.0	7.5	7.0
Venezuela[8]	22.3	27.1	21.1	38.5	57.3	111.8	254.4	493.6	929,789.5	10,000,000	10,000,000	10,000,000	1,555,146	10,000,000	10,000,000
Middle East, North Africa, Afghanistan, and Pakistan	**7.1**	**9.3**	**9.8**	**9.2**	**6.7**	**5.4**	**4.7**	**6.4**	**10.4**	**9.7**	**9.3**	**7.8**	**12.5**	**9.1**	**9.3**
Afghanistan	. . .	11.8	6.4	7.4	4.7	–0.7	4.4	5.0	0.6	1.9	3.5	5.0	0.8	3.0	4.0
Algeria	3.6	4.5	8.9	3.3	2.9	4.8	6.4	5.6	4.3	5.6	6.7	14.0	2.7	4.2	9.4
Bahrain	1.8	–0.4	2.8	3.3	2.7	1.8	2.8	1.4	2.1	3.3	3.2	2.2	1.9	3.8	3.2
Djibouti	3.7	5.2	4.2	1.1	2.3	0.9	0.4	0.8	–0.1	0.8	1.2	1.5	0.6	1.0	1.3
Egypt	7.9	11.1	8.6	6.9	10.1	11.0	10.2	23.5	20.9	14.5	12.3	6.9	14.4	12.8	10.7
Iran	14.7	21.5	30.6	34.7	15.6	11.9	9.1	9.6	31.2	37.2	31.0	25.0	51.1	31.2	30.0
Iraq	. . .	5.6	6.1	1.9	2.2	1.4	0.5	0.1	0.4	2.0	2.0	2.0	–0.1	2.0	2.0
Jordan	4.0	4.2	4.5	4.8	2.9	–0.9	–0.8	3.3	4.5	2.0	2.5	2.5	3.6	2.5	2.5
Kuwait	3.2	4.9	3.2	2.7	3.1	3.7	3.5	1.5	0.7	2.5	2.7	3.0	1.1	2.8	3.0
Lebanon	2.6	5.0	6.6	4.8	1.8	–3.7	–0.8	4.5	6.1	2.0	2.3	2.3	4.0	2.2	2.4
Libya[8]	0.4	15.9	6.1	2.6	2.4	9.8	25.9	28.5	23.1	15.0	15.0	15.0	15.0	15.0	15.0
Mauritania	6.5	5.7	4.9	4.1	3.8	0.5	1.5	2.3	3.1	3.9	4.0	4.3	3.2	4.0	4.1
Morocco	1.8	0.9	1.3	1.9	0.4	1.5	1.6	0.8	1.9	1.4	2.0	2.0	0.4	1.4	2.0
Oman	2.9	4.0	2.9	1.2	1.0	0.1	1.1	1.6	0.9	1.5	1.8	2.5	0.9	1.5	1.8
Pakistan	8.1	13.7	11.0	7.4	8.6	4.5	2.9	4.1	3.9	7.6	7.0	5.0	5.2	8.4	6.8
Qatar	5.1	2.0	1.8	3.2	3.4	1.8	2.7	0.4	0.2	0.1	3.7	2.0	. . .	. . .	. . .
Saudi Arabia	2.1	3.8	2.9	3.5	2.2	1.3	2.0	–0.9	2.5	–0.7	2.2	2.1	2.5	–0.7	2.2
Somalia	. . .	. . .	. . .	. . .	. . .	. . .	. . .	. . .	. . .	. . .	. . .	. . .	3.5	3.0	2.8
Sudan[9]	10.8	18.1	35.6	36.5	36.9	16.9	17.8	32.4	63.3	49.6	58.1	72.8	72.9	56.2	59.4
Syria[10]	5.7	. . .	. . .	. . .	. . .	. . .	. . .	. . .	. . .	. . .	. . .	. . .	. . .	. . .	. . .
Tunisia	3.5	3.5	5.1	5.8	4.9	4.8	3.6	5.3	7.3	7.5	5.6	4.0	7.5	6.8	5.2
United Arab Emirates	5.5	0.9	0.7	1.1	2.3	4.1	1.6	2.0	3.1	2.1	2.1	2.2	3.1	2.1	2.1
Yemen	10.9	19.5	9.9	11.0	8.2	12.0	–12.6	24.7	41.8	20.0	7.5	5.0	30.0	10.0	5.0

Table A7. Emerging Market and Developing Economies: Consumer Prices[1] *(continued)*

(Annual percent change)

	Average									Projections			End of Period[2]	Projections	
	2001–10	2011	2012	2013	2014	2015	2016	2017	2018	2019	2020	2024	2018	2019	2020
Sub-Saharan Africa	**9.9**	**9.3**	**9.2**	**6.6**	**6.4**	**7.0**	**11.2**	**11.0**	**8.5**	**8.1**	**7.4**	**6.6**	**8.0**	**8.0**	**7.3**
Angola	42.4	13.5	10.3	8.8	7.3	9.2	30.7	29.8	19.6	17.5	11.1	6.0	18.6	15.0	9.0
Benin	3.0	2.7	6.7	1.0	–1.1	0.3	–0.8	0.1	1.0	2.0	2.0	2.0	1.0	2.0	1.9
Botswana	8.6	8.5	7.5	5.9	4.4	3.1	2.8	3.3	3.2	3.6	3.8	3.9	3.5	3.7	3.8
Burkina Faso	2.8	2.8	3.8	0.5	–0.3	0.9	–0.2	0.4	2.0	2.0	2.0	2.0	2.0	2.0	2.0
Burundi	8.9	9.6	18.2	7.9	4.4	5.6	5.5	16.6	1.2	7.3	9.0	9.0	5.3	9.0	9.0
Cabo Verde	2.4	4.5	2.5	1.5	–0.2	0.1	–1.4	0.8	1.3	1.6	2.0	2.0	1.5	1.6	2.0
Cameroon	2.6	2.9	2.4	2.1	1.9	2.7	0.9	0.6	0.9	1.2	1.5	2.0	1.1	1.2	1.5
Central African Republic	3.3	1.2	5.9	6.6	11.6	4.5	4.6	4.1	3.0	3.0	2.5	2.4	2.5	2.3	2.7
Chad	2.9	1.9	7.7	0.2	1.7	6.8	–1.1	–0.9	2.5	2.9	3.0	2.4	3.5	–1.2	5.0
Comoros	4.2	2.2	5.9	1.6	1.3	2.0	1.8	1.0	2.0	2.0	2.0	2.0	2.0	1.8	2.2
Democratic Republic of the Congo	36.8	14.9	0.9	0.9	1.2	1.0	18.2	41.5	29.3	8.4	6.7	3.5	7.2	7.1	7.0
Republic of Congo	2.9	1.8	5.0	4.6	0.9	3.2	3.2	0.4	1.2	1.5	1.8	3.0	0.9	2.0	2.5
Côte d'Ivoire	2.9	4.9	1.3	2.6	0.4	1.2	0.7	0.8	0.3	2.0	2.0	2.0	1.1	2.0	2.0
Equatorial Guinea	5.6	4.8	3.4	3.2	4.3	1.7	1.4	0.7	1.3	2.6	2.7	3.0	2.6	2.6	2.7
Eritrea	17.8	3.9	6.0	6.5	10.0	9.0	9.0	9.0	9.0	9.0	9.0	9.0	9.0	9.0	9.0
Eswatini	7.1	6.1	8.9	5.6	5.7	5.0	7.8	6.2	4.8	5.6	5.5	5.5	5.3	5.2	5.8
Ethiopia	11.1	33.2	24.1	8.1	7.4	9.6	6.6	10.7	13.8	9.3	8.0	8.0	10.4	8.0	8.0
Gabon	1.2	1.3	2.7	0.5	4.5	–0.1	2.1	2.7	4.8	3.0	2.5	2.5	6.3	3.0	2.5
The Gambia	7.0	4.8	4.6	5.2	6.3	6.8	7.2	8.0	6.5	6.3	6.0	5.0	6.4	6.5	5.5
Ghana	15.9	7.7	7.1	11.7	15.5	17.2	17.5	12.4	9.8	9.1	8.4	6.0	9.4	8.7	8.0
Guinea	16.0	21.4	15.2	11.9	9.7	8.2	8.2	8.9	9.7	8.9	8.3	7.8	9.6	8.6	8.1
Guinea-Bissau	2.3	5.1	2.1	0.8	–1.0	1.5	1.5	1.1	1.4	2.0	2.1	3.0	5.4	2.1	2.3
Kenya	7.0	14.0	9.4	5.7	6.9	6.6	6.3	8.0	4.7	4.4	5.0	5.0	5.7	4.7	5.0
Lesotho	7.0	6.0	5.5	5.0	4.6	4.3	6.2	4.5	5.2	5.4	5.6	5.5	5.2	5.4	5.6
Liberia	10.0	8.5	6.8	7.6	9.9	7.7	8.8	12.4	23.4	22.3	20.5	13.5	27.2	21.8	19.0
Madagascar	10.2	9.5	5.7	5.8	6.1	7.4	6.7	8.3	7.3	6.7	6.3	5.0	6.1	6.4	6.0
Malawi	8.1	7.6	21.3	28.3	23.8	21.9	21.7	11.5	9.2	8.7	8.2	5.0	9.9	8.3	7.7
Mali	2.7	3.1	5.3	–2.4	2.7	1.4	–1.8	1.8	1.7	1.7	2.2	2.2	1.0	2.2	2.2
Mauritius	5.7	6.5	3.9	3.5	3.2	1.3	1.0	3.7	3.2	2.1	3.7	3.4	1.8	4.1	3.6
Mozambique	11.0	11.2	2.6	4.3	2.6	3.6	19.9	15.1	3.9	4.2	5.5	5.5	3.5	5.5	5.5
Namibia	7.1	5.0	6.7	5.6	5.3	3.4	6.7	6.1	4.3	5.2	5.5	5.5	5.1	5.2	5.4
Niger	2.5	2.9	0.5	2.3	–0.9	1.0	0.2	2.4	3.0	2.4	2.1	2.0	1.6	2.2	2.0
Nigeria	12.9	10.8	12.2	8.5	8.0	9.0	15.7	16.5	12.1	11.7	11.7	11.0	11.4	12.1	11.7
Rwanda	7.9	5.7	6.3	4.2	1.8	2.5	5.7	4.8	1.4	3.5	5.0	5.0	1.1	5.0	5.0
São Tomé and Príncipe	16.2	14.3	10.6	8.1	7.0	5.2	5.4	5.7	7.9	7.8	5.5	3.0	9.0	6.0	5.0
Senegal	2.1	3.4	1.4	0.7	–1.1	0.1	0.8	1.3	0.5	1.3	1.5	1.5	1.3	1.9	1.5
Seychelles	7.6	2.6	7.1	4.3	1.4	4.0	–1.0	2.9	3.7	3.4	3.0	3.0	3.4	3.9	3.2
Sierra Leone	8.3	6.8	6.6	5.5	4.6	6.7	10.9	18.2	16.9	15.8	13.0	8.2	17.5	14.0	12.0
South Africa	5.9	5.0	5.6	5.8	6.1	4.6	6.3	5.3	4.6	5.0	5.4	5.5	4.9	5.3	5.5
South Sudan	. . .	. . .	45.1	0.0	1.7	52.8	379.8	187.9	83.5	24.5	16.9	8.0	40.1	35.9	10.8
Tanzania	6.6	12.7	16.0	7.9	6.1	5.6	5.2	5.3	3.5	3.5	4.5	4.9	3.3	4.1	4.9
Togo	3.0	3.6	2.6	1.8	0.2	1.8	0.9	–0.7	0.7	1.8	2.0	2.0	2.0	2.8	1.4
Uganda	6.4	15.0	12.7	4.9	3.1	5.4	5.5	5.6	2.6	3.6	4.4	5.0	2.2	4.0	4.8
Zambia	15.4	8.7	6.6	7.0	7.8	10.1	17.9	6.6	7.0	10.7	12.0	10.0	8.0	13.5	10.5
Zimbabwe[11]	–5.6	3.5	3.7	1.6	–0.2	–2.4	–1.6	0.9	10.6	73.4	9.4	3.0	42.1	40.1	4.8

[1]Movements in consumer prices are shown as annual averages.
[2]Monthly year-over-year changes and, for several countries, on a quarterly basis.
[3]For many countries, inflation for the earlier years is measured on the basis of a retail price index. Consumer price index (CPI) inflation data with broader and more up-to-date coverage are typically used for more recent years.
[4]Georgia, Turkmenistan, and Ukraine, which are not members of the Commonwealth of Independent States, are included in the group for reasons of geography and similarity in economic structure.
[5]Starting in 2014, data exclude Crimea and Sevastopol.
[6]Based on Eurostat's harmonized index of consumer prices.
[7]Excludes Venezuela but includes Argentina starting from 2017 onward.
[8]See country-specific notes for Argentina, Libya, and Venezuela in the "Country Notes" section of the Statistical Appendix.
[9]Data for 2011 exclude South Sudan after July 9. Data for 2012 and onward pertain to the current Sudan.
[10]Data for Syria are excluded for 2011 onward owing to the uncertain political situation.
[11]The Zimbabwe dollar ceased circulating in early 2009. Data are based on IMF staff estimates of price and exchange rate developments in US dollars. IMF staff estimates of US dollar values may differ from authorities' estimates.

Table A8. Major Advanced Economies: General Government Fiscal Balances and Debt[1]

(Percent of GDP unless noted otherwise)

	Average 2001–10	2013	2014	2015	2016	2017	2018	Projections 2019	2020	2024
Major Advanced Economies										
Net Lending/Borrowing	–4.5	–4.1	–3.4	–2.8	–3.1	–2.8	–2.9	–3.2	–3.0	–2.6
Output Gap[2]	–0.4	–1.7	–1.3	–0.6	–0.6	0.0	0.5	0.7	0.7	0.5
Structural Balance[2]	–4.2	–3.7	–3.0	–2.7	–3.0	–2.9	–3.1	–3.5	–3.3	–2.8
United States										
Net Lending/Borrowing[3]	–4.8	–4.1	–3.7	–3.2	–3.9	–3.8	–4.3	–4.6	–4.4	–3.7
Output Gap[2]	–0.4	–1.9	–1.2	–0.1	–0.2	0.2	1.1	1.4	1.3	1.0
Structural Balance[2]	–4.3	–4.0	–3.4	–3.2	–3.9	–4.0	–4.7	–5.2	–5.0	–4.1
Net Debt	47.8	80.9	80.5	80.4	81.7	80.7	80.9	83.4	86.2	94.3
Gross Debt	68.3	104.8	104.4	104.7	106.9	106.2	105.8	106.7	107.5	110.3
Euro Area										
Net Lending/Borrowing	–3.0	–3.1	–2.5	–2.0	–1.6	–1.0	–0.6	–1.0	–0.9	–1.1
Output Gap[2]	0.4	–2.7	–2.3	–1.8	–1.2	–0.2	0.2	0.2	0.3	0.1
Structural Balance[2]	–3.2	–1.3	–1.0	–0.9	–0.8	–0.7	–0.7	–0.9	–1.1	–1.2
Net Debt	56.4	74.6	75.0	73.8	72.8	70.9	68.9	67.9	66.7	62.3
Gross Debt	70.5	91.6	91.8	89.9	89.1	86.8	85.0	83.6	81.8	75.7
Germany										
Net Lending/Borrowing	–2.8	–0.1	0.6	0.8	0.9	1.0	1.7	1.1	1.1	0.7
Output Gap[2]	–0.5	–0.3	0.1	0.1	0.2	0.9	1.0	0.8	0.6	0.0
Structural Balance[2]	–2.2	0.2	0.9	0.8	1.0	0.9	1.3	0.7	0.6	0.7
Net Debt	53.9	57.5	54.0	51.0	48.2	44.5	41.0	38.6	36.2	28.4
Gross Debt	66.1	77.4	74.5	70.8	67.9	63.9	59.8	56.9	53.8	43.7
France										
Net Lending/Borrowing	–3.8	–4.1	–3.9	–3.6	–3.4	–2.7	–2.6	–3.3	–2.4	–2.6
Output Gap[2]	0.2	–0.8	–0.9	–0.8	–0.8	0.1	0.2	0.1	0.1	0.0
Structural Balance[2]	–4.0	–3.5	–3.3	–3.0	–2.8	–2.6	–2.5	–2.5	–2.5	–2.6
Net Debt	59.1	83.0	85.5	86.4	87.5	87.5	87.6	88.2	87.7	85.2
Gross Debt	68.3	93.4	94.9	95.6	96.6	98.5	98.6	99.2	98.7	96.2
Italy										
Net Lending/Borrowing	–3.4	–2.9	–3.0	–2.6	–2.5	–2.4	–2.1	–2.7	–3.4	–3.8
Output Gap[2]	0.0	–4.1	–4.1	–3.4	–2.7	–1.5	–0.9	–1.0	–0.5	0.0
Structural Balance[2,4]	–4.0	–0.6	–1.1	–0.7	–1.4	–1.6	–1.7	–2.1	–3.1	–4.1
Net Debt	95.7	116.7	118.8	119.5	118.9	119.0	120.1	121.5	122.5	127.8
Gross Debt	104.2	129.0	131.8	131.6	131.3	131.3	132.1	133.4	134.1	138.5
Japan										
Net Lending/Borrowing	–6.4	–7.9	–5.6	–3.8	–3.7	–3.2	–3.2	–2.8	–2.1	–2.1
Output Gap[2]	–1.6	–1.7	–2.0	–1.5	–1.7	–0.5	–0.5	–0.2	–0.2	0.1
Structural Balance[2]	–6.0	–7.5	–5.5	–4.3	–4.1	–3.4	–3.1	–2.8	–2.1	–2.1
Net Debt	99.9	146.4	148.5	147.8	152.6	151.1	153.2	153.6	153.2	154.5
Gross Debt[5]	175.9	232.5	236.1	231.6	236.3	235.0	237.1	237.5	237.0	238.3
United Kingdom										
Net Lending/Borrowing	–4.1	–5.3	–5.3	–4.2	–2.9	–1.8	–1.4	–1.3	–1.2	–0.6
Output Gap[2]	0.6	–1.8	–0.7	–0.1	–0.1	0.1	0.0	–0.3	–0.2	0.0
Structural Balance[2]	–4.6	–3.9	–4.6	–3.9	–2.8	–1.9	–1.4	–1.2	–1.0	–0.6
Net Debt	40.4	76.8	78.8	79.3	78.8	77.5	77.5	76.2	75.0	70.9
Gross Debt	45.4	85.2	87.0	87.9	87.9	87.1	86.9	85.7	84.4	80.3
Canada										
Net Lending/Borrowing	–0.2	–1.5	0.2	–0.1	–0.4	–0.3	–0.4	–0.6	–0.6	–0.6
Output Gap[2]	–0.3	–1.3	–0.8	–2.1	–2.4	–0.8	–0.5	–0.4	0.1	0.1
Structural Balance[2]	–0.1	–0.9	0.3	0.9	0.8	0.1	–0.2	–0.4	–0.7	–0.6
Net Debt[6]	29.7	29.8	28.6	28.5	28.8	27.6	27.9	26.6	25.8	23.0
Gross Debt	74.5	86.2	85.7	91.3	91.8	90.1	90.6	88.0	84.7	72.0

Note: The methodology and specific assumptions for each country are discussed in Box A1. The country group composites for fiscal data are calculated as the sum of the US dollar values for the relevant individual countries.

[1]Debt data refer to the end of the year and are not always comparable across countries. Gross and net debt levels reported by national statistical agencies for countries that have adopted the System of National Accounts (SNA) 2008 (Australia, Canada, Hong Kong SAR, United States) are adjusted to exclude unfunded pension liabilities of government employees' defined-benefit pension plans. Fiscal data for the aggregated major advanced economies and the United States start in 2001, and the average for the aggregate and the United States is therefore for the period 2001–07.

[2]Percent of potential GDP.

[3]Figures reported by the national statistical agency are adjusted to exclude items related to the accrual-basis accounting of government employees' defined-benefit pension plans.

[4]Excludes one-time measures based on the authorities' data and, if unavailable, on receipts from the sale of assets.

[5]Nonconsolidated basis.

[6]Includes equity shares.

Table A9. Summary of World Trade Volumes and Prices
(Annual percent change)

	Averages										Projections	
	2001–10	2011–20	2011	2012	2013	2014	2015	2016	2017	2018	2019	2020
Trade in Goods and Services												
World Trade[1]												
Volume	5.0	3.9	7.3	3.1	3.6	3.9	2.8	2.2	5.4	3.8	3.4	3.9
Price Deflator												
In US Dollars	3.9	–0.3	11.0	–1.8	–0.7	–1.8	–13.2	–4.0	4.3	5.2	–1.4	0.8
In SDRs	2.4	0.5	7.3	1.2	0.1	–1.7	–5.8	–3.4	4.5	3.1	–0.1	0.1
Volume of Trade												
Exports												
Advanced Economies	3.9	3.5	6.1	2.9	3.2	3.9	3.8	1.8	4.4	3.1	2.7	3.1
Emerging Market and Developing Economies	8.1	4.5	8.9	3.6	4.7	3.2	1.4	2.9	7.2	4.3	4.0	4.8
Imports												
Advanced Economies	3.5	3.4	5.3	1.7	2.5	3.9	4.9	2.5	4.3	3.3	3.0	3.2
Emerging Market and Developing Economies	9.1	5.0	11.6	5.4	5.2	4.3	–1.0	1.8	7.5	5.6	4.6	5.3
Terms of Trade												
Advanced Economies	–0.1	0.1	–1.5	–0.7	0.9	0.3	1.9	1.2	–0.2	–0.6	–0.3	0.1
Emerging Market and Developing Economies	1.0	–0.2	3.5	0.6	–0.6	–0.6	–4.3	–1.6	0.8	1.3	–0.9	0.0
Trade in Goods												
World Trade[1]												
Volume	5.0	3.8	7.4	2.8	3.4	3.0	2.2	2.1	5.6	3.9	3.3	3.9
Price Deflator												
In US Dollars	3.9	–0.5	12.2	–1.9	–1.3	–2.4	–14.4	–4.8	4.8	5.7	–1.6	0.7
In SDRs	2.4	0.3	8.4	1.1	–0.5	–2.3	–7.1	–4.2	5.1	3.5	–0.3	–0.1
World Trade Prices in US Dollars[2]												
Manufactures	1.9	–0.1	4.1	2.7	–3.0	–0.5	–2.3	–5.2	–0.3	2.7	1.0	0.2
Oil	10.8	–2.9	31.7	0.9	–0.9	–7.5	–47.2	–15.7	23.3	29.4	–13.4	–0.2
Nonfuel Primary Commodities	8.9	–1.2	20.0	–7.8	–5.4	–5.4	–17.1	–1.0	6.4	1.6	–0.2	1.1
Food	5.6	–0.3	18.8	–3.8	0.7	–1.4	–16.8	0.0	3.9	–0.6	–2.9	2.1
Beverages	8.4	–1.4	24.1	–18.1	–13.7	20.1	–7.2	–3.1	–4.7	–8.2	–2.1	6.8
Agricultural Raw Materials	5.9	–2.3	24.3	–20.5	–4.4	–7.5	–11.5	0.0	5.2	1.9	–3.7	–0.2
Metal	14.5	–3.5	12.7	–17.8	–3.9	–12.2	–27.3	–5.3	22.1	6.2	2.4	–2.2
World Trade Prices in SDRs[2]												
Manufactures	0.5	0.7	0.6	5.9	–2.2	–0.4	6.0	–4.6	0.0	0.6	2.3	–0.5
Oil	9.2	–2.1	27.2	4.0	–0.1	–7.5	–42.7	–15.1	23.6	26.7	–12.3	–0.9
Nonfuel Primary Commodities	7.4	–0.4	15.9	–4.9	–4.7	–5.4	–10.0	–0.4	6.7	–0.5	1.1	0.4
Food	4.0	0.5	14.8	–0.8	1.5	–1.3	–9.7	0.7	4.2	–2.6	–1.6	1.3
Beverages	6.8	–0.6	20.0	–15.6	–13.0	20.1	0.7	–2.5	–4.5	–10.1	–0.8	6.0
Agricultural Raw Materials	4.3	–1.5	20.1	–18.1	–3.7	–7.5	–4.0	0.6	5.5	–0.2	–2.4	–0.9
Metal	12.9	–2.7	8.9	–15.3	–3.1	–12.1	–21.1	–4.7	22.5	4.0	3.8	–2.9
World Trade Prices in Euros[2]												
Manufactures	–1.7	1.3	–0.7	11.2	–6.1	–0.5	17.0	–5.0	–2.3	–1.9	4.3	–0.9
Oil	6.9	–1.5	25.5	9.2	–4.1	–7.6	–36.8	–15.4	20.8	23.6	–10.6	–1.3
Nonfuel Primary Commodities	5.1	0.2	14.4	–0.2	–8.5	–5.5	–0.7	–0.8	4.3	–2.9	3.1	0.0
Food	1.8	1.1	13.3	4.2	–2.6	–1.4	–0.4	0.3	1.8	–5.0	0.4	1.0
Beverages	4.5	–0.1	18.4	–11.4	–16.4	20.0	11.1	–2.8	–6.6	–12.3	1.2	5.6
Agricultural Raw Materials	2.1	–0.9	18.5	–14.0	–7.5	–7.6	5.9	0.3	3.1	–2.6	–0.5	–1.2
Metal	10.4	–2.2	7.4	–11.0	–7.0	–12.2	–12.9	–5.0	19.7	1.5	5.8	–3.2

Table A9. Summary of World Trade Volumes and Prices *(continued)*

(Annual percent change)

	Averages										Projections	
	2001–10	2011–20	2011	2012	2013	2014	2015	2016	2017	2018	2019	2020
Trade in Goods												
Volume of Trade												
Exports												
Advanced Economies	3.8	3.3	6.4	2.6	2.7	3.1	3.2	1.5	4.5	3.2	2.3	3.0
Emerging Market and Developing Economies	8.0	4.2	7.9	3.9	4.7	2.7	1.1	2.9	6.9	3.9	3.8	4.7
Fuel Exporters	4.8	1.9	5.8	2.8	2.1	–0.3	2.9	1.5	1.0	–0.1	0.3	3.1
Nonfuel Exporters	9.3	4.9	8.7	4.3	5.9	3.9	0.4	3.3	8.4	4.9	4.8	5.1
Imports												
Advanced Economies	3.6	3.3	6.0	1.1	2.2	3.4	3.8	2.2	4.9	3.6	3.2	3.3
Emerging Market and Developing Economies	9.2	4.8	11.4	5.1	4.8	2.6	–0.9	2.2	7.6	5.6	4.6	5.4
Fuel Exporters	11.0	1.9	12.0	8.6	3.7	1.1	–7.5	–5.5	3.1	0.4	1.5	3.2
Nonfuel Exporters	8.9	5.4	11.3	4.4	5.0	3.0	0.6	3.8	8.4	6.5	5.1	5.8
Price Deflators in SDRs												
Exports												
Advanced Economies	1.7	0.2	6.1	–0.4	0.3	–1.8	–6.5	–2.2	4.4	2.7	–0.5	0.1
Emerging Market and Developing Economies	4.4	0.4	13.0	3.0	–1.3	–3.1	–8.8	–7.2	6.7	4.8	–0.7	–0.4
Fuel Exporters	7.8	–1.0	25.6	4.4	–2.6	–6.9	–29.7	–12.8	17.0	15.2	–6.7	–1.0
Nonfuel Exporters	3.0	0.8	8.0	2.4	–0.7	–1.5	–0.8	–5.6	4.1	2.1	1.1	–0.2
Imports												
Advanced Economies	1.7	0.1	8.1	0.6	–0.6	–2.0	–8.1	–3.5	4.5	3.4	–0.2	0.1
Emerging Market and Developing Economies	3.2	0.5	8.1	2.4	–0.8	–2.6	–4.5	–5.6	5.5	3.6	0.2	–0.4
Fuel Exporters	3.7	0.6	6.2	3.1	0.0	–2.4	–3.1	–3.3	3.7	1.3	1.2	–0.4
Nonfuel Exporters	3.0	0.5	8.6	2.3	–1.0	–2.7	–4.8	–6.0	5.9	4.1	0.1	–0.4
Terms of Trade												
Advanced Economies	–0.1	0.0	–1.8	–1.0	0.9	0.2	1.7	1.4	–0.1	–0.7	–0.3	0.0
Emerging Market and Developing Economies	1.2	–0.1	4.5	0.6	–0.5	–0.4	–4.5	–1.7	1.1	1.1	–0.9	0.0
Regional Groups												
Commonwealth of Independent States[3]	3.0	–0.9	21.2	1.8	–6.5	–1.8	–22.2	–13.6	12.0	12.7	–5.6	0.4
Emerging and Developing Asia	–1.3	0.6	–2.7	1.4	1.1	2.4	8.5	0.0	–3.4	–2.1	1.3	0.1
Emerging and Developing Europe	1.0	–0.1	–0.1	–0.8	1.7	0.9	–0.2	0.3	–2.7	–2.1	1.6	0.6
Latin America and the Caribbean	2.3	–0.7	5.1	–1.7	–1.2	–2.5	–8.9	0.6	3.5	–0.4	–0.5	–0.1
Middle East, North Africa, Afghanistan, and Pakistan	3.4	–1.5	12.8	0.0	–0.1	–4.6	–25.1	–5.3	10.6	10.6	–6.6	–1.0
Middle East and North Africa	3.5	–1.5	13.0	0.5	0.0	–4.7	–25.9	–5.9	10.9	11.0	–6.7	–1.1
Sub-Saharan Africa	3.9	–0.7	12.7	–1.5	–2.3	–2.8	–15.0	–0.6	7.5	3.6	–6.5	0.4
Analytical Groups												
By Source of Export Earnings												
Fuel	3.9	–1.5	18.3	1.3	–2.6	–4.6	–27.5	–9.9	12.9	13.7	–7.8	–0.6
Nonfuel	0.0	0.3	–0.5	0.1	0.3	1.3	4.3	0.5	–1.7	–1.9	1.0	0.2
Memorandum												
World Exports in Billions of US Dollars												
Goods and Services	13,467	23,299	22,306	22,602	23,324	23,751	21,101	20,714	22,774	24,838	25,206	26,375
Goods	10,664	18,106	17,923	18,124	18,546	18,633	16,201	15,743	17,436	19,082	19,264	20,107
Average Oil Price[4]	10.8	–2.9	31.7	0.9	–0.9	–7.5	–47.2	–15.7	23.3	29.4	–13.4	–0.2
In US Dollars a Barrel	54.25	74.23	104.05	105.01	104.07	96.25	50.79	42.84	52.81	68.33	59.16	59.02
Export Unit Value of Manufactures[5]	1.9	–0.1	4.1	2.7	–3.0	–0.5	–2.3	–5.2	–0.3	2.7	1.0	0.2

[1]Average of annual percent change for world exports and imports.
[2]As represented, respectively, by the export unit value index for manufactures of the advanced economies and accounting for 83 percent of the advanced economies' trade (export of goods) weights; the average of UK Brent, Dubai Fateh, and West Texas Intermediate crude oil prices; and the average of world market prices for nonfuel primary commodities weighted by their 2014–16 shares in world commodity imports.
[3]Georgia, Turkmenistan, and Ukraine, which are not members of the Commonwealth of Independent States, are included in this group for reasons of geography and similarity in economic structure.
[4]Percent change of average of UK Brent, Dubai Fateh, and West Texas Intermediate crude oil prices.
[5]Percent change for manufactures exported by the advanced economies.

Table A10. Summary of Current Account Balances

(Billions of US dollars)

	2011	2012	2013	2014	2015	2016	2017	2018	Projections 2019	2020	2024
Advanced Economies	**–39.9**	**25.5**	**212.8**	**238.8**	**286.6**	**328.0**	**423.3**	**371.9**	**303.8**	**267.8**	**354.4**
United States	–445.7	–426.8	–348.8	–365.2	–407.8	–432.9	–449.1	–468.8	–513.4	–583.3	–548.8
Euro Area	–12.4	173.5	300.7	340.4	342.6	383.6	410.6	403.6	394.8	399.6	361.4
Germany	229.7	248.9	252.5	291.0	301.2	297.5	295.0	294.3	279.6	282.0	305.7
France	–24.6	–25.9	–14.3	–27.3	–9.0	–18.5	–14.8	–19.6	–10.2	–0.5	–25.4
Italy	–68.3	–7.0	21.0	41.1	27.1	47.4	54.2	53.5	58.9	54.3	36.5
Spain	–47.4	–3.1	20.7	14.9	13.9	27.9	24.3	11.1	11.8	12.5	14.5
Japan	129.8	59.7	45.9	36.8	136.4	194.9	196.1	174.1	180.4	196.6	237.9
United Kingdom	–51.6	–100.9	–141.9	–149.6	–142.4	–139.3	–88.1	–109.1	–117.4	–115.9	–128.1
Canada	–49.6	–65.7	–59.4	–43.2	–55.1	–49.0	–46.3	–45.3	–53.7	–51.7	–54.7
Other Advanced Economies[1]	262.0	272.7	343.7	357.0	360.9	344.4	324.8	345.7	338.3	344.5	395.4
Emerging Market and Developing Economies	**376.0**	**346.2**	**173.5**	**173.9**	**–57.0**	**–76.3**	**–9.5**	**–23.7**	**–149.4**	**–200.9**	**–471.5**
Regional Groups											
Commonwealth of Independent States[2]	107.3	67.4	17.9	57.6	53.0	0.6	20.4	109.3	83.6	78.0	46.7
Russia	97.3	71.3	33.4	57.5	67.7	24.5	33.3	114.9	92.1	84.4	56.9
Excluding Russia	10.0	–3.9	–15.5	0.1	–14.7	–23.9	–12.9	–5.6	–8.6	–6.5	–10.2
Emerging and Developing Asia	97.6	123.1	101.2	230.2	310.6	227.9	151.7	–25.1	–16.2	–44.2	–186.6
China	136.1	215.4	148.2	236.0	304.2	202.2	164.9	49.2	59.6	40.8	–40.4
India	–78.2	–87.8	–32.3	–26.8	–22.1	–14.4	–48.7	–68.5	–73.6	–77.9	–117.6
ASEAN-5[3]	49.4	6.3	–3.6	22.4	30.7	43.2	47.8	13.7	14.5	11.4	–7.5
Emerging and Developing Europe	–119.4	–81.8	–71.9	–59.0	–35.7	–33.5	–49.1	–44.4	–18.1	–29.8	–60.6
Latin America and the Caribbean	–111.0	–146.4	–169.2	–183.0	–169.1	–98.5	–79.0	–100.2	–103.6	–110.0	–136.2
Brazil	–76.3	–83.8	–79.8	–101.4	–54.5	–24.0	–7.2	–14.5	–33.2	–33.1	–46.6
Mexico	–12.5	–18.7	–31.8	–24.8	–30.5	–24.3	–19.4	–22.2	–21.1	–24.7	–29.3
Middle East, North Africa, Afghanistan, and Pakistan	410.1	410.7	331.3	190.8	–123.6	–119.4	–20.3	79.3	–31.5	–25.6	–65.6
Sub-Saharan Africa	–8.7	–26.9	–35.9	–62.8	–92.2	–53.4	–33.2	–42.6	–63.6	–69.2	–69.2
South Africa	–9.2	–20.3	–21.2	–17.8	–14.6	–8.2	–8.3	–12.4	–12.7	–14.4	–17.0
Analytical Groups											
By Source of Export Earnings											
Fuel	619.8	596.9	465.4	311.8	–78.0	–73.7	80.5	274.5	114.7	112.3	52.9
Nonfuel	–243.9	–250.7	–292.0	–137.9	21.0	–2.6	–90.0	–298.2	–264.1	–313.3	–524.4
Of Which, Primary Products	–31.6	–67.6	–86.9	–59.2	–66.1	–43.9	–58.3	–72.1	–54.6	–60.0	–64.4
By External Financing Source											
Net Debtor Economies	–338.9	–412.7	–384.5	–354.4	–306.3	–212.3	–221.7	–294.7	–305.6	–327.0	–452.9
Net Debtor Economies by Debt-Servicing Experience											
Economies with Arrears and/or Rescheduling during 2013–17	–37.0	–54.7	–53.9	–39.2	–49.3	–50.2	–41.5	–37.8	–39.5	–41.2	–43.4
Memorandum											
World	**336.1**	**371.7**	**386.3**	**412.7**	**229.5**	**251.7**	**413.8**	**348.2**	**154.5**	**66.9**	**–117.1**
European Union	77.1	208.3	284.8	302.5	299.1	321.8	445.1	388.0	367.0	373.3	332.8
Low-Income Developing Countries	–22.5	–31.0	–37.8	–44.9	–78.6	–40.7	–33.7	–50.4	–62.9	–72.0	–79.4
Middle East and North Africa	405.1	413.2	333.8	192.8	–121.5	–115.9	–8.6	97.3	–17.2	–13.3	–44.2

Table A10. Summary of Current Account Balances *(continued)*

(Percent of GDP)

									Projections		
	2011	2012	2013	2014	2015	2016	2017	2018	2019	2020	2024
Advanced Economies	**–0.1**	**0.1**	**0.5**	**0.5**	**0.6**	**0.7**	**0.9**	**0.7**	**0.6**	**0.5**	**0.6**
United States	–2.9	–2.6	–2.1	–2.1	–2.2	–2.3	–2.3	–2.3	–2.4	–2.6	–2.1
Euro Area	–0.1	1.4	2.3	2.5	2.9	3.2	3.2	3.0	2.9	2.8	2.2
Germany	6.1	7.0	6.7	7.5	8.9	8.5	8.0	7.4	7.1	6.8	6.2
France	–0.9	–1.0	–0.5	–1.0	–0.4	–0.8	–0.6	–0.7	–0.4	0.0	–0.8
Italy	–3.0	–0.3	1.0	1.9	1.5	2.5	2.8	2.6	2.9	2.6	1.6
Spain	–3.2	–0.2	1.5	1.1	1.2	2.3	1.8	0.8	0.8	0.8	0.8
Japan	2.1	1.0	0.9	0.8	3.1	4.0	4.0	3.5	3.5	3.6	3.5
United Kingdom	–2.0	–3.8	–5.1	–4.9	–4.9	–5.2	–3.3	–3.9	–4.2	–4.0	–3.8
Canada	–2.8	–3.6	–3.2	–2.4	–3.5	–3.2	–2.8	–2.6	–3.1	–2.8	–2.4
Other Advanced Economies[1]	4.0	4.1	5.0	5.2	5.7	5.3	4.7	4.7	4.6	4.4	4.2
Emerging Market and Developing Economies	**1.4**	**1.2**	**0.6**	**0.6**	**–0.2**	**–0.3**	**0.0**	**–0.1**	**–0.4**	**–0.5**	**–0.9**
Regional Groups											
Commonwealth of Independent States[2]	4.1	2.4	0.6	2.1	2.8	0.0	1.0	5.0	3.8	3.4	1.7
Russia	4.8	3.2	1.5	2.8	5.0	1.9	2.1	7.0	5.7	5.1	3.0
Excluding Russia	1.7	–0.6	–2.2	0.0	–2.8	–5.1	–2.5	–1.0	–1.5	–1.1	–1.2
Emerging and Developing Asia	0.8	1.0	0.7	1.5	2.0	1.4	0.9	–0.1	–0.1	–0.2	–0.6
China	1.8	2.5	1.5	2.2	2.7	1.8	1.4	0.4	0.4	0.3	–0.2
India	–4.3	–4.8	–1.7	–1.3	–1.0	–0.6	–1.8	–2.5	–2.5	–2.4	–2.5
ASEAN-5[3]	2.6	0.3	–0.2	1.1	1.5	2.0	2.1	0.6	0.6	0.4	–0.2
Emerging and Developing Europe	–6.3	–4.4	–3.6	–2.9	–2.0	–1.8	–2.5	–2.2	–0.9	–1.4	–2.1
Latin America and the Caribbean	–1.9	–2.5	–2.8	–3.1	–3.2	–1.9	–1.4	–1.9	–1.9	–2.0	–2.0
Brazil	–2.9	–3.4	–3.2	–4.1	–3.0	–1.3	–0.4	–0.8	–1.7	–1.6	–1.9
Mexico	–1.1	–1.6	–2.5	–1.9	–2.6	–2.3	–1.7	–1.8	–1.7	–1.9	–1.9
Middle East, North Africa, Afghanistan, and Pakistan	12.7	12.4	9.8	5.5	–4.0	–3.9	–0.6	2.3	–0.9	–0.7	–1.5
Sub-Saharan Africa	–0.6	–1.7	–2.2	–3.6	–5.9	–3.7	–2.1	–2.6	–3.7	–3.7	–2.8
South Africa	–2.2	–5.1	–5.8	–5.1	–4.6	–2.8	–2.4	–3.4	–3.4	–3.7	–3.7
Analytical Groups											
By Source of Export Earnings											
Fuel	10.5	9.6	7.3	5.1	–1.6	–1.6	1.6	5.2	2.2	2.0	0.8
Nonfuel	–1.2	–1.1	–1.2	–0.6	0.1	0.0	–0.3	–1.1	–0.9	–1.0	–1.2
Of Which, Primary Products	–1.8	–3.6	–4.5	–3.2	–3.5	–2.5	–3.0	–3.8	–2.9	–3.0	–2.5
By External Financing Source											
Net Debtor Economies	–2.6	–3.0	–2.7	–2.4	–2.3	–1.6	–1.5	–2.0	–2.0	–2.0	–2.0
Net Debtor Economies by Debt-Servicing Experience											
Economies with Arrears and/or Rescheduling during 2013–17	–4.8	–6.6	–6.1	–4.4	–5.7	–5.9	–5.3	–4.5	–4.3	–4.2	–3.5
Memorandum											
World	**0.5**	**0.5**	**0.5**	**0.5**	**0.3**	**0.3**	**0.5**	**0.4**	**0.2**	**0.1**	**–0.1**
European Union	0.4	1.2	1.6	1.6	1.8	1.9	2.6	2.1	2.0	1.9	1.4
Low-Income Developing Countries	–1.5	–1.9	–2.1	–2.3	–4.2	–2.3	–1.8	–2.5	–2.9	–3.1	–2.4
Middle East and North Africa	13.5	13.5	10.6	6.0	–4.3	–4.2	–0.3	3.1	–0.5	–0.4	–1.1

Table A10. Summary of Current Account Balances *(continued)*

(Percent of exports of goods and services)

	2011	2012	2013	2014	2015	2016	2017	2018	Projections 2019	2020	2024
Advanced Economies	**–0.3**	**0.2**	**1.5**	**1.6**	**2.1**	**2.4**	**2.9**	**2.4**	**1.9**	**1.6**	**1.8**
United States	–21.0	–19.2	–15.2	–15.4	–18.0	–19.5	–19.1	–18.7	–20.1	–22.1	–17.4
Euro Area	–0.4	5.4	8.8	9.5	10.5	11.8	11.6	10.6	. . .	. . .	. . .
Germany	13.6	15.3	14.8	16.3	19.0	18.5	16.9	15.7	14.8	14.2	12.8
France	–3.0	–3.2	–1.7	–3.1	–1.2	–2.4	–1.8	–2.2	–1.1	–0.1	–2.2
Italy	–11.1	–1.2	3.4	6.5	4.9	8.6	8.9	8.2	9.0	7.9	4.4
Spain	–11.0	–0.8	4.7	3.3	3.5	6.8	5.4	2.3	2.4	2.4	2.3
Japan	13.9	6.5	5.5	4.3	17.4	24.0	22.4	18.8	19.6	20.7	21.7
United Kingdom	–6.4	–12.6	–17.3	–17.5	–17.9	–18.5	–11.1	–12.9	–13.6	–13.1	–13.0
Canada	–9.1	–11.9	–10.7	–7.6	–11.2	–10.3	–9.1	–8.3	–10.1	–9.4	–8.5
Other Advanced Economies[1]	6.7	6.8	8.3	8.6	9.7	9.5	8.2	8.1	7.8	7.6	7.3
Emerging Market and Developing Economies	**4.5**	**3.7**	**2.0**	**2.2**	**–0.6**	**–1.0**	**–0.1**	**–0.3**	**–1.6**	**–2.0**	**–3.8**
Regional Groups											
Commonwealth of Independent States[2]	12.1	7.4	2.0	6.8	9.0	0.1	3.3	14.7	11.5	10.2	5.1
Russia	17.0	12.1	5.6	10.2	17.2	7.4	8.1	22.6	18.8	16.5	9.2
Excluding Russia	3.2	–1.2	–5.1	0.0	–7.5	–13.9	–6.3	–2.3	–3.6	–2.6	–3.4
Emerging and Developing Asia	2.8	3.4	2.6	5.7	8.2	6.2	3.7	–0.6	–0.3	–0.9	–2.9
China	6.8	9.9	6.3	9.6	12.9	9.2	6.8	1.9	2.2	1.4	–1.2
India	–17.2	–19.4	–6.9	–5.6	–5.3	–3.2	–9.7	–12.1	–11.9	–11.4	–11.8
ASEAN-5[3]	5.5	0.7	–0.4	2.3	3.4	4.7	4.6	1.2	1.2	0.9	–0.4
Emerging and Developing Europe	–17.2	–11.8	–9.7	–7.5	–5.0	–4.6	–6.0	–4.9	–1.9	–3.0	–4.8
Latin America and the Caribbean	–9.0	–11.5	–13.4	–14.7	–15.6	–9.4	–6.7	–8.0	–8.1	–8.2	–8.1
Brazil	–26.1	–29.8	–28.5	–38.4	–24.3	–11.0	–2.9	–5.3	–11.6	–11.1	–12.7
Mexico	–3.4	–4.8	–8.0	–5.9	–7.5	–6.1	–4.4	–4.6	–4.3	–4.8	–4.4
Middle East, North Africa, Afghanistan, and Pakistan	26.8	24.3	20.8	13.6	–10.0	–10.6	–1.9	5.7	–2.4	–1.6	–4.2
Sub-Saharan Africa	–1.8	–5.6	–7.5	–13.8	–26.8	–16.9	–9.0	–10.2	–15.6	–16.0	–12.9
South Africa	–7.3	–17.3	–18.7	–16.1	–15.2	–9.1	–8.0	–11.3	–11.3	–12.4	–12.3
Analytical Groups											
By Source of Export Earnings											
Fuel	25.3	22.5	18.4	13.8	–4.2	–4.7	4.5	13.5	6.1	6.0	2.6
Nonfuel	–4.2	–4.1	–4.6	–2.1	0.3	0.0	–1.4	–4.2	–3.5	–3.9	–5.2
Of Which, Primary Products	–6.5	–14.0	–18.2	–12.8	–16.6	–11.2	–13.1	–15.2	–11.2	–11.8	–10.2
By External Financing Source											
Net Debtor Economies	–8.6	–10.3	–9.4	–8.6	–8.4	–5.8	–5.4	–6.5	–6.4	–6.4	–6.7
Net Debtor Economies by Debt-Servicing Experience											
Economies with Arrears and/or Rescheduling during 2013–17	–14.6	–21.8	–21.5	–16.7	–25.3	–28.3	–20.6	–16.4	–16.2	–15.6	–13.0
Memorandum											
World	**1.5**	**1.5**	**1.7**	**1.8**	**1.1**	**1.2**	**1.8**	**1.4**	**0.6**	**0.3**	**–0.4**
European Union	1.0	2.8	3.7	3.8	4.1	4.4	5.6	4.5	4.2	4.1	3.0
Low-Income Developing Countries	–4.8	–6.5	–7.3	–8.5	–16.4	–8.5	–6.0	–8.0	–9.3	–9.7	–7.4
Middle East and North Africa	27.1	24.9	21.4	14.0	–10.1	–10.6	–0.9	7.2	–1.3	–0.7	–2.9

[1]Excludes the Group of Seven (Canada, France, Germany, Italy, Japan, United Kingdom, United States) and euro area countries.

[2]Georgia, Turkmenistan, and Ukraine, which are not members of the Commonwealth of Independent States, are included in this group for reasons of geography and similarity in economic structure.

[3]Indonesia, Malaysia, Philippines, Thailand, Vietnam.

Table A11. Advanced Economies: Balance on Current Account

(Percent of GDP)

									Projections		
	2011	2012	2013	2014	2015	2016	2017	2018	2019	2020	2024
Advanced Economies	**–0.1**	**0.1**	**0.5**	**0.5**	**0.6**	**0.7**	**0.9**	**0.7**	**0.6**	**0.5**	**0.6**
United States	–2.9	–2.6	–2.1	–2.1	–2.2	–2.3	–2.3	–2.3	–2.4	–2.6	–2.1
Euro Area[1]	–0.1	1.4	2.3	2.5	2.9	3.2	3.2	3.0	2.9	2.8	2.2
Germany	6.1	7.0	6.7	7.5	8.9	8.5	8.0	7.4	7.1	6.8	6.2
France	–0.9	–1.0	–0.5	–1.0	–0.4	–0.8	–0.6	–0.7	–0.4	0.0	–0.8
Italy	–3.0	–0.3	1.0	1.9	1.5	2.5	2.8	2.6	2.9	2.6	1.6
Spain	–3.2	–0.2	1.5	1.1	1.2	2.3	1.8	0.8	0.8	0.8	0.8
Netherlands	9.0	10.7	9.7	8.5	6.3	8.0	10.5	9.8	9.3	8.9	7.5
Belgium	–1.1	–0.1	–0.3	–0.9	–1.0	–0.6	0.7	0.4	0.3	0.5	0.4
Austria	1.6	1.5	1.9	2.5	1.7	2.5	2.0	2.3	2.0	1.9	1.9
Greece	–10.0	–2.4	–2.6	–2.3	–1.5	–2.3	–2.4	–3.4	–2.7	–2.6	–3.4
Portugal	–6.0	–1.8	1.6	0.1	0.1	0.6	0.5	–0.6	–0.4	–0.5	–1.2
Ireland	–1.6	–3.4	1.6	1.1	4.4	–4.2	8.5	10.0	9.1	8.3	6.4
Finland	–1.7	–2.3	–2.2	–1.8	–0.7	–0.7	–0.7	–0.5	0.1	0.4	0.9
Slovak Republic	–5.0	0.9	1.9	1.1	–1.7	–2.2	–2.0	–2.0	–1.0	–0.7	0.0
Lithuania	–4.5	–1.4	0.8	3.2	–2.8	–0.8	0.9	1.4	1.1	0.6	–1.5
Slovenia	0.2	2.1	4.4	5.8	4.5	5.5	7.2	6.5	4.4	3.4	–0.4
Luxembourg	6.0	5.6	5.4	5.2	5.1	5.1	4.9	5.2	5.0	5.0	4.9
Latvia	–3.2	–3.6	–2.7	–1.7	–0.5	1.6	0.7	–1.0	–1.4	–1.7	–3.0
Estonia	1.3	–1.9	0.5	0.8	1.8	2.0	3.2	1.7	1.5	1.1	–0.4
Cyprus	–4.1	–6.0	–4.9	–4.3	–1.5	–5.1	–8.4	–5.6	–7.3	–6.5	–5.8
Malta	–0.2	1.7	2.7	8.7	2.4	3.4	10.4	10.1	9.3	8.8	8.0
Japan	2.1	1.0	0.9	0.8	3.1	4.0	4.0	3.5	3.5	3.6	3.5
United Kingdom	–2.0	–3.8	–5.1	–4.9	–4.9	–5.2	–3.3	–3.9	–4.2	–4.0	–3.8
Korea	1.4	4.0	5.9	5.9	7.6	6.9	4.9	4.7	4.6	4.5	4.5
Canada	–2.8	–3.6	–3.2	–2.4	–3.5	–3.2	–2.8	–2.6	–3.1	–2.8	–2.4
Australia	–3.1	–4.3	–3.4	–3.1	–4.6	–3.3	–2.6	–2.1	–2.1	–2.1	–2.5
Taiwan Province of China	7.8	8.9	10.0	11.5	14.2	13.7	14.4	11.6	11.4	10.7	9.5
Switzerland	7.8	10.7	11.6	8.5	11.2	9.4	6.7	9.8	9.0	9.0	9.0
Sweden	5.6	5.6	5.2	4.5	4.1	3.8	2.8	2.0	2.4	2.5	2.9
Singapore	21.6	16.9	15.8	17.9	17.0	17.5	16.0	17.7	17.6	17.1	15.0
Hong Kong SAR	5.6	1.6	1.5	1.4	3.3	4.0	4.6	3.5	3.2	3.4	3.5
Norway	12.4	12.5	10.3	10.5	7.9	4.0	5.6	8.1	7.4	7.2	6.8
Czech Republic	–2.1	–1.6	–0.5	0.2	0.2	1.6	1.1	0.2	–0.6	–0.8	–1.8
Israel	2.0	0.6	3.0	4.3	5.3	3.7	2.6	1.9	1.7	1.4	1.7
Denmark	6.6	6.3	7.8	8.9	8.2	7.9	8.0	6.0	5.5	5.1	4.4
New Zealand	–2.8	–3.9	–3.2	–3.1	–3.0	–2.2	–2.9	–4.0	–4.4	–4.3	–3.7
Puerto Rico	. . .	. . .	. . .	. . .	. . .	. . .	. . .	. . .	. . .	. . .	. . .
Macao SAR	40.9	39.3	40.2	34.2	25.3	27.2	33.0	35.0	37.4	38.7	41.7
Iceland	–5.1	–3.8	5.8	3.9	5.1	7.5	3.6	2.9	0.8	1.1	1.1
San Marino	. . .	. . .	. . .	. . .	. . .	. . .	–0.5	0.4	0.4	0.2	0.2
Memorandum											
Major Advanced Economies	–0.8	–0.9	–0.7	–0.6	–0.4	–0.3	–0.1	–0.3	–0.4	–0.5	–0.4
Euro Area[2]	0.8	2.3	2.8	3.0	3.4	3.4	3.8	3.5	3.5	3.4	2.7

[1]Data corrected for reporting discrepancies in intra-area transactions.
[2]Data calculated as the sum of the balances of individual euro area countries.

Table A12. Emerging Market and Developing Economies: Balance on Current Account
(Percent of GDP)

									Projections		
	2011	2012	2013	2014	2015	2016	2017	2018	2019	2020	2024
Commonwealth of Independent States[1]	**4.1**	**2.4**	**0.6**	**2.1**	**2.8**	**0.0**	**1.0**	**5.0**	**3.8**	**3.4**	**1.7**
Russia	4.8	3.2	1.5	2.8	5.0	1.9	2.1	7.0	5.7	5.1	3.0
Excluding Russia	1.7	–0.6	–2.2	0.0	–2.8	–5.1	–2.5	–1.0	–1.5	–1.1	–1.2
Armenia	–10.4	–10.0	–7.3	–7.6	–2.6	–2.3	–2.8	–6.2	–4.6	–4.3	–4.5
Azerbaijan	26.0	21.4	16.6	13.9	–0.4	–3.6	4.1	12.6	11.7	13.3	12.8
Belarus	–8.2	–2.8	–10.0	–6.6	–3.3	–3.4	–1.6	–2.3	–4.0	–2.3	–2.3
Georgia	–12.8	–11.9	–5.9	–10.8	–12.6	–13.1	–8.8	–7.9	–8.0	–7.8	–7.0
Kazakhstan	5.3	0.5	0.5	2.8	–2.8	–6.5	–3.3	0.6	0.1	0.6	1.5
Kyrgyz Republic	–2.9	3.7	–13.3	–16.0	–16.0	–11.6	–6.2	–9.8	–10.9	–8.6	–9.3
Moldova	–9.8	–6.4	–4.1	–4.4	–4.8	–3.3	–6.2	–9.9	–7.7	–8.0	–6.8
Tajikistan	–7.3	–9.2	–7.8	–2.8	–6.0	–5.2	2.1	–5.3	–7.0	–6.8	–6.3
Turkmenistan	–0.8	–0.9	–7.3	–6.1	–15.6	–20.2	–10.3	3.1	–2.3	–3.2	–5.7
Ukraine[2]	–6.3	–8.1	–9.2	–3.9	1.7	–1.5	–2.2	–3.7	–2.5	–2.4	–2.6
Uzbekistan	5.7	1.2	2.8	1.7	0.7	0.3	1.4	–7.8	–5.6	–4.7	–4.4
Emerging and Developing Asia	**0.8**	**1.0**	**0.7**	**1.5**	**2.0**	**1.4**	**0.9**	**–0.1**	**–0.1**	**–0.2**	**–0.6**
Bangladesh	–1.0	0.7	1.2	1.3	1.9	0.6	–2.1	–2.8	–1.9	–1.7	–1.9
Bhutan	–29.8	–21.4	–25.4	–26.4	–28.3	–29.4	–22.8	–22.7	–15.0	–10.6	6.2
Brunei Darussalam	34.7	29.8	20.9	31.9	16.7	12.9	16.7	11.0	17.1	17.4	16.7
Cambodia	–7.9	–8.6	–8.4	–8.5	–8.7	–8.4	–8.0	–10.5	–9.1	–9.0	–7.9
China	1.8	2.5	1.5	2.2	2.7	1.8	1.4	0.4	0.4	0.3	–0.2
Fiji	–5.1	–1.4	–9.7	–6.6	–2.7	–3.2	–6.2	–5.9	–5.1	–4.4	–3.9
India	–4.3	–4.8	–1.7	–1.3	–1.0	–0.6	–1.8	–2.5	–2.5	–2.4	–2.5
Indonesia	0.2	–2.7	–3.2	–3.1	–2.0	–1.8	–1.6	–3.0	–2.7	–2.6	–2.4
Kiribati	–13.1	–4.4	8.3	24.9	46.2	20.1	20.5	10.3	4.3	0.4	–7.2
Lao P.D.R.	–15.3	–29.0	–32.4	–29.3	–26.8	–16.9	–16.9	–17.1	–16.4	–14.9	–10.3
Malaysia	10.9	5.2	3.5	4.4	3.0	2.4	3.0	2.3	2.1	2.1	0.5
Maldives	–14.8	–6.6	–4.3	–3.7	–7.5	–23.5	–22.1	–24.0	–18.9	–13.6	–10.4
Marshall Islands	–2.2	–6.3	–10.7	–1.7	14.4	9.7	4.8	3.8	3.4	2.4	0.9
Micronesia	–20.0	–14.6	–11.6	–0.9	1.6	3.9	7.5	21.3	2.4	2.4	–5.0
Mongolia	–26.5	–27.4	–25.4	–11.3	–4.0	–6.3	–10.1	–14.6	–11.8	–10.8	–4.7
Myanmar	–2.2	–1.6	–2.1	–2.9	–5.2	–4.3	–4.7	–4.3	–4.9	–4.9	–4.6
Nauru	26.1	38.1	18.8	–13.5	–9.5	1.7	4.1	–7.7	–7.5	–7.1	–5.7
Nepal	–1.0	4.8	3.3	4.5	5.0	6.3	–0.4	–8.2	–9.6	–12.5	–4.5
Palau	–10.7	–10.5	–11.3	–13.8	–6.5	–10.5	–17.9	–17.3	–16.0	–15.8	–11.8
Papua New Guinea	–24.0	–36.1	–30.8	1.3	12.0	24.0	23.5	23.5	21.5	18.3	13.5
Philippines	2.5	2.8	4.2	3.8	2.5	–0.4	–0.7	–2.6	–2.2	–1.8	–1.4
Samoa	–6.9	–9.0	–1.7	–8.1	–3.1	–4.7	–1.8	2.3	–0.6	–0.3	–1.2
Solomon Islands	–8.3	1.7	–3.4	–4.3	–3.0	–3.9	–4.2	–6.4	–8.3	–8.8	–6.8
Sri Lanka	–7.1	–5.8	–3.4	–2.5	–2.3	–2.1	–2.6	–3.2	–2.8	–2.6	–2.1
Thailand	2.5	–0.4	–1.2	3.7	8.0	11.7	11.0	7.7	7.1	6.3	4.6
Timor-Leste	39.1	39.7	42.3	27.0	6.6	–21.6	–10.2	–2.4	1.8	–1.8	–7.5
Tonga	–16.9	–12.3	–8.0	–10.0	–10.7	–6.6	–6.3	–9.9	–11.8	–9.6	–8.0
Tuvalu	–37.1	18.2	–6.6	2.9	–52.8	23.2	4.2	3.5	–2.0	–12.5	–4.1
Vanuatu	–7.8	–6.5	–3.3	2.4	–10.7	–4.6	–1.5	–6.9	–8.0	–7.5	–6.0
Vietnam	0.2	6.0	4.5	4.9	–0.1	2.9	3.0	3.0	3.1	2.6	1.3
Emerging and Developing Europe	**–6.3**	**–4.4**	**–3.6**	**–2.9**	**–2.0**	**–1.8**	**–2.5**	**–2.2**	**–0.9**	**–1.4**	**–2.1**
Albania	–13.2	–10.1	–9.2	–10.8	–8.6	–7.6	–7.5	–6.3	–6.0	–5.8	–6.1
Bosnia and Herzegovina	–9.5	–8.7	–5.3	–7.4	–5.3	–4.7	–4.7	–4.5	–5.1	–6.2	–5.3
Bulgaria	0.3	–0.9	1.3	1.2	0.0	2.6	6.5	3.9	1.9	1.3	–0.1
Croatia	–0.7	–0.1	0.9	2.0	4.5	2.6	4.0	2.9	2.1	1.6	0.3
Hungary	0.7	1.8	3.8	1.5	2.8	6.2	2.8	0.5	0.5	0.6	0.7
Kosovo	–12.7	–5.8	–3.4	–6.9	–8.6	–7.9	–6.4	–8.3	–10.5	–10.1	–8.0
Montenegro	–14.8	–15.3	–11.4	–12.4	–11.0	–16.2	–16.1	–18.5	–17.5	–14.5	–9.6
North Macedonia	–2.5	–3.2	–1.6	–0.5	–2.0	–2.9	–1.0	–0.3	–1.2	–1.5	–2.0
Poland	–5.2	–3.7	–1.3	–2.1	–0.6	–0.5	0.1	–0.7	–1.1	–1.5	–1.8
Romania	–5.0	–4.8	–1.1	–0.7	–1.2	–2.1	–3.2	–4.6	–5.2	–4.8	–3.5
Serbia	–8.1	–10.8	–5.7	–5.6	–3.5	–2.9	–5.2	–5.2	–5.5	–5.0	–4.0
Turkey	–8.9	–5.5	–6.7	–4.7	–3.7	–3.8	–5.6	–3.6	0.7	–0.4	–2.4

Table A12. Emerging Market and Developing Economies: Balance on Current Account *(continued)*
(Percent of GDP)

									Projections		
	2011	2012	2013	2014	2015	2016	2017	2018	2019	2020	2024
Latin America and the Caribbean	**–1.9**	**–2.5**	**–2.8**	**–3.1**	**–3.2**	**–1.9**	**–1.4**	**–1.9**	**–1.9**	**–2.0**	**–2.0**
Antigua and Barbuda	. . .	. . .	. . .	0.0	5.2	–2.2	–6.9	–4.7	–3.5	–3.7	–3.8
Argentina	–1.0	–0.4	–2.1	–1.6	–2.7	–2.7	–4.9	–5.4	–2.0	–2.5	–2.5
Aruba	–10.5	3.5	–12.9	–5.1	4.2	5.1	1.0	0.9	2.6	2.2	0.6
The Bahamas	–11.8	–14.0	–14.1	–17.3	–12.0	–10.6	–16.3	–15.5	–11.3	–8.8	–4.9
Barbados	–11.8	–8.5	–8.4	–9.2	–6.1	–4.3	–3.8	–2.4	–1.2	–1.3	–2.6
Belize	–1.1	–1.2	–4.5	–7.9	–9.8	–9.0	–7.0	–5.9	–5.7	–5.4	–4.8
Bolivia	0.3	7.4	3.5	1.7	–5.9	–5.7	–5.3	–4.7	–5.2	–5.1	–4.7
Brazil	–2.9	–3.4	–3.2	–4.1	–3.0	–1.3	–0.4	–0.8	–1.7	–1.6	–1.9
Chile	–1.7	–3.9	–4.1	–1.7	–2.3	–1.6	–2.1	–3.1	–3.2	–2.8	–1.7
Colombia	–2.9	–3.1	–3.3	–5.2	–6.3	–4.3	–3.3	–3.8	–3.9	–3.8	–3.8
Costa Rica	–5.3	–5.1	–4.8	–4.8	–3.5	–2.2	–3.0	–3.2	–3.2	–3.3	–3.4
Dominica	. . .	. . .	. . .	–6.9	–6.9	–8.4	–7.3	–46.2	–31.0	–22.8	–8.7
Dominican Republic	–7.5	–6.5	–4.1	–3.3	–1.9	–1.1	–0.2	–1.4	–1.2	–1.4	–3.0
Ecuador	–0.5	–0.2	–1.0	–0.7	–2.2	1.3	–0.4	–0.7	0.4	1.4	1.6
El Salvador	–5.5	–5.8	–6.9	–5.4	–3.2	–2.1	–2.0	–4.8	–4.4	–4.5	–5.0
Grenada	. . .	. . .	. . .	–10.9	–11.0	–10.1	–13.8	–14.6	–14.6	–14.0	–15.6
Guatemala	–3.4	–2.6	–2.5	–2.1	–0.2	1.5	1.6	0.3	–0.3	–0.6	–2.0
Guyana	–12.2	–11.3	–13.3	–9.5	–5.1	0.4	–6.7	–7.1	–5.8	8.6	50.3
Haiti	–4.3	–5.7	–6.6	–8.5	–3.1	–1.0	–3.7	–4.1	–3.9	–2.2	–2.3
Honduras	–8.0	–8.5	–9.5	–6.9	–4.7	–2.7	–1.8	–4.2	–3.7	–3.7	–4.0
Jamaica	–12.2	–11.1	–9.2	–7.5	–3.1	–1.4	–2.6	–2.8	–2.3	–2.2	–1.6
Mexico	–1.1	–1.6	–2.5	–1.9	–2.6	–2.3	–1.7	–1.8	–1.7	–1.9	–1.9
Nicaragua	–11.9	–10.7	–10.9	–7.1	–9.1	–7.5	–5.0	–1.0	–0.1	1.2	–1.9
Panama	–13.0	–10.3	–9.7	–13.5	–7.9	–8.0	–7.9	–8.5	–5.3	–4.0	–3.3
Paraguay	0.6	–0.9	1.6	–0.1	–0.4	3.5	3.1	0.5	–0.8	0.4	0.6
Peru	–1.8	–2.8	–4.6	–4.4	–4.8	–2.7	–1.2	–1.5	–1.4	–1.5	–1.6
St. Kitts and Nevis	. . .	. . .	. . .	–0.7	–10.3	–12.6	–8.7	–0.8	–5.4	–9.5	–9.5
St. Lucia	. . .	. . .	. . .	0.8	4.2	–3.4	–2.6	–1.2	–2.5	–0.4	0.4
St. Vincent and the Grenadines	. . .	. . .	. . .	–25.8	–14.5	–15.2	–17.2	–15.8	–14.4	–13.5	–11.7
Suriname	9.8	3.3	–3.8	–7.9	–16.4	–5.4	–0.1	–2.9	–3.8	–3.2	–2.1
Trinidad and Tobago	16.9	12.9	19.9	14.6	7.4	–4.0	4.9	4.9	0.6	1.1	2.7
Uruguay	. . .	–4.0	–3.6	–3.2	–0.9	0.6	0.7	–0.6	–0.8	–1.2	–1.9
Venezuela	4.9	0.8	2.0	2.3	–5.0	–1.4	6.1	6.0	1.4	–1.9	–2.1
Middle East, North Africa, Afghanistan, and Pakistan	**12.7**	**12.4**	**9.8**	**5.5**	**–4.0**	**–3.9**	**–0.6**	**2.3**	**–0.9**	**–0.7**	**–1.5**
Afghanistan	26.6	10.9	0.3	5.8	2.9	7.2	4.7	4.8	1.0	1.2	–1.7
Algeria	9.9	5.9	0.4	–4.4	–16.4	–16.5	–13.2	–9.1	–12.5	–9.3	–2.5
Bahrain	8.8	8.4	7.4	4.6	–2.4	–4.6	–4.5	–5.8	–3.6	–3.4	–3.0
Djibouti	–13.1	–18.8	–23.3	–25.1	–31.8	–9.4	–13.8	–14.3	–14.9	–15.4	–9.6
Egypt	–2.5	–3.6	–2.2	–0.9	–3.7	–6.0	–6.1	–2.4	–2.4	–1.7	–1.0
Iran	10.4	6.0	6.7	3.2	0.3	4.0	3.8	4.3	–0.4	–0.6	–0.6
Iraq	10.9	5.1	1.1	2.6	–6.5	–7.8	2.1	4.9	–6.7	–2.9	–4.8
Jordan	–10.2	–15.0	–10.3	–7.2	–9.0	–9.4	–10.6	–7.4	–8.2	–8.0	–6.0
Kuwait	42.9	45.5	40.3	33.4	3.5	–4.6	5.9	12.7	7.4	8.0	5.5
Lebanon	–15.7	–25.2	–27.4	–28.2	–19.3	–23.1	–25.7	–27.0	–28.2	–28.4	–22.1
Libya[3]	9.9	29.9	0.0	–78.4	–54.4	–24.7	7.9	2.0	–0.2	–7.8	–3.6
Mauritania	–5.0	–24.2	–22.0	–27.3	–19.8	–15.1	–14.4	–18.0	–17.1	–17.8	–5.2
Morocco	–7.6	–9.3	–7.6	–5.9	–2.1	–4.2	–3.6	–4.5	–4.1	–3.5	–3.3
Oman	13.0	10.2	6.6	5.2	–15.9	–18.7	–15.2	–5.9	–8.7	–5.4	–6.5
Pakistan	0.1	–2.1	–1.1	–1.3	–1.0	–1.7	–4.1	–6.1	–5.2	–4.3	–5.4
Qatar	31.1	33.2	30.4	24.0	8.5	–5.5	3.8	9.3	4.6	4.1	3.1
Saudi Arabia	23.6	22.4	18.1	9.8	–8.7	–3.7	1.4	8.3	3.5	2.8	–0.9
Somalia	. . .	. . .	–1.8	–5.0	–4.4	–5.9	–5.6	–5.6	–5.3	–5.2	–4.2
Sudan[4]	–4.0	–12.8	–11.0	–5.8	–8.4	–7.6	–10.5	–11.5	–9.9	–10.0	–9.9
Syria[5]	. . .	. . .	. . .	. . .	. . .	. . .	. . .	. . .	. . .	. . .	. . .
Tunisia	–8.4	–9.1	–9.7	–9.8	–9.7	–9.3	–10.2	–11.2	–10.1	–9.1	–5.8
United Arab Emirates	12.6	19.7	19.0	13.5	4.9	3.7	6.9	6.6	5.9	5.1	3.5
Yemen	–3.0	–1.7	–3.1	–0.7	–6.1	–2.8	–0.1	0.0	0.7	–1.9	–3.9

Table A12. Emerging Market and Developing Economies: Balance on Current Account *(continued)*

(Percent of GDP)

									Projections		
	2011	2012	2013	2014	2015	2016	2017	2018	2019	2020	2024
Sub-Saharan Africa	**–0.6**	**–1.7**	**–2.2**	**–3.6**	**–5.9**	**–3.7**	**–2.1**	**–2.6**	**–3.7**	**–3.7**	**–2.8**
Angola	11.7	10.8	6.1	–2.6	–8.8	–4.8	–0.3	1.3	–3.8	–1.9	–1.2
Benin	–7.3	–7.4	–8.4	–9.9	–10.0	–9.4	–9.9	–8.9	–8.4	–7.4	0.2
Botswana	3.1	0.3	8.9	15.4	7.8	13.7	12.3	9.6	8.6	8.0	9.6
Burkina Faso	–4.0	–7.1	–11.3	–8.1	–8.6	–7.6	–9.4	–7.5	–5.8	–4.8	–7.0
Burundi	–14.4	–18.6	–19.3	–18.5	–17.7	–13.1	–12.3	–13.4	–12.6	–11.9	–8.8
Cabo Verde	–16.3	–12.6	–4.9	–9.1	–3.2	–2.4	–6.2	–7.1	–7.3	–6.5	–5.0
Cameroon	–2.7	–3.3	–3.6	–4.0	–3.8	–3.2	–2.7	–4.0	–3.7	–3.4	–3.1
Central African Republic	–7.6	–6.5	–3.3	–14.8	–9.7	–5.5	–8.3	–8.6	–6.1	–6.0	–4.5
Chad	–5.8	–7.8	–9.1	–8.9	–13.6	–9.2	–5.7	–4.8	–6.1	–4.3	–5.6
Comoros	–6.0	–5.5	–7.0	–6.3	–0.4	–6.5	–4.0	–9.1	–8.9	–8.8	–8.4
Democratic Republic of the Congo	–5.2	–4.6	–5.0	–4.6	–3.7	–3.1	–0.5	–0.5	–1.8	–2.9	–2.3
Republic of Congo	13.9	17.7	13.8	1.3	–54.2	–46.2	–3.9	5.5	4.7	5.9	–1.1
Côte d'Ivoire	10.4	–1.2	–1.4	1.4	–0.6	–1.2	–2.8	–3.4	–3.0	–2.8	–2.5
Equatorial Guinea	–5.7	–1.1	–2.4	–4.3	–16.4	–13.0	–5.8	–3.6	–4.7	–5.7	–9.4
Eritrea	3.2	2.7	3.6	4.0	–1.4	–2.1	–2.4	–1.6	–2.0	–2.0	–2.5
Eswatini	1.0	12.2	17.0	17.5	18.0	14.3	12.5	9.9	10.0	11.6	10.7
Ethiopia	–2.5	–7.1	–6.1	–6.6	–10.4	–9.3	–8.6	–6.5	–6.0	–5.4	–3.4
Gabon	24.0	17.9	7.3	7.6	–5.6	–9.9	–4.4	–1.9	–3.6	–1.2	3.0
The Gambia	–7.5	–4.5	–6.8	–7.2	–9.8	–9.4	–7.1	–11.5	–9.8	–12.7	–10.5
Ghana	–6.6	–8.7	–9.0	–7.0	–5.8	–5.2	–3.4	–3.2	–3.0	–3.5	–3.1
Guinea	–18.4	–19.9	–12.5	–12.9	–12.9	–31.6	–6.8	–16.1	–20.1	–17.3	–9.4
Guinea-Bissau	–1.3	–8.4	–4.6	0.5	1.9	1.3	–0.6	–1.6	–3.9	–3.3	–2.7
Kenya	–9.2	–8.4	–8.8	–10.4	–6.7	–5.2	–6.3	–5.4	–5.0	–4.9	–4.8
Lesotho	–13.4	–8.4	–5.1	–4.8	–3.9	–8.4	–4.6	–5.8	–12.6	–4.3	–3.3
Liberia	–17.6	–17.3	–21.7	–26.4	–26.7	–18.6	–23.4	–23.3	–23.4	–23.6	–17.8
Madagascar	–7.7	–8.9	–6.3	–0.3	–1.9	0.6	–0.5	0.3	–1.4	–3.5	–4.2
Malawi	–8.6	–9.2	–8.4	–8.2	–8.9	–12.9	–11.0	–9.2	–6.8	–7.6	–7.7
Mali	–5.1	–2.2	–2.9	–4.7	–5.3	–7.2	–5.9	–7.3	–5.6	–6.1	–6.9
Mauritius	–13.5	–7.1	–6.2	–5.4	–3.6	–4.0	–5.6	–6.2	–7.4	–6.7	–5.0
Mozambique	–25.3	–44.7	–42.9	–38.2	–40.3	–39.3	–20.2	–34.4	–51.1	–63.8	–34.7
Namibia	–3.0	–5.7	–4.0	–10.8	–12.4	–12.8	–6.2	–4.3	–3.9	–3.2	–5.0
Niger	–22.3	–14.7	–15.0	–15.8	–20.5	–15.5	–15.7	–16.3	–21.0	–23.1	–12.3
Nigeria	2.6	3.8	3.7	0.2	–3.2	0.7	2.8	2.1	–0.4	–0.2	0.0
Rwanda	–7.5	–10.0	–8.7	–11.8	–13.3	–14.3	–6.8	–7.8	–9.2	–8.7	–8.0
São Tomé and Príncipe	–27.7	–21.9	–15.2	–22.1	–12.3	–6.5	–12.7	–10.6	–9.4	–8.2	–5.1
Senegal	–6.5	–8.7	–8.2	–7.0	–5.6	–4.0	–7.3	–7.2	–7.3	–10.2	–4.1
Seychelles	–23.0	–21.1	–11.9	–23.1	–18.6	–20.1	–20.5	–16.3	–16.0	–15.7	–16.0
Sierra Leone	–65.0	–31.8	–17.5	–9.3	–15.5	–2.3	–10.9	–13.8	–10.9	–9.7	–6.0
South Africa	–2.2	–5.1	–5.8	–5.1	–4.6	–2.8	–2.4	–3.4	–3.4	–3.7	–3.7
South Sudan	18.2	–15.9	–3.9	–1.5	–7.1	0.1	–6.6	–12.5	–12.0	–19.3	–10.1
Tanzania	–10.8	–11.5	–10.3	–9.7	–8.1	–4.4	–3.3	–3.7	–3.9	–4.2	–4.4
Togo	–7.8	–7.6	–13.2	–10.0	–11.0	–9.7	–7.9	–7.9	–6.2	–5.2	–4.9
Uganda	–9.9	–6.7	–7.2	–8.1	–7.3	–3.4	–5.0	–6.8	–8.2	–9.1	–3.0
Zambia	4.7	5.4	–0.6	2.1	–3.9	–4.5	–3.9	–5.0	–2.9	–2.7	–0.2
Zimbabwe[6]	–17.2	–10.7	–13.2	–11.6	–7.6	–3.6	–1.3	–4.0	–3.0	–4.6	–4.7

[1]Georgia, Turkmenistan, and Ukraine, which are not members of the Commonwealth of Independent States, are included in this group for reasons of geography and similarity in economic structure.
[2]Starting in 2014, data exclude Crimea and Sevastopol.
[3]See country-specific note for Libya in the "Country Notes" section of the Statistical Appendix.
[4]Data for 2011 exclude South Sudan after July 9. Data for 2012 and onward pertain to the current Sudan.
[5]Data for Syria are excluded for 2011 onward owing to the uncertain political situation.
[6]The Zimbabwe dollar ceased circulating in early 2009. Data are based on IMF staff estimates of price and exchange rate developments in US dollars. IMF staff estimates of US dollar values may differ from authorities' estimates.

Table A13. Summary of Financial Account Balances

(Billions of US dollars)

									Projections	
	2011	2012	2013	2014	2015	2016	2017	2018	2019	2020
Advanced Economies										
Financial Account Balance	–261.7	–155.0	224.6	354.6	332.3	434.0	439.9	355.9	311.9	282.2
Direct Investment, Net	359.2	109.8	154.9	220.8	–27.9	–191.6	190.8	–37.3	83.7	125.2
Portfolio Investment, Net	–1,112.1	–246.0	–552.6	76.3	263.4	492.5	63.6	203.3	354.8	325.1
Financial Derivatives, Net	–5.4	–97.8	74.8	–11.0	–104.7	21.7	6.8	5.6	–30.5	–55.0
Other Investment, Net	146.9	–194.3	394.6	–66.3	–25.0	–67.4	–65.6	60.1	–193.5	–211.0
Change in Reserves	349.8	273.2	153.1	134.9	226.8	178.6	244.3	124.4	97.4	98.0
United States										
Financial Account Balance	–526.0	–448.2	–400.3	–297.3	–325.9	–385.1	–331.9	–465.2	–507.1	–574.4
Direct Investment, Net	173.1	126.9	104.7	135.7	–202.0	–181.5	24.4	–373.4	–178.8	–178.0
Portfolio Investment, Net	–226.3	–498.3	–30.7	–114.9	–53.5	–195.1	–212.5	–44.0	–274.0	–230.5
Financial Derivatives, Net	–35.0	7.1	2.2	–54.3	–27.0	7.8	23.1	–2.4	9.3	9.0
Other Investment, Net	–453.7	–88.4	–473.4	–260.1	–37.1	–18.4	–165.2	–48.2	–63.6	–174.8
Change in Reserves	15.9	4.5	–3.1	–3.6	–6.3	2.1	–1.7	2.9	0.0	0.0
Euro Area										
Financial Account Balance	–40.9	182.6	439.0	337.6	296.5	381.5	473.2	466.7	. . .	. . .
Direct Investment, Net	124.9	58.9	13.5	69.1	158.3	196.2	140.6	354.0	. . .	. . .
Portfolio Investment, Net	–383.3	–177.0	–168.5	75.4	221.1	529.5	300.8	80.9	. . .	. . .
Financial Derivatives, Net	5.5	38.9	41.8	65.8	90.9	20.4	19.3	109.1	. . .	. . .
Other Investment, Net	197.7	242.8	544.2	123.0	–185.6	–381.7	14.1	–106.7	. . .	. . .
Change in Reserves	14.3	19.0	8.0	4.4	11.8	17.1	–1.6	29.3	. . .	. . .
Germany										
Financial Account Balance	167.7	194.3	300.0	317.8	264.9	284.3	316.3	274.7	279.6	282.0
Direct Investment, Net	10.3	33.6	26.0	95.3	74.8	33.2	47.1	59.3	48.9	55.2
Portfolio Investment, Net	–51.4	66.8	209.6	177.7	213.5	228.8	228.1	134.5	189.9	179.5
Financial Derivatives, Net	39.8	30.9	31.8	43.3	29.0	35.8	10.3	25.2	22.8	18.8
Other Investment, Net	165.1	61.1	31.4	4.8	–49.9	–15.4	32.3	55.4	18.0	28.5
Change in Reserves	3.9	1.7	1.2	–3.3	–2.4	1.9	–1.5	0.5	0.0	0.0
France										
Financial Account Balance	–78.6	–48.0	–19.2	–10.3	–0.8	–14.4	–36.0	–45.7	–7.9	1.8
Direct Investment, Net	19.8	19.4	–13.9	47.2	7.9	28.1	8.3	45.1	47.9	52.6
Portfolio Investment, Net	–335.1	–50.6	–79.3	–23.8	43.2	23.8	22.4	18.6	67.9	83.9
Financial Derivatives, Net	–19.4	–18.4	–22.3	–31.8	14.5	–17.6	–1.4	–20.1	–27.8	–37.9
Other Investment, Net	263.8	–3.6	98.2	–2.9	–74.2	–51.1	–61.9	–101.5	–98.3	–99.3
Change in Reserves	–7.7	5.2	–1.9	1.0	8.0	2.5	–3.4	12.3	2.5	2.6
Italy										
Financial Account Balance	–79.9	–4.1	29.0	68.5	39.1	66.3	58.0	40.0	60.2	55.7
Direct Investment, Net	17.2	6.8	0.9	3.1	2.7	–10.7	3.7	11.7	12.3	13.3
Portfolio Investment, Net	25.6	–22.4	–5.4	5.5	108.2	176.5	98.8	138.9	93.2	24.2
Financial Derivatives, Net	–10.1	7.5	4.0	–4.8	2.6	–3.3	–8.2	–3.0	–1.2	–0.4
Other Investment, Net	–113.9	2.1	27.5	65.9	–75.0	–95.0	–39.2	–110.8	–44.1	18.6
Change in Reserves	1.3	1.9	2.0	–1.3	0.6	–1.3	3.0	3.1	0.0	0.0

Table A13. Summary of Financial Account Balances *(continued)*
(Billions of US dollars)

	2011	2012	2013	2014	2015	2016	2017	2018	Projections 2019	Projections 2020
Spain										
Financial Account Balance	–43.4	0.5	41.6	14.8	21.1	26.0	24.6	14.7	15.3	16.2
Direct Investment, Net	12.8	–27.2	–24.6	8.6	28.4	16.0	19.1	17.3	17.4	18.4
Portfolio Investment, Net	43.1	53.7	–83.6	–12.1	11.8	56.1	28.6	19.4	19.3	17.7
Financial Derivatives, Net	2.9	–10.7	1.4	1.7	–1.3	–3.3	–2.5	0.0	0.0	0.0
Other Investment, Net	–116.2	–18.2	147.8	11.5	–23.3	–52.0	–24.5	–22.0	–21.4	–19.8
Change in Reserves	13.9	2.8	0.7	5.1	5.6	9.1	4.0	0.0	0.0	0.0
Japan										
Financial Account Balance	158.4	53.9	–4.3	58.9	180.9	263.7	158.0	183.8	177.4	192.9
Direct Investment, Net	117.8	117.5	144.7	118.6	133.3	134.4	149.7	134.4	144.6	157.4
Portfolio Investment, Net	–162.9	28.8	–280.6	–42.2	131.5	276.5	–53.5	88.1	69.6	62.1
Financial Derivatives, Net	–17.1	6.7	58.1	34.0	17.7	–16.1	30.5	0.5	0.6	0.6
Other Investment, Net	43.4	–61.1	34.8	–60.1	–106.7	–125.4	7.7	–63.3	–48.4	–38.7
Change in Reserves	177.3	–37.9	38.7	8.5	5.1	–5.7	23.6	24.0	11.0	11.5
United Kingdom										
Financial Account Balance	–43.3	–92.6	–132.5	–154.2	–142.6	–145.8	–115.7	–85.8	–120.0	–118.6
Direct Investment, Net	53.4	–34.8	–11.2	–176.1	–106.0	–219.5	16.3	–14.6	–0.8	–12.6
Portfolio Investment, Net	–215.5	275.0	–284.2	16.4	–201.8	–195.4	–134.9	–361.7	0.0	0.0
Financial Derivatives, Net	7.4	–65.8	63.4	31.2	–128.6	29.3	13.3	17.7	–5.2	–11.2
Other Investment, Net	103.4	–279.1	91.8	–37.5	261.6	231.0	–19.2	248.1	–129.5	–111.7
Change in Reserves	7.9	12.1	7.8	11.7	32.2	8.8	8.8	24.8	15.6	16.9
Canada										
Financial Account Balance	–49.4	–62.7	–56.9	–42.2	–56.2	–49.5	–40.4	–37.8	–53.7	–51.7
Direct Investment, Net	12.5	12.8	–12.0	1.3	23.6	34.0	55.0	10.8	–5.0	–2.5
Portfolio Investment, Net	–104.3	–63.8	–27.1	–32.9	–48.1	–118.6	–80.5	–8.8	–33.0	–34.5
Financial Derivatives, Net	...	...	...	...	...	...	...	...	...	...
Other Investment, Net	34.3	–13.4	–22.5	–15.9	–40.2	29.5	–15.6	–38.2	–15.7	–14.7
Change in Reserves	8.1	1.7	4.7	5.3	8.5	5.6	0.8	–1.5	0.0	0.0
Other Advanced Economies[1]										
Financial Account Balance	283.6	251.5	373.9	345.0	293.4	333.9	310.3	314.4	332.0	340.2
Direct Investment, Net	–6.2	–33.7	30.8	–6.3	–100.8	–71.1	–77.3	–49.3	–42.8	–40.4
Portfolio Investment, Net	47.2	150.0	139.6	181.5	337.0	265.9	190.8	263.5	203.7	210.4
Financial Derivatives, Net	31.1	–28.8	–33.5	–23.5	–12.7	3.4	–7.9	16.7	2.8	–1.0
Other Investment, Net	86.4	–110.7	135.9	87.0	–105.9	–14.7	–8.4	30.1	105.3	110.0
Change in Reserves	125.1	274.7	101.3	106.3	175.9	150.2	213.1	53.4	63.0	61.1
Emerging Market and Developing Economies										
Financial Account Balance	234.0	110.5	28.4	19.0	–270.8	–413.7	–255.6	–83.8	–106.0	–158.7
Direct Investment, Net	–531.7	–494.4	–485.8	–432.6	–344.5	–256.8	–325.5	–381.0	–380.2	–401.5
Portfolio Investment, Net	–144.7	–233.7	–157.5	–106.2	105.7	–57.0	–180.2	–51.1	–33.4	–57.4
Financial Derivatives, Net	...	...	...	...	...	...	...	...	...	...
Other Investment, Net	161.7	410.0	86.5	418.4	475.4	390.2	82.8	273.2	185.5	182.8
Change in Reserves	744.6	431.4	589.4	128.6	–512.6	–476.8	164.3	74.6	115.2	109.7

Table A13. Summary of Financial Account Balances *(continued)*
(Billions of US dollars)

									Projections	
	2011	2012	2013	2014	2015	2016	2017	2018	2019	2020
Regional Groups										
Commonwealth of Independent States[2]										
Financial Account Balance	100.7	52.1	2.5	12.2	53.1	2.7	22.8	113.3	84.8	79.1
Direct Investment, Net	–15.3	–27.7	–3.7	19.1	–0.2	–35.8	–4.3	13.7	11.3	15.3
Portfolio Investment, Net	17.9	3.5	–0.2	28.8	12.0	–2.4	–17.4	9.7	5.4	3.8
Financial Derivatives, Net	. . .	. . .	. . .	. . .	. . .	. . .	. . .	. . .	. . .	. . .
Other Investment, Net	64.3	44.3	27.5	73.0	38.8	30.4	15.2	46.5	10.6	17.3
Change in Reserves	32.1	30.5	–21.5	–114.1	–4.9	10.1	28.9	43.2	57.1	42.5
Emerging and Developing Asia										
Financial Account Balance	64.5	16.9	35.6	146.9	85.8	–32.0	–95.2	–95.5	–11.3	–39.5
Direct Investment, Net	–277.5	–220.5	–273.4	–203.6	–139.8	–26.9	–144.1	–188.4	–187.9	–199.0
Portfolio Investment, Net	–58.0	–115.6	–64.8	–124.4	81.7	30.9	–47.5	–27.1	–23.0	–27.1
Financial Derivatives, Net	–0.3	1.5	–2.0	0.7	–1.3	–10.0	2.6	1.7	2.0	2.2
Other Investment, Net	–29.3	215.6	–73.6	279.1	460.6	356.5	–102.3	110.4	136.4	119.3
Change in Reserves	431.3	139.1	450.6	195.3	–316.1	–381.8	197.1	8.4	61.5	65.6
Emerging and Developing Europe										
Financial Account Balance	–107.2	–66.7	–62.7	–43.6	–9.6	–12.2	–48.5	–4.5	–3.1	–14.9
Direct Investment, Net	–39.9	–27.7	–26.5	–32.0	–36.1	–30.0	–30.8	–38.4	–27.5	–29.0
Portfolio Investment, Net	–53.5	–70.2	–40.0	–19.4	24.3	–4.0	–24.2	7.1	6.4	–5.1
Financial Derivatives, Net	1.6	–3.0	–1.4	0.3	–1.8	0.2	–2.7	–3.7	3.6	3.2
Other Investment, Net	–30.1	6.4	–13.3	7.8	14.3	–1.8	20.8	24.5	17.2	4.1
Change in Reserves	14.6	27.8	18.5	–0.2	–10.4	23.5	–11.7	6.0	–2.7	12.0
Latin America and the Caribbean										
Financial Account Balance	–128.0	–154.8	–194.2	–200.5	–188.9	–100.4	–85.9	–110.0	–102.4	–109.0
Direct Investment, Net	–146.4	–158.5	–150.6	–138.5	–131.8	–125.9	–121.1	–141.2	–133.5	–135.7
Portfolio Investment, Net	–106.7	–79.8	–100.7	–112.3	–57.1	–51.7	–39.0	–8.8	6.2	–11.7
Financial Derivatives, Net	5.5	2.5	1.8	7.0	1.3	–2.9	3.9	3.9	3.6	4.1
Other Investment, Net	11.7	21.9	43.6	4.0	27.6	59.6	53.1	26.0	18.6	20.8
Change in Reserves	108.1	59.1	11.8	39.1	–28.8	20.5	17.2	10.2	2.8	13.6
Middle East, North Africa, Afghanistan, and Pakistan										
Financial Account Balance	317.7	287.5	301.1	180.7	–131.4	–205.6	–14.6	66.3	–21.9	–15.3
Direct Investment, Net	–20.0	–25.4	–7.9	–28.8	0.7	–7.0	–4.3	–2.5	–7.4	–12.8
Portfolio Investment, Net	75.0	56.7	70.6	130.3	68.0	–12.5	–24.7	–3.9	–11.4	–2.0
Financial Derivatives, Net	. . .	. . .	. . .	. . .	. . .	. . .	. . .	. . .	. . .	. . .
Other Investment, Net	125.5	101.4	111.4	62.9	–61.4	–47.1	94.8	69.7	0.2	28.2
Change in Reserves	137.8	155.0	127.2	16.2	–138.2	–138.6	–80.1	3.8	–2.5	–27.9
Sub-Saharan Africa										
Financial Account Balance	–13.7	–24.5	–54.0	–76.6	–79.8	–66.4	–34.2	–53.6	–52.2	–59.1
Direct Investment, Net	–32.7	–34.6	–23.7	–48.8	–37.2	–31.3	–20.9	–24.2	–35.0	–40.2
Portfolio Investment, Net	–19.4	–28.4	–22.3	–9.3	–23.2	–17.3	–27.3	–28.1	–16.9	–15.4
Financial Derivatives, Net	–1.7	–1.7	–0.8	–1.5	–0.4	0.9	0.3	–0.2	–0.2	–0.2
Other Investment, Net	19.7	20.4	–9.3	–8.4	–4.5	–7.3	1.1	–3.8	2.5	–6.8
Change in Reserves	20.8	20.0	2.8	–7.8	–14.2	–10.5	12.9	3.1	–1.1	4.0

Table A13. Summary of Financial Account Balances *(continued)*

(Billions of US dollars)

	2011	2012	2013	2014	2015	2016	2017	2018	Projections 2019	2020
Analytical Groups										
By Source of Export Earnings										
Fuel										
Financial Account Balance	513.5	445.7	374.5	226.5	–85.7	–156.6	71.2	246.9	121.2	121.6
Direct Investment, Net	–24.0	–29.3	13.0	6.0	5.9	–24.7	16.3	31.9	19.0	22.4
Portfolio Investment, Net	90.1	50.4	78.9	164.0	81.2	–9.5	–31.9	7.4	–10.1	4.4
Financial Derivatives, Net	. . .	. . .	. . .	. . .	. . .	. . .	. . .	. . .	. . .	. . .
Other Investment, Net	252.0	188.0	182.9	157.6	9.0	31.5	138.9	153.3	65.7	82.8
Change in Reserves	194.7	235.2	99.2	–106.6	–189.1	–154.4	–52.6	54.2	46.6	12.2
Nonfuel										
Financial Account Balance	–279.5	–335.2	–346.1	–207.5	–185.1	–257.2	–326.8	–330.7	–227.3	–280.3
Direct Investment, Net	–507.7	–465.1	–498.8	–438.6	–350.5	–232.1	–341.8	–412.9	–399.2	–423.9
Portfolio Investment, Net	–234.8	–284.1	–236.5	–270.2	24.5	–47.5	–148.3	–58.5	–23.3	–61.8
Financial Derivatives, Net	5.8	–0.9	–2.4	6.5	–2.2	–11.7	4.1	1.7	8.9	9.3
Other Investment, Net	–90.2	222.0	–96.4	260.8	466.5	358.7	–56.1	120.0	119.8	100.0
Change in Reserves	549.9	196.2	490.2	235.2	–323.6	–322.4	216.8	20.4	68.6	97.6
By External Financing Source										
Net Debtor Economies										
Financial Account Balance	–363.2	–414.8	–409.4	–373.4	–282.0	–231.7	–243.4	–290.5	–269.7	–293.5
Direct Investment, Net	–278.1	–282.0	–274.4	–283.5	–292.7	–285.1	–270.5	–300.6	–309.6	–327.0
Portfolio Investment, Net	–189.2	–218.8	–176.3	–191.4	–34.8	–53.3	–111.9	–15.8	–26.8	–44.2
Financial Derivatives, Net	. . .	. . .	. . .	. . .	. . .	. . .	. . .	. . .	. . .	. . .
Other Investment, Net	–72.8	–29.9	–22.4	–8.6	45.4	31.5	28.3	31.7	20.5	–10.0
Change in Reserves	174.1	121.1	67.6	103.3	1.8	90.2	108.3	–6.5	39.1	79.6
Net Debtor Economies by Debt-Servicing Experience										
Economies with Arrears and/or Rescheduling during 2013–17										
Financial Account Balance	–31.2	–58.8	–52.7	–33.3	–43.0	–52.6	–40.0	–36.9	–35.1	–35.9
Direct Investment, Net	–21.4	–28.1	–24.5	–19.8	–26.9	–23.7	–24.7	–23.3	–27.8	–31.7
Portfolio Investment, Net	1.0	–1.6	–12.1	–5.4	0.5	–1.9	–24.3	–18.9	3.7	–3.7
Financial Derivatives, Net	. . .	. . .	. . .	. . .	. . .	. . .	. . .	. . .	. . .	. . .
Other Investment, Net	1.6	–5.2	–19.0	–0.1	–22.8	–23.4	8.6	–0.9	–15.8	–7.9
Change in Reserves	–12.0	–23.7	4.0	–7.0	6.9	–2.2	0.9	7.1	6.7	8.5
Memorandum										
World										
Financial Account Balance	–27.7	–44.5	253.0	373.6	61.5	20.3	184.4	272.1	205.9	123.5

Note: The estimates in this table are based on individual countries' national accounts and balance of payments statistics. Country group composites are calculated as the sum of the US dollar values for the relevant individual countries. Some group aggregates for the financial derivatives are not shown because of incomplete data. Projections for the euro area are not available because of data constraints.

[1]Excludes the Group of Seven (Canada, France, Germany, Italy, Japan, United Kingdom, United States) and euro area countries.

[2]Georgia, Turkmenistan, and Ukraine, which are not members of the Commonwealth of Independent States, are included in this group for reasons of geography and similarity in economic structure.

Table A14. Summary of Net Lending and Borrowing
(Percent of GDP)

	Averages								Projections		
											Average
	2001–10	2005–12	2013	2014	2015	2016	2017	2018	2019	2020	2021–24
Advanced Economies											
Net Lending and Borrowing	–0.7	–0.6	0.5	0.5	0.6	0.7	0.8	0.7	0.6	0.5	0.5
Current Account Balance	–0.8	–0.6	0.5	0.5	0.6	0.7	0.9	0.7	0.6	0.5	0.5
Savings	21.6	21.4	21.9	22.5	22.7	22.2	22.7	22.7	22.7	22.7	22.9
Investment	22.3	22.0	21.1	21.4	21.5	21.3	21.6	21.9	22.1	22.2	22.5
Capital Account Balance	0.0	0.0	0.0	0.0	0.0	0.0	0.0	0.0	0.0	0.0	0.0
United States											
Net Lending and Borrowing	–4.4	–4.0	–2.1	–2.1	–2.2	–2.3	–2.2	–2.3	–2.4	–2.6	–2.4
Current Account Balance	–4.4	–4.0	–2.1	–2.1	–2.2	–2.3	–2.3	–2.3	–2.4	–2.6	–2.4
Savings	17.3	16.8	19.2	20.3	20.1	18.6	18.9	19.0	19.2	18.9	19.2
Investment	21.5	20.8	20.4	20.8	21.0	20.3	20.6	21.1	21.6	21.6	21.7
Capital Account Balance	0.0	0.0	0.0	0.0	0.0	0.0	0.1	0.0	0.0	0.0	0.0
Euro Area											
Net Lending and Borrowing	0.1	0.1	2.4	2.6	3.1	3.2	3.1	3.1	. . .	. . .	. . .
Current Account Balance	0.0	0.0	2.3	2.5	2.9	3.2	3.2	3.0	2.9	2.8	2.4
Savings	22.7	22.6	22.4	22.9	23.7	24.2	24.7	24.8	24.8	24.9	25.1
Investment	22.3	22.0	19.6	19.9	20.4	20.8	20.9	21.5	21.5	21.7	22.3
Capital Account Balance	0.1	0.1	0.2	0.1	0.2	0.0	–0.2	0.1	. . .	. . .	. . .
Germany											
Net Lending and Borrowing	4.1	5.9	6.7	7.6	8.9	8.6	8.0	7.4	7.1	6.8	6.3
Current Account Balance	4.1	5.9	6.7	7.5	8.9	8.5	8.0	7.4	7.1	6.8	6.3
Savings	24.0	25.7	26.2	27.1	28.1	28.2	28.1	28.6	28.2	28.3	28.6
Investment	19.9	19.8	19.5	19.6	19.2	19.7	20.1	21.2	21.1	21.5	22.2
Capital Account Balance	0.0	0.0	0.0	0.1	0.0	0.1	0.0	0.0	0.0	0.0	0.0
France											
Net Lending and Borrowing	0.7	–0.3	–0.5	–1.0	–0.4	–0.7	–0.5	–0.6	–0.3	0.1	–0.2
Current Account Balance	0.7	–0.3	–0.5	–1.0	–0.4	–0.8	–0.6	–0.7	–0.4	0.0	–0.2
Savings	23.0	22.5	21.8	21.8	22.3	21.9	22.9	22.1	22.2	22.5	22.7
Investment	22.4	22.9	22.3	22.7	22.7	22.7	23.5	22.8	22.6	22.6	22.9
Capital Account Balance	0.0	0.0	0.0	–0.1	0.0	0.1	0.0	0.1	0.1	0.1	0.1
Italy											
Net Lending and Borrowing	–1.2	–1.8	0.9	2.1	1.7	2.4	2.7	2.5	3.0	2.7	2.0
Current Account Balance	–1.3	–1.9	1.0	1.9	1.5	2.5	2.8	2.6	2.9	2.6	2.0
Savings	19.9	18.7	17.9	18.9	18.8	20.1	20.4	20.6	20.6	20.5	20.1
Investment	21.1	20.7	17.0	17.0	17.3	17.6	17.6	18.0	17.7	17.9	18.2
Capital Account Balance	0.1	0.1	0.0	0.2	0.2	–0.2	–0.1	–0.1	0.1	0.1	0.1
Spain											
Net Lending and Borrowing	–5.5	–5.4	2.2	1.6	1.8	2.5	2.1	1.0	1.1	1.1	1.1
Current Account Balance	–6.1	–5.9	1.5	1.1	1.2	2.3	1.8	0.8	0.8	0.8	0.8
Savings	21.9	20.7	20.2	20.5	21.6	22.7	22.9	22.7	22.9	23.0	23.1
Investment	28.0	26.5	18.7	19.5	20.4	20.4	21.1	21.9	22.0	22.1	22.3
Capital Account Balance	0.6	0.5	0.6	0.5	0.7	0.2	0.2	0.3	0.3	0.3	0.3
Japan											
Net Lending and Borrowing	3.2	3.0	0.7	0.7	3.1	3.8	4.0	3.5	3.4	3.5	3.4
Current Account Balance	3.3	3.1	0.9	0.8	3.1	4.0	4.0	3.5	3.5	3.6	3.5
Savings	27.4	26.3	24.1	24.7	27.1	27.4	27.9	27.9	28.4	28.6	28.6
Investment	24.1	23.2	23.2	23.9	24.0	23.4	23.9	24.4	24.9	25.0	25.1
Capital Account Balance	–0.1	–0.1	–0.1	0.0	–0.1	–0.1	–0.1	0.0	–0.1	–0.1	–0.1
United Kingdom											
Net Lending and Borrowing	–2.9	–3.2	–5.2	–5.0	–5.0	–5.3	–3.4	–4.0	–4.2	–4.1	–3.9
Current Account Balance	–2.9	–3.2	–5.1	–4.9	–4.9	–5.2	–3.3	–3.9	–4.2	–4.0	–3.8
Savings	14.3	13.4	11.1	12.3	12.3	12.0	13.9	13.3	13.1	13.2	13.8
Investment	17.2	16.6	16.2	17.3	17.2	17.3	17.2	17.2	17.2	17.2	17.6
Capital Account Balance	0.0	0.0	–0.1	–0.1	–0.1	–0.1	–0.1	–0.1	–0.1	–0.1	–0.1

Table A14. Summary of Net Lending and Borrowing *(continued)*
(Percent of GDP)

	Averages								Projections		
											Average
	2001–10	2005–12	2013	2014	2015	2016	2017	2018	2019	2020	2021–24
Canada											
Net Lending and Borrowing	0.4	–1.1	–3.2	–2.4	–3.5	–3.2	–2.8	–2.6	–3.1	–2.8	–2.6
Current Account Balance	0.5	–1.1	–3.2	–2.4	–3.5	–3.2	–2.8	–2.6	–3.1	–2.8	–2.6
Savings	22.6	22.5	21.7	22.5	20.3	19.7	20.7	20.4	19.8	20.5	21.0
Investment	22.1	23.6	24.9	24.9	23.8	22.9	23.5	23.0	22.9	23.3	23.6
Capital Account Balance	0.0	0.0	0.0	0.0	0.0	0.0	0.0	0.0	0.0	0.0	0.0
Other Advanced Economies[1]											
Net Lending and Borrowing	4.0	4.0	5.1	5.0	5.3	5.4	4.5	4.7	4.5	4.4	4.2
Current Account Balance	4.0	4.0	5.0	5.2	5.7	5.3	4.7	4.7	4.6	4.4	4.3
Savings	29.8	30.3	30.3	30.5	30.8	30.1	30.1	29.9	29.6	29.4	29.1
Investment	25.5	26.0	25.1	25.2	24.8	24.7	25.2	25.2	25.0	24.9	24.9
Capital Account Balance	0.0	0.0	0.1	–0.1	–0.4	0.1	–0.2	0.0	–0.1	–0.1	0.0
Emerging Market and Developing Economies											
Net Lending and Borrowing	2.5	2.7	0.7	0.6	0.0	–0.2	0.0	0.0	–0.3	–0.4	–0.7
Current Account Balance	2.5	2.6	0.6	0.6	–0.2	–0.3	0.0	–0.1	–0.4	–0.5	–0.8
Savings	30.3	32.6	32.8	33.0	32.4	31.9	32.2	32.7	32.1	31.8	31.3
Investment	28.1	30.3	32.4	32.6	32.8	32.1	32.4	32.8	32.6	32.4	32.1
Capital Account Balance	0.1	0.2	0.1	0.0	0.1	0.1	0.1	0.1	0.1	0.1	0.1
Regional Groups											
Commonwealth of Independent States[2]											
Net Lending and Borrowing	4.9	4.2	0.6	0.6	2.8	0.0	1.0	5.0	3.9	3.5	2.3
Current Account Balance	5.6	4.5	0.6	2.1	2.8	0.0	1.0	5.0	3.8	3.4	2.2
Savings	26.7	26.8	24.2	25.0	25.9	24.4	25.4	29.0	29.1	29.1	28.5
Investment	21.2	22.4	23.5	22.8	22.7	23.9	24.3	24.0	25.1	25.5	26.1
Capital Account Balance	–0.7	–0.3	0.0	–1.5	0.0	0.0	0.0	0.0	0.0	0.0	0.0
Emerging and Developing Asia											
Net Lending and Borrowing	3.7	3.7	0.8	1.5	2.0	1.4	0.9	–0.1	–0.1	–0.2	–0.5
Current Account Balance	3.6	3.6	0.7	1.5	2.0	1.4	0.9	–0.1	–0.1	–0.2	–0.5
Savings	39.7	43.0	43.1	43.6	42.5	41.1	41.0	40.1	39.3	38.7	37.5
Investment	36.4	39.6	42.3	42.1	40.5	39.7	40.1	40.2	39.4	38.9	38.0
Capital Account Balance	0.1	0.1	0.1	0.0	0.0	0.0	0.0	0.0	0.0	0.0	0.0
Emerging and Developing Europe											
Net Lending and Borrowing	–4.5	–5.1	–2.5	–1.6	–0.7	–1.2	–1.9	–1.3	–0.1	–0.6	–1.4
Current Account Balance	–4.8	–5.7	–3.6	–2.9	–2.0	–1.8	–2.5	–2.2	–0.9	–1.4	–1.9
Savings	19.6	20.0	21.4	22.0	22.9	22.3	22.9	23.1	22.4	21.9	21.1
Investment	24.2	25.7	24.9	24.9	24.8	24.1	25.4	24.8	23.2	23.1	22.9
Capital Account Balance	0.4	0.6	1.1	1.3	1.3	0.6	0.6	1.0	0.9	0.8	0.5
Latin America and the Caribbean											
Net Lending and Borrowing	–0.1	–0.5	–2.8	–3.0	–3.2	–1.9	–1.4	–1.9	–1.9	–1.9	–2.0
Current Account Balance	–0.2	–0.6	–2.8	–3.1	–3.2	–1.9	–1.4	–1.9	–1.9	–2.0	–2.0
Savings	20.4	21.0	19.1	17.9	16.5	16.9	16.8	17.6	17.6	17.5	17.9
Investment	20.6	21.6	22.3	21.5	21.1	18.5	18.5	19.6	19.5	19.5	19.9
Capital Account Balance	0.1	0.1	0.1	0.0	0.0	0.0	0.0	0.0	0.0	0.0	0.0
Middle East, North Africa, Afghanistan, and Pakistan											
Net Lending and Borrowing	7.8	10.0	10.0	6.3	–3.7	–3.7	–0.7	2.4	–0.8	–0.5	–1.0
Current Account Balance	8.2	10.6	9.8	5.5	–4.0	–3.9	–0.6	2.3	–0.9	–0.7	–1.2
Savings	35.0	37.9	36.1	32.9	24.8	24.6	26.7	29.3	27.0	26.7	25.7
Investment	27.7	28.2	26.1	27.0	28.7	28.1	27.5	27.1	27.5	26.9	26.4
Capital Account Balance	0.1	0.1	0.0	0.2	0.0	0.0	0.0	0.1	0.1	0.1	0.2
Sub-Saharan Africa											
Net Lending and Borrowing	1.8	2.0	–1.7	–3.2	–5.5	–3.0	–1.6	–2.2	–3.2	–3.3	–2.8
Current Account Balance	0.5	0.5	–2.2	–3.6	–5.9	–3.7	–2.1	–2.6	–3.7	–3.7	–3.2
Savings	20.7	21.6	19.4	19.2	17.2	18.0	18.9	17.8	17.1	17.4	18.4
Investment	20.7	21.5	21.6	22.5	22.7	21.2	21.0	20.2	20.8	21.1	21.2
Capital Account Balance	1.3	1.5	0.4	0.4	0.4	0.7	0.6	0.4	0.5	0.4	0.4

Table A14. Summary of Net Lending and Borrowing *(continued)*

(Percent of GDP)

	Averages								Projections		
	2001–10	2005–12	2013	2014	2015	2016	2017	2018	2019	2020	Average 2021–24
Analytical Groups											
By Source of Export Earnings											
Fuel											
Net Lending and Borrowing	8.7	10.0	7.4	4.7	–1.5	–1.5	1.6	5.2	2.2	2.1	1.3
Current Account Balance	9.1	10.4	7.3	5.1	–1.6	–1.6	1.6	5.2	2.2	2.0	1.2
Savings	33.5	35.1	32.0	30.2	24.7	24.9	27.0	30.4	28.5	28.2	27.0
Investment	24.8	25.2	24.8	25.3	27.3	25.4	25.5	25.1	25.9	25.7	25.4
Capital Account Balance	–0.2	0.0	0.0	–0.6	–0.1	0.0	0.0	0.0	0.0	0.0	0.1
Nonfuel											
Net Lending and Borrowing	0.8	0.6	–1.0	–0.4	0.3	0.1	–0.2	–0.9	–0.8	–0.9	–1.1
Current Account Balance	0.6	0.4	–1.2	–0.6	0.1	0.0	–0.3	–1.1	–0.9	–1.0	–1.1
Savings	29.4	31.9	33.1	33.7	33.9	33.2	33.2	33.1	32.7	32.4	32.0
Investment	29.0	31.7	34.3	34.3	33.9	33.2	33.6	34.1	33.7	33.4	33.1
Capital Account Balance	0.2	0.2	0.2	0.2	0.2	0.1	0.1	0.1	0.1	0.1	0.1
By External Financing Source											
Net Debtor Economies											
Net Lending and Borrowing	–0.7	–1.3	–2.4	–2.2	–2.0	–1.4	–1.3	–1.8	–1.8	–1.8	–1.9
Current Account Balance	–1.0	–1.7	–2.7	–2.4	–2.3	–1.6	–1.5	–2.0	–2.0	–2.0	–2.0
Savings	22.8	23.8	22.7	22.8	22.5	22.5	22.9	22.9	23.0	23.2	23.6
Investment	24.1	25.6	25.4	25.2	24.7	24.1	24.4	24.8	25.0	25.1	25.6
Capital Account Balance	0.3	0.4	0.3	0.3	0.3	0.2	0.2	0.2	0.2	0.2	0.1
Net Debtor Economies by Debt-Servicing Experience											
Economies with Arrears and/or Rescheduling during 2013–17											
Net Lending and Borrowing	–0.8	–2.8	–5.9	–4.1	–5.4	–5.8	–5.0	–4.3	–4.1	–4.0	–3.7
Current Account Balance	–1.4	–3.4	–6.1	–4.4	–5.7	–5.9	–5.3	–4.5	–4.3	–4.2	–4.0
Savings	20.4	19.1	13.2	14.3	12.2	12.4	13.4	15.4	16.1	17.0	18.3
Investment	22.1	22.5	19.3	18.8	18.2	18.5	18.9	19.9	20.5	21.2	22.3
Capital Account Balance	0.5	0.6	0.3	0.4	0.3	0.1	0.3	0.2	0.2	0.2	0.2
Memorandum											
World											
Net Lending and Borrowing	0.1	0.4	0.6	0.5	0.3	0.4	0.5	0.5	0.2	0.1	0.0
Current Account Balance	0.1	0.3	0.5	0.5	0.3	0.3	0.5	0.4	0.2	0.1	–0.1
Savings	24.0	25.0	26.2	26.7	26.5	26.0	26.5	26.7	26.5	26.4	26.5
Investment	23.9	24.7	25.5	25.8	25.9	25.4	25.8	26.2	26.3	26.3	26.5
Capital Account Balance	0.1	0.1	0.1	0.0	0.0	0.0	0.0	0.0	0.1	0.1	0.0

Note: The estimates in this table are based on individual countries' national accounts and balance of payments statistics. Country group composites are calculated as the sum of the US dollar values for the relevant individual countries. This differs from the calculations in the April 2005 and earlier issues of the *World Economic Outlook,* in which the composites were weighted by GDP valued at purchasing power parities as a share of total world GDP. The estimates of gross national savings and investment (or gross capital formation) are from individual countries' national accounts statistics. The estimates of the current account balance, the capital account balance, and the financial account balance (or net lending/net borrowing) are from the balance of payments statistics. The link between domestic transactions and transactions with the rest of the world can be expressed as accounting identities. Savings (*S*) minus investment (*I*) is equal to the current account balance (*CAB*) (*S* – *I* = *CAB*). Also, net lending/net borrowing (*NLB*) is the sum of the current account balance and the capital account balance (*KAB*) (*NLB* = *CAB* + *KAB*). In practice, these identities do not hold exactly; imbalances result from imperfections in source data and compilation as well as from asymmetries in group composition due to data availability.

[1]Excludes the Group of Seven (Canada, France, Germany, Italy, Japan, United Kingdom, United States) and euro area countries.

[2]Georgia, Turkmenistan, and Ukraine, which are not members of the Commonwealth of Independent States, are included in this group for reasons of geography and similarity in economic structure.

Table A15. Summary of World Medium-Term Baseline Scenario

	Averages				Projections			
							Averages	
	2001–10	2011–20	2017	2018	2019	2020	2017–20	2021–24
				Annual Percent Change				
World Real GDP	**3.9**	**3.6**	**3.8**	**3.6**	**3.3**	**3.6**	**3.6**	**3.6**
Advanced Economies	1.7	1.9	2.4	2.2	1.8	1.7	2.0	1.6
Emerging Market and Developing Economies	6.2	4.9	4.8	4.5	4.4	4.8	4.6	4.9
Memorandum								
Potential Output								
Major Advanced Economies	1.8	1.4	1.5	1.6	1.5	1.5	1.5	1.4
World Trade, Volume[1]	**5.0**	**3.9**	**5.4**	**3.8**	**3.4**	**3.9**	**4.1**	**3.8**
Imports								
Advanced Economies	3.5	3.4	4.3	3.3	3.0	3.2	3.4	3.3
Emerging Market and Developing Economies	9.1	5.0	7.5	5.6	4.6	5.3	5.7	5.1
Exports								
Advanced Economies	3.9	3.5	4.4	3.1	2.7	3.1	3.3	3.2
Emerging Market and Developing Economies	8.1	4.5	7.2	4.3	4.0	4.8	5.0	4.5
Terms of Trade								
Advanced Economies	–0.1	0.1	–0.2	–0.6	–0.3	0.1	–0.2	0.2
Emerging Market and Developing Economies	1.0	–0.2	0.8	1.3	–0.9	0.0	0.3	0.1
World Prices in US Dollars								
Manufactures	1.9	–0.1	–0.3	2.7	1.0	0.2	0.9	0.9
Oil	10.8	–2.9	23.3	29.4	–13.4	–0.2	8.3	–0.5
Nonfuel Primary Commodities	8.9	–1.2	6.4	1.6	–0.2	1.1	2.2	0.6
Consumer Prices								
Advanced Economies	2.0	1.6	1.7	2.0	1.6	2.1	1.8	2.0
Emerging Market and Developing Economies	6.6	5.1	4.3	4.8	4.9	4.7	4.7	4.4
Interest Rates				*Percent*				
Real Six-Month LIBOR[2]	0.7	–0.3	–0.4	0.2	1.4	1.8	0.8	0.9
World Real Long-Term Interest Rate[3]	1.9	0.3	–0.2	–0.1	0.4	0.0	0.0	0.5
Current Account Balances				*Percent of GDP*				
Advanced Economies	–0.8	0.5	0.9	0.7	0.6	0.5	0.7	0.5
Emerging Market and Developing Economies	2.5	0.2	0.0	–0.1	–0.4	–0.5	–0.3	–0.8
Total External Debt								
Emerging Market and Developing Economies	30.4	28.6	30.3	29.9	30.1	29.3	29.9	27.6
Debt Service								
Emerging Market and Developing Economies	9.1	10.2	9.8	10.3	10.4	10.2	10.2	9.6

[1]Data refer to trade in goods and services.
[2]London interbank offered rate on US dollar deposits minus percent change in US GDP deflator.
[3]GDP-weighted average of 10-year (or nearest-maturity) government bond rates for Canada, France, Germany, Italy, Japan, the United Kingdom, and the United States.

WORLD ECONOMIC OUTLOOK SELECTED TOPICS

World Economic Outlook Archives

World Economic Outlook: Financial Systems and Economic Cycles	September 2006
World Economic Outlook: Spillovers and Cycles in the Global Economy	April 2007
World Economic Outlook: Globalization and Inequality	October 2007
World Economic Outlook: Housing and the Business Cycle	April 2008
World Economic Outlook: Financial Stress, Downturns, and Recoveries	October 2008
World Economic Outlook: Crisis and Recovery	April 2009
World Economic Outlook: Sustaining the Recovery	October 2009
World Economic Outlook: Rebalancing Growth	April 2010
World Economic Outlook: Recovery, Risk, and Rebalancing	October 2010
World Economic Outlook: Tensions from the Two-Speed Recovery—Unemployment, Commodities, and Capital Flows	April 2011
World Economic Outlook: Slowing Growth, Rising Risks	September 2011
World Economic Outlook: Growth Resuming, Dangers Remain	April 2012
World Economic Outlook: Coping with High Debt and Sluggish Growth	October 2012
World Economic Outlook: Hopes, Realities, Risks	April 2013
World Economic Outlook: Transitions and Tensions	October 2013
World Economic Outlook: Recovery Strengthens, Remains Uneven	April 2014
World Economic Outlook: Legacies, Clouds, Uncertainties	October 2014
World Economic Outlook: Uneven Growth—Short- and Long-Term Factors	April 2015
World Economic Outlook: Adjusting to Lower Commodity Prices	October 2015
World Economic Outlook: Too Slow for Too Long	April 2016
World Economic Outlook: Subdued Demand—Symptoms and Remedies	October 2016
World Economic Outlook: Gaining Momentum?	April 2017
World Economic Outlook: Seeking Sustainable Growth: Short-Term Recovery, Long-term Challenges	October 2017
World Economic Outlook: Cyclical Upswing, Structural Change	April 2018
World Economic Outlook: Challenges to Steady Growth	October 2018
World Economic Outlook: Growth Slowdown, Precarious Recovery	April 2019

I. Methodology—Aggregation, Modeling, and Forecasting

Measuring Inequality: Conceptual, Methodological, and Measurement Issues	October 2007, Box 4.1
New Business Cycle Indices for Latin America: A Historical Reconstruction	October 2007, Box 5.3
Implications of New PPP Estimates for Measuring Global Growth	April 2008, Appendix 1.1
Measuring Output Gaps	October 2008, Box 1.3
Assessing and Communicating Risks to the Global Outlook	October 2008, Appendix 1.1
Fan Chart for Global Growth	April 2009, Appendix 1.2
Indicators for Tracking Growth	October 2010, Appendix 1.2
Inferring Potential Output from Noisy Data: The Global Projection Model View	October 2010, Box 1.3
Uncoordinated Rebalancing	October 2010, Box 1.4
World Economic Outlook Downside Scenarios	April 2011, Box 1.2

II. Historical Surveys

III. Economic Growth—Sources and Patterns

Output Synchronicity in the Middle East, North Africa, Afghanistan, and Pakistan and in the Caucasus and Central Asia	October 2013, Box 3.1
Spillovers from Changes in U.S. Monetary Policy	October 2013, Box 3.2
Saving and Economic Growth	April 2014, Box 3.1
On the Receiving End? External Conditions and Emerging Market Growth before, during, and after the Global Financial Crisis	April 2014, Chapter 4
The Impact of External Conditions on Medium-Term Growth in Emerging Market Economies	April 2014, Box 4.1
The Origins of IMF Growth Forecast Revisions since 2011	October 2014, Box 1.2
Underlying Drivers of U.S. Yields Matter for Spillovers	October 2014, Chapter 2, Spillover Feature
Is It Time for an Infrastructure Push? The Macroeconomic Effects of Public Investment	October 2014, Chapter 3
The Macroeconomic Effects of Scaling Up Public Investment in Developing Economies	October 2014, Box 3.4
Where Are We Headed? Perspectives on Potential Output	April 2015, Chapter 3
Steady As She Goes—Estimating Sustainable Output	April 2015, Box 3.1
Macroeconomic Developments and Outlook in Low-Income Developing Countries—The Role of External Factors	April 2016, Box 1.2
Time for a Supply-Side Boost? Macroeconomic Effects of Labor and Product Market Reforms in Advanced Economies	April 2016, Chapter 3
Road Less Traveled: Growth in Emerging Market and Developing Economies in a Complicated External Environment	April 2017, Chapter 3
Growing with Flows: Evidence from Industry-Level Data	April 2017, Box 2.2
Emerging Market and Developing Economy Growth: Heterogeneity and Income Convergence Over the Forecast Horizon	October 2017, Box 1.3
Manufacturing Jobs: Implications for Productivity and Inequality	April 2018, Chapter 3
Is Productivity Growth Shared in a Globalized Economy?	April 2018, Chapter 4
Recent Dynamics of Potential Growth	April 2018, Box 1.3
Growth Outlook: Advanced Economies	October 2018, Box 1.2
Growth Outlook: Emerging Market and Developing Economies	October 2018, Box 1.3
The Global Recovery 10 Years after the 2008	October 2018, Chapter 2

IV. Inflation and Deflation and Commodity Markets

The Boom in Nonfuel Commodity Prices: Can It Last?	September 2006, Chapter 5
International Oil Companies and National Oil Companies in a Changing Oil Sector Environment	September 2006, Box 1.4
Commodity Price Shocks, Growth, and Financing in Sub-Saharan Africa	September 2006, Box 2.2
Has Speculation Contributed to Higher Commodity Prices?	September 2006, Box 5.1
Agricultural Trade Liberalization and Commodity Prices	September 2006, Box 5.2
Recent Developments in Commodity Markets	September 2006, Appendix 2.1
Who Is Harmed by the Surge in Food Prices?	October 2007, Box 1.1
Refinery Bottlenecks	October 2007, Box 1.5
Making the Most of Biofuels	October 2007, Box 1.6
Commodity Market Developments and Prospects	April 2008, Appendix 1.2
Dollar Depreciation and Commodity Prices	April 2008, Box 1.4
Why Hasn't Oil Supply Responded to Higher Prices?	April 2008, Box 1.5
Oil Price Benchmarks	April 2008, Box 1.6
Globalization, Commodity Prices, and Developing Countries	April 2008, Chapter 5
The Current Commodity Price Boom in Perspective	April 2008, Box 5.2

Is Inflation Back? Commodity Prices and Inflation	October 2008, Chapter 3
Does Financial Investment Affect Commodity Price Behavior?	October 2008, Box 3.1
Fiscal Responses to Recent Commodity Price Increases: An Assessment	October 2008, Box 3.2
Monetary Policy Regimes and Commodity Prices	October 2008, Box 3.3
Assessing Deflation Risks in the G3 Economies	April 2009, Box 1.3
Will Commodity Prices Rise Again When the Global Economy Recovers?	April 2009, Box 1.5
Commodity Market Developments and Prospects	April 2009, Appendix 1.1
Commodity Market Developments and Prospects	October 2009, Appendix 1.1
What Do Options Markets Tell Us about Commodity Price Prospects?	October 2009, Box 1.6
What Explains the Rise in Food Price Volatility?	October 2009, Box 1.7
How Unusual Is the Current Commodity Price Recovery?	April 2010, Box 1.2
Commodity Futures Price Curves and Cyclical Market Adjustment	April 2010, Box 1.3
Commodity Market Developments and Prospects	October 2010, Appendix 1.1
Dismal Prospects for the Real Estate Sector	October 2010, Box 1.2
Have Metals Become More Scarce and What Does Scarcity Mean for Prices?	October 2010, Box 1.5
Commodity Market Developments and Prospects	April 2011, Appendix 1.2
Oil Scarcity, Growth, and Global Imbalances	April 2011, Chapter 3
Life Cycle Constraints on Global Oil Production	April 2011, Box 3.1
Unconventional Natural Gas: A Game Changer?	April 2011, Box 3.2
Short-Term Effects of Oil Shocks on Economic Activity	April 2011, Box 3.3
Low-Frequency Filtering for Extracting Business Cycle Trends	April 2011, Appendix 3.1
The Energy and Oil Empirical Models	April 2011, Appendix 3.2
Commodity Market Developments and Prospects	September 2011, Appendix 1.1
Financial Investment, Speculation, and Commodity Prices	September 2011, Box 1.4
Target What You Can Hit: Commodity Price Swings and Monetary Policy	September 2011, Chapter 3
Commodity Market Review	April 2012, Chapter 1, Special Feature
Commodity Price Swings and Commodity Exporters	April 2012, Chapter 4
Macroeconomic Effects of Commodity Price Shocks on Low-Income Countries	April 2012, Box 4.1
Volatile Commodity Prices and the Development Challenge in Low-Income Countries	April 2012, Box 4.2
Commodity Market Review	October 2012, Chapter 1, Special Feature
Unconventional Energy in the United States	October 2012, Box 1.4
Food Supply Crunch: Who Is Most Vulnerable?	October 2012, Box 1.5
Commodity Market Review	April 2013, Chapter 1, Special Feature
The Dog That Didn't Bark: Has Inflation Been Muzzled or Was It Just Sleeping?	April 2013, Chapter 3
Does Inflation Targeting Still Make Sense with a Flatter Phillips Curve?	April 2013, Box 3.1
Commodity Market Review	October 2013, Chapter 1, Special Feature
Energy Booms and the Current Account: Cross-Country Experience	October 2013, Box 1.SF.1
Oil Price Drivers and the Narrowing WTI-Brent Spread	October 2013, Box 1.SF.2
Anchoring Inflation Expectations When Inflation Is Undershooting	April 2014, Box 1.3
Commodity Prices and Forecasts	April 2014, Chapter 1, Special Feature
Commodity Market Developments and Forecasts, with a Focus on Natural Gas in the World Economy	October 2014, Chapter 1, Special Feature

V. Fiscal Policy

VI. Monetary Policy, Financial Markets, and Flow of Funds

VII. Labor Markets, Poverty, and Inequality

VIII. Exchange Rate Issues

Measuring Real Effective Exchange Rates and Competitiveness: The Role of Global Value Chains	October 2015, Box 3.2
Labor Force Participation Rates in Advanced Economies	October 2017, Box 1.1
Recent Wage Dynamics in Advanced Economies: Drivers and Implications	October 2017, Chapter 2
Labor Market Dynamics by Skill Level	October 2017, Box 2.1
Worker Contracts and Nominal Wage Rigidities in Europe: Firm-Level Evidence	October 2017, Box 2.2
Wage and Employment Adjustment after the Global Financial Crisis: Firm-Level Evidence	October 2017, Box 2.3

IX. External Payments, Trade, Capital Movements, and Foreign Debt

Capital Flows to Emerging Market Countries: A Long-Term Perspective	September 2006, Box 1.1
How Will Global Imbalances Adjust?	September 2006, Box 2.1
External Sustainability and Financial Integration	April 2007, Box 3.1
Large and Persistent Current Account Imbalances	April 2007, Box 3.2
Multilateral Consultation on Global Imbalances	October 2007, Box 1.3
Managing the Macroeconomic Consequences of Large and Volatile Aid Flows	October 2007, Box 2.3
Managing Large Capital Inflows	October 2007, Chapter 3
Can Capital Controls Work?	October 2007, Box 3.1
Multilateral Consultation on Global Imbalances: Progress Report	April 2008, Box 1.3
How Does the Globalization of Trade and Finance Affect Growth? Theory and Evidence	April 2008, Box 5.1
Divergence of Current Account Balances across Emerging Economies	October 2008, Chapter 6
Current Account Determinants for Oil-Exporting Countries	October 2008, Box 6.1
Sovereign Wealth Funds: Implications for Global Financial Markets	October 2008, Box 6.2
Global Imbalances and the Financial Crisis	April 2009, Box 1.4
Trade Finance and Global Trade: New Evidence from Bank Surveys	October 2009, Box 1.1
From Deficit to Surplus: Recent Shifts in Global Current Accounts	October 2009, Box 1.5
Getting the Balance Right: Transitioning out of Sustained Current Account Surpluses	April 2010, Chapter 4
Emerging Asia: Responding to Capital Inflows	October 2010, Box 2.1
Latin America-5: Riding Another Wave of Capital Inflows	October 2010, Box 2.2
Do Financial Crises Have Lasting Effects on Trade?	October 2010, Chapter 4
Unwinding External Imbalances in the European Union Periphery	April 2011, Box 2.1
International Capital Flows: Reliable or Fickle?	April 2011, Chapter 4
External Liabilities and Crisis Tipping Points	September 2011, Box 1.5
The Evolution of Current Account Deficits in the Euro Area	April 2013, Box 1.3
External Rebalancing in the Euro Area	October 2013, Box 1.3
The Yin and Yang of Capital Flow Management: Balancing Capital Inflows with Capital Outflows	October 2013, Chapter 4
Simulating Vulnerability to International Capital Market Conditions	October 2013, Box 4.1
The Trade Implications of the U.S. Shale Gas Boom	October 2014, Box 1.SF.1
Are Global Imbalances at a Turning Point?	October 2014, Chapter 4
Switching Gears: The 1986 External Adjustment	October 2014, Box 4.1
A Tale of Two Adjustments: East Asia and the Euro Area	October 2014, Box 4.2
Understanding the Role of Cyclical and Structural Factors in the Global Trade Slowdown	April 2015, Box 1.2
Small Economies, Large Current Account Deficits	October 2015, Box 1.2
Capital Flows and Financial Deepening in Developing Economies	October 2015, Box 1.3
Dissecting the Global Trade Slowdown	April 2016, Box 1.1
Understanding the Slowdown in Capital Flows to Emerging Markets	April 2016, Chapter 2
Capital Flows to Low-Income Developing Countries	April 2016, Box 2.1
The Potential Productivity Gains from Further Trade and Foreign Direct Investment Liberalization	April 2016, Box 3.3
Global Trade: What's behind the Slowdown?	October 2016, Chapter 2

The Evolution of Emerging Market and Developing Economies' Trade Integration with China's Final Demand	April 2017, Box 2.3
Shifts in the Global Allocation of Capital: Implications for Emerging Market and Developing Economies	April 2017, Box 2.4
Macroeconomic Adjustment in Emerging Market Commodity Exporters	October 2017, Box 1.4
Remittances and Consumption Smoothing	October 2017, Box 1.5
A Multidimensional Approach to Trade Policy Indicators	April 2018, Box 1.6
The Rise of Services Trade	April 2018, Box 3.2
Role of Foreign Aid in Improving Productivity in Low-Income Developing Countries	April 2018, Box 4.3
Global Trade Tensions	October 2018, Scenario Box
The Price of Capital Goods: A Driver of Investment under Threat?	April 2019, Chapter 3
Evidence from Big Data: Capital Goods Prices across Countries	April 2019, Box 3.2
Capital Goods Tariffs and Investment: Firm-Level Evidence from Colombia	April 2019, Box 3.4
The Drivers of Bilateral Trade and the Spillovers from Tariffs	April 2019, Chapter 4
Gross versus Value-Added Trade	April 2019, Box 4.1
Bilateral and Aggregate Trade Balances	April 2019, Box 4.2
Understanding Trade Deficit Adjustments: Does Bilateral Trade Play a Special Role?	April 2019, Box 4.3
The Global Macro and Micro Effects of a US–China Trade Dispute: Insights from Three Models	April 2019, Box 4.4
A No-Deal Brexit	April 2019, Scenario Box

X. Regional Issues

EMU: 10 Years On	October 2008, Box 2.1
Vulnerabilities in Emerging Economies	April 2009, Box 2.2
East-West Linkages and Spillovers in Europe	April 2012, Box 2.1
The Evolution of Current Account Deficits in the Euro Area	April 2013, Box 1.3
Still Attached? Labor Force Participation Trends in European Regions	April 2018, Box 2.3

XI. Country-Specific Analyses

Why Is the U.S. International Income Account Still in the Black, and Will This Last?	September 2005, Box 1.2
Is India Becoming an Engine for Global Growth?	September 2005, Box 1.4
Saving and Investment in China	September 2005, Box 2.1
China's GDP Revision: What Does It Mean for China and the Global Economy?	April 2006, Box 1.6
What Do Country Studies of the Impact of Globalization on Inequality Tell Us? Examples from Mexico, China, and India	October 2007, Box 4.2
Japan after the Plaza Accord	April 2010, Box 4.1
Taiwan Province of China in the Late 1980s	April 2010, Box 4.2
Did the Plaza Accord Cause Japan's Lost Decades?	April 2011, Box 1.4
Where Is China's External Surplus Headed?	April 2012, Box 1.3
The U.S. Home Owners' Loan Corporation	April 2012, Box 3.1
Household Debt Restructuring in Iceland	April 2012, Box 3.2
Abenomics: Risks after Early Success?	October 2013, Box 1.4
Is China's Spending Pattern Shifting (away from Commodities)?	April 2014, Box 1.2
Public Investment in Japan during the Lost Decade	October 2014, Box 3.1
Japanese Exports: What's the Holdup?	October 2015, Box 3.3
The Japanese Experience with Deflation	October 2016, Box 3.2
Permanently Displaced? Labor Force Participation in US States and Metropolitan Areas	April 2018, Box 2.2

XII. Special Topics

IMF EXECUTIVE BOARD DISCUSSION OF THE OUTLOOK, APRIL 2019

The following remarks were made by the Chair at the conclusion of the Executive Board's discussion of the Fiscal Monitor, Global Financial Stability Report, *and* World Economic Outlook *on March 21, 2019.*

Executive Directors broadly shared the assessment of global economic prospects and risks. They observed that global economic activity had recently lost momentum, reflecting a confluence of factors in a number of large economies. Global trade had slowed sharply, and concerns over trade tensions weakened business confidence. Directors noted that while growth is expected to level off in the first half of this year and firm up thereafter, this short-term outlook is subject to considerable uncertainty.

Directors noted that, over the medium term, growth is expected to moderate further in advanced economies, as population aging constrains the expansion of the labor force and labor productivity growth remains tepid. In emerging market and developing economies, growth is expected to increase modestly. Convergence toward advanced economy income levels, however, remains slow for many of these economies, due to structural bottlenecks and, in some cases, high debt, subdued commodity prices, and civil strife.

Directors agreed that risks to the global outlook remain skewed to the downside amid high policy uncertainty. These include a reescalation of trade tensions and disruptions from a no-deal Brexit. Given still-accommodative financial conditions, the global economy also remains susceptible to a sudden shift in market sentiment and associated tightening in financial conditions. Downside risks in systemic economies, if they were to materialize, also weigh on the outlook. On the upside, if recent tariff increases are rolled back and trade tensions resolved, rising business confidence could lift growth. Over the medium term, many Directors noted risks from rising inequality, climate change, cyber risks, political uncertainty, and declining trust in institutions.

Directors noted that the current conjuncture highlights the urgent need for strong global cooperation and coordination to tackle shared challenges. Many Directors attached priority to resolving trade disagreements cooperatively without raising further distortionary barriers, and reiterated the importance of strengthening the open, rules-based multilateral trading system. Directors stressed that broadening the gains from global economic integration would also require closer cooperation in the areas of financial regulatory reforms, the global financial safety net, international corporate taxation, and climate change. Progress on external rebalancing relies on macroeconomic and structural policies, mindful of countries' domestic conditions and objectives, to increase demand and growth potential in surplus countries, and initiatives to boost supply and potential output in deficit countries.

Against the backdrop of waning global growth momentum and limited policy space in many countries, Directors underscored the need to avoid policy missteps, contain risks, and enhance resilience while raising inclusive growth prospects. Macroeconomic policies should be carefully calibrated, aiming to support growth where output may fall below potential and policy space exists, and ensuring a soft landing where policy support needs to be withdrawn. In the event of a deeper or protracted downturn, policies should become more accommodative where feasible.

Directors stressed that fiscal policy should strike the right balance between growth and debt sustainability objectives as appropriate in individual countries. In countries with high debt, gradual fiscal adjustment is needed, particularly if financing risks are large. In countries with fiscal space, fiscal policy should boost aggregate demand where there is slack and raise potential growth where the economy is operating above potential. In this regard, a few Directors noted the role of automatic stabilizers during cyclical downswings. In the event of a more protracted slowdown in growth, care should be taken to avoid a procyclical fiscal stance. Directors concurred that fiscal policy should also adapt to shifting demographics, advancing technology, and deepening global integration. Where there is limited budgetary room, such a response will have to occur through budget recomposition and reprioritization.

Amid signs of weakening growth and muted inflation in most advanced economies, Directors welcomed the more gradual approach to monetary policy normalization by major central banks since the beginning of this year, which has helped boost positive market sentiment. They urged policymakers to clearly communicate any reassessment of the pace of monetary policy normalization that reflects either changes in the economic outlook or risks surrounding the outlook, to avoid excessive market swings or unduly compressed market volatility.

With financial conditions still accommodative as the credit cycle matures, Directors noted that financial vulnerabilities would likely continue to build in different parts of the global economy. These include rising corporate debt, sovereign–financial sector nexus, maturity and liquidity mismatches, house price misalignment, and sensitivity of portfolio flows and asset prices in emerging markets to changes in global financial conditions. The tightening in financial conditions late last year was too short-lived to meaningfully slow the buildup of vulnerabilities, leaving medium-term risks to global financial stability broadly unchanged. Where needed, policymakers should deploy prudential tools proactively, expand macroprudential toolkits, and continue to repair public and private balance sheets.

Across all economies, growth-enhancing structural reforms remain key to improving potential output, inclusiveness, and resilience. Directors emphasized that high debt levels in many countries require a multipronged approach, including to enhance debt transparency and management. Broader structural reforms should aim to lift productivity, encourage labor force participation, and upgrade skills. Further deregulation in product markets and services, supported by stronger competition law and policy, could help deter the rise in corporate market power in advanced economies.

Noting that corruption could undermine inclusive growth, public finances, and poverty reduction efforts, Directors highlighted the need to improve fiscal institutions, transparency, and governance in the public sector. Greater cooperation is also essential at the global level, including combating foreign bribery and money laundering of proceeds from corrupt activities, as well as improving the sharing of information to fight tax evasion and prosecute corrupt acts.

Directors stressed that, with external conditions remaining uncertain, emerging market and developing economies should focus monetary policy on anchoring inflation expectations where inflation remains high, and support domestic activity as needed where expectations are well anchored. Depending on country circumstances, efforts should continue to raise revenue, reduce debt-related vulnerabilities, and make steady progress on economic and financial rebalancing.

Directors underscored the need for low-income developing economies to adopt policies that focus on drivers of growth, raise resilience to volatile external conditions, durably reduce debt vulnerabilities, and advance toward the 2030 Sustainable Development Goals, with continued support from the international community. Priorities include improving macroeconomic and macroprudential policy frameworks, strengthening domestic resource mobilization, and gearing fiscal policy toward supporting growth and development objectives, including protection for social spending and carefully selected capital projects. Commodity exporters need to continue diversifying their economies through policies that improve education quality, narrow infrastructure gaps, enhance financial inclusion, and boost private investment.